LET THEM NOT RETURN

War and Genocide

General Editors: Omer Bartov, Brown University; A. Dirk Moses, University of Sydney

In recent years there has been a growing interest in the study of war and genocide, not from a traditional military history perspective, but within the framework of social and cultural history. This series offers a forum for scholarly works that reflect these new approaches.

"The Berghahn series Studies on War and Genocide *has immeasurably enriched the English-language scholarship available to scholars and students of genocide and, in particular, the Holocaust."* —**Totalitarian Movements and Political Religions**

For a full volume listing, please see back matter

LET THEM NOT RETURN

Sayfo – The Genocide against the Assyrian, Syriac and Chaldean Christians in the Ottoman Empire

Edited by David Gaunt, Naures Atto and
Soner O. Barthoma

berghahn
NEW YORK · OXFORD
www.berghahnbooks.com

Published in 2017 by
Berghahn Books
www.berghahnbooks.com

Library of Congress Cataloging-in-Publication Data

A C.I.P. cataloging record is available from the Library of Congress

British Library Cataloguing in Publication Data

A catalogue record for this book is available from the British Library

ISBN 978-1-78533-498-6 hardback
ISBN 978-1-78920-051-5 paperback
ISBN 978-1-78533-499-3 ebook

CONTENTS

PREFACE

⁓

This book appears in a political atmosphere in which great parts of the Middle East have been set alight, where massacres and ethnic and religious cleansing have become part of our daily lives and indigenous minorities that were the target of massacres and ethnic cleansing in the Ottoman Empire during the First World War are again faced with extinction. In their demonstrations worldwide, Assyrians are appealing to the international community to put an end to the ongoing genocide; they have been holding placards on which is written '1915, 1933, now 2014: No more genocide!' – referring to the genocidal events in the last century and today. The year 2015 marked the centenary of the genocide during the First World War in Ottoman Turkey. Assyrians refer to this genocide as 'the year of the sword' (*i Shato du Sayfo*[1]). In a broader context it is more commonly known as the Assyrian genocide, which took place in the borderlands between Turkey, Iran and present-day Iraq and decimated an indigenous population with a unique ethno-religious heritage. Hundreds of thousands were murdered or driven into exile with survivors scattered all over the world. Today they are greatly dispersed in a worldwide diaspora, with large populations in the United States, Europe and Australia, and in the Middle East in Iraq and Lebanon, with only tiny remnants of once vibrant communities in Turkey, Syria and Iran. Although it happened a century ago, among the descendants of its victims and survivors the genocide is still a living trauma. The denial of this genocide, the continued oppression of the Assyrians and their recent expulsion from their ancestral homeland have all served to trigger the remembrance of this traumatic past.

This book is a result of the international research project, 'An Intergenerational Approach to the Study of Genocide: Seyfo', organized in the Netherlands by the Inanna Foundation in 2011. The impetus for this book stemmed from a shared conviction among its contributors that there are many issues regarding the Assyrian genocide that have not been dealt with or that still require further investigation. Although the genocide of Ottoman Armenians, Assyrians and Pontic Greeks took place in the same time frame and in the same political context, most of the academic publications that have hitherto appeared discuss only the Armenian genocide. So far, existing literature about the Assyrian genocide has been composed principally of a few monographs and articles mainly by historians. Therefore, the primary aim of this volume is to fill the gap in academic research about the Assyrian genocide and develop a greater interest in the Sayfo among scholars. This work is the first academic anthology dealing specifically with the Sayfo. The book aims to provide an interdisciplinary account of the study of the Sayfo by bringing together scholars from history, philosophy, anthropology, linguistics, theology, political science and law in order to open up new avenues of research to the study of this less-researched genocide. We believe that the volume will be an important contribution to comparative genocide studies.

Naming

In this volume, the reader will notice the use of various names for the group(s) discussed in this study. Some of the writers apply the cross-denominational term Assyrian or Syriac to denote what can be seen as an ethnic group originally from Anatolia and Mesopotamia who adhere to several indigenous Christian churches.[2] Other authors use a cross-denominational name when referring to the victim group(s) in general terms, as well as their use of the church name when discussing specific experiences. Yet other authors might use only confessional names. In all cases authors have made it clear in their specific chapters how they refer to the group(s) concerned.

This multiple naming is the result of a historical condition arising from the *millet* system of the Ottoman Empire in which the formal status of the Assyrians was that of separate church communities and not an ethno-national group. The national awakening of Assyrians came about in the late Ottoman period but rapidly collapsed as, in the period before and during the First World War, their intellectuals were among the first to be killed. Only after the relocation of large numbers of the group to Western countries in the twentieth century did they begin to express a cross-denominational national identity *en masse*, first as 'Assyrian' and later also as 'Aramean'.[3] The name 'Chaldean' has also been used to indicate a community when referring to both a religious and an ethnic group. The use of the respective names 'Assyrians' and 'Arameans' reflects a particular (perceived) ancient ancestry. Many who use the name 'Arameans' focus on a more religious identity and stress the importance of their collective identity after their conversion to Christianity. Hence they also use either the name 'Syriac' or 'Aramean' interchangeably; the latter highlights a more ethno-national identity. In this context, the present-day use of 'Arameans' has been developed in opposition to the use and identification as 'Assyrians' which has a more political and secular orientation. Despite the heated dispute over what name to use when translating the emic name 'Suryoye'/'Suryaye' into Western languages, all sides suffered from the Sayfo and request recognition of it as a genocide from the international community.

Notes

1. *Sayfo* is also spelled *Seyfo* and *Saypa*.
2. These churches are the Syriac Orthodox Church, the Church of the East, the Chaldean Catholic Church, the Syriac Catholic Church and their Protestant offshoots.
3. Atto (2011) details the disagreement over self-identity. Cetrez, Donabed and Makko (2013) present the case for Assyrian continuity. For the case of Aramean continuity, see Brock et al. (2001).

Bibliography

Atto, N. 2011. *Hostages in the Homeland. Orphans in the Diaspora.* Leiden: Leiden University Press.

Brock, Sebastian, et al. 2001. *The Hidden Pearl: The Syrian Orthodox Church and its Ancient Aramaic Heritage.* Rome: Trans World Film Srl.

Cetrez, Ö.A., S.G. Donabed and A. Makko (eds). 2013. *The Assyrian Heritage. Threads of Continuity and Influence.* Uppsala: Uppsala University Library.

ACKNOWLEDGEMENTS

We are thankful to the Inanna Foundation, which covered the editing costs of this publication. We would also like to thank our series editors at Berghahn and anonymous reviewers of this volume for their useful feedback and their help in the publication of this book. We are very grateful for the work of Mrs Rosemary Robson in the English editing.

INTRODUCTION

CONTEXTUALIZING THE SAYFO IN THE FIRST WORLD WAR

David Gaunt, Naures Atto and Soner O. Barthoma

"We should not let them return to their homelands"

—From a telegram of Talaat to the governors of Mosul and Van provinces,
30 June, 1915.

This book focuses on a little-known genocide of the Assyrian peoples that took place at the same time as the well-known Armenian genocide during the First World War. The sorrow and loss caused by the killing and displacement of ancestors has been a painful memory for the Assyrians ever since. But the memory of the massacres, deportations and expulsions of the Assyrians has long been confined inside families and religious communities, only seldom told to outsiders. As with the Armenian genocide, the official stance of Turkey has been to deny that anything near a genocide ever befell the Assyrians. Representatives of the various traditionally Syriac-speaking Christian minorities, here referred to collectively by the cross-denominational name 'Assyrians', estimated that 250,000 of their number perished between 1914 and 1918. The population had been reduced to half its original size (Namik and Nedjib 1919). Before 1914 the Assyrians lived in a wide region in what is now south-east Turkey, north-western Iran and the northern parts of Syria and Iraq. Academic source-based research on their fate has only recently started (de Courtois 2004; Gaunt 2006; Hellot-Bellier 2014). Fortunately, it is becoming integrated into the overall history of the Armenian genocide and in that way is increasingly recognized as a genocide in its own right (Suny, Göçek and Naimark 2011; Kaiser 2014; Kévorkian and Ternon 2014; Suny 2015; De Waal 2015). But there are still many aspects that need further investigation.

The genocide during the First World War did not come without warning. For decades the Assyrian peoples had been the victims of increasing violence and dispossession, to which the Ottoman governments were constant bystanders. Much of this violence had a colonial aspect, that is, to seize land and property, but other aspects were religious, that is, forced conversion to Islam or death; another aspect that came late into the overall picture was political, to create a homogeneous Turkish national identity by destroying those peoples and cultures that were considered impossible to assimilate. Although the motives varied, the long chain of massacres kept a feeling of vulnerability alive. When the genocide began, it was preceded by posters spreading jihad propaganda among the local Muslim population, in the manner of an announcement (Hellot-Bellier 2014).

The first instance of mass violence that specifically targeted Assyrians in the nineteenth century was in the 1840s, when the Kurdish emir of Bohtan, Badr Khan, invaded the Hakkari mountains twice and attacked the Assyrian tribes. According to European newspapers, tens of thousands were murdered. Further mass violence followed in the 1870s and in the so-called Hamidiye massacres of the 1890s. In most parts of south-eastern Anatolia, when Armenians were attacked, their Assyrian neighbours suffered the same brutality.

Massacres and ethnic cleansing in Anatolia proceeded in a manner that makes it difficult to generalize (Gaunt 2015a). Basically, the events reflected territorial and religious divisions among the Assyrians, thus shaping three very different patterns. One pattern, that of ethnic cleansing, refers to the Hakkari mountain area populated by people belonging to the Church of the East (formerly also known as Nestorians); the second pattern is that of imperialist invasion and concerns the district of Urmia, a part of north-western Iran populated both by members of the Church of the East and the Chaldean Church; and the third is that of the systematic attacks on towns and villages in the neighbourhood of the province of Diyarbakir (also spelled Diyarbekir) populated mostly by Syriac Orthodox and Syriac Catholic believers. Details of these events will be presented later in this introduction.

In a nutshell, the official Ottoman government's deportations and massacres of Assyrians started on 26 October 1914.[1] Through a ciphered telegram, Minister of the Interior Talaat ordered the deportation of Assyrians living along the border with Iran. They were to be sent inwards to central Anatolia and dispersed so that only a few would be living in any particular village. This order was never implemented because war with Russia broke out a few days later. Instead, irregular Kurdish cavalry perpetrated massacres intended to cause the population to flee. From this starting point, attacks on Assyrians spread eastwards into Iran and westwards into the provinces of Bitlis, Diyarbakir, Harput and Aleppo. Ottoman troops, irregular Kurdish cavalry, pardoned criminals, local jihadists and specially formed death squads were the prime perpetrators. In all territories the Assyrians tried to mount armed resistance and in a few cases were successful. The houses and other property of the victims were confiscated by the state and redistributed to Muslim refugees. The bulk of the government-sponsored killing ceased with an order by Interior Minister Talaat to stop the hostility against the Assyrians (but not the Armenians) on 25 December 1915.[2] After that date, Assyrians were still being attacked but on an individual basis and without the commitment of government resources. The war ended in November 1918 and some of those Assyrians who had survived tried to return to their homes. When the Republic of Turkey was established in 1923, a new wave of state violence was directed against the Assyrians remaining in Turkey. Those trying to revive their villages in Hakkari were driven out by a large military operation. The Syriac Orthodox patriarch was sent into exile and members of his church living in the town of Urfa were deported in 1924. Only a tiny enclave of Assyrians remained in the tiny south-eastern district of Midyat (also known as Tur Abdin).

Most of the killings and deportations had a local background. The case of the Assyrian mountaineers of Hakkari differs greatly from the story of the Syriac Orthodox and Chaldeans. The Assyrian tribes of the Hakkari mountains had an autonomous legal position under the traditional secular-religious leader Patriarch Mar Shimun, who combined both religious and secular tasks in his leadership. The Ottomans called these people *Nasturi* (Nestorians). These Assyrians lived on both sides of the Turkish-Iranian border and this position was becoming increasingly precarious. Russia and Turkey both had ambitions in Iran and this conflict affected all of the many different ethnic groups living in the border zone, primarily Sunni and Shia Kurds, Turkish-speaking Azeris, Armenians, Assyrians, Chaldeans and Jews. The Assyrian tribes on the Turkish side of the border were isolated, living in small villages in alpine terrain. By the end of the nineteenth century, they were in contact with

Russian diplomats, military and religious figures, who promised them
protection (Lazarev 1964). In all fairness, the Ottomans also sought
to woo the Assyrians but had less success as siding with Russia gave
the Assyrians hope of greater autonomy. Even the British government
had contact with the Assyrians through its consular officer in Van who,
under the terms of the Treaty of Berlin of 1878, was to monitor the
human rights of the Christian minorities, and the Anglican Church
established a mission (Coakley 1992). As the war loomed, Russian influence increased and some Assyrian communities joined the Russian
Orthodox Church. Inter-ethnic clan conflicts undermined the unity of
the Assyrians. Before the outbreak of the First World War, the Russians
intensified their contact, but the Ottomans had efficient spies and knew
of the communications. Obviously worried, on 12 July 1914, Minister
of the Interior Talaat Pasha telegraphed the provincial government of
Mosul and ordered a report on the 'Nestorians' – how many they were,
where they were settled, what their political orientation was and what
steps the provincial governor considered appropriate.[3]

After weeks of border skirmishes along the Iranian border, the
Ottoman Empire commenced formal hostilities with the Russian Empire
in November 1914. Although Iran declared neutrality, the Ottoman military plans included a violation of Iranian territory in order to encircle
the Russians and seize the oilfields at Baku. This manoeuvre involved
the invasion of the north-western border district of Urmia, which had
a large number of Armenian, Assyrian and Chaldean settlements.
On the eve of war, as an important matter of security, Minister of the
Interior Talaat Pasha sent a decree to the province of Van to deport the
Assyrians from the Ottoman side of the border. His order of 26 October
1914 stated:

> The position of the Nestorians has always remained dubious in the eyes of
> the government on account of their predisposition to be influenced by for-
> eigners and to act as a channel and an instrument for them. Because of the
> operation and efforts in Iran, the importance of the Nestorians to the gov-
> ernment has increased. Especially those who are found at our border area
> with Iran, because of the government's lack of trust ... [they will be punished
> by their] deportation and expulsion from their locations to appropriate such
> provinces as Ankara and Konya, to be transferred in a dispersed fashion so
> that henceforth they will not be together *en masse* and be settled exclusively
> among Muslim people, and in no location to exceed twenty dwellings.[4]

The Assyrians resisted deportation, and confrontations with civil and
military authorities continued throughout the autumn and winter of
1914–15. Massacres of villagers were carried out as an instrument to

terrify the population into fleeing across the border into the part of Iran occupied by Russia. Some of the leaders responded by activating the provisions of their agreement with the Russians for mutual help. On the Iranian side of the border, the Russians organized an Assyrian self-defence militia, armed with army-surplus rifles, and gave them some training (Matveev and Mar-Yukhanna 1968; Genis 2003). The Christian militias existed up to New Year's Day 1915, when a makeshift Ottoman army under the provincial governor of Van, Jevdet Bey, rushed into the Urmia district to fill a vacuum of power as the Russians pulled back their troops to face an offensive in the southern Caucasus. The Ottomans occupied the district until May 1915. During the occupation, numerous atrocities were committed against those Armenians, Assyrians and Chaldeans who had not managed to flee. Returning Russian soldiers discovered a huge massacre of 707 Armenian and Assyrian civilian males in the village of Haftevan (near Salamas) when they arrived on 10 March 1915. Reports of similar atrocities in this and other places came from American and French missionaries who had remained in Iran to care for refugees seeking asylum in mission complexes (Toynbee and Bryce 2000). The Iranian government also informed foreign embassies of the atrocities (Empire de Perse 1919). Alarmed by these reports, the governments of Great Britain, France and Russia issued a joint statement published in major newspapers such as the *New York Times* and the London-based *Times* on 24 May 1915 declaring that in consideration of the Ottoman 'crimes against humanity and civilization ... all members of the Turkish government ... together with its agents implicated in the massacres' will be held personally responsible and punished (Gaunt 2006). This warning was proclaimed on 24 May, just at the official start of the anti-Armenian deportations inside Turkey, and had no effect there. Inside Iran, the Russian army, led by Russian-Armenian generals and supported by local Armenian and Assyrian volunteers, defeated troops under General Halil, who retreated into the Hakkari mountains. The defeated Ottoman army withdrew deep into Turkish territory, destroying whatever Christian communities they happened to come into contact with, most notoriously slaughtering the Armenian and Chaldean populations of the towns of Bashkala, Siirt and Bitlis. A Venezuelan mercenary in Ottoman service witnessed these events (Nogales 1926). It has to be said that the victorious army manned by Armenian and Assyrian volunteers was no better disciplined than the Ottoman, and it took revenge by pillaging Muslim villages, slaughtering the men and raping their women. The Russian civil authorities constantly complained about the atrocities committed by these soldiers and their allies during punitive raids (Holquist 2013: 347–348).

The most important assistance given to the Russians was during the Turkish bombardment of the Armenian quarters in the town of Van, which began on 20 April 1915. Assyrian warriors joined forces with a Russian detachment, which had rushed to relieve the Armenians. During this campaign, in mid-May the Assyrian warriors fought against and stopped General Halil's army, which had intended to reinforce the Turkish troops in Van. Of course, the Turks considered this an act of revolt, even though it was devised as a tactical protective measure. This defiance resulted in a concentration of civil and military might for the purpose of punishing the Assyrians. The governor of Mosul, Haydar Bey, was granted extraordinary powers to invade the Hakkari mountains, which had been transferred to his jurisdiction.[5] Soldiers under Haydar Bey's command joined forces with several local Kurdish tribes to mount an attack from several sides. Although the Assyrians fought well, they were outnumbered, outgunned and had difficulty in finding supplies and food. They retreated high up into the mountains, where they had no chance of survival. Talaat Pasha ordered Haydar Bey to drive them out and concluded, 'Let them not return to their homelands'.[6] By September, driven by desperation, most of the Assyrians from Hakkari had fled into Russian-occupied Iran, never to return, even though many of the males had volunteered for service in the Russian army in the hope of being able to return. Assyrian military units remained part of the Russian army until the Bolshevik Revolution of October 1917, and after that time they continued to defend the area, retaining sporadic contact with the British. The Assyrian militia was still in place in 1918 when a Turkish army invaded present-day northern Iran and a great many Assyrians fled south to join up with the British in Iraq. During this mass flight on foot, many of the refugees were killed in attacks by Turkish units. In effect, by the end of the First World War the border zone between Iran and Turkey had been ethnically cleansed, an operation in which the Ottoman army played the most important role, but which had also been supported by local Kurdish tribes.

These examples of the activities of the Ottoman army in repressing and expelling Assyrians from their homes are documented in Ottoman sources because their resistance brought the matter to the attention of the highest civil and military authorities. However, many other Christian communities were haphazardly annihilated, for which there was felt to be no need to consult with the central government, and hence relevant archival documentation is unavailable. Throughout the province of Diyarbakir, Syriac villages were systematically destroyed at the same time as those of their Armenian neighbours. In many places, like the important administrative city of Harput, the Assyrians had assimilated into Armenian society and spoke the Armenian language. One of the professors of Armenian literature at the Protestant college in Harput, Ashur Yusef, was a Syriac Protestant and he was murdered together with his colleagues in Diyarbakir in June 1915. The organizers of the massacres made little distinction between the two groups. For example, in the Beshire district east of Diyarbakir, although both the Assyrians and Armenians spoke Kurdish, they retained their different religions. In the town of Mardin, all of the Christian groups spoke a local variety of Arabic, particularly the large Catholic community into which were integrated the Armenian Catholic, Syriac Catholic and Chaldean congregations. Any violence targeting Armenians in such places as Harput, Mardin and Beshire became a general massacre of Christians rather than a specific Armenian massacre. Levene has proposed the term 'zone of violence' to describe eastern Anatolia during late Ottoman times. There was not one single Armenian genocide, but rather a 'series of genocidal and near genocidal massacres encompassing ... additional national groups' (Levene 1998: 394).

The Question of Genocide

Assyrians today usually refer to their genocide by the term *Sayfo* (also spelled *Seyfo*), Aramaic for 'sword'.[7] The year 1915 has become the symbol of this genocide and has been referred to in terms of 'the year of the sword' (see more on this term in the chapter by Shabo Talay in this volume). Sayfo as a designation has been in oral use since the event itself and was obviously used even earlier as a metaphor for massacre. Nevertheless, in publications it has only been used since roughly the 1980s, when the first publications of witness testimonies and oral history appeared in Europe.[8] Previously, in addition to Sayfo, the Arabic word for catastrophe, *nakba*, was used.[9] In some areas the Turkish word *firman*, which means an 'official decree', was commonly used because many people in rural Anatolia, both victims and perpetrators, believed the sultan had ordered the massacres (Talay 2010).

Since the 1990s, Assyrian political activists have advanced the idea that what happened to their people in the First World War and its immediate aftermath can be considered genocide. Agitation and lobbying began against the background of increasing international recognition that what happened to the Armenians was genocide. Assyrian groups patterned their activities on the Armenians: commemorations were held on or around 24 April, memorials were raised throughout the world in localities where there were large diaspora communities, youth

groups created educational materials, organizations urged parliamentarians to submit bills for the recognition of Sayfo as genocide and, in
a few cases such as in Sweden, such a bill was actually passed. In 2007
the International Association of Genocide Scholars issued a statement
to the effect that what happened to the Assyrians was genocide. This
activity of recognition began before there was much scientific research,
so discussions of whether the facts fit any definition of genocide became
a matter of choice within a 'black and white' dichotomy of cruel perpetrators against innocent victims.

There are many definitions of genocide, but nearly all see it as a systematic campaign organized by governments and their apparatuses to
destroy targeted ethnic and religious groups. The UN convention of
1948 talks of full genocide but also refers to 'partial' genocide, in which
a substantial part of a targeted population, but not all of it, is destroyed.
Therefore, it is not dependent on the total eradication of the target.
The concept of 'partial destruction' has not been sufficiently discussed.
Genocide is directed at the destruction of a national group as a conscious
community; it does not matter that some individuals survive if the community to which they had belonged no longer exists (Feierstein 2012).
Genocide is not just the outright murder of a people; it can also take
the form of forcing a people into conditions in which they cannot survive (ghettos, camps in the desert, death marches). Massacres are also
combined with forced expulsion or acts of extreme terror to drive people
to abandon their homes voluntarily. In this sense, it is close to 'ethnic
cleansing'. The purpose is usually to win a piece of territory completely
or nearly completely emptied of the target population.

The intention of the Ottoman government to remove the Assyrians
from their homelands is not in doubt. The government definitely knew
it was acting against populations that were not Armenians. In the documents cited in Turkish, the members of the Church of the East are called
Nasturi, the members of the Syriac Orthodox Church are called *Süryani*
and the Chaldeans are called *Keldani*. It is not a case of mistaken identity,
except in those places where language assimilation with the Armenians
had taken place. As mentioned above, Minister of the Interior Talaat
Pasha expressed suspicions about the loyalty of 'Nestorians' in July
1914 and sent a deportation order to expel the Nestorians along the borderlands with Iran as early as October 1914. When they resisted, in July
1915 he ordered the army to drive them from the Hakkari mountains,
never to return. In the case of Azakh, one of the last entrenched positions of Syriac defenders, Minster of War Enver ordered the suppression
of the village using the 'utmost severity'.[10] Talaat even sent a contingent
of *mujaheddin* under his command to lend the siege a Muslim-Christian

twist. After the attack failed, Enver conferred with the Commander of the Third Army about returning to finish the job when a better opportunity should present itself. Other high-ranking Committee of Union and Progress (CUP) members were involved: Naci Bey had been the committee's Inspector General for Anatolia and both he and the provincial governor, Reshid Bey, were well-respected members of the Young Turks' old guard.

That Enver intended the destruction of Azakh and its defenders is beyond question. Because of the presence of German military advisors, these events came to the notice of the German government. Obviously that government understood that the task of the Ottoman army was to exterminate the defenders and therefore it insisted that no German soldiers should be involved.

Members of the Syriac Orthodox Church in Azakh and members of the Church of the East in Hakkari took up arms in order to confront the Ottoman civil and military authorities. Therefore, the Ottoman government officials were able to describe the actions they took against them as punitive measures against rebels and traitors. However, as the German consul in Mosul pointed out, they were simply trying to save themselves from certain annihilation or expulsion. This point seemed to have been recognized by the government as, on 25 December 1915, an order arrived in the eastern provinces bringing news of a change of policy. 'Instead of deporting all of the Syriac people found within the territory', they should be 'detained in their present locations'.[11] However, by that date most of the Christian heartland in the Mardin sub-district had been destroyed, with the exception of the defended villages, some families who had found asylum in monasteries and some isolated villages in forested areas. It was therefore an ongoing genocide that was only halted at the eleventh hour.

Another point that indicates the intention to annihilate all Christians in the eastern provinces is the way the Ottoman government turned a deaf ear to international criticism. Against the background of the atrocities committed against Armenians, Assyrians and Chaldeans in the Turkish-Iranian borderlands, the declaration of 24 May 1915 had no effect. Furthermore, German diplomatic protests decrying the atrocities of the governor of Diyarbakir, Reshid Bey, in instigating a general massacre of all Christians received only a *pro forma* response from the Ottoman government. Nevertheless, Germany did lodge a protest about the killing of more than four hundred Armenian, Syriac Catholic, Chaldean and Protestant leaders from Mardin and its vicinity on the night of 10–11 June 1915.[12] This had come to the attention of the German consul in Mosul who immediately informed his ambassador and government. The German response was to insist that the universal massacre of Christians should be stopped and that Reshid be dismissed. Talaat telegraphed Reshid on 12 July saying that 'measures adopted against the Armenians are under no circumstances to be extended to other Christians ... you are ordered to put an immediate end to these acts'.[13] However, despite this warning, the general massacre of Christians did not stop, Reshid was not replaced and, at the end of his term of office in Diyarbakir, he was rewarded with the provincial governorship of Ankara. His closest ally in orchestrating the general massacres, his deputy-governor, Bedreddin Bey, took over his position. Whether or not Talaat's telegram was genuine, or merely a ploy to appease the diplomats, is a matter of debate. Its importance lies in showing that Talaat was aware that Christians who were not Armenians had been arrested, tortured and murdered, and that he had not intervened to stop it. Certainly Reshid had a long-standing reputation for brutality and hostility towards Christians and this was one of the reasons the local Diyarbakir CUP group insisted on his appointment to replace an alleged too 'Christian-friendly' governor, Hamid, in March 1915 (Bilgi 1997).

Another indication of the occurrence of genocide is the high number of victims. In a rare show of inter-sectarian cooperation, in 1919 Assyrians of all denominations presented a petition to the Paris Peace Conference stating that altogether 250,000 of their number had been killed in Anatolia or Turkish-occupied Iran during the war. They calculated that this was about half of the original population. By 1922, at the Lausanne peace negotiations, they raised that number to 275,000. However, the delegate, Afram Barsoum, Archbishop of the Syriac Orthodox archdiocese in Syria, gave a lower figure of 90,000 for the Syriac Orthodox and 90,000 for the combined Church of the East and Chaldeans, resulting in a total of 180,000. In other words, the earliest stated numbers of victims range from as low as 180,000 to as high as 275,000. The accuracy of these figures is impossible to check. How they could obtain information from a decimated population that had been dispersed all over the world is also hard to understand. The various churches lacked their own precise statistics that would give an accurate starting point from which to calculate the percentage population loss. Most estimates from the immediate prewar years indicate a total Assyrian population ranging from 500,000 to 600,000 (Gaunt 2006: 19–28, 300–303). Given the nature of the peace process and the desire of the Christians to be compensated in proportion to the extent of their suffering, it would have been natural for them to give somewhat exaggerated figures. However, the estimate of 50 per cent is an overall figure and contemporary observers found much higher percentages in certain important localities. Jacques Rhétoré, a French

Dominican monk interned in Mardin from 1915 to 1916, recorded that in the sub-district of Mardin, 86 per cent of Chaldeans had disappeared along with 57 per cent of the Syriac Orthodox, 48 per cent of the Syriac Protestants and 18 per cent of the Syriac Catholics (Rhétoré 2005: 136).[14] The manner in which people were murdered had been extreme in places and had been proceeded by the gratuitous public humiliation of local leaders and their families. For instance, in Mardin on 10 June 1915, four hundred prisoners were paraded through the main street of the town in heavy chains. The deputy-governor of Diyarbakir and the chief of police organized the march. Many of the Christian leaders, particularly the heads of churches, displayed visible injuries caused by torture and beatings (Armale 1919: part 3 chapters 4–5; Rhétoré 2005: 72–74; Sarafian 1998: 264; Simon 1991: 65–71; Ternon 2002: 133, Gaunt 2006: 170–173). As they trudged through the centre of town, the Muslim population was encouraged to insult them, while the families of the victims were forbidden to leave their houses. Female Assyrian witnesses claimed sexual abuse, rape and other forms of gender-based atrocities (Naayem 1920 reveals many such cases).

In conclusion, a number of conditions make it possible to recognize the Sayfo as a genocide. Chief among them was the deep involvement of the civil and military commands of the Ottoman government in plans to target Assyrians of all denominations. Secondly, hundreds of thousands out of a relatively small population fell victim. Thirdly, the Assyrian homeland in Hakkari was completely destroyed and never re-established. Fourthly, the Syriac Orthodox were nearly wiped out and only saved by an order of December 1915 calling a temporary reprieve to the aggression. The Chaldeans had the best chance of survival as the majority of the members of this church lived in the southern provinces of Mosul, Bagdad and Basra, which were not part of the 1915 anti-Christian campaign. However, those Chaldeans who lived in the Anatolian province of Bitlis, particularly in or around the towns of Siirt and Cizre or in the Urmia district of Iran, were subject to great cruelty and had little chance of survival unless they had been able to flee beforehand.[15]

What Were the Causes?

Genocides are complex. There are usually multiple and entangled ideological, economic and social causes. The Assyrian case is no exception. There were geopolitical as well as regional and local causes over which the groups had little control. Alongside these were Turkish nationalistic ideological causes and, finally, there were social and economic causes specific to the localities in which the target populations lived.

On a macro level, these peoples lived in a historically very unstable borderland. These regions are territories prone to ethnic and religious mass violence. Bartov and Weitz (2013) have identified what they term a geographic 'shatterzone' of extreme violence extending from the Baltic region of Northern Europe through Eastern Europe down to the Middle East. This 'shatterzone' emerged in the borderland friction between the German, Habsburg, Russian and Ottoman empires. To the cases described in this book can be added the fact that these Oriental Christian peoples were caught up in the additional friction between Turks, Iranians, Kurds and Arabs, all with their nascent national movements. In this type of violent territory, all people needed to be on their guard against personal attack. In a genocidal situation, even the target population might respond with violence and seek revenge.

A similar concept of a territory prone to persistent extreme religious or ethnic violence is Mark Levene's idea of the 'zone of genocide', which he applies directly to eastern Anatolia in the period 1878–1923 (Levene 1998). The date 1878 refers to the Treaty of Berlin, which ended the Russo-Turkish War and provided for the appointment of foreign consuls inside Turkey to act as guardians of the rights of Armenians. Christian Gerlach's (2006) term 'extremely violent society' is also relevant here. His concept seeks to avoid some of the pitfalls inherent in the term genocide – particularly that of the implied moral dichotomy of perpetrators and victims. The above-mentioned theories place extreme ethnic and religious violence within a particular type of disputed geography, creating a certain type of social structure – one in which there are persistent unresolved and long-standing ethnic conflicts. They also have the advantage of removing the role of complete innocence from the target population. In a zone of extreme violence, even the victims can be armed defenders.

Another high-level explanation comes from Donald Bloxham (2005), who emphasizes the perfidious influence of Great Power involvement as a background to genocide. The nineteenth-century rivalry known as the Great Game between Russia, Britain, Germany, Austria and France in bids to gain influence over the declining Ottoman Empire destabilized that country. The Great Powers became increasingly involved in the situation of the non-Muslim minorities and what today is called their human rights. Their not-so-altruistic involvement included plans for grabbing territory under the premise of protecting the non-Muslims. This outside interference created a backlash that put the minorities at risk of retribution through the connivance of officials. In 1908, the patriarch of the

Church of the East, Mar Shimun, begged the British consul in Van to stop protesting about the pillaging of Assyrian villages as the protests only made matters worse (Heazell and Margoliuth 1913: 205–8). French consuls at Diyarbakir were equally ineffectual, although they did document numerous cases of seizure of Christian property and unsolved murders and kidnappings (de Courtois 2004). During the First World War, the Russians and then the British promised the Assyrians that they would be granted independence if they participated in the struggle against the Ottomans. Despite the Assyrians siding with these powers, in the end their dreams were crushed, resulting in a justified feeling of betrayal (Stafford 1935; Malek 1935). The German intervention was connected with that country's need for a socially stable Turkey in order to benefit German economic interests. Consequently, it supported the idea of making Turkey homogeneous so as to rid itself of the (potential) internal conflicts caused by unassimilated minorities. At the outbreak of the world war, German diplomats and military advisors agreed to the deportation of the Armenians, even though they thought the measures unnecessarily cruel. And, as already mentioned, they protested when non-Armenians were made victims (Weitz 2013).

On the national level, there was an acute demographic crisis a few years after the Young Turk revolution of 1908. Turkey had to cede a large amount of territory in Europe through the Balkan Wars of 1912–13 and large waves of Muslim refugees streamed into Istanbul and western Anatolia. By and large, the refugees were rural families and needed farmland and places to live. The Minister of the Interior, Talaat, developed a scheme of demographic engineering that would disperse them in Anatolia to encourage the Turkification of those many Balkan refugees who were not already Turkish speaking. The refugees would be resettled in eastern Anatolia on land possessed by people suspected of disloyalty. The upshot was orders to move populations. The order to resettle the Assyrians of Hakkari was just one step in this greater scheme. New waves of Muslim refugees were created as people fled from front-line regions. During the world war, the Directorate for the Settlement of Tribes and Immigrants controlled the conditions and direction of resettlement (Akçam 2012). The forced removal of Christian farmers greatly facilitated the resettlement of Muslim refugees.

This general and national background intertwined with local factors to create a very violent situation. Among the local factors was the emergence of a provincial civil administration prone to violence against non-Muslims. Genocide in the Ottoman Empire was not accomplished in the set-up of a modern bureaucratic system as was the Jewish Holocaust, but depended instead mainly on the enthusiasm of brutal local leaders who could build up an *ad hoc* organization of volunteer death squads, reinforced in places by pardoned criminals. The massacres were organized by a provincial committee that determined the times and places of depredations. In Diyarbakir, a political and administrative symbiosis could build upon an already-existing, fatal anti-Christian hostility alive among the Muslim population. Some of the highest administrators, like governor Reshid of Diyarbakir, belonged to the so-called *Teshkilat-i Mahsusa* (Special Organization), the combined espionage and assassination group of the CUP. To implement the planned eradications, local leaders and administrators created paramilitary militias under their own control.

The local political club of the Young Turks in Diyarbakir was dominated by the Pirinççizâde clan, which had a history of violence against non-Muslims. They were close to the CUP leadership through their relative Ziya Gökalp, the principal ideologue and a member of the party's Central Committee. When Pirinççizâde Arif was mayor of Diyarbakir, in 1895, he instigated a bloody pogrom against Armenian and Assyrian businesses, leading to more than a thousand deaths in the city and the destruction of eighty-five Assyrian villages in the vicinity (Gaunt 2013: 320). In 1908, Arif also ordered the slaughter of the non-Muslim Yezidis living to the west of Diyarbakir (Kaiser 2014). His son, Aziz Feyzi, became a delegate to the newly established National Assembly, where he was noted for his hostility towards the Armenian delegates. Allegedly he had assassinated Ohannes Kazazian from Mardin, his political rival in elections, in 1913 (Üngör 2011: 48). He was also instrumental in having Reshid Bey appointed governor of Diyarbakir in March 1915. Reshid brought with him a personal bodyguard of Circassian warriors and hitmen who became embroiled in all sorts of anti-Christian violence as well as in the assassinations of Muslim dissidents. Furthermore, the provincial administration created local militias of Muslim males exempted from conscription and they were based in the major towns, given military rifles and led by reserve officers. They made up a collection of death squads that could be rapidly deployed.

The politicians and governors of Diyarbakir may or may not have been Turkish nationalists, but they did take part in the plundering of Christian wealth and property. In Van province, where most of the members of the Church of the East in the Ottoman Empire lived, the governor was Jevdet Bey, a close relative of Minister of War Enver. Jevdet also had a private army composed of gendarmes and others whose activities were an embarrassment to the regular army. His anti-Christian hostility was unleashed in early 1915 when he was the acting commander of the Turkish army that invaded north-western Iran. The mass killing of seven hundred Armenian and Assyrian men in Haftevan was reported to have been undertaken on his orders. He called his cut-throat private army the 'butcher battalion' (*kassablar taburu*). Jevdet can be seen as the initiator of the Armenian deportations by creating an atmosphere of panic by means of a series of reports of 'Armenian rebellions', which he sent to Enver throughout March and April 1915 (Gaunt 2006: 106–7). His forces fired the first artillery shells against the Ottoman Armenians when they began to bombard the Armenian quarters in Van on 20 April 1915.

Another local factor, which might not have caused the genocide but certainly contributed to its complexity and prevented stronger and more strategic resistance, was the lack of unity among the members of the Church of the East, Syriac and Chaldean churches. This disunity made possible incidents in which some Christian communities stood to one side as bystanders while their neighbours were massacred. The lack of a common, non-ecclesiastical identity was compounded by the instability of the major institutions – their churches. The Syriac Orthodox of Tur Abdin with numerous farm villages were embroiled in long-term conflict with the Syriac Orthodox patriarch based in Mardin. The authority of the patriarch of the Church of the East, Mar Shimun, was in question. One archdiocese joined the Russian Orthodox Church and the leaders of the Jilu tribe converted to Roman Catholicism. The Chaldeans were equally split and in some places cooperated with Armenian and Syriac Catholics in the use of church buildings. The instability of the churches was matched by the divisions created by the social structure, which was based on large clans in Tur Abdin, or on tribes in the Hakkari mountains. Clans and tribes were rivals. All of these persistent hostilities enabled the Ottoman authorities to play the game of 'divide and rule'. In Midyat, for instance, the Syriac Orthodox secular leadership was enticed by the municipal authorities to turn over the rival Syriac Protestant minority, who were said to be richer, to certain death. In Mardin, when the Syriac Catholic, Protestant and Chaldean prisoners were being sent to execution in June 1915, the Syriac Orthodox bribed their way to freedom. In Hakkari, when most of the other tribes united to fight the Turkish army, the Jilu tribe, whose leaders had just been assassinated on Mar Shimun's orders, declined to participate, and instead retreated into Iran. Efforts by the few Assyrian intellectuals in the different churches to unite their communities were to little avail (Gaunt 2013).

Many of the above-mentioned factors affected all non-Muslim minorities in Anatolia, particularly the Armenians. This would partially explain why Assyrians were caught up in a genocide despite not being clearly defined as a target, as the Armenians were. The same background factors that were relevant to the extermination of the Armenians resulted in the partial genocide of the other Christian peoples. We are aware that the background causes enumerated here are descriptive factors. They do not actually explain why these groups were annihilated, not even when all these aspects are combined.

The genocide perpetrated against the various Assyrian denominations of northern Mesopotamia can be viewed from several perspectives, each of which is legitimate. One approach focuses only on the great catastrophe during the First World War, instigated by the Young Turk government and its extreme nationalist Committee of Union and Progress. This approach emphasizes the political ideology of the political leaders and their desire to 'Turkify' the country by eliminating all members of the population who were expected to resist. Indisputably, the main actors were Talaat, the Minister of the Interior, who orchestrated the genocide, and Enver, the Minister of War, who supplied the support of the army when needed. The second approach emphasizes the long-term escalation of anti-Christian violence from the mid-nineteenth century, culminating in the great annihilation of 1915, followed by continued persecution in Turkey and even in the new successor state of Iraq. The first approach, with a short historical background, emphasizes the role of the Young Turk government in radicalizing politics and systematically orchestrating the murders, and places them in the context of modern *political genocides*. This point of view stresses the importance of ideology and nationalism to mass politics and of gaining popular support for the repression of minorities (Mann 2005). The second approach, with a longer historical background, places the killing inside an increasingly lethal local inter-ethnic and inter-religious conflict, and puts it in the context of *colonial genocides*, pushing native peoples off their land. The genocide can be seen as an extreme form of a 'culture of violence', and some would call it genocide 'by attrition' (Fein 1997).

In this context, the slow evolution approach as an explanation of the genocide distinguishes the following phases. Sporadic but later on recurring bloody anti-Christian pogroms commenced in the mid-nineteenth century and as a consequence of which non-Armenian Christians were also increasingly caught up in the Armenian Question. This phase continued in varying intensity up to the outbreak of the First World War. The second phase began at the time of Turkey's mobilization at the outbreak of the First World War in August 1914 until the spring of 1915. In the mobilization phase, adult men were drafted into slave labour battalions on the pretext of suspicions about disloyalty. Searches for suspected army deserters in Christian quarters of towns led to indiscriminate violence and the arrests of Christian leaders. The third phase, from May 1915, was marred by an outburst of general genocidal atrocities over a wide area, characterized by mass executions, destruction of entire districts, death marches and rape warfare, continuing unabated until November 1915. The fourth phase was that of the mopping-up operations, in which the last survivors were pushed out of Hakkari and the Urfa area and revenge was exacted on those who had led village defences, and the final expulsion of the Syriac Orthodox patriarch from Turkey in 1924. In this volume both short-term and long-term perspectives are represented.

Roots and Settlement

The various Syriac-speaking church communities are indigenous to eastern Anatolia and Mesopotamia and most of their members trace their heritage to the Assyrians, Arameans and/or Chaldeans. Ethnically, they are probably a composite of people who converted to Christianity in the first centuries AD, long before its acceptance by the Roman Empire. They came to be known as Syrian(/c) Christians; *Suryoye/Suryaye* in Syriac Aramaic. Originally, they spoke a variety of Aramaic local dialects and used Syriac as their liturgical language. This hybrid ancient past is very much reflected in the hotly disputed discourses about their origin, especially within the group itself in its diaspora communities. Leaving aside what happened in the past, contemporary identity debates in the diaspora should be understood from the present-day perspective of the context of having to establish a new life in secular states in which religious identity is seen as a private matter and other forms of identification (such as ethno-national) have become dominant instead. This process of redefining the collective identity of the group concerned in the diaspora has been discussed in several studies (Deniz 1999; Cetrez 2005; Atto 2011). For a better understanding of the present ethno-politics in a historical context, it is necessary to reflect briefly on the divisions within the church in the early centuries of Christianity.

The first main split within Syriac Christianity goes back to the fifth century AD, and emanated from various inner-Christian conflicts and splits over sophisticated theological points dealing with the nature of Christ. In 410, the Christians in Persia proclaimed their independence from the patriarch of Antioch and the emperor in Constantinople at a time when war was raging between Byzantium and Persia. The church leadership of the Christians in Persia needed to adopt an independent position in relation to the Byzantine Church if it was to win greater acceptance from the Persian rulers. Thereafter, it became known as the

Church of the East.[16] This church has also been known under the name East Syrian Church, in contrast to the West Syrian Church, which grew inside the Byzantine Empire.

Theological debates in the Byzantine Empire resulted in the establishment of various Christian churches of the Near East and the Mediterranean. Archbishop Nestorius's ideas about his concept of Christology and the Virgin Mary were declared heretical at the Synod of Ephesus (431). When as a consequence of this he settled in Persia, he gained ascendancy in the recently established Church of the East, which was already independent and chose to adopt a Dyophysite Christology, which was closely, but not exactly, related to Nestorius's position. This is the reason the Church of the East has also been known by the erroneous name Nestorian Church, after Nestorius. Throughout Ottoman official documents and censuses, its members are referred to as *Nasturiler*. The Church of the East was the first institution in modern times to use the term Assyrian to express its collective identity (Surma 1920; Coakley 1992).

In the sixth century, the West Syriac Church continued to oppose the Chalcedonian Creed to which the Roman rulers had committed themselves. The persecution by these rulers forced the Syriac Orthodox hierarchy and monastic orders to seek to escape the influence of the emperor. Jacob Baradaeus (Bishop of Edessa, ca 500–578) played a fundamental role in the setting up of a new, independent, stable organizational structure for the Syriac Orthodox Church. Therefore, the Syriac Miaphysites have erroneously been called Jacobites. In official Ottoman documents they are sometimes referred to as *Süryaniler* and sometimes as *Yakubiler*.

Having been pushed to the periphery, Syriac-speaking Christians gradually began to express their own traditional cultural identity. In retrospect, it is possible to see that the divisions in the church were also heavily influenced by non-theological struggles: political (mainly rivalry between Byzantium and Persia), ethnic, social and geographical, not to mention personal antagonisms between the clergy (Rompay 1997).

With the spread of Islam throughout the Middle East, Syriac Christians hoped they would escape the persecution to which they had been subjected under the Byzantines. In many places, the Christians formed a majority, although their rulers were Muslims. Under Arab Muslim rule, all Christians acquired the status of *dhimmis* and no major difference was made between the various Christian sects. As the non-Muslim subjects of an Islamic state, they lived under Sharia law, and had the right of residence and protection from the ruler in return for the payment of a special tax (*jizya*). Moreover, they had to abide by certain rules that did not apply to Muslims. However, centuries after the initial Islamic conquest, the combined negative consequences of the failure of the Crusades and the Mongol invasions (Bagdad was taken in 1258 and razed by Timur Lenk in 1401) brought near total destruction to the indigenous Christian communities of Mesopotamia. By the fifteenth century, the once-flourishing indigenous Christians found themselves a decimated minority.

In their subsequent steady decline, the Oriental churches splintered even more as they struggled with internal and external strife. The Church of the East became a local church in the vast isolation of the Hakkari mountains and, after a while, the office of patriarch became hereditary to the Shimun dynasty, whose base was in an inaccessible Hakkari mountain hamlet. In the mid-sixteenth century, a group within the Church of the East split off and created a separate church. Its base became the provinces that make up Iraq, with enclaves inside Turkey and Iran. It sought union with the Vatican and was accepted under the name of the Chaldean Catholic Church and the leader was termed the Catholicos-Patriarch of Babylon. Throughout, the Ottomans designated the members of this Church *Keldaniler*. In the second half of the seventeenth century, under the influence of French missionaries, a group of Syriac Orthodox split away and established the first Syriac Catholic patriarchate in Aleppo. Later Protestant churches were also founded.

Each church had a core area in which nearly everyone was a member of the same church. The Syriac Orthodox core area was in the southern part of Diyarbakir province, with concentrations around the market towns of Mardin and Midyat as well as in the large rural district of Midyat (known as Tur Abdin) consisting of about a hundred villages. There were outlying enclaves near the towns of Harput, Adiyaman and Urfa. The core area of the Church of the East was in the remote Hakkari mountains, forming the Turco-Iranian frontier. It also had an enclave around the Iranian administrative town of Urmia. The majority of the Chaldeans lived in Mosul province, with enclaves around the Turkish towns of Cizre and Siirt and Salamas in Iran.

All of these sects were small and their leaders bitterly reviled their opponents as dangerous heretics, an attitude that promoted sectarian exclusion and effectively hindered the growth of a cross-denominational collective identity or common national movement. However internally important these divisions were, outsiders paid little attention to them. In the face of rising Turkish nationalism and Islamic radicalism in the late 1800s, the term *gavur* (infidel) for all non-Muslims became a general part of verbal abuse in Muslim discourse, blurring the fine distinctions between the various Assyrian denominations and even those with the Armenians and Greeks.

In the mid-nineteenth century, lethal conflicts between the Assyrians and Kurds began when Kurdistan was rocked by a confrontation between the Ottoman government and Badr Khan, the ambitious Kurdish emir of Bohtan. Cizre, the town in which he resided on the Tigris River, had many Christian settlements in its immediate neighbourhood. Then, suddenly, a civil war erupted in the nearby Emirate of Hakkari, which had been split over a disputed succession to its leadership. The upshot was a breach between the Kurds and the Assyrians. Badr Khan used the problem caused by the dispute as a pretext to launch an invasion targeting the Assyrians who were on the losing side. An initial military campaign in the summer of 1843 singled out the Assyrians for massacre and European newspapers reported that an estimated seven to ten thousand were killed. Hundreds were captured and sold as slaves. A second invasion in 1846 destroyed any Assyrian village that had been previously overlooked. It is a matter of speculation as to why Badr Khan targeted the Christians, but he was known for his Muslim piety. His operations were not confined to Hakkari, which lay east of Bohtan, but also encompassed much of Tur Abdin, which was situated to the west. Bowing to British pressure, the Ottoman government finally put a halt to Badr Khan's activities (Hirmis 2008; Gaunt 2012; Gaunt 2015b).

Controlling peripheral areas was a chronic problem confronting all Ottoman governments. Centrally appointed provincial governors were underpaid and quickly slipped under the thumbs of local clans and their interests. State finances were so strapped that it proved impossible to station regular troops in the area on a permanent basis (Hartmann 2013). Therefore, the state compromised with local power holders, particularly the Kurdish emirs and the urban notables. The Ottomans adopted a policy of binding the loyalty of selected Kurdish tribes to the sultan. One fateful step in the 1880s was the establishment of irregular Kurdish cavalry regiments (*Hamidiye Alayları*) on the same model as the notorious Russian Cossacks. In return for loyalty to the sultan, these tribes received a special extra-legal status and could behave with impunity. The chief was given a military officer's rank and the warriors were supplied with uniforms and military arms. These regiments proved a highly disruptive factor to Muslims and non-Muslims alike. As military regiments, they were outside the jurisdiction of the civil authority and, as irregular troops, they were beyond normal bounds of military discipline (Klein 2011). Their activities in the borderland region wrecked the delicate balance of power between the Kurds and the Assyrians (see Gaunt's chapter in this volume).

In the late Ottoman period, politically motivated persecution focused on the relatively strong Armenian nationalist movement. Several Armenian political parties worked underground to achieve co-determination in eastern Anatolia, and a small number of revolutionaries struggled for total independence and in their campaign committed occasional acts of violence. In response, Sultan Abdulhamid sought and found enthusiastic support from latent Islamist forces. In 1895 and 1896, riots directed against Armenians broke out in many towns and Assyrians were sucked into these events haphazardly, even though they had no political movement themselves. In November and December 1895, mobs destroyed Christian homes and shops, over a thousand were murdered in Diyarbakir and an untold number were killed in Harput. Most victims were Armenians, but hundreds of Assyrians were killed and many Assyrian villages were plundered. As Uğur Ümit Üngör points out in his contribution to this volume, the victimhood of the Assyrians was almost always eclipsed by the greater interest given to the plight of the Armenians. It has required painstaking research to rediscover the Assyrian genocide behind the Armenian genocide.

Although general anti-Christian violence grew steadily in the final years of the Ottoman Empire, violence specifically targeting Assyrians had been common for centuries. The motives for the violence were complex, but included a lethal mix of the land hunger of Kurdish nomadic tribes, the urgent need to find homes for Muslim refugees streaming in after the defeats in the Balkan Wars of 1912–13, newly radicalized Turkish political and cultural nationalism and, on top of all that, popular religious hatred which the authorities found easy to manipulate. The Assyrian Christians were deeply divided – isolated from each other by denomination, distance and dialects. These divisions prevented any unified resistance, but the administration of the Ottoman government nonetheless depicted them as dangerous insurgents threatening the very existence of the nation.

At the end of the First World War, most of eastern Anatolian Turkey had been cleansed of Oriental Christians. There were a few Assyrian exceptions: some Tur Abdin villages had been passed over and some refugees had been permitted to return from the Arab provinces to which they had fled by local Kurdish *aghas*. Other refugees made their way to Europe (particularly France) or the United States of America. Tens of thousands of survivors were scattered in refugee camps in the Caucasus states, which were later part of the Soviet Union, and in the emerging countries of Iraq, Lebanon and Syria. Their leaders were not able to do much for them. As the chapter by Naures Atto and Soner O. Barthoma reveals, although the Syriac Orthodox patriarch did everything in his

support – including expressing full loyal support for the new political line of the Turkish governing elite and downplaying the genocide
– he was forced to leave Turkey in 1924 by Atatürk. Thereafter, the
new Patriarchal See was established in Homs in Syria (1933). Jan van
Ginkel focuses on the role that one church leader played during the
time of genocide. He asks such questions as: what was the response of
the church leaders during the genocide itself and later? How did the
genocide influence the behaviour of religious leaders after the event?
How did the community respond to the behaviour of their secular and
religious leaders? In his chapter, he introduces a new, more or less forgotten church leader from that time, Mor Dionysius 'Abd an-Nur Aslan,
Metropolitan of Harput, Homs and Diyarbakir, to illustrate some aspects
of these questions.

The Aftermath of the Sayfo

After the First World War, the allied victors met at the Paris Peace
Conference (1919) to lay down the terms for the defeated powers, among
them the once mighty but by then long-crumbling Ottoman Empire.
The terms were quite severe and the vanquished empires were carved
up to make new states based on the principle of the rights of nationalities to independence. In the midst of negotiations, a large but uninvited
group turned up calling itself the Assyro-Chaldean delegation, claiming
authority to speak for what they called the 'Assyro-Chaldean nation'.
To complicate matters, other Assyrian groups turned up, one claiming to speak for the Assyrians of Persia, another for the Assyrians of
Transcaucasia (Gaunt 2013). All told, these rival delegates hailed from
many places – the United States, Russia, Iran, Lebanon and Turkey –
and had had different experiences during the war. Most delegates had
been born inside the Ottoman, Persian or Russian empires. Those who
lived outside the war area had little direct knowledge of the destruction,
but had high hopes for independence. The delegates told a remarkable
tale: their people formed Christian minorities which for centuries had
been dominated and persecuted by Muslim majorities. They insisted
that they had been promised their own country, first by Russia and
then by Great Britain, provided they joined them in fighting against the
Ottoman army. Some of them had done so, particularly those who lived
along the Turkish-Persian border. Now their representatives turned up
in Paris expecting to collect their reward. Their motive for fighting the
Turkish army was to defend their homes from ethnic cleansing and to
avert aggression. The British made many promises of independence.

The Balfour Declaration made to Jewish leaders assigned them a home-land in Palestine and Sheriff Hussein of Mecca was promised Arab independence in return for launching a revolt. But the Assyrians lacked solid proof that similar oral promises made by middle-ranking officers were the official standpoint of the British government. A number of diplomats and military officers did give testimonies that such promises had been made, but they were not confirmed by the British government. Similar promises of independence made by Tsarist Russia were of course worthless after the Bolshevik Revolution. Although they included many influential public figures, supporters of the Assyrians in Britain lobbied unsuccessfully for those whom they called 'our smallest ally' (Wigram 1920, Bentinck 1924).[17]

Far from all of the Assyrians had joined the allies in military campaigns – fighting was mostly confined to the tribes living on the Turkish side of the border and the village militias armed by the Russians on the Iranian side of the border (Holquist 2015). They had been the target of persecution and violen Abdulmesih ce for a long time and their plight had been exacerbated after the Young Turk revolution of 1908. Prewar Ottoman violations of the Iranian border were daily occurrences and ambitions were clear about annexing territory where Turkish speakers lived. For this reason, the Assyrians maintained contacts with representatives of Tsarist Russia in order to discuss the possibilities of Russian protection (Lazarev 1964; Matveev and Mar-Yukhanna 1968; Hellot-Bellier 2014). Apologists for the decision to rid Turkey of Assyrians usually generalize by arguing that because the Assyrians took up arms against the government, full military suppression and ethnic cleansing was their due reward (see the chapter by Abdulmesih BarAbraham in this volume). For Turkish apologists, the issue of resistance is – no matter how limited and unsuccessful – the main legitimation for Ottoman state aggression. However, under no circumstances are states allowed to annihilate an entire population simply because it refuses to comply with a hostile government order to vacate their ancestral homes.

The conflicting claims of the various Assyrian delegates to the peace conferences led to deep disappointment. The Syriac Orthodox Archbishop of Syria, Afram Barsoum, demanded the independence of the provinces of Diyarbakir, Bitlis, Harput and Urfa – a region where a majority of Syriac Orthodox lived – but he did not include the Hakkari mountains or Urmia. Representing the most extreme claim, Joel Werda, an Assyrian-American journalist born in Iran, called for the rebirth of the ancient Assyrian Empire extending from the Persian Gulf to the Mediterranean Sea. He illustrated his journal, *Izgadda: Persian American Courier*, with a map showing this 'new Assyria'. His group made claims for Iranian territory, something the Peace Conference refused to discuss since Iran had been neutral. Furthermore, many of the territorial demands clashed with the Sykes-Picot Agreement, which divided a large part of the Middle East between Britain and France. Some Assyrians curried favour with the French, others with the British.

The Assyro-Chaldean delegation was never officially recognized and therefore had no authority to plead its case before the Peace Conference. Some of the delegates did manage to obtain private audiences with the British diplomat Robert Vansittart and Philip Kerr, Lloyd George's private secretary. One very active Assyrian delegate, A.K. Yousef, a doctor in the US army although born in Harput, tried to encourage the delegation to coordinate its efforts with the Armenian delegations, but to no avail. The Assyrian voices were submerged in a cacophony of similar demands, often for the same territory, from other larger and therefore more politically 'valuable' nationalities, such as the equally victimized Armenians and the Kurds. However, all of these conflicting nationality claims eventually came to nothing. Neither the Assyrians, Armenians nor the Kurds were rewarded with parts of the Ottoman lands. Relatively vague statements of the recognition of a need for the special protection of the Christian minorities were made in the first peace treaty dictated in the Parisian palace of Sèvres in 1920, and there was mention of possible Kurdish and Armenian states. However, that treaty was never ratified and by 1922 the Turkish war of independence had created a completely new situation. A state of Kurdistan had been proposed at Sèvres, in which the Assyrians would become a protected minority. Nonetheless, even these weak expressions of support vanished into thin air in the final treaty negotiated with the new Republic of Turkey at Lausanne in 1922–23. Thereafter, European awareness of the destitution of the Assyrians faded as the survivors were dispersed to all corners of the globe.

In 1933, a new crisis drew international concern to the Assyrians. The British mandate in Iraq was drawing to a close. In the new states of Syria and Iraq, the British mandatory administration had actively recruited Assyrian warriors into special military detachments named Levies and used them to put down Kurdish and Arab rebellions, which caused considerable ill will among the new Iraqi rulers. The League of Nations recognized that they ran the risk of massacre once Iraq became independent. Various projects for resettlement in other countries saw the light of day, but none came to fruition. After the British relinquished their mandate and Iraq became independent, the Iraqi army took revenge and targeted Assyrian settlements, the largest Simele, with a series of massacres in August 1933. Many Assyrians then fled from Iraq to Syria. Raphael Lemkin had collected clippings of newspaper articles dealing with these attacks in preparation for his ongoing, worldwide comparative research on genocide.

New Results

One of the intentions of this volume is to stimulate researchers working on the Sayfo to strike out in new directions. In several instances, this has meant focusing on local studies rather than searching through the political statements of high-ranking politicians to try to discover the intentions of the Young Turk government. One local study has the added importance of highlighting the situation of women during the massacres. In her chapter, Florence Hellot-Bellier deals with the abduction, rape and forced conversion of Assyrian women by Muslim men in the region of Urmia, and attempts by the Assyrians to protect themselves from Muslim violence. Systematic rape is not included as a criterion in the 1948 United Nations convention on punishing and preventing genocide, but it has been increasingly included in legal cases as a condition calculated to destroy a national group (Stiglmayer 1995). There are widespread accusations of rape warfare in the contemporary testimonies of survivors.

Other contributions to this volume describe and analyse previously unknown or little-used sources. Sebastian Brock takes up a recently discovered colophon in a liturgical manuscript which gives an account of mass killings of Assyrians in the Mardin area. It was written in the Zafaran Monastery, and he compares it with another source, that of Qarabashi, from the same monastery (Qarabashi 1997). Simon Birol interprets an epic poem in the classical Syriac language written by Gallo Shabo, who was the leader of a village in Tur Abdin which managed to defend itself successfully against the assaults of Turkish troops and Kurds. One key explanation offered by Gallo Shabo for what happened to his people is God's punishment for their sins.

One very important field of research is the consequences of genocide for the families of the victims and the efforts of the survivors to commemorate their victimization. This research goes in two directions. One leads to the psychological effects of collective trauma. The other leads to efforts to spread knowledge and to have the genocide recognized and acknowledged. Taking the first line of reasoning, Önver Cetrez applies psychological categories of Post-Traumatic Stress Disorder to determine the degree to which the Assyrian community has been marked by internal dissent and distrust of outsiders. He advances the idea that present-day Assyrians suffer from the death of time, that is, they are unable to distinguish between today and what happened in the past.

Finally, several of our contributors deal with the international repercussions of genocide in the form of pressure put on the governments of the countries in which they now live as citizens by the Assyrian diaspora to officially acknowledge that these peoples were victims of genocide. Throughout the Western world, parliaments are being asked to make declarations recognizing that inside the Ottoman Empire the Assyrian, Armenian and Greek peoples were victims of genocide. This is not a demand usually placed on the agenda of a government or a parliament, and deliberations are not always fruitful. The Republic of Turkey has invested enormous resources in denying that anything criminal was perpetrated against the Assyrians. Racho Donef describes such denial activities produced by the recently created Assyrian section of the Turkish Historical Society. The aim of this new section is to challenge the Assyrian claims. As a rule, this is done by casting doubt on the statistics presented and by claiming that the testimony of survivors is flawed and therefore inadmissible. Abdulmesih BarAbraham describes the key arguments employed by Turkish government officials when denying genocide. He also makes an analysis of several recent 'denialist' publications by the Turkish Historical Society. Christophe Premat, a political scientist, compares how the French and the Swedish parliaments have dealt with diaspora demands for the recognition of genocide. His study shows that the larger the group is, and the more votes it can muster, the greater the possibility of getting a recognition bill passed.

The purpose of this volume is to initiate further research on the Sayfo, as the results have led to more burning issues. Foremost is the role of the Assyrian religious and political leadership, that is, to explain the contacts between the Assyrians and the Russians and British before, during and after the First World War and to explain the degree to which some of the religious leaders were collaborating with the Turkish authorities both during and after the war – whether out of necessity to avoid worse, or otherwise. How much of a role did personal rivalry between the leaders play in the failure of the Assyrians to develop a united resistance? There is an acute need to recover documentation, particularly from the archives and libraries of the religious institutions of Assyrians. There should be plenty of material in the correspondence between the patriarchs and the Ottoman authorities. Moreover, there should be primary documents used by the Assyro-Chaldean delegation to the Peace Conference in its estimation of the total number of victims. Much more effort needs to be exerted to clarify the ambiguity of the CUP government's reaction when it realized that Assyrians were caught up in a persecution that outwardly targeted only Armenians. How and why were the two groups conflated as enemy targets? Hardly anyone has yet touched on the impact of the Sayfo on the socio-economic position of Assyrians in the post-genocidal period as a consequence of the confiscation of their property. Furthermore, how has the Sayfo affected institutions like their churches and secular organizations, their emigration, their future orientation and their relationship with their Muslim neighbours? What forms of collective trauma are to be found in the post-genocide period and how are Sayfo memories transmitted and reconstructed? How has the Sayfo affected different fields of art, including the disappearance of some, and how is it expressed in art created by post-genocide Assyrian generations? What are the effects of the Sayfo on language and culture? These and many other questions raised by this book should be on the agenda for future study.

David Gaunt is professor of History at the Centre for Baltic and East European Studies at Södertörn University, Stockholm, Sweden. He has published widely on ethnic and religiously motivated violence against minorities in Eastern Europe and the Middle East. His monograph on the Armenian and Assyrian genocides *Massacres, Resistance, Protectors: Muslim-Christian Relations in Eastern Anatolia during World War I* (2006) has been translated into Turkish.

Naures Atto is Senior Research Associate at the Faculty of Asian and Middle Eastern Studies and former Mellon Postdoctoral Fellow in World Christianities and their Diaspora in the European Context at the University of Cambridge. She is the author of *Hostages in the Homeland, Orphans in the Diaspora: Identity Discourses among the Assyrian/Syriac elites in the European Diaspora* (2011).

Soner O. Barthoma is Research Fellow at Freie Universität Berlin, and coordinator of the EC Horizon 2020 'Respond' project at Uppsala University. He is the author of several articles about the modern history of Assyrians in Turkey.

Notes

1. Minister of Interior to governor of Van province, 26 October 1914, the President's Ottoman Archive, Istanbul (BOA) DH. ŞFR 46/78.

2. Talaat to the Directorate of General Security for the Eastern Provinces, 25 December 1915, BOA DH. ŞFR 57/112, as cited in Akçam (2012: xx).
3. BOA DH. ŞFR 42/263, as cited in Akçam (2012: xx).
4. Minister of Interior to governor of Van province, 26 October 1914, BOA DH. ŞFR 46/78.
5. Ministry of the Interior to Mosul *vilayet*, 7 June 1915, BOA DH. ŞFR 53/276.
6. Talaat to *valis* of Mosul and Van, 30 June 1915, BOA DH. ŞFR 54/240.
7. Smith (1903: 376) translates the Syriac *Mawto dsayfo* as 'death by the sword'.
8. Julius Yesu' Cicek, *Ktobo d-Seyfe* (1981) is one of the first publications to use Sayfo.
9. See the witness testimony of Ishaq Armale, in *Al-Qusara fi nakabat al-nasara* [1919] 1970. During the war he was secretary to the Syriac Catholic Archbishop of Mardin.
10. Enver to Third Army Command, 27 November 1015. ATASE (Turkish Military Historical Archive, Ankara) Kol.: BDH, Kls.: 81, Dos.: 81/, Fih. 35-14. Reprinted in Gaunt 2006 482–483.
11. Talaat to the Directorate of General Security for the Eastern Provinces, 25 December 1915, BOA DH. ŞFR 57/112, as cited in Akçam (2012: xx).
12. According to Rhétoré (2005), 410 persons: 230 Armenian Catholics, 113 Syriac Catholics, 30 Chaldeans and 27 Protestants. Somehow, 85 Syriac Orthodox males already imprisoned managed to get released (Gaunt 2006: 170–73).
13. Holstein to German Embassy, 10 July 1915; German Ambassador to Minister of the Interior Talaat, 12 July 1915, in Lepsius (1919: 101–3). Talaat to Reshid, 12 July 1915, in Turkey General Directorate of Ottoman Archives (1995: 75), and BOA DH. ŞFR 54/406.
14. For other local estimates, see Gaunt (2006: 300–303).
15. From a legal perspective, the Sayfo also meets the criteria mentioned in the Memorandum of the International Centre for Transitional Justice (ICTJ) on the *Applicability of the UN Convention on the Prevention and Punishment of the Crime of Genocide to Events which Occurred during the Early Twentieth Century*. 1 January 2002. The memorandum deals specifically with the Armenian issue. Access through www.ictj.org/publications.
16. Today this church has two patriarchates and two different names: Holy Apostolic Catholic Assyrian Church of the East (largest) and the Ancient Holy Apostolic Catholic Church of the East.
17. The Petition of the Persian Assyrians to the Peace Conference (June 1919), a copy of which can be found in the Hoover Library, elaborates on the numerous promises made by British, Russian and French military officers and diplomats; some of the battles are described in Eva Haddad (1996).

Bibliography

Akçam, T. 2006. *A Shameful Act: The Armenian Genocide and the Question of Turkish Responsibility*. New York: Metropolitan Books.
────── 2012. *The Young Turks' Crime against Humanity: The Armenian Genocide and Ethnic Cleansing in the Ottoman Empire*. Princeton, NJ and Oxford: Princeton University Press.
Armale, I. [1919] 1970. *Al-Qusara fi nakabat al-nasara*. Beirut. This work was published anonymously and without specifying publisher; it has been reprinted in Beirut in 1970 giving the name of the author, but not specifying any publishing house.

Atto, N. 2011. *Hostages in the Homeland. Orphans in the Diaspora: Identity Discourses among the Assyrian/Syriac Elites in the European Diaspora*. Leiden: Leiden University Press.

Bartov, O., and E.D. Weitz (eds). 2013. *Shatterzone of Empires: Coexistence and Violence in the German, Habsburg, Russian, and Ottoman Borderlands*. Bloomington: Indiana University Press.

Bentinck, A. D. W. 1924. 'The Assyrians', in *Journal of the Royal Central Asian Society*, vol. 11, 85–89.

Bilgi, N. 1997. *Dr. Mehmed Reşid Şahingiray'in Hayatı ve Hâtıraları: İttihâd ve Terraki Dönemi ve Ermeni Meselesi*. Istanbul: Akademi Kitapevi.

Bloxham, D. 2005. *The Great Game of Genocide: Imperialism, Nationalism, and the Destruction of the Ottoman Armenians*. Oxford: Oxford University Press.

Brock, S., et al. 2001. *The Hidden Pearl: The Syrian Orthodox Church and its Ancient Aramaic Heritage*. Rome: Trans World Film Srl.

Cicek, J.Y. (ed.) 1981. *Mimre d'cal Seyfe [Poems about Swords]*. Losser, Netherlands: St Ephrem der Syrier Kloster.

Cetrez Ö.A 2005. *Meaning-Making Variations in Acculturaltion and Ritualization: A Multi-generational Study of Suroyo Migrants in Sweden*. Uppsala: Acta Universitatis Upsaliensis.

Cetrez, Ö.A., S.G. Donabed and A. Makko (eds.). 2013. *The Assyrian Heritage: Threads of Continuity and Influence*. Uppsala: Acta Universitatis Upsaliensis.

Coakley, J.F. 1992. *The Church of the East and the Church of England: A History of the Archbishop of Canterbury's Assyrian Mission*. Oxford: Clarendon.

de Courtois, S. 2004. *The Forgotten Genocide: Eastern Christians, the Last Arameans*. Piscataway, NJ: Gorgias Press.

De Waal, T. 2015. *Great Catastrophe: Armenians and Turks in the Shadow of Genocide*. New York: Oxford University Press.

Deniz, F. 1999. *En Minoritets Odyssé: Upprätthållande till moderniseringsprocesser – Det assyriska exemplet*. Uppsala: Department of Sociology, Uppsala University.

Donef, R. 2009. *Massacres and Deportation of Assyrians in Northern Mesopotamia: Ethnic Cleansing by Turkey 1924–1925*. Stockholm: Nsibin.

Empire de Perse, Ministère des affaires étrangers. 1919. *Neutralité Persane: Documents diplomatiques*. Paris: Georges Cadet.

Feierstein, D. 2012. 'The Concept of Genocide and the Partial Destruction of the National Group', *Logos: A Journal of Modern Society and Culture* (11:1), accessed online 19 September 2012.

Fein, H. 1997. 'Genocide by Attrition 1939–1993: The Warsaw Ghetto, Cambodia, and Sudan: Links between Human Rights, Health, and Mass Atrocities', *Health and Human Rights* 2(2): 10–45.

Gaunt, D. 2006. *Massacres, Resistance, Protectors: Muslim–Christian Relations in Eastern Anatolia during World War I*. Piscataway, NJ: Gorgias Press.

——— 2012. 'Relations between Kurds and Syriacs and Assyrians in Late Ottoman Diyarbekir', in J. Jongerden and J. Verheij (eds), *Social Relations in Ottoman Diyarbekir, 1870–1915*. Leiden: Brill, pp. 241–266.

——— 2013. 'Failed Identity and the Assyrian Genocide', in O. Bartov and E.D. Weitz (eds), *Shatterzone of Empires: Coexistence and Violence in the German, Habsburg, Russian and Ottoman Empires*. Bloomington: Indiana University Press, pp. 317–33.

——— 2015a. 'The Complexity of the Assyrian Genocide', *Genocide Studies International* 9(1): pp. 83–103.

——— 2015b. 'Too Close for Comfort. Relations between Kurds, Syriacs and Assyrians in Late Ottoman Times', *Vienna Kurdology Yearbook* 3: pp. 45–64.

Genis, V. 2003. *Vitse-konsul Vvedenskii sluzhba v Persii i Bukharskom khanstve (1906–1920 gg.): Rossiiskaya diplomatiya v sud'bakh*. Moscow: Izdatel'stvo Sotsialno-politicheskaya Mysl'.

Gerlach, C. 2006. 'Extremely Violent Society – an Alternative to the Concept of Genocide', *Journal of Genocide Research* (Vol 8(4): pp. 455–71.

Haddad, E. (pseudonym) 1996. *The Assyrian, Rod of my Anger*. Australia, private publisher.

Hartmann, E. 'The Central State in the Borderlands: Ottoman Eastern Anatolia in the Late Nineteenth Century', in O. Bartov and E. D. Weitz (eds), *Shatterzone of Empires: Coexistence and Violence in the German, Habsburg, Russian and Ottoman Empires*. Bloomington: Indiana University Press, pp. 172-192.

Heazell, F.N., and Mrs. Margoliuth (eds). 1913. *Kurds and Christians*. London: Wells Gardner.

Hellot-Bellier, F. 2014. *Chroniques de massacres annoncés: Les Assyro-Chaldéens d'Iran et Hakkari face aux ambitions des empires 1896–1920*. Paris: Geuthner.

Henno, S. 1987. *Gunhe d-Suryoye d-Tur Abdin*. Losser: Bar Hebreaus Verlag.

Hirmis, Aboona. 2008. *Assyrians, Kurds and Ottomans: Intercommunal Relations on the Periphery of the Ottoman Empire*. New York: Amherst.

Holquist, P. 2013. 'Forms of Violence during the Russian Occupation of Ottoman Territory and in Northern Persia (Urmia and Astrabad)', in O. Bartov and E.D. Weitz (eds), *Shatterzone of Empires: Coexistence and Violence in the German, Habsburg, Russian, and Ottoman Borderlands*. Bloomington: Indiana University Press, pp. 334–361.

————— 2015. 'The World Turned Upside Down: Refugee Crisis and Militia Massacres in Occupied Northern Persia, 1917–1918', in Conseil scientifique internationale pour l'étude de génicide des Arméniens, *Le génocide des Arméniens*. Paris: Armand Colin, pp. 130–54.

Kaiser, H. 2014. *The Extermination of Armenians in the Diarbekir Region*. Istanbul: Bilgi University Press.

Kévorkian, R. 2006. *Le génocide des armeniens*. Paris: Jacob.

Kévorkian, R., and Y. Ternon (eds). 2014. *Mémorial du génocide des Arméniens*. Paris: Seuil.

Kiernan, B. 2007. *Blood and Soil: A World History of Genocide and Extermination from Sparta to Darfur*. New Haven, CT: Yale University Press.

Klein, J. 2011. *The Margins of Empire: Kurdish Militias in the Ottoman Tribal Zone*. Palo Alto, CA: Stanford University Press.

Lazarev, M.S. 1964. *Kurdistan i kurdskaya problema (90-e gody XIX vecka – 1917g.)*. Moscow: Izdatel'stvo Nauka.

Lepsius, J. 1919. *Deutschland und Armenien: Sammlung diplomatischer Aktenstücke*. Potsdam: Der Tempelverlag.

Levene, M. 1998. 'Creating a Modern "Zone of Genocide": The Impact of Nations and State on Eastern Anatolia 1878–1923', *Holocaust and Genocide Studies* 12: pp. 93–433.

Leverkuehn, P. 1938. *Posten auf ewiger Wache: Aus dem abenteuerreichen Leben des Max von Scheubner-Richter*. Essen: Essener Verlagsanstalt.

Malek, Y. 1935. *The British Betrayal of the Assyrians*. Warren Point NJ: The Kimball Press.

Mann, M. 2005. *The Dark Side of Democracy: Explaining Ethnic Cleansing*. Cambridge: Cambridge University Press.

Matveev, K.P., and I.I. Mar-Yukhanna. 1968. *Assiriskii vopros vo vremya i posle pervoi mirovoi voiny*. Moscow: Izdatel'stvo Nauka.

Naayem, J. 1920. *Les Assyro-Chaldéens et les Arméniens massacreés par les Turcs: Documents inédits recueillis par un témoin oculaire*. Paris: Bloud et Guy.

Namik, S.A., and R. Nedjib. 1919. *La Question assyro-chaldéenne devant la conference de la paix (July 16)*. Paris: private distribution to Peace Conference Delegations. A copy can be found in the Hoover Library, Stanford University.

Nogales, R. 1926. *Four Years beneath the Crescent*. London: Charles Scribner.

Qarabashi, A.M.N. 1997. *Dmo Zliho: Vergossenes Blut, 1915–1918*. Augsburg: A.D.O.

Rhétoré, J. 2005. *'Les Chrétiens aux bêtes': Souvenirs de la guerre sainte proclamée par les Turcs contre les chrétiens en 1915*. Paris: Cerf.

Rompay, L. van. 1997. 'Opkomst en groei van onafhankelijke volkskerken in het Oosten tot aan de Arabisch-Islamitische veroveringen (451–641)', in H. Teule and A. Wessels (eds), *Oosterse Christenen binnen de Wereld van de Islam*. Kampen: Uitgeverij Kok, pp. 451–641.

Sarafian, A. 1998. 'The Disasters of Mardin during the Persecutions of the Christians, Especially the Armenians, 1915', in *Haigazian Armenological Review* 18: 261–71.

Simon, H. 1991. *Mardine la ville heroique: Autel et tombeau de l'Arménie (Asie Mineure) Durant les massacres de 1915*. Jounieh, Lebanon: Maison Naaman pour la Culture.

Smith, J.P. 1903. *A Compendious Syriac Dictionary*. Oxford: Calderon Press.

Stafford, R.S. 1935. *The Tragedy of the Assyrians*. London: Allen and Unwin.

Stiglmayer, A. (ed.). 1995. *Mass Rape: The War against Women in Bosnia-Herzegovina*. Lincoln: University of Nebraska Press.

Suny, R.G. 2015. *'They Can Live in the Desert But Nowhere Else': A History of the Armenian Genocide*. Princeton, NJ: Princeton University Press.

Suny, R.G., F.M. Göçek and N.M. Naimark (eds). 2011. *A Question of Genocide: Armenians and Turks at the End of the Ottoman Empire*. New York: Oxford University Press.

Surma d'Bait Mar Shimun. 1920. *Assyrian Church Customs and the Murder of Mar Shimun*. London: Faith Press.

Talay, T. 2010. 'Sayfo, Firman, Qafle: Der Erste Weltkrieg aus der Sicht der syrischen Christen', in R.M. Voigt (ed.), *Akten des 5. Symposiums zur Sprache, Geschichte, Theologie und Gegenwartslage der syrischen Kirchen* (V. Deutsche Syrologentagung), Berlin 14.-15. Juli 2006. Semitica et Semitohamitica Berolinensia 9. Aachen: Shaker Verlag.

Ternon, Y. 2002. 'Mardin 1915: Anatomie pathologique d'une destruction', Special issue of *Revue d'Histoire Arménienne Contemporaine* 4.

Tevetoğlu, F. 1987. *Ömer Naci*. Ankara: Kültur ve Turizm Bakanlığı Yayınları.

Toynbee, A., and J. Bryce (eds). 2000. *The Treatment of Armenians in the Ottoman Empire 1915–1916*. Originally printed 1916. Uncensored edition edited by Ara Sarafian. Princeton, NJ: Gomidas Institute.

Turkey General Directorate of Ottoman Archives. 1995. *Armenians in Ottoman Documents (1915–1920)*. Retrieved from http://onlinebooks.library.upenn.edu/webbin/book/lookupid?key=olbp30433, 24 July 2014.

Üngör, U.Ü. 2006. 'When Persecution Bleeds into Mass Murder: The Processive Nature of Genocide', *Genocide Studies and Prevention* 1(2): pp. 173–96.

——— 2011. *The Making of Modern Turkey: Nation and State in Eastern Anatolia, 1913–1950*. Oxford: Oxford University Press.

Weitz, E.D. 2013. 'Germany and the Ottoman Borderlands: The Entwining of Imperial Aspirations, Revolution, and Ethnic Violence', in O. Bartov and E.D. Weitz (eds), *Shatterzone of Empires: Coexistence and Violence in the German, Habsburg, Russian, and Ottoman Borderlands*. Bloomington: Indiana University Press, pp. 152–171.

Wigram, W.A. 1920. *Our Smallest Ally: A Brief Account of the Assyrian Nation in the Great War.* London: Society for Promoting Christian Knowledge.

Winter, J. (ed.). 2008. *America and the Armenian Genocide of 1915.* Cambridge: Cambridge University Press.

Zaken, M. 2007. *Jewish Subjects and Their Tribal Chieftains in Kurdistan. A Study in Survival* (Jewish Identities in a Changing World 9). Leiden: Brill.

CHAPTER 1

HOW ARMENIAN WAS THE 1915 GENOCIDE?

Uğur Ümit Üngör

Introduction

Much like other modern genocides, the Armenian Genocide can be considered a complex process of sequential and overlapping developments. At the outbreak of the First World War, persecution, stigmatization, expropriation and emigration ushered in the first phase of the process. This was followed by an economic and social boycott and exclusion from civil service in the early winter of 1914. Harassment and sporadic violence became commonplace as the Young Turk regime launched its policy of cultural and economic 'nationalization'. The Young Turk military failures in the Caucasus and Persia sparked a severe radicalization of anti-Armenian policy at the political centre. The second phase was the threat of defeat and invasion by the British in the west and the Russians in the east. It is no exaggeration to state that the effect of these threats on the Ottoman political elite was nothing short of apocalyptic. It fuelled a fear of disappearance among the Ottoman elites and spurred persecutions in the winter of 1914–15 when, for example, all Armenian civil servants were fired from their positions and Armenian soldiers were disarmed and placed in labour battalions (Bloxham 2002: 101–28). The third phase developed out of the delusional fear of an organized Armenian insurrection, which reached boiling point when Allied forces launched the Gallipoli campaign on the night of 24 April 1915. The same night, Ottoman Interior Minister Mehmed Talaat (1871–1921) ordered the arrest of the Armenian elites of the entire Ottoman Empire. In Istanbul, 235 to 270 Armenian clergymen, physicians, editors, journalists, lawyers, teachers and politicians were rounded up and deported to the interior, where most were murdered (Shamtanchian 2007; Odian 2009). Other provinces followed. This effectively stripped a community of their political, intellectual, cultural and religious leaders. Armenian men in the labour battalions were disarmed and massacred.

By this time, sporadic deportations had already been launched. The fourth phase followed when on 23 May 1915 the regime officially authorized the general deportation of all Ottoman Armenians to the Syrian desert. This consisted of expulsion and deportation, policies that were expected to offer a territorial solution to the 'Armenian question' (Bloxham 2002: 101–28). From the spring of 1915 onwards, the Ministry of the Interior began deporting Armenians locally, first to central Anatolia, then to the Syrian desert. From May 1915, mass deportations developed into veritable death marches. There were no proper provisions for those who reached the scorching desert, giving way to exposure and hunger. This final phase of the process consisted of two pillars. First was an escalation into outright mass murder as special units began murdering Armenian soldiers, elites and deportation convoys. Second, the killings became categorical and targeted the abstract category of group identity: *all* Armenians, loyal or disloyal, were deported and massacred. This is what made the massacres genocidal. By the end of the war, the approximately 2,900 Anatolian Armenian settlements (villages, towns, neighbourhoods) were depopulated and about a million Armenians were dead.[1]

The identities of the organizers and perpetrators of the 1915 Young Turk genocide have been explored relatively well. There can be little doubt that the Committee of Union and Progress (CUP) elite mobilized local party members and certain families and tribes to achieve their aim of destroying the Armenian community of the Ottoman Empire. On the other hand, little is known regarding the categorical nature of victims targeted. The notion that official CUP policy targeted only Armenians clearly contradicts the broad diversity of non-Armenian victims, especially in the provinces of Diyarbekir and Hakkari, as well as in Persia.[2] In other words, how *Armenian* was the genocide supposed to be? The

Mardin district can serve as a fitting backdrop for an exploration of this discrepancy because of the district's religious diversity. The evidence, admittedly patchy, supports the argument that Diyarbekir governor Dr Mehmed Reshid (1873–1919) amplified the anti-Armenian persecution into a more general anti-Christian persecution, and by the time he was reproached for this policy, it was too late.

Diyarbekir Province in the Spring of 1915

Most Christian notables in Diyarbekir city were incarcerated in May 1915. By this time, there had been little persecution in Mardin, the citadel city south of Diyarbekir. As in other provincial towns, Reshid had ordered the *mutasarrif*,[3] Hilmi Bey, to arrest the Christian notables of the city. Hilmi reportedly answered that the Armenians of Mardin were Arabic-speaking Catholics, and had little in common with the Gregorian Armenians. The *mutasarrif* also added that they were unarmed and honourable citizens, and that there was no reason at all to arrest any other Christians either (Sarafian 1998: 263). Reshid was not interested in this reply and sent local CUP strongman Pirinççizâde Aziz Feyzi (1878–1933) in May to incite Muslim notables to destroy the Mardin Christians. Feyzi toured the region and bribed and persuaded the chieftains of the Deşi, Mışkiye, Kiki and Helecan tribes to carry out this destruction. From 15 May, the scenario in Diyarbekir was repeated in Mardin. Police chief Memduh Bey, a ruthless opportunist, moved into the house of the notable Syriac Yonan family and began organizing the process of persecution. First he arrested dozens of Armenian and Syriac men and tortured them to extract confessions of disloyalty and high treason. In the meantime, he extorted large sums of money from the families of the arrested men, who offered Memduh financial compensation in exchange for the release of their children (Sarafian 1998: 263).

Reshid sent the new mayor of Mardin, İbrahim Bedreddin and militiamen Çerkez Şakir and Çerkez Harun to Mardin to organize the physical destruction of the Christian population of Mardin. Together they organized a militia of five hundred men and placed them under command of the brothers Nuri and Tahir El Ensari, both of them sheikhs of the Ensari family (Rhétoré 2005: 65). While Hilmi was still in office, the group bypassed standard bureaucratic procedures and began arresting Christian notables, such as Anton Gasparian (Armalto 1970).[4] However, Reshid and his men probably considered the presence of an uncooperative *mutasarrif* an intransigent obstacle to the organization of a massacre, which was a complex undertaking. Therefore, Reshid attempted to apply his tested method of having the *mutasarrif* removed, but his appeal only achieved the reinstatement of the equally unwilling official Mehmed Şefik Bey to his old district of Mardin. Moreover, Talaat suggested that İbrahim Bedri be 'assigned to a vacant office of district governor' (BOA, DH.SFR 53/291).[5] Having replaced Hilmi with Mehmed Şefik, Reshid did not respect this new constellation either. He ignored Şefik and treated his emissary Bedri as a shadow-official with the authority of a district governor. In Mardin, Bedri was assisted by Halil Edib, who was made a judge on 17 June 1915. Bedri himself officially became district governor only on 12 September (Aydin et al. 2000: 242; Armalto 1970: 33). The CUP had not completely taken over the Ottoman bureaucracy, but it was sufficient for the genocidal process to be launched in Mardin.

On 3 June 1915, at eight o'clock in the evening, Mardin was surrounded by Reshid's militiamen, headed by Çerkez Harun. Memduh Bey arrested Bishop Ignatius Maloyan and his entire Armenian Catholic clergy and locked them up in the Mardin castle, a fortress overlooking the city. Over the following days he arrested hundreds of Christian notables, according to a French eyewitness, 'all taken from various ranks of society, without differences of age, nor of rite, nor of condition' (Simon 1991: 17–18). The men were all taken to prison and severely tortured for a week by judge Halil Edib. On 9 June a group of militiamen arrived from Diyarbekir with dozens of sets of chains and galloped up to the fort. The prisoners were told they were summoned by Governor Reshid and would be taken to Diyarbekir the next morning. The notables realized at this point they were going to be killed (Rhétoré 2005: 70).

The treatment of the Mardin notables was a copy of that of the Diyarbekir notables, who had already been massacred in the Reman gorge by that time. The first convoy, just over four hundred Christians of all denominations, left Mardin on 10 June and was marched off to Diyarbekir by Memduh on horseback. After having walked for two hours in the burning heat, Memduh took away four notables (Iskender Adem, his son August, Naum Cinanci and Iskender Hammal) and killed them (Simon 1991: 64). Three hours later, the convoy was halted at the Kurdish village of Adirshek, near the Şeyhan caves. Memduh Bey gathered the convoy and read their death sentence aloud. He added that conversion to Islam would avert death and gave those who refused conversion one hour to prepare for their deaths. Memduh had barely finished his words when Bishop Maloyan responded that he would never convert and preferred to die as a Christian rather than to live as a Muslim. The great majority of the convoy agreed, whereupon Memduh took a hundred men, led them away to the Şeyhan caves and had them all murdered and burnt. After this first massacre he returned and took another hundred men off to the Roman castle Zirzawan, where he slaughtered them and threw them in large wells (Rhétoré 2005: 78). Those who agreed to convert were taken away by the Kurdish villagers to their shaikh and became Muslims. The next day, the rest of the convoy was marched further and halted four hours from Diyarbekir. For the last time, Memduh turned to Maloyan and urged him to convert. When he refused, Memduh pulled out his handgun and shot the bishop in the head.[6] He then ordered the firing squad to massacre the rest of the convoy (Armalto 1970: 47). The work was finished and the perpetrators rode to Diyarbekir and reported their accomplishment to Governor Reshid (PAAA, R14087, 21 August 1915).[7] Two weeks later, Talaat asked Reshid about the whereabouts of Maloyan (BOA, DH.SFR 54-A/178).

The killings in Diyarbekir province had become so explicit that national and international political actors began speaking about them freely. The genocide had definitively broken through the circle of CUP secrecy. Apart from the Catholic clergymen in Mardin, another Western observer of the massacres in Diyarbekir province was the German vice-consul at Mosul, Walter Holstein. On 10 June he wired the German embassy, expressing his abhorrence of the crimes. When Holstein spoke to the governor of Mosul about the killings, the latter responded 'that only the governor of Diyarbekir bears responsibility' (PAAA, Botschaft Konstantinopel 169, 10 June 1915).[8] However, Holstein was not content with this evasive reply and dispatched a second, more indignant telegram to the embassy two days later:

> The massacre of Armenians in Diyarbekir province is becoming more and more known here every day and causes a growing unrest among the local population which, with the foolish unscrupulousness and weakness of the local authorities can easily bring about unforeseen consequences. In the Mardin district ... the circumstances have grown to a veritable persecution of Christians. It is undoubtedly the government that bears guilt for it. (PAAA, Botschaft Konstantinopel 169, 13 June 1915)

This well-intentioned message made its way through the German bureaucracy to Talaat and most probably to Reshid too. Talaat seemingly was not moved much by these protests. He listened to the stories about the massacres and replied to an employee at the German embassy named Dr Mordtmann, 'that the Porte wants to use the World War, to thoroughly settle scores [*gründlich aufzuräumen*] with its inner enemies – the domestic Christians – without being disturbed by diplomatic intervention from abroad' (PAAA, R14086, 17 June 1915).[9] What Holstein did not know was that preparations were underway for a second convoy of Christian notables in Mardin, the day after his cable.

In the meantime, the second convoy of Mardin Christians, 266 people of all denominations, was sent off on 14 June. It was led by militia commander Abdul Kadir (a subordinate of Çerkez Şakir) and Tevfik Bey, who had eliminated the Armenians of Derik (Rhétoré 2005: 83; Simon 1991: 69–70). As had been done with the first convoy, the group was halted at the Şeyhan caves, where they were forced to pay tribute to the Sultan Şeyhmus cult. The men noticed that Kurdish tribesmen, armed with rifles, axes and spades, had surrounded them. The militiamen invited the Christians to descend to the cave to drink from the cold spring water, but those who went never returned. The killings continued during the night and the next day. More than a hundred men were killed at the Şeyhan caves, after which the rest of the convoy was marched off to Diyarbekir. All of a sudden, the convoy came across three mounted gendarmes approaching at high speed. They reached the convoy and proclaimed that the sultan had pardoned the non-Armenian Christians from persecution. Their hands were untied and they were allowed to drink water and eat bread. The Armenians were not fed and continued the deportation with their hands tied. The convoy was marched off again and reached Diyarbekir on 16 June, where they were sent to the caravanserai prison (Armalto 1970: 52–53, 103).

As in Diyarbekir, after the elimination of the notables, the remaining Christians were sent to their deaths. These were mainly women, children and the elderly, although many men were still alive as well. On 2 July, a convoy of six hundred men was taken away and slaughtered just outside the city walls. Before sending the victims down the Mardin road to the valley, İbrahim Bedri and Memduh resorted to large-scale extortion. On 13 July, Memduh negotiated with the families of the Christian men still in custody about a considerable ransom, which amounted to several hundred liras per family. The men were sent off and killed on the Mardin–Diyarbekir road (Sarafian 1998: 263). After the men, their families were targeted. From late June to late October, several convoys comprising hundreds of women and children were led away and destroyed. For example, on 10 August, a convoy of six hundred women and children was taken through the Mardin plain further south. Some had already died of exhaustion and sunstroke when the convoy was halted in the district of the Kiki tribe. After Kurdish tribesmen had finished selecting the women and children they fancied, the three hundred remaining victims were massacred with axes and swords. A small batch of survivors was able to flee and hide in the desert caves (Rhétoré 2005: 164–6). Within a month or two, the Christian population of Mardin city had been drastically reduced.

The district of Mardin numbered several substantial villages with large numbers of Christian inhabitants. The largest among these were Eqsor (Gulliye) and Tell Ermen, each harbouring several thousand souls. Tell Ermen had already experienced some persecution and arrests by Memduh's militia, but mass violence was not employed until 1 July. On that day, the militia and a large number of Kurdish tribesmen invaded the village, where the terrified villagers had fled to the church. On the orders of the militia commander and with assistance from the village headman Derwiş Bey, the church was attacked and a massacre ensued. The killers did not distinguish between men and women and decapitated many of the victims. Some were drawn and quartered, or hacked to pieces with axes. A little girl who crawled out from under the corpses was battered to death when she refused to convert to Islam. Approximately seventy women were raped in the church before being put to the sword. After the massacre, Kurdish women entered the church and used daggers to stab to death any survivors (Armalto 1970: 102–3). The bodies were disposed of by being thrown into wells or burnt to ashes (PAAA, R14087, 21 August 1915, enclosure no. 5). When Rafael de Nogales visited the village a few weeks later, he met a few severely traumatized survivors, and was shocked by 'corpses barely covered with heaps of stone from which emerged here and there a bloody tress or an arm or leg gnawed on by hyenas' (Nogales 2003: 171–2). A German navy officer visited Tell Ermen too and saw severed children's hands and women's hair.[10] A week after the massacre, a Major von Mikusch reported to Vice-Consul Holstein that he had met the militia, who had 'told about the massacre, beaming with joy' [*freudestrahlend von Massacres erzählt*] (PAAA, R14086, 9 July 1915).

The next day, on 2 July at eight o'clock in the evening, Memduh Bey ordered the attack on the village of Eqsor (Gulliye), a predominantly Jacobite Syriac agricultural centre on the Mardin plain. The militia was headed by Sergeant Yusuf, son of Nuri Ensari, and aided by chieftain Mohammed Ağa of the Milli tribe. Kurdish tribesmen of the Deşi, Mişkiye and Helecan tribes, as well as some Arabs, had come over to Eqsor to participate. The village was invaded and the population was massacred. Children were thrown from roofs and mutilated with axes. Many villagers were crammed together in the house of the village headman Elias Cabbar Hinno, and burnt alive (Armalto 1970: 102). After the massacre, the village was burnt down, a spectacle visible from Mardin, where the inhabitants looked on in awe. According to Hyacinthe Simon,

İbrahim Bedreddin watched the bloodbath too, cheering and applauding (Noel 1919: part I, p. 11):

> During this bloody tragedy a man was seated on the balcony of his terrace, breathing the fresh morning air and gazing at the roseate glow of the fire raging on the plane: it was the governor of Mardin, it was Bedreddin Bey. The barbarians were cutting throats and burning his subjects, he was smoking his cigarette. (Simon 1991: 53)

Dozens of pretty women were raped and dozens more were carried off. According to survivor Abdulaziz Jacob, Yusuf Ensari had kept at least fifty women in his home in Mardin for serial rape (Yeghiayan 1991: 229). The mass looting went on for two more days and by the third day the once prosperous village of Eqsor had been reduced to a state of complete devastation (Rhétoré 2005: 195–6).

Protests and Response

The massacres in Mardin were a major component of the 'reign of terror' that Dr Reshid pursued all over Diyarbekir province. It is probable that due to Reshid's fanaticism, the CUP genocide in Diyarbekir exceeded in efficiency, scope, speed and cruelty that of any other province of the Ottoman Empire. Reshid's militia murdered without mercy, without distinction and without consequences. His bloody rule obviously did not go unnoticed, since Vice-Consul Holstein had already denounced the governor's policy. Other international observers were disturbed by his campaign as well. A French report noted Reshid's treatment of the Christians he imprisoned: 'It is difficult to describe here in detail the suffering and torture that these unfortunates have suffered in prison during all this time' (Beylerian 1983: 49).[11] Likewise, Aleppo Consul Jesse Jackson wrote on 28 June that the persecution of the Armenians in his city was intensifying. Jackson informed Ambassador Morgenthau specifically about 'the horrible things taking place in Diarbekir. Just such a reign of terror has begun in this city also'.[12]

Most protests emanated from German officials, stationed in the eastern provinces. Aleppo Consul Walter Rößler wrote about Diyarbekir province that they received 'the most gruesome rumours, which remind us of the Spanish Inquisition' (PAAA, R14086, 29 June 1915). Ambassador Wangenheim forwarded to Berlin the news about 'the province of Diyarbekir, where the Armenians are persecuted particularly cruelly' (PAAA, R14086, 9 July 1915). When Holstein received the news about the Eqsor and Tell Ermen massacres, he wrote an even more indignant telegram to Wangenheim:

> The former district governor of Mardin, briefly here, informed me as follows: the governor of Diyarbekir, Reshid Bey, is raging among the Christians of his province like an insane bloodhound; recently, in Mardin too he had seven hundred Christians (mostly Armenians) including the Armenian bishop gathered during a night by gendarmerie specially dispatched from Diyarbekir, and had them slaughtered like sheep [*wie Hammel abschlachten lassen*] near the city. Reshid Bey is continuing his bloody work among the innocents, the number of which, the district governor assured me, now surpasses two thousand. If the government does not immediately take quite vigorous measures against Reshid Bey, the common Muslim population of this local province will launch similar massacres against Christians. The situation from this point of view is becoming more threatening every day. Reshid Bey should immediately be recalled, which would document that the government does not condone his infamous acts so that a general uproar here can be allayed. (PAAA, Botschaft Konstantinopel 169, 10 July 1915)

The insistence of this message impelled Wangenheim to take a stand in regard to the reports. The next day he replied to Holstein that he would convey the content of his message to the Sublime Porte. On 12 July 1915, Wangenheim slightly adjusted the telegram, translated it into French and sent it to Talaat, who knew French. Wangenheim reproduced the exact wording of 'wie Hammel abschlachten lassen' as 'égorgé comme des moutons' (PAAA, Botschaft Konstantinopel 169, 12 July 1915).

After this sequence of written communication, Talaat officially reproached Reshid for 'overdoing' the carnage. Several instances of reprehension are especially significant as they contain intimations of the scope of the massacres. On the same day Talaat received Wangenheim's message about the indiscriminate killings in Diyarbekir province, he dispatched the following telegram to Dr Reshid:

> Lately it has been reported that massacres have been organized against the Armenians of the province and Christians without distinction of religion, and that recently for example people deported from Diyarbekir together with the Armenians and the Bishop of Mardin and seven hundred persons from other Christian communities have been taken out of town at night and slaughtered like sheep, and that an estimated two thousand people have been massacred until now, and if this is not ended immediately and unconditionally, it has been reported that it is feared the Muslim population of the neighbouring provinces will rise and massacre all Christians. It is absolutely unacceptable for the disciplinary measures and policies procured to the Armenians to include other Christians as this would leave a very bad impression upon

public opinion and therefore these types of incidents that especially threaten the lives of all Christians need to be ended immediately, and the truth of the conditions needs to be reported. (BOA, DH.ŞFR 54/406)

In this important telegram, Talaat not only literally reproduced Holstein's words, 'slaughtered like sheep', but also used the euphemism 'disciplinary measures and policies' to endorse what Reshid had been doing correctly so far: destroying the Armenians of Diyarbekir.

In July, Reshid's excesses became notorious among anyone who even came near his province, strewn as it was with corpses. The governor of Baghdad, Süleyman Nazif (1870–1927), a noted intellectual hailing from Diyarbekir, travelled to his hometown during this period. Nazif later wrote that the pungent smell of decaying corpses pervaded the atmosphere and that the bitter stench clogged his nose, making him gag (Kocahanoğlu 1998: 522–3). Nazif had seen only the tip of the iceberg, as most bodies were disposed of in the rivers Euphrates and Tigris. Rößler wrote that the 'floating along of corpses on the Euphrates' had been going on for twenty-five days, adding: 'The bodies were all tied in the same manner two by two, back to back' (PAAA, R14087, 27 July 1915). Cemal Pasha, in charge of the Syrian region south of Diyarbekir, reproached Dr Reshid with an urgent and personal telegram on 14 July, complaining that 'the corpses floating down the Euphrates are probably those of the Armenians killed in the rebellion, these need to be buried on the spot, leave no corpses out in the open'.[13] Two days later, Reshid answered Cemal by pointing out that the Euphrates bore little relation to Diyarbekir province, and that the floating corpses were coming from the Erzurum and Mamuret-ul Aziz directions. Reshid noted that burials were exceptional and that 'those who were killed here are either being thrown into deep deserted caves or, as has been the case for the most part, are being burnt'.[14] Faiz Al-Ghusayn was a witness to the burning of dead bodies when he entered Diyarbekir province near Karapınar. He saw hundreds of bodies burnt to ashes. He also saw that there were many women and children among the dead, consumed by fire (Al-Ghusayn 1917: 20). The rumours of Diyarbekir having become an open-air morgue reached Talaat, who ordered Reshid on 3 August to 'bury the deceased lying on the roads, throw their corpses into brooks, lakes, and rivers, and burn their property left behind on the roads'.[15] Alongside these reports, there is photographic evidence that the two men met during the war, possibly because Reshid was summoned to Istanbul.

Reshid did not pay much attention to, let alone seriously consider the wave of negative feedback, and his reputation grew more and more nefarious. The German protests became much more explicit by the end of July. An employee at the German embassy wrote to German Chancellor Bethmann-Hollweg a most explicit report, which read: 'Since the beginning of this month the governor of Diyarbekir, Reshid Bey, has begun the systematic extermination of the Christian population under his jurisdiction, without distinction of race and religion' (PAAA, R14086, 31 July 1915). As reports of massacres poured into Mosul province, Walter Holstein became increasingly enraged and wrote a bitter telegram to his colleagues in Istanbul:

> Everyone knows that the governor of Diyarbekir ... is the instigator of the terrible crimes committed against the Christians in his province; everyone rightly presumes that we are also aware of the atrocities and they are asking themselves why we allow a notorious mass murderer to remain unpunished and continue to be the governor. It would hardly suffice merely to express our disapproval of the atrocities effectively to counteract the various compromising attitudes towards us. Not until we have forced the Porte ruthlessly to demand that the criminals who are sitting in official positions in Diyarbekir, Mardin, Siirt, etc., account for these allegations and do so as quickly as possible, only then will they drop the suspicions held against us. I read in various German newspapers official Turkish denials of the atrocities committed against the Christians and am surprised at the naivety of the Porte in believing they can obliterate facts about the crimes by Turkish officials by telling blatant lies. Up to now the world has not experienced such atrocities, which have provenly been and are still being committed by officials in Diyarbekir province! (PAAA, Botschaft Konstantinopel 170, 14 August 1915)

This report too was forwarded to Talaat, who began losing his patience, since he was forced to explain Reshid's compromising and embarrassing actions to German officials. Reshid obviously had taken no measures to act according to his instructions a month previously. To clear things up, two days after Holstein's cable, Talaat sent a second telegram admonishing Reshid, reiterating that the persecution and massacre of all Christians in the province was not permitted. He also urged him to dismantle the militia that was causing the provincial authorities to be held responsible for the killings (BOA, DH.ŞFR 54-A/248). This was not yet the end of Talaat's reprimands to his zealous subordinate. It had become clear that Reshid had persecuted and murdered not only non-Armenian Ottoman Christians, but also non-Ottoman Armenians. His indiscriminate slaughter of *ethnic* Armenians without consideration of *political* identity had become a serious problem. One of the victims was Stepan Katosian, an Armenian American who had summarily been put to death in the Diyarbekir prison. His execution could have caused a diplomatic incident since the Ottoman Empire was not at war with the

United States, in which case it still would have been a legal violation. Talaat therefore asked Reshid for information about Katosian's execution (BOA, DH.ŞFR 56/131). To ensure that this was the last instance in which Reshid transgressed the rules of the genocide, Talaat ordered the consistent screening of the political identities of Armenians from then on (BOA, DH.ŞFR 57/50).[16] The purpose of this order was that non-Ottoman Armenians should not be persecuted. For example, an Iranian Armenian named Mıgırdiç Stepanian was allowed to leave for Persia via Mosul (BOA, DH.ŞFR 57/57).[17]

Fine-Tuning the Scope of Victims

Apart from specific instructions readjusting Reshid's extreme behaviour, Talaat released several national decrees defining the categories of those to be persecuted and deported. At first, he excluded the Armenian converts to Islam from deportation to the south (BOA, DH.ŞFR 54/100). Most converts were not persecuted any further and, provided they kept their silence, were allowed to continue living in their homes. Two weeks later, he reincorporated the converts into the deportation programme. Talaat's order read that 'some Armenians are converting collectively or individually just to remain in their home towns', and that 'this type of conversion should never be lent credence'. Talaat contended that 'whenever these types of people perceive threats to their interests they will convert as a means of deception' (BOA, DH.ŞFR 54/254). On 4 August, Talaat excluded the Armenian Catholics from deportation, requesting their numbers in the respective provinces (BOA, DH.ŞFR 54-A/252). On 15 August, the Protestant Armenians were also excluded from deportation to Der ez-Zor. Again, Talaat requested statistical data (BOA, DH.ŞFR 55/20). Besides these official directions, the general methodology of the genocide consisted of killing the men and deporting those women and children who were not absorbed into Muslim households. This means that, in general, Armenian women were not to be subjected to immediate on-the-spot killing as the men were (Derderian 2005). Finally, a specific order excluding the Jacobite Syriacs from deportation was issued for those provinces with Syriac communities (BOA, DH.ŞFR 57/112).[18]

There is contradictory evidence on the precise nature of Reshid's local implementation of Talaat's national instructions. On the one hand, Reshid observed the commands for exclusion of non-Armenian Christians from further genocidal destruction; on the other hand, he disregarded all narrowing of victim categories. According to another interpretation, it is conceivable that the series of rebukes compelled him to mitigate the persecution, even though the harm was already done. In other words, Reshid discontinued the persecution of the non-Armenian Christian communities when they had already been largely destroyed. These restrictions of time may have added to restrictions of location. It is also possible that this turn of events only happened in and around Diyarbekir city, since in Mardin İbrahim Bedreddin, Aziz Feyzi and Memduh Bey had taken over the district. The most compelling example of selective persecution, steered from above, is the causal link between Holstein's telegram of 12 June and the fate of the second convoy of Mardin notables. In that chain of events, Reshid indeed seems to have followed orders and limited the scope of the genocide.

One of the first villages to be thoroughly destroyed was Kabiye, on 23 April 1915. According to one survivor from that village, a group of survivors from all over the Diyarbekir plain had assembled in Qarabash some time after the massacre, probably around mid-June. Pirinççizâde Sıdkı had drawn up a list of these survivors and had the list read aloud in front of the group. Those with Armenian names were carefully separated from those with Syriac names. Sıdkı declared that the Syriacs were exempted from persecution on orders of the government. When a young man named Dikran was also placed into the Armenian group, he protested to Sıdkı, pleading that he was a Syriac Orthodox. Although he had spoken the truth, his protests were futile and he was led away with the rest of the Armenians and butchered (Jastrow 1981: 327–9). The survivors of the second Mardin convoy had been in prison for a week when Memduh Bey arrived and ordered all cells opened. The prisoners were led outside, where Memduh addressed them: 'Those of your who are Syriac, Chaldean and Protestant, raise your hands and state your names'. The Syriacs, Chaldeans and Protestants were separated from the Armenians and were allowed to go home (Armalto 1970: 54). A similar selection was remembered by a Syriac survivor from a labour battalion working on road construction near Akpınar, between Diyarbekir and Mardin. On 17 June Sıdkı reportedly arrived at the road-building site, where he separated the Armenians from the other Christians. An Armenian named Migirditch from Qarabash village was moved to the Armenian side but claimed to be a Syriac Orthodox. Though his identity was confirmed by a native of Qarabash, Sıdkı did not believe him and swore at him: 'Filthy dog, your name is Migirditch and you are supposed to be a Syriac?!' The unfortunate man was then sent off to his death with the other Armenians (Qarabashi 2002: 69–70). A Syriac conscript in a labour battalion working between Urfa and Diyarbekir in mid-August related his tale to the Swiss missionary Jacob Künzler, who reported as follows:

'In the evening', the Syriac recounted, 'a large crowd of well-armed gendarmes had come from the city. They immediately ordered the segregation
of the Armenians from the Syriacs. Thereupon the Armenians were tied
together and were taken about a quarter of an hour away. Soon one heard
many shots ... It became clear to us, that our Armenian comrades were now
being slaughtered ... When the gendarmes returned to the village, we Syriacs
thought that soon it would also be our turn. We were provided with lanterns
and had to go towards the place of slaughter ... We had to throw the murdered Armenians in a deep well. There were several among them, who were
still breathing, one could even still walk, he dove into the well voluntarily.
When all the dead and half-dead had been dropped down, we had to seal off
the well and heap earth and ashes on it'. (Künzler [1921] 1999: 47–8)

These instances of selection of Armenians illustrate that Reshid delegated the implementation of Talaat's orders to Sıdkı. After Talaat's
telegrams, some form of selective killing seems to have been applied. By
that time, many Syriacs had already been murdered.

These telling examples notwithstanding, there is also evidence that
runs counter to Reshid's ostensible pardon of non-Armenian Christians
after Talaat's telegrams. The case of the Eqsor massacre shows that
orders for differentiation between Christians were simply brushed
aside. Reportedly, the executioner of Eqsor, Nuri Ensari, had personally
proclaimed the 'amnesty' accorded to the Syriacs, while the predominantly Syriac and Catholic village had just been exterminated and was
at that time still being razed (Yeghiayan 1991: 230). The same treatment befell the Christian women and children, who were supposed to
be excluded from immediate massacre as routine. As early as June,
Aleppo Consul Jackson reported about the village of Redwan that 'they
even killed little children'.[19] A deportation convoy trudging to Mardin
was halted by Reshid's militia at the village of Golikê, where dozens of
women were first raped and then killed (Qarabashi 2002: 72).[20] There
was even a report – though highly suspect – that Reshid himself 'took
800 children, enclosed them in a building and set light to it', burning the
children alive (*Morning Post*, 7 December 1918, quoted in Dadrian 2003:
430, 436, fn 24).[21]

The few Orthodox or Catholic Greeks were not spared either. The
wife of a Catholic Greek citizen of Diyarbekir complained to German
Vice-Consul Rößler that she had not heard from her husband Yorgi
Obégi since he, her daughter and four of her brothers had gone into
hiding with a Muslim colleague in Diyarbekir. It became known that
they were found and deported, but shortly outside of Diyarbekir stripped
of their valuables and killed. The Greek Orthodox priest of Diyarbekir
had disappeared without a trace, and was probably murdered as well.

Rößler was informed by an Ottoman officer that the then police chief of Diyarbekir, most probably Memduh Bey, had confessed the murder to him: 'The commissar had told him that he had killed them himself' (PAAA, R14087, 3 September 1915, enclosure no. 2).[22] In the Silvan district, 425 Greeks out of a total 583 were killed (Noel 1919: part II, p. 1).

The most compelling evidence supporting the interpretation that Talaat's orders were ignored are the massacres organized in Nusaybin and Cizre. On 16 August 1915, İbrahim Bedri sent militia officer Abdulkadir and chieftain of the Deşi tribe Abdulaziz to Nusaybin (Rhétoré 2005: 220). They incarcerated all the Christian men of Nusaybin with no distinction of denomination: Syriac Jacobites, Chaldeans, Protestants and Armenians. In the middle of the night, the men were led away to a desolate canyon, butchered one by one and thrown into the ravine. Many were decapitated, and each victim was urged to convert to Islam before being killed and hurled down the abyss (Hinno 1993: 30–33). Hanna Shouha, the Chaldean priest of Nusaybin, had already been deported to Kharput and died on the road. His wife was violated and killed; his family were sent to Mardin and Diyarbekir and were eliminated either on the road or on arrival. Within two days, the population of Nusaybin dropped from 2,000 to 1,200, as 800 Christians were destroyed. The Jewish community of 600 persons was left unharmed (Armalto 1970: 97–8; Qarabashi 2002: 124–5).

Almost two weeks later, Cizre was targeted. On orders of Reshid, deputies Zülfü Bey and Aziz Feyzi had toured the province in April 1915 to organize the genocide. They had also frequented Cizre and spoken to local Kurdish leaders (*Épisodes des massacres* 1920: 14).[23] On 29 August, Aziz Feyzi led a group of men, including the mufti of Cizre Ahmed Hilmi and Reman chieftain Ömer, in the attack.[24] All Christian men were arrested and tortured under the pretext that they had arms hidden in secret depots. They were then bound with ropes and chains, and marched out of the city, where they were stripped of their belongings and murdered. The naked bodies were dumped downstream in the Tigris, for the obvious reason that the killers did not want the victims' relatives to see the corpses and panic. Two days later, the families were placed on *kelek* rafts and sent off, after local Muslims had selected a number of children. Their river journey was short, as their vessels were moored at a Kurdish village shortly downstream. Most women were raped, shot dead and thrown in the river (Armalto 1970: 89–90). The pollution the decaying corpses caused to the Tigris was of such a nature that the population of Mosul was forbidden to drink from the river for a month (Merigoux 2000: 462). In Cizre, the only survivors were four women absorbed into a Muslim household. Three of them were killed

anyway; the other, Afife Mimarbashi, bribed her kidnapper and fled
to Mardin as the only survivor of the Cizre massacre (Sarafian 1998:
263). A total of 4,750 Armenians (2,500 Gregorians, 1,250 Catholics,
1,000 Protestants), 250 Chaldeans and 100 Jacobite Syriacs were killed
(PAAA, Botschaft Konstantinopel 170, 11 September 1915). A week
after the mass murder, Holstein reported to his superiors that 'gangs
of Kurds, who were recruited for this purpose by Feyzi Bey, deputy for
Diyarbekir, with connivance of the local authorities and participation of
the army, have massacred the entire Christian population of the town of
Cizre (in Diyarbekir province)' (PAAA, Botschaft Konstantinopel 170, 9
September 1915).

Discussion

It is evident that the indiscriminate killings were by no means spontaneous outbursts of popular bloodlust. Nor were they meticulously
premeditated and prepared by conspiracy the year before. Talaat's
telegraphic reprimands had arrived late, and were not taken into consideration. As the Minister of the Interior, he was aware of this, as he
was continuously informed of it by German officials in Istanbul, who
noted 'that the instructions of the Turkish government to the provincial authorities for a large part defeat their purpose as a result of their
arbitrariness' (PAAA, R14093, 27 September 1916). In the summer of
1915, all Christian communities of Diyarbekir were equally struck by
the genocide, although the Armenians were often singled out for immediate destruction. As Norman Naimark (2002: 41–2) wrote, 'Protestant
and Catholic Armenians could be formally exempted from deportation,
even if in practice local authorities made no distinction among the various Christian sects'. Consul Rößler reported that the Ottoman government lost 'control over the elements they had brought into existence'
(PAAA, R14087, 27 July 1915). These 'elements', as Rößler described
the genocidal measures, proved particularly ferocious in Diyarbekir
province. Major Noel was aware of this, but he incorrectly noted about
the Syriacs:

> In Diarbekir itself the Syrian Jacobites were scarcely molested. Of all the
> Christian communities they know how best to get on with the Turks, and
> when the massacres were ordered they were officially excluded. In the dis-
> tricts, however, the Government very soon lost control of the passions they
> had loosed (if they ever wanted to keep them in control), with the result that
> the Jacobites suffered there as much as anybody else. (Noel 1919: part II,
> p. 14)

Contrary to Rößler's perception, Reshid had a firm control of his murderous infrastructure. Especially in and around Diyarbekir district, most instances of massacre in which the militia engaged were directly ordered by him. An exploration of the perpetrators involved, the timing, scope and methodology of the killings clearly reveals Reshid's will propelling them. Due to his personal disposition, Dr Mehmed Reshid gave a distinct shape to the genocide, configuring the range of victims from the outset, even when his superior tried to modify it.

What does this mean for the conventional understanding of the 1915 Young Turk genocide? Hannibal Travis has argued, in a sweeping statement, that the shorthand 'Armenian Genocide' became entrenched in genocide studies in the 1970s, as scholars came to use it without properly questioning the broader range of victims, thereby 'unremembering' the victimization of Assyrians and Greeks (Travis 2013). In recent years this trend has changed. Edited volumes by Tessa Hofmann (2010) and Matthias Bjørnlund (2011) have sketched, with precise empirical strokes, a more complex picture of Christian victimization in the Ottoman Empire. In some provinces, all Christians were targeted from the outset; in other provinces, only Armenians were; again in others, a mosaic of persecution fluctuated throughout the First World War. The arguments might be reconcilable: yes, the Armenians were singled out across the vast country for complete annihilation, and yes, although not necessarily planned by Istanbul, the mass murder of Assyrians quantitatively and qualitatively meets the criteria for genocide, by any definition. The 1915 genocide was a multi-layered, chequered process of destruction with a broad range of victims. Like most genocides are.

Uğur Ümit Üngör gained his PhD in 2009 (cum laude) at the University of Amsterdam. He is Associate Professor in the Department of History at Utrecht University and Research Fellow at the NIOD: Institute for War, Holocaust, and Genocide Studies in Amsterdam. His main area of interest is the historical sociology of mass political violence. His most recent publications include *Confiscation and Destruction: The Young Turk Seizure of Armenian Property* (Continuum, 2011) and the award-winning *The Making of Modern Turkey: Nation and State in Eastern Anatolia, 1913–1950* (Oxford University Press, 2011).

Notes

Parts of this chapter have been reprinted from Uğur Ümit Üngör, *The Making of Modern Turkey: Nation and State in Eastern Anatolia, 1913–1950*, Chapter 2: 'Genocide of

Christians, 1915–1916', published in 2011 by Oxford University Press. By permission of
Oxford University Press, www.oup.com.

1. For a bibliography on the Armenian genocide see Vassilian (1992). All translations in
   this chapter are mine.
2. For example, for detailed studies of the genocidal process in Mardin, see Ternon
   (2002) and Gaunt (2006).
3. An administrative authority in the Ottoman system.
4. This detailed chronicle was written in 1919 in Arabic by the Syriac Catholic priest
   Ishaq Armalto, who was also secretary to Mardin's bishop Gabriel Tappouni. It
   provides a very valuable account of Diyarbekir province before and during the war.
   The book has recently been translated by Ingvar Rydberg (2005) into Swedish.
   This author has used an unofficial Turkish translation by Turan Karataş (Sweden,
   1993), p. 40.
5. Hilmi was demoted and assigned to a minor office in the Mosul province. Just as he
   left for Mosul, Reshid sent orders for him to be murdered. Hilmi escaped assassination because the *mutasarrif* who was assigned this task was a personal friend who
   procrastinated in carrying out the order. In the meantime, Hilmi crossed into Mosul
   province, out of the jurisdiction of the Diyarbekir provincial authorities, and thereby
   out of Reshid's deadly reach (Sarafian 1998: 263).
6. Bishop Maloyan was later beatified by the Vatican. See *Ciliciae Armenorum seu
   Mardinen* (2000).
7. See enclosure no. 6: 'In the Mardin too the district governor was deposed, for he did
   not obey the will of the governor. From here, they brought to D[iyarbekir] first 500
   and then again 300 notables of all sects. The first 600 never arrived, from the others
   nothing was ever heard.' (*In Mardin wurde der Mutessarif auch abgesetzt, da er nicht
   nach dem Willen des Walis. Von hier hat man einmal 500 und dann wieder 300 der
   Notabeln aller Konfessionen nach D. bringen lassen. Die ersten 600 sind nie angekom-
   men, von den anderen hat man nichts mehr gehört.*)
8. This telegram contains a footnote which reads: 'Herrn Kap Humann für Enver'.
   The note refers to Lieutenant Commander and Marine Attaché Hans Humann, a
   personal friend of Enver Pasha's and a staunch advocate of Ottoman expansion into
   the Caucasus. According to an intimate observer, Humann had unfettered access to
   the CUP elite and held 'an outstanding position of extraordinary influence' (Jäckh
   1944: 119).
9. When Kâmil Bey, a member of parliament for Diyarbekir who opposed the massacres,
   travelled to Istanbul to complain to Talaat about Reshid and Feyzi's genocidal campaign in Diyarbekir, Talaat threatened to have him assassinated if he did not quieten
   down (Yeghiayan 1991: 482).
10. Bundesarchiv (Freiburg), Reichsmarine 40/434, G.B.N. 8289, Engelking to Fleet
    Command, 11 November 1915, quoted in Kaiser (2002: 84).
11. Document no. 156: 'Note du Département sur les massacres arméniens'.
12. National Archives, RG 59, 867.4016/92, Jackson to Morgenthau, 28 June 1915, in
    Sarafian (2004: 84).
13. Cemal to Reshid, 14 July 1915, quoted in Kocahanoğlu (1998: 519).
14. Reshid to Cemal, 16 July 1915, quoted in Kocahanoğlu (1998: 519).
15. Talaat to Reshid, 3 August 1915, quoted in Kocahanoğlu (1998: 519).
16. Talaat later specified the order and requested information on 'Armenian officials
    employed at consulates of allied and neutral countries' (BOA, DH.ŞFR 70/152).
17. Whereas his superordinate Talaat was scolding him continuously, two days later
    Reshid received an appreciative telegram from his subordinate Halil Edib in Mardin.

Edib expressed his praise on the Eid el-Adha, the important Muslim festival involving sacrifice of cattle: 'I congratulate you with your Eid, and kiss your hands that have gained us the six provinces and opened up the gateways to Turkistan and the Caucasus'. Halil Edib to Reshid, 19 October 1915, quoted in Bilgi (1997: 29, fn 73).

18. A year later, an even more lenient instruction was issued towards the Syriacs, requesting information about their numbers and at the same time allowing them to travel within the country for the sake of trade (BOA, DH.ŞFR 68/98). Although tens of thousands of Syriacs had been massacred by that time, it did allow a terrified and traumatized remnant of the Syriac community to live in their native regions. Still, their relative comfort was probably contingent on the appointment of Süleyman Necmi, Reshid's successor in Diyarbekir. The new governor was merciful compared to Reshid, and permitted the Syriacs to take a breath, before İbrahim Bedreddin became governor of Diyarbekir province and launched a second attack against the Syriacs of Tur Abdin.

19. Jackson to Morgenthau, 8 June 1915, in Sarafian (2004: 60).

20. There is some propagandistic evidence that Aziz Feyzi became known for his habit of collecting trophies from female victims. On several occasions he reportedly had the militia retrieve a necklace of women's nipples and a rope of women's hair. See more in *Épisodes des massacres* (1920: 50) and Yeghiayan (1991: 152).

21. Dr Reshid's reputation would hardly accord him the benefit of the doubt regarding incidents such as these. This source, however, seems highly dubious and the massacre is not reported in any of the other sources from Diyarbekir province.

22. Additionally, Memduh seems to have murdered a Russian and an Englishman. The murdered Englishman was probably Albert Atkinson, a missionary. Talaat later asked Reshid questions on his whereabouts (BOA, DH.ŞFR 56/238).

23. On his way back to Diyarbekir, Feyzi reportedly visited the Reman district and convinced the brothers Ömer and Mustafa that the time had come to destroy all Christians.

24. PRO, FO 371/4191, 9 April 1919, reproduced in Mesut (1992: 29). For biographical information on the then Muslim clerics of Cizre, see Yaşın (1983: 147–65).

Bibliography

Al-Ghusayn, F. 1917. *Martyred Armenia*. London: C.A. Pearson Ltd.

Armalto, I. 1970. *Al-Qousara fi Nakabat an-Nasara*, 2nd edn. Beirut: Al-Sharfe Monastery.

———— 2005. *De Kristnas Hemska Katastrofer: Osmanernas och Ung-turkarnas Folkmord i norra Mesopotamien 1895 / 1914–1918*, trans. Ingvar Rydberg. Stockholm: Beth Froso Nsibin.

Aydın, S., et al. (eds). 2000. *Mardin: Aşiret-Cemaat-Devlet*. Istanbul: Tarih Vakfı.

Başbakanlık Osmanlı Arşivi [Ottoman Archives], Istanbul (BOA) DH.ŞFR 53/291, Talaat to Reshid, 8 June 1915.

———— DH.ŞFR 54/100, Talaat to provinces, 22 June 1915.

———— DH.ŞFR 54/254, Talaat to provinces, 1 July 1915.

———— DH.ŞFR 54/406, Talaat to Reshid, 12 July 1915.

———— DH.ŞFR 54-A/178, Talaat to Reshid, 29 July 1915.

———— DH.ŞFR 54-A/252, Talaat to provinces, 4 August 1915.

———— DH.ŞFR 55/20, Talaat to provinces, 15 August 1915.

———— DH.ŞFR 54-A/248, Talaat to Reshid, 16 August 1915.

———— DH.ŞFR 56/131, Talaat to Reshid, 24 September 1915.

—— DH.ŞFR 57/50, Talaat to Reshid, 17 October 1915.
—— DH.ŞFR 57/57, Talaat to Reshid, 17 October 1915.
—— DH.ŞFR 57/112, Talaat to the provinces of Diyarbekir, Bitlis, Haleb and Urfa, 25 October 1915.
—— DH.ŞFR 56/238, Talaat to Reshid, 30 October 1915.
—— DH.ŞFR 68/98, Mamuret-ul Aziz, Diyarbekir, Bitlis, Musul and Urfa, 23 September 1916.
—— DH.ŞFR 70/152, Talaat to provinces, 30 November 1916.
Beylerian, A. 1983. *Les grandes puissances l'Empire ottoman et les Arméniens dans les archives françaises, 1914–1918. Recueil de documents*. Cambridge, MA: Avon Hill Books.
Bilgi, N. 1997. *Dr. Mehmed Reşid Şahingiray'ın hayatı ve hâtıraları*. İzmir: Akademi.
Bjørnlund, M. et al. (eds). 2011. *The Genocide of the Ottoman Greeks: Studies on the State-Sponsored Campaign of Extermination of the Christians of Asia Minor 1912–1922 and Its Aftermath*. New York: Aristide D. Caratzas.
Bloxham, D. 2002. 'The Beginning of the Armenian Catastrophe: Comparative and Contextual Considerations', in H.-L. Kieser and D.J. Schaller (eds), *Der Völkermord an den Armeniern und die Shoah: The Armenian Genocide and the Shoah*. Zürich: Chronos, pp. 101–28
Ciliciae Armenorum seu Mardinen: Beatificationis seu Canonizationis servi Dei Ignatii Choukrallah Maloyan, archiepiscopi mardinensis in opium fidei, uti fertur, interfecti (1915): Positio super vita, martyrio et fama martyrii. 2000. Rome: Tipografia Guerra.
Dadrian, V.N. 2003. 'Children as Victims of Genocide: The Armenian Case', *Journal of Genocide Research* 5(3): 421–37.
Derderian, K. 2005. 'Common Fate, Different Experience: Gender-Specific Aspects of the Armenian Genocide, 1915–1917', *Holocaust and Genocide Studies* 19(1): 1–25.
Épisodes des massacres armèniens de Diarbekir: Faits et Documents. 1920. Constantinople: Kéchichian Fr.
Gaunt, D. 2006. *Massacres, Resistance, Protectors: Muslim–Christian Relations in Eastern Anatolia during World War I*. Piscataway, NJ: Gorgias.
Hinno, H.H. 1993. *Farman: Tur'Abdinli Süryanilerin Katliamı 1914–1915*. Athens: n.p.
Hofmann, T. (ed.). 2010. *Verfolgung, Vertreibung und Vernichtung der Christen im Osmanischen Reich 1912–1922*. Berlin: LIT Verlag.
Jäckh, E. 1944. *The Rising Crescent: Turkey Yesterday, Today, and Tomorrow*. New York: Farrar & Rinehart.
Jastrow, O. (ed.). 1981. *Die mesopotamisch-arabischen Qəltu-Dialekte: vol. II, Volkskundliche Texte in Elf Dialekten*. Wiesbaden: Kommissionsverlag Franz Steiner GmbH.
Kaiser, H. 2002. *At the Crossroads of Der Zor: Death, Survival, and Humanitarian Resistance in Aleppo, 1915–1917*. London: Gomidas.
Kocahanoğlu, O.S. 1998. *İttihat-Terakki'nin Sorgulanması ve Yargılanması*. Istanbul: Temel.
Künzler, J. [1921] 1999. *Im Lande des Blutes und der Tränen: Erlebnisse in Mesopotamien während des Weltkrieges (1914–1918)*. Zürich: Chronos.
Merigoux, J.M. 2000. *Va a Ninive! Un dialogue avec l'Irak: Mosul et les villages chrétiens, pages d'histoire dominicaine*. Paris: Cerf.
Mesut, A. (ed.). 1992. *İngiliz Belgelerinde Kürdistan 1918–1958*. Istanbul: Doz.
Naimark, N. 2002. *Fires of Hatred: Ethnic Cleansing in Twentieth-Century Europe*. Cambridge, MA: Harvard University Press.
Noel, E.W.C. 1919. *Diary of Major E. Noel on Special Duty in Kurdistan*. Basra: n.p.

Nogales, R. 2003. *Four Years beneath the Crescent*. London: Sterndale Classics.

Odian, Y. 2009. *Accursed Years: My Exile and Return from Der Zor, 1914–1919*. London: Gomidas.

Politisches Archiv Auswärtiges Amt [German National Archives], Berlin (PAAA), Botschaft Konstantinopel 169, Holstein to embassy, 10 June 1915.

——— Botschaft Konstantinopel 169, Holstein to embassy, 13 June 1915.

——— R14086, Wangenheim to Bethmann-Hollweg, 17 June 1915.

——— R14086, Rößler to Bethmann-Hollweg, 29 June 1915.

——— R14086, Wangenheim to Bethmann-Hollweg, 9 July 1915.

——— Botschaft Konstantinopel 169, Holstein to Embassy, 10 July 1915.

——— Botschaft Konstantinopel 169, Wangenheim to Talaat, 12 July 1915.

——— R14087, Rößler to Bethmann-Hollweg, 27 July 1915.

——— R14086, Hohenlohe-Langenburg to Bethmann-Hollweg, 31 July 1915.

——— Botschaft Konstantinopel 170, Holstein to Embassy, 14 August 1915.

——— R14087, director of the Deutscher Hülfsbund für christliches Liebeswerk im Orient (Frankfurt am Main) Friedrich Schuchardt to the Auswärtiges Amt, 21 August 1915.

——— R14087, Rößler to Bethmann-Hollweg, 3 September 1915.

——— Botschaft Konstantinopel 170, Holstein to embassy, 9 September 1915.

——— Botschaft Konstantinopel 170, Hohenlohe-Langenburg to Auswärtige Amt, 11 September 1915.

——— R14093, 'Aufzeichnung über die Armenierfrage', Berlin, 27 September 1916.

Qarabashi, N. 2002. *Dmo Zliho*, trans. J. Jonk from German into Dutch, *Vergoten Bloed*. Glanerburg: Bar Habreus Uitgeverij.

Rhétoré, J. 2005. *Les chrétiens aux bêtes: souvenirs de la guerre sainte proclamée par les Turcs contre les chrétiens en 1915*. Paris: Éditions du Cerf.

Sarafian, A. 1998. 'The Disasters of Mardin during the Persecutions of the Christians, Especially the Armenians, 1915', *Haigazian Armenological Review* 18: 261–271.

——— (ed.). 2004. *United States Official Records on the Armenian Genocide 1915–1917*. London: Gomidas.

Shamtanchian, M. 2007. *The Fatal Night: An Eyewitness Account of the Extermination of Armenian Intellectuals in 1915*. Studio City, CA: H. and K. Majikian Publications.

Simon, H. 1991. *Mardine: la ville heroïque: Autel et tombeau de l'Arménie (Asie Mineure) durant les massacres de 1915*. Jounieh: Maison Naaman pour la culture.

Ternon, Y. 2002. 'Mardin 1915: Anatomie pathologique d'une destruction', *Revue d'Histoire Arménienne Contemporaine* 4.

Travis, H. 2013. 'Constructing the "Armenian Genocide": How Scholars Unremembered the Assyrian and Greek Genocides in the Ottoman Empire', in A.L. Hinton, T. La Pointe and D. Irvin-Erickson (eds.), *Hidden Genocides: Power, Knowledge, Memory*. Rutgers, NJ: Rutgers University Press, 170–192.

Vassilian, H.B. 1992. *The Armenian Genocide: A Comprehensive Bibliography and Library Resource Guide*. Glendale, CA: Armenian Reference Books Co.

Yaşın, A. 1983. *Bütün yönleriyle Cizre*. Cizre: n.p.

Yeghiayan, V. (ed.). 1991. *British Foreign Office Dossiers on Turkish War Criminals*. Pasadena, CA: American Armenian International College.

CHAPTER 2

SAYFO GENOCIDE

THE CULMINATION OF AN ANATOLIAN CULTURE OF VIOLENCE

David Gaunt

⸻𝒮𝓈𝓈⸻

Scholars seeking to identify the background causes of genocide often point to the crucial importance of a long history of violence inside the territory where the genocide later takes place. The aim of this research is to see if it is possible to predict risk of mass murder or genocide in advance in order to prevent it. The indicators can also be used in describing historical events. Helen Fein points out that the perpetrators of genocide are often repeat offenders who have committed mass killings before and want to complete the destruction of a target group (Fein 1993). Barbara Harff shows that perpetrators of genocide and their victims are brought through the repeated instances of inter-ethnic and inter-religious violence into a condition of being 'habituated' to mass killing and repeated attacks (Harff 2003). Here I will examine the increasing instances of anti-Christian violence building up in south-eastern Anatolia before the First World War and its connection with the genocide perpetrated against the native Assyrian, Chaldean and Syriac Christians. This was a region so accustomed to mass violence in late Ottoman times that one scholar has termed it a 'zone of genocide' (Levene 1998).

The Ottoman Empire and its successor the Republic of Turkey have been plagued by unresolved tension between the centre and its periphery (Mardin 1973, 2006). Efforts to integrate the multicultural borderlands, which historically were semi-autonomous, led often to violence that proved irreversible. The harder the central government strove to control the periphery, the more bloodshed came in its wake. The regimes of the sultan's court and even the Young Turk rule after their revolution of 1908 ruled the provinces with an underpaid bureaucracy appointed for a short term and staffed by persons who were strangers to the communities they administered. The local population was composed of an undifferentiated mass of agriculturalists dominated by a higher stratum of patriarchal extended families, the *ayan*. Upon arrival, the agents of the central government immediately became dependent on collaborating with the local strongmen, which made the provinces almost immune to national policies, unless they were compatible with the wishes of the *ayan* or could be manipulated to its advantage. This made the process of top-down modernization protracted and frustrated. In the course of time, it created a condition in the borderlands of Turkey that can be seen as a culture of violence or a society of violence (Gerlach 2006; Speitkamp 2013). Using Ottoman documents, Hilmar Kaiser describes the province of Diyarbakir in the years after the Young Turk revolution of 1908 as in near total Hobbesian anarchy, with Kurdish tribal feuds, attacks against Christians and Yezidis, and ineffective governors. This situation continued up to and even after the Ottoman Empire entered the First World War on the side of Germany and Austria-Hungary (Kaiser 2014).

Inside a culture of violence, force is one of the prime tactics used to resolve social, economic and political issues. It neutralizes the functioning of the legal system and forces the victims to develop means of defence and makes for an atmosphere of guarded suspicion. One remarkable aspect of the Sayfo genocide was the capacity of the Assyrians, once they realized that even they were targeted, not just the Armenians, to put up resistance. Depending on lucky circumstance, they organized self-defence units, made barricades, found weapons and made ammunition. At times they were able to repel large Kurdish attacks and even sieges by the regular army. Only rarely did this resistance result in an Assyrian victory, such as in the villages of Azakh and Ayn-Wardo. The Assyrians were pushed out of Hakkari after a three-month military campaign and the medium-sized Christian town of Midyat was crushed after a week-long battle. But the Ottomans did not always find it easy to annihilate them.

Genocide by definition is a criminal act made up of a long series of massacres and other bloody activities instigated by authorities in order to remove or destroy an ethnic, religious or racial group. Genocide does not need to be seen as an 'event', but can also be seen as a process of steadily increasing killing until the target population is extremely decimated. It may have a vague beginning, but the final phase is definite. The reasons for a government to start a genocide and choose a victim group vary, but normally have some sort of ideological background and a belief that this is a necessary step to benefit the majority (Mann 2005). The members of the targeted population are murdered regardless of sex or age, whether they are unarmed captives or simply peaceful residents. The indiscriminate killing of women and children is a particularly telling sign that the aim is total eradication. Usually genocides are preceded by a long period in which the targeted population is subjected to spontaneous or less well-organized forms of violence, which do not lead to total removal or destruction. During the First World War, Armenians, Assyrians and Greeks were the object of genocide initiated by the Ottoman regime. They were easy targets because they differed from the majority Muslim population through language and religion. These differences became steadily more visible as the Ottoman Empire struggled to survive in confrontation with European Great Power pressure. Particularly the divide between Muslims and non-Muslims became politicized in the final decades of the empire's existence. Muslims, despite actions to the contrary by Kurds and Arabs, were perceived as the backbone of society, while non-Muslims were often assumed, despite their protests of loyalty, to be an internal threat to the survival of the empire.

The cause of the genocide is not completely researched, but the main factors are presumed to be a mix of newborn nationalistic Turkish ideology in collision with embryonic Armenian and Kurdish nationalism, growing religious friction between popular Muslim extremists and the peoples they termed *gavur* (infidels), ethnic commercial competition that the non-Muslims were clearly winning, failed constitutional reforms for granting non-Muslims equal citizenship, coupled with acute material needs for land to settle Muslim refugees from the Caucasus and Balkans. The genocide perpetrated against the non-Muslims during the First World War can be seen as the culmination of a process of forcefully assimilating the distant provinces of Anatolia into a state modernization project. And at that particular moment, the plans of the central government to eradicate a perceived non-Muslim threat were compatible with the local notables in removing their non-Muslim neighbours and seizing their wealth. Sociologically the various local militias and death squads established for the purpose of exterminating the Armenians and Assyrians created powerful new links between the state and the local communities. At the same time, it solidified a culture of violence inside the new republic in relation to its Anatolian border-lands (Üngör 2011).

Under the dark shadow of a total war, the Committee of Union and Progress (CUP) nationalist government, which seized power in a military coup in 1913, intensified a programme for the 'Turkification' of the country through state-orchestrated violence and large-scale forced dislocation of groups that either resisted outright or were assumed to be impossible to turn into Turks (Seker 2007). These were mostly Christian Armenians and Assyrians of various confessions. Since the 1878 Treaty of Berlin, they had Great Power support, at least on paper, for their claims to cultural autonomy and state-guaranteed freedom from harassment from Kurdish and Caucasian tribes. But it proved impossible to attain this protection and after a while the Assyrians of Hakkari even stopped complaining to the authorities as doing so only made matters worse (Heazell and Margoliuth 1913: 205–7). Instead, the Ottoman project of replacing Anatolia's Christian population fitted well into the desires of local Muslim notables hoping to grasp the wealth of their urban rivals, and to seize the farm land from Christian villagers. This linked into the desires of local religious leaders to decrease the status of the non-Muslim community. For their part, the local notables echoed national suspicions accusing the Christians of being spies for the enemies literally on the cusp of revolt, even though no evidence of this existed. Directly after the massacres and deportations, Muslim refugees were resettled into confiscated homes and farms. For perhaps for the first time ever in Anatolia, it proved possible to mobilize the provincial elites for a central state project. The combination of economic and religious motives deepened the link between local elites and their political structure so that their traditional distrust of high officials was temporarily neutralized. This is most evident in the situation of the governor of Diyarbakir, Reshid Bey, who was appointed in March 1915 on the insistence of the local elite. He was in the hands of the city's powerful Pirinççizâde clan, who convinced him to attack the Assyrians as well as the Armenians (Üngör 2011: 61–5; Kieser 2002: 245–80). The Pirinççizâdes were in Fein's meaning repeat perpetrators: Arif as mayor had organized the massacres of 1895 and the extermination of a Yezidi tribe; his son Feyzi inherited his role and organized the massacres of local Armenians and Assyrians. Both joined the local CUP club and became national assembly delegates. This integration of national and local interests made possible a hitherto unparalleled expansion of genocidal activities that almost totally eradicated the Christians. After the war, the traditional conflict of interests between centre and periphery resumed, particularly in Kurdistan. However, above-mentioned Feyzi became a minister in the new Kemalist government (Üngör 2011).

A Spiralling Conflict

There is some difference of opinion as to the level of inter-ethnic warfare in eastern Anatolia at the start of the twentieth century. The Anglican minister W.A. Wigram, who worked closely with the Assyrian tribes in the Hakkari mountains, reported unparalleled growth of violence. According to him, the Kurdish tribes no longer observed the unwritten moral code of tribal fighting and had become increasingly deadly. The Assyrian tribesmen told him that inter-religious strife assumed ever more brutal proportions. Battles between the groups were

> ... by no means intolerable a generation ago ... arms were approximately equal; and the Christians, though outnumbered, had strong positions to defend, and were of good fighting stock, as men of Assyrian blood should be. So, until [Sultan] Abdul Hamid's day, the parties were fairly matched on the whole; and generations of 'cross-raiding' had evolved an understanding in the matter, capable of summary statement as 'Take all you like, but do not damage what you leave; and do not touch the women'. Thus livestock were fair lot, and so were carpets and other house-furniture, and arms of course. But the house must not be burnt, and standing crops and irrigating channels not touched, while a gentlemanly brigand would leave the corn-store alone. Women were never molested when a village of *ashirets* [tribesmen] was raided, until a few years ago. And this was so thoroughly understood that it was not necessary even to guard them ... Of late things have changed for the worse in this respect. Women are not always respected now; and the free distribution of rifles among the Kurds has done away with all the old equality. This was done, when the late Sultan raised the '*Hamidiye*' battalions; partly for the defence of his throne, partly perhaps with the idea of keeping the Christians in subjection. Now when to odds in numbers you add the additional handicap implied in the difference between Mauser and flintlock, the position becomes impossible; and the balance has since inclined steadily against the Christian tribes. (Wigram and Wigram 1914: 167–8)

The British archaeologist and later famous government advisor on Iraq, Gertrude Bell, passed through Diyarbakir and noted in 1909 the inter-communal tension. She wrote to her mother:

> [t]he nervous anxiety which is felt by both Christians and Moslems – each believing that the other means to murder him at the first opportunity – is in itself a grave danger and very little in Diyarbakir is needed to set them at each other's throats. During the three days that I was there tales of outbreaks in

different parts of the empire were constantly being circulated in the bazaars. I have no means of knowing whether they were true, but after each new story people went home and fingered their rifles.[1]

Among all the foreign observers, few downplay the level of conflict in the borderlands. Those with long experience of the area – missionaries and foreign consuls above all – stressed the debilitating effects of tribal warfare on the Christian communities. All are agreed that everyday life was characterized by tension and distrust and the need to think defensively.

Throughout the nineteenth century, Diyarbakir province was marked by increasingly brutal violence. Simple small-scale cattle stealing developed into full-blown battles, with thousands of tribesmen ranged against large Ottoman armies. The battles aimed at bringing new territory under control of the emirs and at the same time crush rival tribes into total defencelessness. Several factors were at play – one was the ambition of certain local Kurdish chiefs to create enlarged emirates by conquering or coercing their neighbours. The other was the concerted effort by the Ottoman leadership to bring the previously self-governing emirates of Kurdistan under direct government control. The balance of power between the Kurdish emirs and the Ottoman authorities shifted over time, but from the second half of the nineteenth century the government tightened its grip over the region, succeeding in buying the loyalty of some tribes, by forming the so-called Hamidiye irregular cavalry.

A decisive confrontation between the central government and an ambitious Kurdish prince came when the emir of Bohtan, Badr Khan, had built up a new tribal federation that he ruled from his main town, Jezire-ibn-Omar (now renamed Cizre), on an island in the Tigris River. The neighbouring emirate of Hakkari was in uproar after a disputed choice of a new emir, resulting in a breach between the majority of the Kurds on one side and the majority of the Assyrians on the other. Badr Khan used the issue of the disputed succession as a pretext to invade. Up until then it was said that the so-titled Mar Shimun, as the religious and secular head of the Assyrian tribes, was always the second in command to the Muslim emir of Hakkari and ruled in his absence. During a first invasion in 1843, the Assyrian mountaineers were singled out for massacre and an estimated seven to ten thousand were killed in what one missionary saw as a 'war of extermination' ('Letter of Dr. Grant' 1843: 434). Badr Khan appeared to be preparing to form an independent state. He established a rifle and ammunition factory, formed a standing army and even minted his own coins. An Ottoman army sent to defeat him had considerable difficulty with several heavy battles in and around Cizre, but he eventually surrendered in 1847. Still, his many heirs continued to claim influence over much of the surrounding district, revolted at any opportunity and started the Kurdish nationalist movement (Hakan 2007; Aprim 2006; Jwaideh 2006).

After Badr Khan was brought under control, other Kurdish warlords fought to fill his position, but most of them seldom held power for long periods and the regions they controlled were usually small. The Ottoman army modernized and could defeat Kurdish forces in a running battle. Among the rivals for Kurdish leadership was Êzdan Şêr, who invaded the then predominantly Christian Tur Abdin in 1855. An Assyrian family history describes these incursions in almost the same terms as Wigram, quoted above. Kurdish tribesmen 'savagely killed and enslaved the Syriac people, making them homeless and raped their property, destroyed their houses'. The invaders burned the 'green and dry' crops, pulled down houses and kidnapped women and children. The Assyrians attempted to defend themselves, but were defeated and the tribes of Bohtan continued to ravage Tur Abdin for about thirty years (Safar ca. 1970). In 1877, against the background of the ongoing Russo-Turkish war, two of Badr Khan's sons attempted to revive the emirate. They rebelled and occupied a vast stretch of territory extending far westwards to the towns of Mardin, Midyat and Nusaybin, which they held for about eight months (Bruinessen 1992). The government sent an army under General Shevket Bey and he sought and received local support from the non-Muslims. This was perhaps the first time non-Muslims supported the policy of the central government against the Kurdish tribes. They supplied warriors, scouts and advisors, which proved an essential resource. The Ottomans brought in canons and heavy armament. After the Kurdish defeat, the sultan rewarded the leading Assyrian family of Midyat, the Safars, with the honorary title of pasha for their loyalty. A young son of the Safar family, Hanne, as one of the few who knew Ottoman Turkish, served as advisor to the Ottoman general. Up until his death in the 1915 genocide, he was the main contact between Tur Abdin's Assyrians and the government, and even became a figure inside a Kurdish tribal confederation. As loyal supporters of the government, the Safars were surprised when the authorities turned against the Assyrians and besieged Midyat in July 1915.

A new turn of the screw in the increasing local violence came in the wake of the Turkish-Russian war of 1877–78. In that war the government felt it had sufficient control so that it would be safe to trust Kurdish tribesmen to fight at the Caucasus front. If Kurds volunteered, they would be outfitted with state-of-the-art Martini-Henry rifles (breach-loading rifles). After that war they were requested to return the rifles, but this seldom happened. Thus, the strongest Kurdish tribes now had even more modern weapons plus experience of military operations, but the Assyrians had to make do with home-crafted flintlock hunting rifles. The authority of the Kurdish emirs may have been destroyed, but in their place the Kurdish *shaikhs* rose up as a new type of leader even in secular matters (Bruinessen 1992; McDowall 1996). Since the shaikhs were religious leaders, often also connected with popular sufi orders, they could use their traditional role to mobilize a broad following. This had the effect of introducing religious differences into tribal warfare between the Kurds and Christians and making cooperation over religious boundaries more difficult. In the countryside, shaikhs and their followers would sometimes plunder Christian villages and seize their land and flocks. One shaikh is known to have dismantled a church to use the stone to build his house (Yarman 2010; Astourian 2011).

Hamidiye Regiments

One fateful innovation in the Ottoman policy of binding the loyalty of selected Kurdish tribes was the establishment in 1882 of irregular cavalry regiments (Klein 2011). In return for loyalty to the sultan, these chosen tribes received special privileges. They were termed *Hamidiye* regiments as they were under the personal protection of Sultan Abdulhamid. These regiments proved a greatly disturbing factor and were decisive in creating a culture of violence. As military regiments they were outside civil authority and courts of justice, but as irregular units they were outside normal forms of military discipline. Thus, they could act with impunity inside their home territory and could never be brought to trial no matter how outrageously they behaved. They became a plague to both the Christians and the other Kurdish tribes.

Powerful Hamidiye forces influenced the condition of the Christians in Diyarbakir province. On one side was the *Milli* confederation, which had three regiments led by Ibrahim Pasha based in the town of Viranshehir. On the eastern side around Cizre were the *Miran* confederation led by Mustapha Pasha, which had two regiments. In addition, there were a few smaller tribes with a single regiment such as the *Karakechi*, the *Kiki-Kikan* and the *Bucaks* who lived in Siverek. Although all of them expressed loyalty to the sultan, this did not hinder continual feuds among them. When tribal wars broke out, the brunt of the aggression was directed at burning and plundering the Christian villages that were under the protection of the enemy tribe. A French consul attested to the destructive effect of tribal warfare.

It is difficult for me to describe the deplorable situation in which the province's Christian populations, especially those who live in the countryside, find themselves. Oppressed to no end, stripped of their belongings, they are forced, in order to gain some form of protection from the Kurdish aghas and beys of their region, to work for these people and to accept the harshest conditions of slavery. Despite that, they pay a great deal for their protection and yet are still the most frequent victims of rivalries between Kurdish chieftains, who when wanting to inflict reprisals, find nothing better to do than to kill and pillage each other's fellahs – meaning Christians – and vice versa.[2]

The Assyrians who were victimized were conscious of the need to build defences. One such step was to ally with Kurdish leaders in a patron–client relationship. This could, of course, mean getting involved in the leader's tribal feuds. There are notices that non-Muslims fought alongside the Kurds. The consul in Diyarbakir wrote in 1904:

> Since the beginning of the present year, the Beshiri and Midyat kazas have been in a desperate situation because of the rivalries among the many Kurdish tribes living there ... The Christians and Yezidi that live there have been singled out and denounced to the Sublime Porte as disruptive elements who could cause the Government a great deal of embarrassment. I must not allow you to remain unaware that the situation of the Armenians and Jacobites, and of those Yezidi, is very different from that of other Christians scattered among that vilayet's Kurdish tribes: while the latter are reduced to the most brutal slavery, the ones from Beshiri and Midyat have the privilege of being equal to the Muslims.[3]

This meant they were obliged to follow their *aghas* and to take up their causes and even to help them in tribal warfare (Joseph 2000: 111).

The 1895–96 Pogroms: Relations between Assyrians and Kurds

Popular anti-Christian feelings exploded in widespread massacres in eastern Anatolia in 1895–96. The epidemic-like spreading of the pogroms and the participation of public officials in the agitation indicates a degree of consensus among powerful local Muslims to target Christians. It seems reasonable to assume that the government was in some way involved; the ambassadors of foreign countries certainly believed so and wrote so in the reports they sent to their governments. In Diyarbakir, Arif the mayor, who belonged to the Pirinççizâde extended family, was definitely one of the instigators. Diplomats noted that riots began at a predetermined hour and started on a given signal. Afterwards, the sultan's government participated in a cover-up and was more than passive in pursuing the perpetrators and negligent in aiding the survivors. The French consul advised that what was called the 'Armenian Question' actually included a universal Christian dimension.

> This state of affairs affects all Christians regardless of race, be they Armenian, Chaldean, Syrian or Greek. It is the result of a religious hatred that is all the more implacable in that it is based on the strength of some and the weakness of others. We might even say that the 'Armenian issue' is foreign to this matter, for if the Armenians are indeed the worst treated, it is because they are the most numerous and because it is easy to portray the cruelty with which they are subjected as a form of repression necessary for public safety.[4]

In November 1895, deadly ethnic riots erupted in Diyarbakir with the torching of the bazaars. Mobs struck mainly against the large Armenian community with a thousand deaths and two thousand shops destroyed. But 167 Assyrians of many denominations also perished, 89 of their homes were plundered and 308 shops were looted and burned (Meyrier 2000: 134–5).

What is new here is that destruction struck important urban commercial enterprises, not just the farmers in the rural backwaters. In this form it likens what has been termed the 'deadly ethnic riot'. The definition of this is an 'intense, sudden though not necessarily unplanned, lethal attack by civilian members of one ethnic group on civilian members of another ethnic group, the victims chosen because of their group membership. So conceived, ethnic riots are synonymous with what are variously called "communal", "racial", "religious", "linguistic" or "tribal" disturbances' (Horowitz 2001: 1).

Christians and Kurds reacted differently to news of the Young Turk revolution of 1908. It was expected that the new rulers would stop Abdulhamid's currying of Islamist anti-Christian sentiments. The Assyrians welcomed the new government's statements implying the imminent realization of unfulfilled promises of full Ottoman citizenship to non-Muslims. This was part of the attraction of the revolution and it seemed to open the door wide for non-Muslim political participation. But the Kurds with Hamidiye regiments now found themselves without the patronage of the sultan and feared loss of power and influence and many revolted. Kurdish shaikhs opposed the revolution because of its secular nature, and they combined their customary defence of religion with a new dose of nationalism (Jwaideh 2006: 301–5). One of the first non-Muslim groups to meet with genocidal violence was the Yezidis around the town of Viranshehir. Diyarbakir notables and politicians supported a campaign of eradication against them in 1909 (Kaiser

2013: 207–20). A whole series of Kurdish proto-nationalistic revolts began and the Assyrians were often entangled in these events. The embryonic Assyrian press commented on the chaotic increase of violence since 1908. The *Mürşid-i Âsûriyûn* (Guide of the Assyrians) published in Harput since 1909 attributed the conflicts to Kurdish chiefs who resumed the drive for autonomy. A letter from a correspondent in the town of Hasankeyf described the sacking of nearby villages and monasteries and complained that there was 'no government' (Trigona-Harany 2009: 143–5). In an attempt to master the chaos, the Young Turks soon abandoned their initial multicultural stance, and became increasingly Turk nationalistic, particularly after the Committee of Union and Progress clique took over in 1913. Turkish ideologues tended to combine their nationalism with Islamism (Hanioğlu 2008: 187–8; Landau 1995). The Assyrian peoples had great difficulty in responding to the radical Turkish and Kurdish national feelings. They were caught unaware and were unable to create bonds between the various religious sects (Gaunt 2013: 317–33).

The pre-modern history of Kurdish–Assyrian relations shows a high degree of integration between the Kurds and Assyrians. They were neighbours, they were dependent on each other, but they were entwined in a vicious circle that excluded stable and harmonious relations. This integration was not peaceful; rather it led straight into a world marked by violence, raiding, the kidnapping and rape of women, hostage taking, cattle stealing, robbery, plundering, the torching of villages and a state of chronic unrest.

Culmination of Violence in the Genocide

The complicated structures that intertwined the Assyrians and Kurds broke down to a great extent during the First World War and resulted in genocide and a near permanent rift between Kurds and Christians (Gaunt 2012: 241–66). The rift is even evident in the differing memories of 1915 (Biner 2010). This breakdown can probably be attributed to a new factor in domestic Turkish politics. The radical government policy aimed to forcibly displace Christians from their homelands, and evolved into one of the first examples of a politically motivated genocide (see more in Gaunt 2006).

Despite the weakened bonds of Kurdish–Assyrian loyalty, the Assyrians had a slightly better chance of survival than the Armenians. There were several reasons for this. One has to do with geography. The Assyrians lived mostly south of the Armenian core regions. When massacres and deportations of Armenians started, some of them fled into Assyrian territory and could tell of what was happening. This gave the Assyrians a slight opportunity to start preparing defences. Also the Assyrians of Hakkari bordered Iran, where they could flee, and some of the Syriacs and Chaldeans of Diyarbakir and Bitlis provinces could escape further south to adjacent Arab provinces. The Dominican monk Jacques Rhétoré completed his statistical estimates for population loss for the entire Diyarbakir province up to 1916 when he made his computation. He found that the losses for Gregorian Armenians were 97 per cent of the original population and for Armenian Catholics 92 per cent. Losses for the Syriac Orthodox were slightly less, at 72 per cent. When he investigated the Mardin district, he found that the Syriac Orthodox loss of population was 57 per cent (Rhétoré 2005: 136–8).[5] These figures indicate that although the eradication of the Assyrian population was extreme, it was still not as total as for the Armenians.

Accustomed as they were to a society of everyday violence, many Assyrians reacted by establishing a self-defence. This usually worked, except in the case of surprise attacks. In the cities the Assyrians had a tendency to trust the disinformation coming from the authorities that only the Armenians were the targets. But in the countryside, where people traditionally distrusted all authorities, Assyrians established defensive structures and people from small outlying villages and hamlets swelled into the defensible places like Ayn-Wardo and Azakh.

But even the Kurds were put under government pressure to abandon their Assyrian clients. To a great extent, local Kurdish tribes were caught up in an anti-Christian policy initiated and orchestrated by the government. This made it almost impossible to stand neutral. Death squad militiamen were recruited from among urban Muslims in Diyarbakir, Cizre, Mardin and Nusaybin. They were given uniforms and military weapons and the units were led by an officer. Often they could handle the massacring of a small village by themselves. However, if it was a large village, or if they expected resistance, they would call for a collection of warriors from nomadic tribes on a certain date at a specified place, before mounting a coordinated assault. It was hard to avoid such a summons. The vali of Diyarbakir went out of his way to seek out and recruit outlawed bandits, who were given amnesty if they became the governor's personal assassins (Demirer 2008: 77–87; Aktar and Kirmizi 2013: 289–323).

When news of plans to eliminate the Christian population came, it was impossible for the government-loyal Kurdish confederations to oppose. Thus, the *Milli*, who under Ibrahim Pasha's leadership were famous for their protection, participated in the massacres under his son's chieftaincy (Armale [1919] 1970: 283; Berré 1997: 93). The same was true for the *Dekşuri* despite the fact that they had Assyrian sub-sections and close relations with the Christians of Midyat. But the government-oppositional *Heverkan* confederation's leaders promised to shield their clients. Thus, the sections headed by the families of Çelebi *agha*, Alike Bate, Sarokhano and Sarohan helped Assyrians by escorting them to defendable villages, or hid them in their own villages. One branch, however, turned on its initial promise of help and that was the one led by Hassan Haco in the district east of Nusaybin. It appears that he was pressured by the authorities to participate or be punished. Other chiefs who protected Assyrians in Tur Abdin were Haco of the Kurtak clan and Musa Fatme of the Dayran clan (Gaunt 2006: 211, 240, 271). Armenians found refuge among the Kurds of Dersim and the Yezidis of Sinjar. After the First World War was over, it was close to impossible for survivors and refugees to return to their farms, but Çelebi *agha* of the *Heverkan* who sat out the war in prison because of involvement in a prewar revolt, helped Assyrians to return to their lands in the villages of Boqusyono, Mizizah and Zaz.

Even such a catastrophe as the genocide of 1915 could not entirely break all of the bonds between Diyarbakir's Assyrians and Kurds. But they were never again at the same level of stability and trust.

Conclusion

There was a great difference between the mass murder of 1915 and the previous violence. Before the First World War, the anti-Christian attacks were either a side effect of inter-tribal warfare or the target of local short-term pogroms after which some sort of normality resumed. However, an elaborate net of local organizations implemented the mass killing during the First World War and saw to it that the killing was systematic with a nearly complete geographic spread over almost the whole country north of the Arab provinces. This included mopping-up operations to ensure that few of the targeted victims survived. The main part of the mass murder, with hundreds of thousands of murders, took place from May to October 1915. But a second wave of genocide took place in 1916, targeting people placed in concentration camps near the desert as well as deporting individuals who had been allowed to remain in their hometowns, and stragglers who had run away from the deportation caravans. About 250,000 Assyrians and more than a million Armenians were dead or missing at war's end.[6] Refugees were seldom able to return to their homes of origin.

David Gaunt is professor of History at the Centre for Baltic and East European Studies at Södertörn University, Stockholm, Sweden. He has published widely on ethnic and religiously motivated violence against minorities in Eastern Europe and the Middle East. His monograph on the Armenian and Assyrian genocides *Massacres, Resistance, Protectors: Muslim-Christian Relations in Eastern Anatolia during World War I* (2006) has been translated into Turkish.

Notes

1. Gertrude Bell to her mother, 6 June 1909, Gertrude Bell Archive, University of Newcastle Library.
2. Diplomatic dispatch from Diyarbakir, no. 2, 9 January 1901, cited in de Courtois (2004: 141).
3. French diplomatic dispatch, no. 10, 3 June 1904, cited in de Courtois (2004: 144–5).
4. French vice-consul in Diyarbakir, report no. 2, 9 February 1895, cited in de Courtois (2004: 101).
5. See Gaunt (2006: 301–3) for more calculations.
6. General surveys are: Raymond Kévorkian (2006) and David Gaunt (2006).

Bibliography

Aktar, A., and A. Kirmizi. 2013. 'Diyarbekir 1915', in *Diyarbakir ve Çevresi Toplumsal ve Ekonomik Tarihi Konferansi*. Istanbul: Hrant Dink Vakfi. 289–323.

Aprim, F. 2006. *Assyrians from Badr Khan to Saddam Hussein*. Verdugo City, CA. Pearlida Publishing.

Armale, I. [1919] 1970. *Al Quosara fi nakabat an-Nasara*. Beirut: n.p.

Astourian, S.H. 2011. 'The Silence of the Land: Agrarian Relations, Ethnicity and Power', in R.G. Suny, F.M. Göçek and N.M. Naimark (eds), *A Question of Genocide: Armenians and Turks at the End of the Ottoman Empire*. Oxford: Oxford University Press 55–81.

Berré, M. 1997. 'Massacres de Mardin', *Haigazian Armenological Journal* 17: 81–106.

Biner, Z. 2010. 'Acts of Defacement, Memory Loss: Ghostly Effects of the Armenian Crisis in Mardin, Southeastern Turkey', *History & Memory* 22(2): 68–94.

Bruinessen, M. 1992. *Agha, Shaikh and State: The Social and Political Structures of Kurdistan*. London: Zed Books.

de Courtois, S. 2004. *The Forgotten Genocide: Eastern Christians, the Last Arameans*. Piscataway, NJ: Gorgias Press.

Demirer, H. 2008. *Ha ver Delal: Emînê Perîxanê'nin Hayati*. Istanbul; Avesta.

Fein, H. 1993. 'Accounting for Genocide after 1945: Theories and Some Findings', *International Journal on Group Rights* 1: 79–106.

Gaunt, D. 2006. *Massacres, Resistance, Protectors: Muslim–Christian Relations in Eastern Anatolia during World War I*. Piscataway, NJ: Gorgias Press.

——— 2012. 'Relations between Kurds and Syriacs and Assyrians in Late Ottoman Diyarbekir', in J. Jongerden and J. Verheij (eds), *Social Relations in Ottoman Diyarbekir, 1870–1915*. Leiden: Brill 241-266.

—— 2013. 'Failed Identity and the Assyrian Genocide', in O. Bartov and E.D. Weitz (eds), *Shatterzone of Empires: Coexistence and Violence in the German, Habsburg, Russian, and Ottoman Borderlands*. Bloomington: Indiana University Press. 317-333

Gerlach, C. 2006. 'Extremely Violent Societies: An Alternative to the Concept of Genocide', *Journal of Genocide Research*, 8(4): 455-71.

Hakan, S. 2007. *Osmanlı Arşiv Belgelerinde Kürtler ve Kürt Direnişleri (1817-1867)*. Istanbul: Presidential Archive.

Hanioğlu, M.S. 2008. *A Brief History of the Late Ottoman Empire*. Princeton, NJ: Princeton University Press.

Harff, B. 2003. 'No Lessons Learned from the Holocaust? Assessing Risks of Genocide and Political Mass Murder since 1955', *American Political Science Review* 97: 57-73.

Heazell, F.N., and Mrs. Margoliuth (eds). 1913. *Kurds and Christians*. London: Wells Gardner.

Horowitz, D.L. 2001. *The Deadly Ethnic Riot*. Berkeley: University of California Press.

Joseph, J. 2000. *The Modern Assyrians of the Middle East: Encounters with Western Christian Missions, Archaeologists, and Colonial Powers*. Leiden: Brill.

Jwaideh, W. 2006. *The Kurdish National Movement: Its Origins and Development*. Syracuse, NY: Syracuse University Press.

Kaiser, H. 2013. 'Ezidi Aşiretleri ve Şehirli Elitler', in Çengiz Aktar ed., *Mardin ve Çevresi Toplumsal ve Ekonomik Tarihi Konferansi*. Istanbul: Hrant Dink Vakfi 123-140.

—— 2014. *The Extermination of Armenians in the Diarbekir Region*. Istanbul: Bilgi University Press.

Kévorkian, R. 2006. *Le genocide des arméniens*. Paris: Odile Jacob.

Kieser, H.-L. 2002. 'Dr. Mehmed Reshid (1873-1919): A Political Doctor', in H.-L. Kieser and Dominik J. Schaller (eds), *Der Völkermord an den Armeniern und die Shoah*. Zürich: Chronos 245-280.

Klein, J. 2011. *The Margins of Empire: Kurdish Militias in the Ottoman Tribal Zone*. Stanford, CA: Stanford University Press.

Landau, J. 1995. *Pan-Turkism: From Irredentism to Cooperation*. Bloomington: Indiana University Press.

'Letter of Dr. Grant July 5'. 1843. *The Missionary Herald* XXXIX, no. 11.

Levene, M. 1998. 'Creating a Modern Zone of Genocide: The Impacts of Nations and State on Eastern Anatolia 1878-1923', *Holocaust and Genocide Studies* 12: 393-433.

Mann, M. 2005. *The Dark Side of Democracy: Explaining Ethnic Cleansing*. Cambridge: Cambridge University Press.

Mardin, S. 1973. *Religion, Society, and Modernity in Turkey*. Syracuse, NY: University of Syracuse Press.

—— 2006. 'Centre-Periphery Relations: A Key to Turkish Politics?' *Daedalus* 102(1): 169-90.

McDowall, D. 1996. *A Modern History of the Kurds*. London: I.B. Tauris.

Meyrier, G. 2000. *Les Massacres de Diarbekir: Correspondance diplomatique du Vice-Consul de France 1894-1896*. Paris: L'Inventaire.

Rhétoré, J. 2005. *Les Chrétiens aux bêtes: Souvenirs de la guerre sainte proclamée par les Turcs contre les chrétiens en 1915*. Paris: Cerf.

Safar, S. (ca 1970). 'Sayfo Rabo: Majzarët Mëdyat wa Nakabat aṭ Ṭor', Unpublished manuscript in Arabic, Mesopotamian Collection, Södertörn University.

Şeker, N. 2007. 'Demographic Engineering in the Late Ottoman Empire and the Armenians', *Middle Eastern Studies* 43: 461-74.

Speitkamp, W. (ed.). 2013. *Gewaltgemeinschaften von Spätantike bis ins 20. Jahrhundert*. Göttingen: V & R.

Trigona-Harany, B. 2009. *The Ottoman Süryânî from 1908 to 1914*. Piscataway, NJ: Gorgias Press.
Üngör, U.Ü. 2011. *The Making of Modern Turkey: Nation and State in Eastern Anatolia, 1913–1950*. Oxford: Oxford University Press.
Wigram, W.A., and E. Wigram. 1914. *The Cradle of Mankind: Life in Eastern Kurdistan*. London: n.p.
Yarman, A. 2010. *Palu-Harput 1878 – Çarsancak, Çemişgezek, Çapakçur, Erzincan, Hizan ve Civar Bölgeler, Vol. 2*. Istanbul: Belge.

CHAPTER 3

THE RESISTANCE OF URMIA ASSYRIANS TO VIOLENCE AT THE BEGINNING OF THE TWENTIETH CENTURY

Florence Hellot-Bellier

Assyro-Chaldeans and Armenians had been living in the Urmia region of north-west Iran for centuries when they fled to the Caucasus (1915), then to Hamadan and Bakuba (1918) to escape from the Ottoman armies. The Church of the East was originally established under the Sassanid Empire (224–651). Its roots lay in the province of Syria and it clearly distinguished itself from Western Christianity, rooted in the Roman Empire and its successor the Byzantine Empire. Later it underwent an expansion and even set up dioceses in the south of India and along the Silk Road all the way to China.

At the end of the fourteenth century, Tamerlane's (1336–1405) attacks on Iran forced Christians who had settled east of the Kurdish uplands to take refuge in Hakkari, a mountainous region where they lived a tribal life until 1915. At a critical stage, in 1552, the Church of the East developed a schism. A dispute over the patriarchal succession resulted in the creation of the Chaldean Church, which eventually entered into communion with the Roman Catholic Church. In the eighteenth century, a number of formerly displaced Christian groups settled back in the Urmia and Salmas Valleys in the Iranian province of Azerbaijan. Throughout the centuries, classical Syriac, derived from Aramaic, was preserved and kept alive in the liturgy, but spoken Syriac was increasingly permeated with borrowings from the surrounding local languages (Murre-van den Berg 1999). In the nineteenth century, the number of native speakers of Syriac living in Azerbaijan was estimated to be between thirty and forty thousand, plus some six hundred Christians from Erbil who had settled in Sina (Iranian Kurdistan). A handful of Christians also lived in the city of Kermanshah.

Ever since the Arab conquest of the seventh century and the proclamation of Shia Islam as the state religion by the Safavids in the sixteenth century, Iranian Christians had been tolerated as 'People of the Book', but this status never entitled them to equal rights with the Muslims, with whom they enjoyed relations of 'trust and violence' (Reemtsma 2008). Although this discrimination on religious grounds was experienced as a form of violence, the practice of 'gift exchange' did manage to succeed in generating a kind of solidarity between Muslims, Christians and Jews, as Marcel Mauss (1923–24) has shown in his famous book *An Essay on the Gift*. Hoping to be able to counter their inequality at the time of the Iranian constitutionalist revolution in 1906, the Urmia Christians took part in the uprising. Their hope was to gain full citizenship and freedom of conscience for themselves and for all other Iranian people as a whole. The outcome disappointed their expectations. On one particular issue, however, they were able to convince a number of Iranian dignitaries, both civilian and military, to rally to their cause and take issue with a practice that had long escaped prosecution: the abduction of Christian women by Muslims.

The Ottoman occupation west of Lake Urmia, which took place between 1907 and 1912, followed by the Russian occupation until 1918, created a situation which the Iranian authorities were powerless to do anything about, and the Christians of the Urmia region found themselves trapped, left to face the endemic violence of raids by Kurdish tribes. As they were hemmed in at the crossroads between the Iranian, Ottoman and Russian Empires, they had no choice but to come together and join forces to protect their villages.

In the modern era, the Eastern Christian societies have undergone a series of decisive transformations. Many of these changes have been introduced by missionary education, as well as emigration to the Caucasus and the United States. These transformations have prompted those Assyrian Christians who had remained behind to react to their conditions and take their history into their own hands, at times sharing the hopes of the Iranian constitutionalists, at times asserting their own national identity, rather than an identity attached solely to the church and religion thrust upon them. The early twentieth century was a time in which the Assyrians claimed their rights, and took a stand against the endemic violence. Given this context, how can the 1915, 1918 and 1919 massacres in Urmia and Salmas be understood? Were they attributable solely to the movements of Ottoman troops in the Iranian province of Azerbaijan, or can they be more cogently explained by a mutual lack of understanding between Iranian Christians and Muslims?

This question can best be answered by looking into the accounts and comments left by the missionaries, such as the Presbyterians or the Roman Catholic Lazarists, who lived among the Urmia Christians. The long-standing presence of a Congregational mission (1835) in areas west of lake Urmia, where they were followed by American Presbyterians (1870), as well as the Congregation of the Mission (French Lazarist Mission) (1841), lends weight to numerous letters written at the height of events by the missionaries themselves: William Ambrose Shedd, Frederick G. Coan, Edmund W. McDowell, Robert M. Labaree plus such Apostolic representatives as Mgr François Lesné and Mgr Jacques Sontag, as well as such Lazarist missionaries as Dilek Shlimun (also known as Désiré Salomon) and Aristide Chatelet.[1] Their fraught relations were stretched beyond breaking point over time, particularly for the Christian community. The reports of the Episcopalian missionaries located in Urmia and in Kurdistan from 1886 have less historical depth as they were replaced every five years. Letters with anti-Islamic undertones written by Russian Orthodox priests who opened their mission in Urmia in 1899 should only be relied on with great caution. Reports of consuls stationed in Tabriz and vice-consuls posted in Iranian Azerbaijan and in Van, in Eastern Anatolia, also contain invaluable information on the state of relations between the various populations in the region, but the impact of the relations Iran maintained with foreign powers at the time must be taken into account when interpreting such reports. This chapter hopes to arrive at a proper reading of these archives, which might help to develop an understanding of how the Urmia Assyrians resisted violence until 1915, when they found themselves thrust into the tumult of the Great War.

Iranian Christians' Fight for a New Legal Status (1905–11)

Iranian Christians' Short-Lived Hopes for a New Status (1905–7)

The Iranian Empire had been ruled by Qajar rulers since the end of the nineteenth century. In the reign of Naser ed-Din Shah (1848–96), Iranians who had spent time in Europe made determined efforts to reform the Iranian political system and to transfer the techniques of government proven successful in European countries to their country. Their struggle was in vain.

However, in the years 1905 and 1906, the Shiite religious leaders who had blocked concessions to foreigners finally joined the reformers and liberals who were seeking to establish a constitutional regime, with powers to oversee the law-making of the Qajar king and contain foreign interference. In August 1906, Mozaffar ed-Din Shah finally yielded to the demonstrations led by merchants and Shiite leaders and signed a document announcing that a National Council or *majles* was to be elected. The constitutionalists in Tabriz gathered for a council or club (*anjuman*) to support and inspire this *majles* in Tehran. On 9 September 1906, a new election law granted suffrage to all men aged twenty-five and older to vote with the exception of the members of the break-away *Babi* Movement; all men aged thirty and over were eligible, with the exception of the *Babis*. Christian Iranians were hoping to share in equal rights with the Muslims, especially as the Fundamental Law signed by Mozaffar ed-Din Shah just a few days before he died, on 30 December 1906, did not discriminate against Iranian believers except for the *Babis*.

In 1906, the inhabitants of Urmia held meetings, as did the people in Tabriz and Tehran. In November, seven Muslim representatives formed an *anjuman* whose composition William A. Shedd described as: 'A sort of censorship of Governmental Affairs, with two influential mullahs, one of whom was a *seyyed* ('descendant of the Prophet', a title that is passed down from father to son), two landowner Khans, two merchants and a representative of the craftsmen of the bazaar'. Hoping that the constitutional movement would bring freedom, Shedd went on to comment: 'So far as I have been able to form an opinion, it seems to me that there is a real popular movement. It recognizes freedom as a necessary condition to national progress' (PHSA, 23 November 1906). The Urmia *anjuman* expressed its willingness to cooperate with the authorities to defend justice and freedom.

The Christians who relied on the Gospel, which states that all God's children are created equal, responded enthusiastically to the calls for more equality and brotherhood expressed by certain constitutionalists. At the beginning of 1907, Urmia Christians, specifically those who had lived in the Caucasus or in the United States, joined the movement. Presbyterian students demonstrated, brandishing banners announcing their desire 'to defend the sacred cause of freedom' (PHSA, 1 September 1907). Dilek Shlimun, a Lazarist priest who had been born into the Assyrian tribe of Tkhuma, mentioned a meeting on 30 January 1907,

at which Christians toyed with the idea of creating their own independent *anjuman*. The Presbyterians dissuaded them because they knew
that the *kargozar* [Iranian Foreign Office officer] in Urmia was attempting to encourage some Assyrians to form a council to compete with the
anjuman established in November 1906, as William A. Shedd wrote to
Secretary Robert E. Speer:

> Our Syrians are being affected by the new spirit of things in Persia and are
> talking about a national assembly etc. It is all very well if they only have
> the sense not to go too fast and get themselves into trouble ... After various
> negotiations a rather stormy meeting of delegates was held and a committee
> elected and empowered to act for the nation. It soon found itself in trouble
> with the *anjuman*, due mainly to the intrigues of certain Syrians with the
> help of the *Kargozar*, the Foreign Secretary's representative. He takes care
> of the foreigners. (PHSA, 1 September 1907)

Dilek Shlimun, like Shedd, emphasized the complexity of the situation
in the Urmia area, pointing out the endemic attacks by some Kurdish
tribes and the difficulty the Assyrians experienced in being able to speak
with a common voice:

> The province is not immune to the turmoil that shook Tabriz and *anju
> man*s have been founded everywhere; there sometimes were two *anjumans*
> inside the walls of a city. Oddly enough, the Chaldeans have been led by
> the movement and, on January 30, a meeting gathered people of all reli
> gions in Urmia: Presbyterians, however, opposed this meeting and those
> who attended it were few. They first decided to send a telegram to His
> Majesty the Shah. Then they created a National Fund and they agreed
> to buy a People's Home. The meeting was of limited scope because of the
> non-participation of the Presbyterians; it confined its work to the limited
> program that I have just indicated. The promoters of the movement are
> the Chaldeans [*sic*] who have been to England and especially to America.
> (FFOA, 17 April 1907)[2]

Some Assyrians joined the ranks of the 'patriotic volunteers' of the
Armenian *fada'is*, a sub-group of the Dashnak Party which had many
branches in Tabriz and in the villages in Urmia and Salmas. In May
1907, Mirza Javad Agha, a representative of the Tabriz *anjuman*,
came to Urmia 'to awaken the revolutionary zeal'. He addressed all
Urmia inhabitants but refrained from mentioning religion, as Dilek
Shlimun commented to the French Consul Alphonse Nicolas:

> He came to Urmia where something unique happened in the annals of
> Islamic Persia. The missionary [Mirza Javad Agha] invited the Muslims,
> Christians and Jews to a lecture which he gave in the great Mosque! The

theme of his speech was 'The situation of Persia, its causes, its cures'. 'We should no more', he said, 'make distinctions between religions and races: every Iranian must endeavour to do his best for Iran!' He began to criticize the current system, reviewing the men in the government, sparing not even the Shah himself, showing in his assessments so ardently his support for the people that the audience asked him if he did not fear to be punished for the violence of his attacks. He replied quietly: 'I am ready to shed my blood to the last drop for the dear and holy cause of the people'. (FFOA, 7 May 1907)

Although some of the Urmia inhabitants did not agree with Mirza Javad Agha, who questioned the status of the non-Muslim Iranians, others were ready to treat all Iranians equally. For example, Jamshid Majid es-Saltaneh Afshar, an influential landowner from Urmia, whom the Episcopalian missionary Oswald H. Parry (1907) considered 'full of liberal and humanitarian ideas, intolerant to any opposition', supported a 'Committee of Syrians appointed to look after their affairs and to represent them in their relations to the government', as the Presbyterian Robert M. Labaree noted. However, when Majid es-Saltaneh enrolled Christians in an expedition to fight the Kurds in July 1907, Labaree admitted that some people in Urmia were worried about the role played by Christians: 'Yesterday the *anjuman* ordered the disbanding of this Christian committee. ... As a result, the sudden turn of affairs gave advantage to some of the most disturbing elements in the Syrian nation who were opposed to the movement'.[3]

In the excitement of the constitutional revolution and what appeared to be the dawning of freedom of the press heralded by the publication of an overwhelming number of new newspapers, a dozen young open-minded Assyrians created a partnership called 'Partnership & Co' to publish the Assyrian newspaper *Kokwa* (The Star) in Syriac. This monthly eight-page newspaper, printed by the Presbyterian press, rapidly became a twelve-page bimonthly, which quickly won support among the Urmia Assyrian emigrants in the United States. This publication represented a step towards the construction of an Assyrian identity whose roots could be traced back to the history of the empires of Assyria and Nineveh rather than to the history of the Church of the East (Naby 1977; De Kelaita 1994). Championing the recently granted press freedom, the *kargozar* also allowed the Presbyterians to print *Faryad* (The Scream) in Farsi on their press.

Finally, in the Salmas Valley, instead of creating an *anjuman*, Chaldeans in the Khosrowabad (Khosrowa) village mandated *qaša* [priest] Lazare Georges to represent them in the Tabriz provincial *anjuman* to issue a demand based on the protection traditionally offered to the village by the Tabriz provincial authorities and in the name of equal

justice the 'constitutional' Iranians were calling for. He announced that
they no longer wanted to be subjected to the arbitrary laws of the tax
collectors. *Jerideh Melli*, the *anjuman*'s newspaper (No. 19) in Tabriz,
commented on the case as follows:[4]

> Amidst all these events, a Christian priest called Lazare Georges, in com-
> pany with a man from Salmas [Gabriel Sefer], arrived and came to the *anju-
> man* [in December 1906] to complain about the acts of violence which he and
> his co-religionists were subject to. He was brought into the chamber where
> he was invited to give his reasons. He said: 'Nasser el-Vezareh had sent a
> *mubasher* [a representative] to Khosrow-Abad and this latter had exercised
> all the violence that pleased him against the *citizens who are the Shah's
> subjects*. Under the title of gifts, loans, or fines, he took all the *money* that
> he wanted and he demanded the payment at 20 *toman* per *kharvar* of the
> sixteen *kharvar* reduction provided by H.I.M. the Shah. The inhabitants of
> Khosrow-Abad asked if this was an order from Tehran or if the *mubasher* did
> as the fancy took him. Then he jailed the old men [*rish sefid*]. Here in Tabriz,
> the man who came with me was arrested. Therefore, I have come on behalf
> of *my compatriots* to ask the *anjuman* for Justice and protection and I wait
> for its verdict with confidence'. The *anjuman* has taken the matter in hand.
> (FFOA, 20 December 1906, emphasis in the original)

Alphonse Nicolas added: 'The case is now settled to the satisfaction
of the inhabitants of Khosrow-Abad' – an indication that in 1907 the
Azerbaijan Assyrians were optimistic that the reforms would take place.

The Special Status Assigned to Non-Muslims Remains in Force (1906–9)

In Tehran and elsewhere in Iran, dissenting voices asserting that civil
rights were for Muslims only were being heard. The question of whether
or not non-Muslim Iranians would have a parliamentary seat was raised.
In 1906, some *ulamas* had pointed out that Iran should adopt European
sciences, but without allowing Christian Iranians to have a seat in the
majles because they were outside the Muslim *umma*. This issue was
debated all year in 1907, because Mohammad-Ali Shah, who succeeded
Mozaffar ed-Din Shah in January 1907, was known for his opposition
to reforms and his subordination to Russia. Therefore, supporters of an
absolutist regime clashed with constitutionalists, as did defenders of an
Islam-based government with supporters of a constitution that made
no reference to Islam. Consequently, the Iranian Christians were disappointed by the Supplementary Fundamental Laws that Mohammad-
Ali Shah implemented in October 1907 and pledged on the Quran to
respect. These laws recognized Islam as the official religion and put legislative control in the hands of a group of *ulamas*:

Article I: The official religion of Persia is Islam according to the orthodox Jafari doctrine of the Twelve Imams, which faith the Shah of Persia must profess and promote. Article II: At no time must any legal enactment of the Sacred national Consultative Assembly be at variance with the sacred principles of Islam or the laws established by His Holiness the Best of Mankind (i.e. Mohammed) on whom and on whose household be the blessings of God and peace. It is therefore officially enacted that there shall always be a committee of five Mujtahid or other devout theologians. ... Article LVIII: No one can attain the rank of Minister unless he be a Moslem by religion, a Persian by birth and a Persian subject. ('The Place of Islam in Persian Constitution' 1911: I, p. 341)

During the course of 1908, Mohammad-Ali Shah gave increasing proof of his determination to override the *majles* and to restore the old regime, going to the extreme in June 1908 of allowing Colonel Liakoff to bombard the *majles*. Many Assyrians joined those who rejected Mohammad-Ali Shah's coup, chief among them Tabriz constitutionalists who were determined to defend the *majles* and the infant constitutional regime, with the help of Caucasian revolutionaries. The upshot was that the Armenian Dashnak Party officially joined forces with Iranian constitutionalists. In the aftermath, the Russians helped the royalist army, which besieged the: city of Tabriz (September 1908–April 1909), and they entered the city in April 1909.

In the Urmia district, Assyrians, Mawana village inhabitants (in Tergawer district on the border) and others, among them Faramarz Khan, never budged an inch in their defence of the constitutionalists. Faramarz Khan was a grandson of Rachel, a Chaldean, who belonged to an Urmia *malek* family (*malek* is a nobility title in the Assyrian tribes and some Assyrian families). Lazare Nazar-e Agha, born to Rachel in 1828 from her first marriage, had been a Lazarist scholar, then a Minister of Iran in Paris from 1873 to 1905 (Hellot-Bellier 2007: 554–6, 560–70). Rachel had two other sons from her second marriage to Colonel Licingof. They both received the title (or *laqab*) of Faramarz and of Burzu, as well as the *Khan* title.[5] They owned Sengar Burzuwi, a village at the gates of Urmia. In 1908, Rachel's grandson, Faramarz, educated in French military schools was working in the Urmia finance department. He was a fierce defender of the Iranian constitution.

Muslims and non-Muslims joined forces to defend the constitution. In 1908, William A. Shedd pointed out 'Armenians' and Iranian nationalists' unity', which had allowed the constitutionalists to score points in Salmas and Khoï. He described the funeral of a *fada'i* killed during a Kurdish raid on Urmia in December 1908. This funeral ceremony provided Muslims with the opportunity to express their solidarity with

Christians. Shedd was delighted by 'the spirit of the Syrians, national rather than religious' and the seriousness of the newspaper *Kokwa* (PHSA-CCIII-Shedd 1908):[6]

> His funeral [the *fada'i*'s funeral] was attended by thousands, including the principal nobility of the city, and speeches were made, such as the streets of Urmia never before heard. After making large allowance for insincerity and fear, the public preaching of equality without regard to religion, and the fraternizing of Christians and Moslems were enough to make one think. Among the speakers were two mullahs and a *Sayyed*. ... The sentiment for liberty has not gone, although the inevitable disappointments of the past few years have destroyed many illusions. We are living in stirring times of wonderful change. The revolution in Turkey has brought new hope to the people in that part of our field, weary as they are of outrage and violence. Among the Syrians there are signs of a new spirit. In the mountains the influence of the young Nestorian patriarch, a man of vigor and liberal impulses, is being felt. ... The new spirit is national rather than religious, but it is healthy and hopeful. (PHSA, 28 December 1908)

The Christians' Hopes Are Dashed

In 1909, the rifts between Mohammad-Ali Shah's followers and the constitutionalists became more blatantly apparent. In Urmia, the Iranian New Year celebration (*Nowruz*), in March, was disturbed by riots. Cries of 'Death to the *anjuman*! Death to patriots!' were heard during the demonstrations. The Armenian *fada'is* of Urmia mounted an operation, assisted by 'Assyrian patriots', among them Faramarz Khan. On 25 March, Governor Muhtasham es-Saltaneh was deposed by nearly twenty *fada'is*; a 'revolutionary' governor was sent from Salmas to take his place. The public was surprised both by the ease with which *fada'is* had managed the operation and by the boldness of the Christians who had conceived and implemented it. Shortly afterwards, however, Russian General Snarsky entered Tabriz, where he put an end to the resistance of the constitutional defenders. Once more, Muhtasham es-Saltaneh became governor of Urmia. On 1 July 1909, Mohammad-Ali Shah decided to save face and announced elections for a new *majles* (parliament): 'Conditions for being elector: to be Iranian subject, to be older than 20, to be well known, to pay a tax of ten toman, exception of those who have renounced Muslim faith (Articles IV and V). Conditions for egilibility: to profess Muslim faith, exception of the representatives of the Christian, Zoroastrian and Jewish nations who have to profess their own religion (Article VII) .. .The Armenian, Chaldean [the term used in the text], Jewish and Zoroastrian nations' (FFOA Téhéran 7 July 1907)[7] would each be represented by one member of parliament' elected by Chaldeans in Tabriz, Armenians in Isfahan, Jews and Zoroastrians in Tehran. The Christians' hopes for civil equality between Muslims and non-Muslims were dashed. Notably, although the Armenians appointed two members of parliament, the Assyrians found it hard to come to an agreement to choose one member.

By now, the Christians who had hoped to become full-fledged members of Iranian society were also interested in the possibility of finding a way to negotiate an end to an ancient practice that acted greatly to their detriment. A custom, attributed to Imam Jafar el-Sadeq (702–765), the sixth Imam, and revived in the seventeenth century under Safavides (1501–1736), allowed the Muslim family of a Christian converted to Islam (*jadid el-Islam*) to claim the Christian family inheritance up to the seventh degree. In 1909, in vain, three priests requested the Urmia *anjuman* and Muhtasham es-Saltaneh to put an end to this practice, as Dilek Shlimun wrote to Alphonse Nicolas:

> A strange thing is that the authorities had taken up the law stating that every Christian converted to Islam is entitled to all the inheritance from his (or her) parents, to the prejudice of his (or her) brothers and sisters. Three priests and several leaders of the community vainly went to ask the *anjuman* not to enforce this law until the case was heard by the *majles*. (FFOA, 11 December 1909)[8]

However, in Iranian society, where the framework for social life was embedded in religion, it was only natural that converting to a different religion was frequently a source of dispute. In 1913, the Presbyterian Samuel Graham Wilson (1880–1916) reported that when Christians converted to the Muslim faith – approximately a dozen individuals each year in Iranian Azerbaijan – the estates of their families were diverted to the benefit of the Muslim families of the new converts, especially as 'the convert was generally a girl who has been beguiled from her home' (Wilson 1913: 342).

In a nutshell, in 1909, the conservative Iranians who opposed fundamental changes finally won out and Assyrians had to relinquish hope of being considered as Iranians with equal rights, even if they could be represented by an MP in the Iranian *majles*.

The Resistance of Abducted Christian Women in the Urmia Region (1910)

Although the abduction of Christian women was another common form of violence perpetrated by Muslims in villages along the Ottoman-Iranian border, most widespread in the western regions of Lake Urmia, the year 1910 was a milestone in the history of such violence because the resistance shown by the abducted women proved stronger than those guilty of abducting them. The abducted women were not only able to go back home, but the legal procedures headed by the Iranian authorities also admitted that their claims were justified.

Although some girls sometimes did consent to marry their abductors, most of the women not only refused to marry their abductors, they also resolutely repudiated conversion to Islam, a condition imposed before such a marriage. This happened to Batisteva from Balulan, Elizabeth from Sardarud, Batisteva from Anhar and Catherine from Urmia (see Figure 3.1 for the locations). The procedures leading to the release of these four women and the involvement of Iranian civil and religious authorities in the process demonstrated that the violence perpetrated in abduction cases could actually be fought on a legal basis. Accounts of these abductions can be read in letters from the Presbyterians and in three issues of the newspaper *Kala d'Shrara* (The Voice of Truth), translated from Syriac into French by the Lazarist Abel Zaya. They were printed on the Lazarist press.

Batisteva, David of Balulan's daughter, was sixteen years old when she was abducted in February 1910 by four Kurds supported by other Kurds hiding in the vineyards. After her refusal to convert to Islam, she was led from village to village, until finally a customs official rescued her from her captors and took her first to the venerable Afshar Monazzam od-Dowleh Vali and then to the Urmia *mojtahed* (Doctor of Islamic Law). Before being summoned before a court, she was lodged with an 'Islamized' woman. In the court, the governor, the community leaders, the *sarparast* – in charge of litigation between non-Muslim Iranians – the Russian vice-consul B.A. Preobrazensky and missionaries handed down their judgements. After she had reiterated her avowal that she wished to remain a Christian, Batisteva was allowed to join the Mission of the Sisters of Charity.

Catherine's abduction on the riverbank was reported in *Esteqlal* (Independence), a Tabriz newspaper, in an article that focused on the Sunni Muslim abductor. She was released thanks to Sherif ed-Din, the Ottoman vice-consul in Urmia, who delivered her first to the governor, then to her mother.

Elizabeth from Sardarud was kidnapped as she was visiting her brother, Nuya. Her abductor was Mahmud, a *seyyed* from Derbarud. She was taken from village to village while three mullahs attempted to convert her to Islam. When Sherif ed-Din realized she was truly obdurate in her refusal to convert to Islam, he took her back to Mar Toma Audo, the Chaldean bishop of Urmia.

Accounts of the abduction of Batisteva, Badal's daughter from Anhar, are numerous as she managed to escape her kidnappers on her own initiative. She was taken to the west of Anhar by Kurds who were serving under their leader, Kordu. Although she refused to eat in order to respect the Chaldean fast, having heard that Shaykh Abd el-Qader was a fair man, she agreed to meet him. However, Kurds had given her clothes to a Kurdish woman who impersonated her and met the shaykh. Batisteva ran away three times and was recaptured three times before she managed to hide first in the vineyards of Anhar and then in Alwach, whose inhabitants, fearful of Kurds' retaliation, denied her protection. Eventually she reached the village of Sengar, where she was taken in by Faramarz Khan. She was tried before Governor Muhtasham es-Saltaneh and asserted she did not wish to become 'Islamized', after which she was released.[9] Presbyterians subsequently informed William F. Doty, the American consul in Tabriz, and Charles W. Russell, their minister in Tehran, of the affair, begging them to communicate with the Ottoman ambassador about this matter, explaining that the intense rivalry between the Ottomans and the Russians in the region left these women and the Iranian and mission authorities with very little power over the situation:[10]

> Several cases of abduction of Syrian girls and women by Kurds have occurred. The missions united in representations and the women were all set free. In one case this was accomplished only by the woman herself escaping from the Kurds at the peril of her life. She was supposedly examined by the Turkish Consul and the Shaykh Abdul Kadir in order to find out her will in the matter; but apparently her clothes and not herself were taken into their presence, for one day while with the Kurds her clothes were taken from her and she shut up in a room. Later the clothes were returned. Doubtless someone had been found to impersonate her. These cases have been reported by letter to the Board. In all of them a great deal of tact as well trouble was called for, not least of all because of the other missions. A concert of the missions here is a very difficult affair because of the delicacy of the relations of the parties included in it. (PHSA, 9 August 1910)

The accounts translated by Abel Zaya for the newspaper *Kala d'Shrara* are highly graphic. They steadfastly compare the violence of the kidnappings with the efficacy of the faith and prayers of the victims of abduction. They highlight the kidnappers' contempt for the law and emphasize the importance of the claims of Christian women filed with the Urmia civil and religious authorities during the trials of the former. Recurrent abduction failures in the spring of 1910 should have reassured Assyrian Christians. Nevertheless, some, namely Faramarz Khan, kept up a resistance, but Dilek Shlimun kept silent for fear of a Christian massacre by Kurds, afraid that 'they will achieve their goal':

> The entry of the escaped woman to the house of our Sisters has irritated the Kurds and turned the Turkish consul against us. The name of France prevents them from launching an attack to remove the woman from the sisters. The Turkish consul is in contact with the Kurds: is it against the Christians? The last few days there have been a host of thefts in the mills, and it has been widely rumoured that the thieves were Christians. The bakers are threatening not to make any bread; they are spreading the rumour that it is because the Christians are stealing the wheat and flour from the mills. Thereby they are whipping up the people's anger against the Christians. Tomorrow they will find some other accusation, but they will reach their goal. (FFOA, 3 June 1910)

Alphonse Nicolas, whose main correspondent was Dilek Shlimun, comments as follows: 'Generally speaking, I do not believe in a massacre of Europeans in Persia, but the case of Urmia is more complex because there, there are Kurds and Turks and I am too far away to be able to form any judgement on my own. The Russian policy is rather aggressive and it gets an unruly minority excited'(FFOA, Tauris 3 June 1910).

The Uprising of the Urmia Christians against Kurdish Raids

The violence arising from various causes – the status of Christians in Iranian society, the conversion of Christians to the Muslim faith and the abduction of women – had simmered for a long time. However, the fact that the Christians began to organize their community and to fight back at the beginning of the twentieth century was something new. At that point in history, several factors combined to lead to increased violence against the Christians. The Russian and Ottoman Empires had both set their sights on Iranian Azerbaijan, the Armenians and Kurds were both harbouring nationalist aspirations and power was ebbing away from the Qajars in Tehran.

The Increasing Violence of Kurdish Tribes

The first problem faced by the region was caused by Kurdish tribes who had cohabited with the Assyrian tribes in the Hakkari mountains and the villagers of the eastern Piedmont Mountains, sometimes peacefully, at other times belligerently. The invasions launched by both the

Ottoman and the Russian Empires into the Hakkari mountain region and the Urmia villages only served to ignite more disputes along an already unstable border. This situation fired the ambitions of a certain number of Kurdish leaders.

The Kurdish tribes in the Hakkari mountain area, like the Assyrian tribes, were divided into the *ashiret*, who were independent tribes, and the *rayat* tribes, the latter being subjects of the former. Their basic income came from their flocks. They had built up two confederations or *bazekke*, and a tribe belonged to the left or right *bazekke* depending on which side the tribe leader would sit next to the emir of Julamerg. In the event of a long absence, the emir would delegate his power to Mar Shimun, both the patriarch of the Eastern Church and head of the Assyrian tribes, who lived in Qodshanes, not far from Julamerg (Bohas and Hellot-Bellier 2008: 91–2).

The abolition of the Kurdish emirates by the Ottomans in the 1840s had sounded the death knell for the *bazekke* structure. The raids of the Kurdish tribes, whose pasture lands stretched on either sides of the border disputed by Ottomans and Iranians until 1913, ensured that a climate of violence dominated in the Urmia and Salmas Valleys, although for a long time the Assyrians and Kurds respected the ancient tribal agreements. This all changed in the early 1890s with the setting up of the *hamidiye* Kurdish battalions along the eastern Ottoman border. This decision by Sultan Abdulhamid increased instability and fed the Kurdish chieftains' misuse of power, thereby driving disturbances to a peak in Eastern Anatolia.

Turmoil reached the Urmia region where, as Consul Nicolas pointed out, Kurdish tribes, Assyrian tribes, Kurdish villages and Christian villages were intertwined:

> They begin in Chara, near Salmas, then stretch as far as Somaï and Baradost (north-west Urmia), Tergawer, Dasht and Mergawer (west and south-west Urmia). Lahijan, Alan and Sardasht are possessions of Sawjbulaq. Chara, Somaï and Bradost are inhabited by the large tribe of the Shakkaks, and are subdivided into small tribes: for example Chara is home to the Shakkaks Abdaï, whose chief, Jaafar Aqa, was recently killed in Tauris [Tabriz]. Another chief of the Shakkaks Mohammadi was taken four and a half years ago and sent to Urmia where he was sentenced to capital punishment – his name was Omer Aqa. Somaï is inhabited by the Shakkaks Nissanaï, Kardari, Hanifeh, etc. whose chieftain was Ismaïl Aqa, Mustafa Khan's brother, who was killed last year by Jaafar Aqa's relatives. Bradost is inhabited by the Shakkaks Hennaraï whose chieftain is Amr Aqa, a very rich man. The tribe of the Shakkaks is very strong and fields 2,000 armed horsemen. Terghaver, or Terghiaver [Tergawer] is partly inhabited by the Chaldeans, who are either Nestorian or Catholic [*sic*], and the Kurds called Harki Mandani. The

Chaldeans have several villages, including Mawana, and are very brave. Their leader, Bijan, who had gone with his men to bring back the herd stolen by the Hennaraï in Harkis two months ago, was killed by Amr Aqa's son. The Harkis are numerous: they are a tribe of more than 3,000 nomad families who move from Terghaver to Mosul during the winter and from Mosul to Terghaver during the summer. Their chieftain is Piru. Dasht is inhabited by the Dashtis or Beyzadehs, who gave birth to the murderers of the American missionary Labaree [B.W. Labaree]. This country is a nest of bandits and brigands who incessantly plunder and ravage the Urmia plain. The Dashtis have several chieftains, and each chieftain has between twenty to forty armed men. ... Merghaver [Mergawer] is inhabited by the Harkis Sidonaïs whose chieftains are Kerim Khan, Qasim Aqa, and Mohammad Aqa. These are the least thieving of all, and the Zapties Turks came to their home. Lahijan is inhabited by the Mameks [Mamashs], whose chieftain is Hamzeh Aqa, and the Mangurs, whose chieftains are Peiz Aqa and Bapera Aqa. The tribe of Piran spreads throughout Persia and Turkey, and the Govriks tribe in Serdasht. In inland Persia, one encounters the Zarzas in Ushnu and the Mokris is in Sawjbulaq whose Serdar Mohammad Qasim is the city governor. (FFOA, 18 June 1907)

The way these Kurdish and Assyrian tribes were intertwined with Christian villages was sometimes a source of peaceful exchange and sometimes a source of violence. The stability of this region located at the crossroads of the Iranian, Ottoman and Russian Empires had yet other dangers to face.

The Assassination of Mar Gawriel (1896) and Kurdish Raids

After massacres of the Armenians in the Ottoman Empire (1894–95), which generated turmoil in Anatolia, the cynical murder of Mar Gawriel probably inspired by Shaykh Sadeq of Neri stood as a warning.

In June 1896, Mar Gawriel, the metropolitan bishop in Urmia for the Church of the East, went with his nephew Esmail, Archdeacon Dinkha and some companions from Tergawer to visit the Matran family who lived in Shemdinan, not far from Shaykh Sadeq of Neri, on the other side of the border. At the Matran's house, they met Shaykh Sadeq, who invited them to visit his house. Before returning home, they spent the evening and night with the shaykh and resumed their journey early the next morning. Their bodies, among them the horribly mutilated corpses of the bishop and the archdeacon, were found near a ravine (Coakley 1992: 212–13).[11] These murders frightened the Assyrians, who were all the more upset since seven thousand Armenian and Assyrian refugees had flocked to the Urmia region, fleeing the massacres in the Ottoman Empire. Most of them were from the Gagoran villages (Gawar), Marbesho and Iyeli, as well as some from the Jelo and Dez Assyrian tribes. Some of the refugees made their way to the Caucasus, but many of them stopped in the Tergawer district, where they were helped by the Christians of Mawana, Balulan, and Qurana. Residents of Marbesho, whose flocks had been stolen, settled in Dustallan, a village in Tergawer. Dilek Shlimun explained the troubles, blaming both the violent acts of the Kurds and the Armenians' plans for autonomy:[12]

> Turkish atrocities against the Christians, many of which happened in Persia. The persecution has increased since the Armenians have demanded autonomy and because of the Kurdish extortions. The migration began before the killings, but since the killings, the Nestorians [i.e. the Christians of the Church of the East] and Armenians flow into Salmas. Many die. (CMA, 1 November 1896)

Unquestionably, at the beginning of the twentieth century, Kurdish tribes did sometimes offer Assyrian tribes a helping hand against Shaykh Rashid of Barwar, who had trapped and killed Yossep Malek, the head of the Bnai-Matha of the Assyrian tribe Tiyari (FFOA, 14 February 1901). Nevertheless, Beyzadeh Kurds looted the Christian villages of the Tergawer district in 1903. Dr Joseph Plumb Cochran, who was the head of the Urmia Presbyterian hospital from 1878 to 1905, analysed the situation of the Christians in a report written in September. He suggested that the Kurds tried to stir up the Muslims against the Christians and he concluded that it would not take much before Christians and Muslims clashed:

> The last summer has been full of anxiety and trouble, due largely to the lawless condition of the country. The weakness of the government, always very evident, becomes painfully so whenever there is any unusual uprising among the Kurds or the rougher elements in the towns and cities. ... Urmia city and country were dwelling in fear and actual danger of general uprising against the Christians first and secondly against the government. A comparatively small affair had been exaggerated, and had become the starting point for a most serious affair against the Christians of Tergawer, a little district lying just over the foothills twenty miles away. The Kurds of this place united to crush or drive out the Christians who resided in different villages of the same district. These Christians are brave and warlike, and not very unlike their Kurdish neighbors in dress, manner or morals, but as the government did not come to their aid, they were badly beaten, and took refuge together in the largest village of the place where they have been huddled together since June. Three villages were burned, 21 men and 4 women have been killed. Others have been wounded, 1,600 sheep have been taken, their hay stacks have been burned, and they have been watched day and night to prevent their moving about freely. They have been unable to feed their flocks and herds at any distance from their village, and have had to go armed and in large numbers to

Figure 3.1. Map illustrating the places mentioned in the Urmia region.

harvest their grain. The Kurds at the head of this trouble were making every effort to excite Moslem ecclesiastics of this city against these Christians, by reporting that they had desecrated their mosques and burned their holy books, and their dead etc. ... The Kurds all along the border, emboldened, threatened to take over the country in a general raid; and now both Christian and Moslem thoroughly frightened, began to desert their villages and move their goods within the City wall. (PHSA, 1 September 1903)

Dilek Shlimun judged the Kurds the same way, whereas Mgr François Lesné, the Apostolic delegate of the Roman Catholic Church in Iran, tried to reassure everyone by demonstrating that the burning of three villages by Kurds was not necessarily synonymous with a universal movement against Christians.[13]

The murder of both the Presbyterian Benjamin W. Labaree, who had been in Iran since 1893 and his servant Israel Guivergis of Gawalan by some Kurds from the Dasht tribe apparently near the town of Khoï, in March 1904, seemed to lend credence to Dr Cochran's opinion. Robert M. Labaree, the murdered Presbyterian's brother, condemned the violence: 'The country is very unsettled, the Kurds committing robbery and murder in every direction' (PHSA, April 1906).

Christian Self-Defence in the Early 1900s

Some groups of Assyrian Christians in Iran decided to oppose this violence being stirred up by international tension, and the Armenians intensified their preparations for defence. The Armenian Dashnak Party, whose members were settled in Tabriz and around Urmia, Salmas and Khoï, had two workshops – in Tabriz and in the Salmas Valley – in which unassembled arms from the Caucasus were reassembled. They distributed these arms to the Armenian *fadais*. The Assyrians of Mawana also decided not to allow the Kurds to loot their village and they were able to repel these would-be invaders, a deed for which they were praised by the Lazarists:

> Mawana, the Chaldean Sparta! Behind its mud walls, three hundred giants from 25 to 40 years old are capable of blocking the way of 3,000 Kurds. The Catholics [Chaldeans] and the Nestorians go into the church dedicated to the Virgin and carry a handful of soil from the church before the battle against the Kurds: one hundred and fifty young men received communion after throwing down to the ground the daggers from which they never separate. (CMA, 5 June 1899)

In the context of the increased rivalry between the Russian and the Ottoman Empires in their bids to control the border of the province of Azerbaijan, the Urmia region was of strategic importance. In August 1907, the Russians and the British signed an agreement splitting Iran into zones of influence: the British would control the Persian Gulf area and the Russians would control northern Iran, especially the Iranian province of Azerbaijan. This agreement urged the Ottomans to occupy the 'disputed territories'[14] west of Lake Urmia which the Iranians considered their own. In Urmia, the archimandrite who was at the head of the Russian Holy Synod Mission did his best to encourage the population to support the Russians. While this was happening, the Ottomans took advantage of the dissension between the Kurdish chieftains to enter Azerbaijan to target Sunni, Shiite and Christian villages.

The Iranians delegated the responsibility of ensuring security along the Ottoman-Iranian border in Azerbaijan to Majid es-Saltaneh Afshar. In 1907, he led a military expedition against the Kurdish tribes suspected of having taken part in Labaree's murder. He intended to enlist Christians to fight in his expeditions. Although the Assyrians of Tergawer agreed to join him, thereby hoping to strengthen the defence of their villages, the Kurds were helped by the Ottomans whose cannons put Majid es-Saltaneh's tiny army to flight in August 1907. The Assyrians covered the retreat. The Kurds retaliated by plundering the villages of Tergawer, whose populations had to find shelter in Urmia. In Tabriz, the Ottoman consul condemned 'the looting and murderous instincts of the Kurds' in strong language, and Consul Nicolas described them as 'the looters and thieves of the Beyzadeh Dashts' (FFOA, 8 August 1907). Tergawer Muslim inhabitants found refuge in the Urmia mosques and the inhabitants of the Christian villages were taken in by Armenian and Assyrian committees; the latter took the situation into their own hands, as Robert M. Labaree reported:

> A committee of the Syrians of Urmia Plain have taken matters in hand and have been trying to raise funds. ... The Moslems and Christians of this plain have made subscriptions for the relief of the sufferers. (PHSA, 27 August 1907)

Even though the Russian vice-consul, A.A. Cherkasov, paid eight *shahi*[15] a day to feed about five hundred Christian refugees until April 1908, some villagers preferred to request Ottoman protection offered by the Ottoman vice-consul or *shahbender* in Urmia. In 1908, the Ottoman *shahbender* was Petros Elia (Agha Petros), an Assyrian from the Baz tribe, a follower of the teachings of the Urmia Presbyterians, who had lived an adventurous life. Having returned from Canada, where he had raised funds for an orphanage, he married Zarifeh, daughter of the Ottoman *shahbender* in Urmia in May 1906. Thereafter he made his way by gradually taking on the functions of the *shahbender*. This elicited Iranian protests and in 1909 the Ottomans appointed another *shahbender*. His rejection drove Agha Petros closer to the Russians. He spoke in favour of Assyrians and in his own defence. He was used to replying in Mar Shimun's place and he gradually inherited a part of the patriarch's power. During WWI he played a leading part in the fights against Ottoman armies. He eventually left Urmia in July 1918 and died in France in 1932.[16]

In 1908, the Lazarist Abel Zaya, from Mawana, found himself in disagreement with Agha Petros. Zaya was convinced, as were most of the Assyrians, that the refugees could only survive under Russian protection – which was a dangerous opinion to hold: 'My parents who were driven out by the Turks and Kurds, and had everything taken away from them, took refuge here in Urmia and sought protection from the Russians' (CMA, 15 April 1908). Shedd (PHSA Urmia, 14 March 1910) claimed that such initiatives might have led to the discrediting of Christians in the eyes of the Muslims.[17]

In 1908, neither the Iranian authorities nor the Ottoman or Russian 'protectors' could prevent the Kurdish attacks on the Christian and Muslim villages. In a letter to the Lazarist Emile Sontag in Tehran, Mgr Lesné detailed the attacks against Christian villages, but failed to mention similar assaults on Muslim villages. He wrongly presented the Christians as passive victims of the Kurds and he deplored the passivity of the Ottomans when faced with the looting of the villages by Kurds, with the object, he suggested, of forcing Iran to give up 'disputed territories':

> Since my last letter, the situation has got worse and gets worse day by day. The Kurds of the regions currently occupied by the Ottomans, driven and urged on by them, have swooped down and continue to swoop down, mainly on the Urmia plain. They put everything to fire and bloodshed, especially in the Christian villages. They loot, burn, and dishonour women and girls, threatening men and women with children, when they cannot flee in time without distinguishing between them. The Christian villages which have been mostly affected in recent times are: Dezatekia, Shemshejian, Tekia, Ardishai, Darbari, Sardarud and Babari. The latter two have been looted and burned, our church in Babari was also ransacked. There were deaths – some say more than a dozen – but one cannot be sure because many do not reappear. Some children, women and young girls were also thrown into the river and drowned. Flocks of several villages were swept away. Everywhere the terror is at its height, people abandon the villages to escape to the city and the city is jam-packed. (FFOA 16 June 1908)

Dilek Shlimun joined the newspaper the *Mojahed*, published in Tabriz, in underlining how the Christians had defended the Iranian territory at considerable risk to their own lives.[18] In a letter sent to the American consul W.F. Doty, W.A. Shedd points out that the Muslim villages in the Salmas Valley were actually subjected to more Kurdish raids than the Christian villages, as the latter were able to profit from the defences organized by the Armenians. In cases of dire emergency, the Armenians and the Assyrians who lived together in small villages were indeed invited to gather in bigger villages where the Armenians tried hard to take defence into their own hands:[19]

> Perhaps it will be no harm to go back a little in reporting affairs here. Very soon after the departure of the Turkish commissioners on February 29, disturbances began. Up till this time, all winter things had been fairly quiet in this region. About the 1st of March, the Shakoik [Shakkak] Kurds in the north between Urmia and Salmas began robbing travellers on the road on the one hand, while on the other hand, to the south, on the way to Sulduz, the Shias turned on the Sunnis, plundering Kurds, carrying their loads and also attacking Kurdish villages. Nearer the city, within three miles' distance, Dashtis attacked two villages, carrying over some plunder. Afterwards Muhtisham es-Saltaneh assumed the governorship of the district and carried on negotiations with the Shakoiks and also with some of the Dashtis who promised to join with the Persians, to maintain order, etc. In the Baranduz, south of the city, the Kurds who had remained with the Persians [Dashtis] and had been charged with the protection of the villages took the opportunity to institute a small reign of terror, quarrelling among themselves and robbing the villagers. One Syrian village was attacked, some eight or ten houses were completely robbed, and one man killed while one or two Moslem [sic] villages also suffered. About two weeks ago the disturbances became more general and more serious, and now all the roads from Salmas to Sulduz region are very disturbed. It is very difficult to get the exact truth about anything in this country, but I will try to give the facts that I am reasonably sure of. Number of the villages of Salmas, especially along the border of the plain, have been robbed, the Moslem villages suffering most. The presence of the Armenian revolutionists keeps the Kurds away from the larger Armenian villages. The road from Salmas towards Urmia is very unsafe and for a considerable distance the telegraph line has been destroyed so that all telegraphic communication has been interrupted for ten days. The villages in the little district of Anzel, this side of the pass to Salmas, are in constant fear of attack. People from Gavilan who had come to get guns and ammunition reported that the Kurds were around the village. The villages along the Nazlu River north of the city some fifteen to twenty miles have been repeatedly attacked by the Shakoiks, at least six of them having either lost flocks or had houses robbed. A good many travellers and several caravans have also been plundered. Two villages near the city had houses robbed last night. One house in the city near the wall was robbed completely a few nights ago and last night there was an alarm of thieves just outside the gate nearest us. ... Naturally the fear is general and the villagers from all directions are crowding into the city. There is no concerted effort to defend the villages, the only landlords who are doing anything being the sons of Agha Khan Mirpanj in Dol and Dr. Aveshalom Khan, Mr. Stevens' agent, in his villages in Nazlu. Muhtisham es-Sultaneh

has not been able to do anything, though he is trying to get some of the soldiers together. ... (PHSA, 25 April 1908)

In the Urmia district, its governor Muhtasham es-Saltaneh supplied weapons to an Assyrian committee led by Faramarz Khan, who was in charge of the protection of four large villages (Dezatakieh, Ardishahi, Shamshajian and Gogtapeh) assigned to serve as places of refuge for the inhabitants of smaller villages. Armenian *fada'is* and Tergawer Assyrians instilled in Christians such a spirit of resistance that the Ottomans were seriously discomposed. The Lazarist Aristide Chatelet praised the feats of 'three mountain Mawananians who, during the attack of Shamshamjian in May 1908, mounted their own siege against sixty Kurds hiding in the poplar woods. The Tergawer refugees have found employment as guards in a good many places and have been really the only people, with the exception of some Christian and a few Muslim villagers ready to offer any effective resistance to the Kurds' (CMA, March 1908).[20]

In May and June 1908, the Kurdish attacks on the village of Jamalabad, where a small unit of Iranian troops was stationed, as well as raids against four Christian villages (Ardishahi, Takieh, Dezzatekieh and Babarud) and many Muslim villages on the Baranduz River, were among the attacks that caused the population the worst damage and the longest-lasting trauma. The American consul W.F. Doty and the British consul A.C. Wratislaw, in Tabriz, the Russian vice-consul of Urmia, Cherkasov, Governor Muhtasham es-Saltaneh and the missionaries of the four missions all put pressure on the Ottoman commissioner Taher Pasha to put an end to the Kurdish violence. Their joint efforts did not meet with much success, even though Taher Pasha consented to acknowledge that the attackers were indeed Kurds who had come from the territories occupied by the Ottomans and he could measure the strength of the resistance of Christians by the large numbers of Kurds killed in battles:[21]

> It gave one a very vivid idea of the terror of the people to see village after village absolutely deserted, to pass hundreds of refugees coming to the city, to find their fields without any labourers and the meadows without cattle. (PHSA, 2 June 1908)

In a letter written to Alphonse Nicolas, Dilek Shlimun in 1910 reported how the Ottomans and the Kurds retaliated against the Christians of Tergawer, because they had taken proper steps to defend themselves and had also managed to free the women abducted by the Kurds and, above all, they remained faithful to the Iranian authorities:

The Turks are furious at the defeat of the Kurds in Sengher [Sengar]. We heard the Turkish officers' threats against the Balulan men. They need forces near their consulate and they want to have their soldiers stationed in Sengher. The defeat and the recovery of the three women [who had been abducted] are an affront to the Kurds. We are fearful that they bear us a grudge. They will not try to massacre Christians, just to give them a lesson that they will not forget. For their part, the Turks note the loyalty of the Christians to the Persian authorities and they do not like it. They let the Kurds seize the fields in Mavana [Mawana], and allowed some others to move the former boundaries. They left the Balulan village entirely to the Kurds, and the Christian inhabitants are all in Urmia, living miserably. (FFOA, 8 July 1910)

The Lazarist priest seized this opportunity to stress the diverging views between the Ottoman troops and the Kurds who had overrun the border and occupied the Urmia region and the Ottoman vice-consul of Urmia who was simultaneously yielding to the resistance of Christians who had been abducted by the Muslims. It was a way for him to pay indirect tribute to the Christians who were resisting both the violence perpetrated against women and the ravages inflicted on Iranian territory by the Ottomans and Kurds. He also sensed that the Ottomans and Kurds would not stop there.

The Assyrians Trapped by the Turkish and Russian Plans

In 1910, the drafting of armed Kurds into 'Tribal Light Cavalry Regiments' and the complexity of the political problems made the cohabitation of Kurdish, Armenian and Assyrian populations in the districts coveted by Russia on both sides of the border more and more difficult. The French vice-consul in Van, Stephan Zarzecki, believed that the nationalist expectations nurtured by Turks, Kurds and Armenians were only making the situation worse. He reported rumours, which distorted the truth as indeed every rumour did: Abd el-Razzak Bederkhan, Simqo Shakkak Abddowi and Shaykh Taha of Neri were allegedly under Russian protection and had settled in Azerbaijan specifically to stir up Kurdish violence against the Ottomans:[22]

The issue is much more complex than in Berlin in 1878. ... The Kurdish claims and the propaganda from the Russian circles of Azerbaijan, the Persian province bordering this *velayat* [Van], militarily occupied by Russia, have been added to the Armenian claims. The Armenians responded by organizing bands of former *fada'is* who attacked the Kurdish chieftains. (FFOA, 11 October 1913)

The Kurdish chieftain Simqo, who lived in Cheheriq Fort two hours from Khosrowa in the Salmas Valley, proved the most opportunist adventurer. After his brother's murder, ordered by the Tabriz governor in 1904, he had made overtures to the Ottomans, but, in 1910, he turned his attention to the Russians. Under Russian pressure, he was appointed a border 'guard' by the Iranians (CMA, 8 February 1913).[23] During the First World War, he fought first on the Russian front before joining the Ottomans.

Through the autumn of 1912, the Ottoman military defeats in the Balkans and the uprisings in Albania hastened the withdrawal of the Ottomans from the Urmia area. The Russians subsequently occupied it and for a while were able to guarantee some sort of security. Nevertheless, they blotted their copybook by encroaching too much on the Iranian authorities, allying themselves with some Kurdish rulers and supplying some Christian villages with weapons to ensure they would receive support for their expansionist policy. Slowly, animosity against Russia spread on both sides of the border and the violence was rekindled (Gaunt 2006: 96).

Russian initiatives in Anatolia raised concerns among Turkish nationalists, already upset by the Ottoman defeats in the Balkans, for which they held the Armenians responsible. In the meantime, the triumvirate trained by Enver Pasha, Talat Pasha and Jamal Pasha (Akçam 2006; Bozarslan 2013), who took over in Constantinople in 1913, were making plans to deport Christians from their Eastern Anatolian villages. Talat Pasha, followed by Enver Pasha, set up 'Special Organization Units' in the form of army corps whose members were put in charge of attacking and exterminating the Christians (Vahakn and Akçam 2010: 122; Bozarslan 2013: 285). Pressure mounted in the years 1913–14, when the nationalist Turks deliberately spread rumours to compromise the Christians, whom they unfairly considered their enemies (Bozarslan 2013: 279). For instance, Mar Shimun Benyamin was rumoured to have yielded to the Russians, who had sent envoys to Qodshanes – as they had heard of the courage of the Assyrian tribes – and because the Russian archimandrite supported the initiative from Urmia.

Initially Mar Shimun trod carefully and did not embrace the Russian cause right away. Also, heeding the advice of some of the patriarchal family emphasized the importance of remaining faithful to the Ottomans. However, when William A. Shedd and the Presbyterian missionary E.W. McDowell visited the patriarch in Qodshanes in May 1913, they heard about the rumour which insinuated that all Christians were under Russian protection. Shedd judged that this rumour campaign, which threatened Christians, wrongly blamed them for supporting

Russian expansionist plans in the region. When he returned to Urmia at the end of May, he wrote a long report and in one paragraph highlighted the risks of protection reversals and swings of power, which could lead to large-scale massacres of Christians. Furthermore, in a serious incident, nine thousand sheep, a massive source of income, had been stolen from the Tkhuma Assyrian tribe. Shedd thought the theft might have had some connection to Shaykh Barzani's recent protection of the Tkhuma tribe, which he viewed as a fair and grateful return for the assistance provided a few years previously:

> When Mr McDowell was in Ashitha last winter he received warnings from different sources, going back ultimately to friendly Kurds, that there was danger of general attack on the Christians in the mountains and especially on the Syrians in Tkhuma and Tiari. About April 20th, when the McDowells were in Tkhuma, a very serious affair took place, which was intended as a part of a larger plan. Nearly 9,000 of the sheep of Tkhuma with over two hundred men, women and children were in the region south of Tkhuma along the Zab, in order to take advantage of the earlier pasturage here. They were under the protection of the Shaykh of Barzani, one of the three or four most powerful of the religious leaders of the Kurds; and they felt secure under his protection, as only a few years ago they had protected this same *Shaykh* against the government at the risk of their own safety. The confidence was misplaced and the followers of the *Shaykh* seized all the sheep and other property of the Christians, the intervention of friendly Kurds saving them from massacre. ... About the same time there was trouble in part from the same Kurds which resulted in the robbing of several thousand sheep and the killing of four or five men from Ashitha and Geramun, districts of Tiari. In other places there were less serious disturbances. From all that can be learned, including information derived from Kurds themselves, it seems very certain that there was an attempt to get up a concerted attack on the Christians. (PHSA, 28 May 1913)

Therefore, on the eve of the First World War, the Assyrian tribes of Ottoman Hakkari, like the Assyrians of the Iranian Azerbaijan, were not at all passive victims of arson attacks: they stood up to protect their own security and their very lives. The Assyrians of Urmia proved their ability and resilience to combat any violence they might have to face, a very real threat that was exacerbated by Turkish and Russian ambitions in the triangle formed by Eastern Anatolia, Iranian Azerbaijan and the southern Caucasus. The Assyrians of Tergawer, who were so vulnerable to Kurdish raids, pragmatically set about developing a protection system for the Assyrian villages. Against all odds, the Assyrians of the Urmia region never gave up hope.

Conclusion

The massacres of the First World War and the genocide inflicted on Armenian and Assyrian Christians in Eastern Anatolia and the Iranian border districts proved William Ambrose Shedd right. The Hakkari Assyrians did fall victim to the Ottoman armies and the Kurdish tribes sent to attack them first on Ottoman, then on Iranian territory. This fate befell the Azerbaijan Assyrians during the first five months of 1915 and again in June and July 1918, despite the fact they had thought they might have been able to forestall this risk by standing up against the injustice which lay at the root of the violence. In 1915 and in July 1918, the attacks against the Assyrian tribes and the massacres of villagers that were an inevitable part of the advance of the Ottoman army in the Urmia and Salmas Valleys were carried out by the 'Special Organization Units' enlisted in the Ottoman troops. Nevertheless, in the face of this onslaught, some Muslim neighbours and some Kurdish chieftains did shelter the Christians who were forced to flee their villages. However, the hundred or so men who had sought refuge in the Urmia missions and were nevertheless shot down by the Ottomans appear to have been the villagers of Tergawer who had defended the Christian villages against Kurdish raids in the years 1900–1910. In 1918, the Urmia and Hakkari Assyrians who had taken refuge in Azerbaijan again felt they were in grave peril after the withdrawal of Russian troops. In their dangerous predicament, Agha Petros played a large part in the organization of the Assyrian troops' fight against the Ottomans: he recruited other Assyrians to fight alongside Urmia Assyrians, reinforcing their sense of unity, even though Patriarch Mar Shimun Benyamin had doubts about seeing the Assyrians siding with the British. The violence reached its peak on both sides: Muslim families were protected by some Assyrians and by the missionaries; however, in March 1918, the Kurdish chieftain Simqo, with the connivance of the Democrat Party of Azerbaijan – it would seem – treacherously murdered Patriarch Mar Shimun Benyamin in Kohnehshehr near Diliman (Kasravi 1380h/1970: 725–8; Yako 1964; Bohas and Hellot-Bellier 2008: 63, 71–87). Afterwards, Agha Petros gradually assumed some of the patriarchal authority, and Surma, Mar Shimun Benyamin's sister, did her best to give the Assyrians guidance. In July 1918, the Ottoman army again entered Urmia: the violence of the 'Special Organization Units' was revived by groups of Iranian Muslims, irritated by Christian claims about their military organizational skills and angered by their support of British plans for the region following a Russian withdrawal. Once again, the Iranian landowners of Urmia sheltered the Christian families of their villages, but despite their help the Christian inhabitants were slaughtered. Those who had been able to flee joined the British in Hamadan. Most of them were sent to Baquba and the Mindan camps in 1919–20.

In May 1919, the starving population of Urmia attacked the Christians who were being assisted by the Presbyterians, who had also never hesitated to distribute aid to the starving Iranians and Kurds. The floodgates of restraint were then broken and the Assyrians were swept away in a storm of distrust, intensified both by the Kurdish attempts to take over the Urmia district and the British attempts to take over Iran.

Florence Hellot-Bellier is a member of the Research Team 'Mondes iranien et indien' (Paris, CNRS), and works on the modern history of Iran, particularly the relations of the Christian minorities with the Iranians and the Western powers. She is the author of *France-Iran, quatre cents ans de dialogue* (Peeters, 2007) and *Chronique de massacres annoncés: Les Assyro-Chaldéens d'Iran et du Hakkari face aux ambitions des empires (1896–1920)* (Geuthner, 2014). She co-authored *Les Assyriens du Hakkari au Khabour: Mémoire et histoire* (Geuthner, 2008) and *La Géorgie entre Perse et Europe* (L'Harmattan, 2009).

Notes

1. W.A. Shedd, from 1892 to 1918, R.M. Labaree from 1904 to 1914, F.G. Coan from 1885 to 1924, E.W. McDowell from 1887 to 1897 and from 1902 to 1922 were Presbyterian missionaries in Urmia. Mgr François Lesné and Mgr Jacques Sontag were the Apostolic delegates in Iran respectively from 1904 to 1910 and from 1910 to 1918. Aristide Chatelet, who remained in Urmia up to 1912, and Dilek Shlimun, who died in September 1914, were Lazarist missionaries.
2. Unless indicated otherwise, all translations from Persian to French have been made by the author, the translations from French to English by Stephanie Wooley.
3. Lambeth Library Palace Archives, LXIX, O.H. Parry, October 1907. US National Archives (USNA), American Consulate Tabriz, IV, Urmia, 23 July 1907.
4. Passages in italics were underlined by the French consul Alphonse Nicolas who translated the article into French from Farsi.
5. Burzu Khan was Urmia's *sarparast* (the governor's representative who took care of Non-Muslim Iranians) in 1872 until he died in 1873.
6. Shedd generally refers to Assyrians as 'Syrians'.
7. Translated by Saugon.
8. See also CMA, 23 April 1882, and Golnazarian-Nichanian (2009).
9. FFOA, 13 June 1910, translated from the French.
10. W. F. Doty arrived in Tabriz in 1907.
11. See also LLPA, *Quarterly Papers*, XXV, October 1896, 190–1 and Coakley 1992: 212–13.

12. See also Golnazarian-Nichanian (2009) and Avedissian (2010).
13. CMA, 29 June 1903, translated from the French.
14. Term used by the diplomats to define the Ottoman territorial claims on Iran.
15. A *shahi* was a silver coin worth one twentieth of a *rial*.
16. Assyrians themselves were divided: some followed the Patriarchal family, others followed Agha Petros. According to Weibel (2007), the British preferred to lean on Surma in 1918, perhaps because Surma represented the ancient traditional power and she had been educated by W.H. Browne (from the Archbishop of Canterbury's Assyrian Mission).
17. State Department Records, Maryland, US (SDR), W.A. Shedd, Urmia, 14 March 1910.
18. FFOA, 3 December 1907, 15 August 1908, translated from the French.
19. See also Avedissian (2010).
20. See also PHSA, 19 May 1908.
21. See also Wratislaw (1924).
22. See also Zarzecki (1914), McDowall (2004: 99) and Vali (2011).
23. See also D'Bait Mar Shimun (1920).

Bibliography

Ahmad, K.M. 1998. 'Les Kurdes et le génocide des Arméniens', trans. Halkawt Abdul Hakem, *Revue du Monde Arménien moderne et Contemporain* IV: 163–84.

Akçam, T. 2006. *A Shameful Act: The Armenian Genocide and the Question of Turkish Responsibility*. New York: Metropolitan Books.

Avedissian, O. 2010. *Du gamin d'Istanbul au fédaï d'Ourmia: Mémoires d'un révolutionnaire arménien*. Paris: Thaddée.

Bayat, K. (ed.). 1369h/1990. *Iran va djang-e djahani-ye avval: Esnad-e vezarat-e dokheleh*. Tehran: K. Bayat ed.

Bloxham, D. 2005. *The Great Game of Genocide*. New York: Oxford University Press.

Bohas, G., and F. Hellot-Bellier. 2008. *Les Assyriens du Hakkari au Khabour: Mémoire et Histoire*. Paris: Geuthner.

Bozarslan, H. 2013. *Histoire de la Turquie, de l'Empire à nos jours*. Paris: Tallandier.

Chaqueri, C. 1988. 'The Role and Impact of Armenian Intellectuals in Iranian Politics 1905–1911', *Armenian Review* XLI(2): 1–51.

Chevalier, M. 1985. *Les Montagnards chrétiens du Hakkari et du Kurdistan septentrional*. Paris: Département de Géographie de l'Université Paris Sorbonne, No. 13.

Coakley, J.F. 1992. *The Church of the East and the Church of England: A History of the Archbishop of Canterbury's Assyrian Mission*. Oxford: Clarendon Press.

Congregation of the Mission Archives, Paris (CMA).

—— Bejan, Urmia, 23 April 1882.

—— Khosrowa, 1 November 1896.

—— *Annals*, LXV, Demuth to Fiat, Urmia, 5 June 1899.

—— Archbishop Lesné's letter, Urmia, 29 June 1903.

—— *Annals*, LXXIII, Chatelet, March 1908.

—— Abel Zaya, Urmia, 15 April 1908.

—— letter of the Lazarist G. Decroo, Khosrowa, 8 February 1913.

Davis, G. (ed.). 1999. *Genocides against the Assyrians*. Unpublished.

D'Bait Mar Shimun, Surma. 1920. *Assyrian Church Customs and the Murder of Mar Shimun*. London: n.p.

De Courtois, S. 2002. *Le Génocide oublié. Chrétiens d'Orient, les derniers Araméens*. Paris: Ellipses.

De Kelaita, R. 1994. 'On the Road to Nineveh: Brief History of Assyrian Nationalism', *Journal of the Academic Society* VIII (1), pp. 26–27.

Dodd, E.M. 1920. 'By the Grace of the Kurds', *Asia Magazine* XX(4), 10 May: 420–25.

French Foreign Office Archives, Paris, Nantes, La Courneuve (FFOA).

—— Constantinople, DCLXIII, Santi to Constans, Mosul, 14 February 1901.

—— Nouvelle Série, Perse, II, Tabriz, 20 December 1906.

—— Nouvelle Série, Perse, II, Téhéran, 17 April 1907.

—— Nouvelle Série, Perse, II, Tabriz, 7 May 1907.

—— Nouvelle Série, Perse, II, Tabriz, 18 June 1907.

—— Téhéran, 'Rules for legislative elections', 7 July 1907.

—— Tauris Consulate, V, Nicolas, Tabriz, 8 August 1907.

—— Nouvelle Série, Perse, III, XIV, Tabriz, 3 December 1907, 15 August 1908.

—— Nouvelle Série, Perse, III, Urmia, 16 June 1908.

—— Nouvelle Série, Perse, XV, Urmia, 11 December 1909.

—— Nouvelle Série, Perse, VII, Tabriz, 3 June 1910.

—— Nouvelle Série, Perse, VII, Tabriz, 13 June 1910.

—— Correspondance Consulaire, Tauris, IX, Urmia, 8 July 1910.

—— Guerre 1914–1918, Van, 11 October 1913.

Gaunt, D. 2006. *Massacres, Resistance, Protectors: Muslim–Christian Relations in Eastern Anatolia during World War I*. Piscataway, NJ: Gorgias Press.

Golnazarian-Nichanian, M. 2009. *Les Arméniens d'Azerbaïdjan: Histoire locale et enjeux régionaux 1828–1918*. Paris: Centre d'histoire arménienne contemporaine.

Heazell, F.N., and D.S. Margoliouth (eds). 1913. *Kurds and Christians*. London: Wells Gordon & Company.

Hellot-Bellier, F. 2002. 'La Première Guerre mondiale à l'ouest du lac d'Urumieh', in O. Bast (ed.), *La Perse et la Grande Guerre*. Tehran: IFRI, pp. 228–52.

—— 2003. 'La fin d'un monde: les Assyro-Chaldéens et la Première Guerre mondiale', in B. Heyberger (ed.), *Chrétiens du Monde Arabe, un Archipel en Terre d'Islam*. Paris: Autrement, pp. 127–45.

—— 2006. 'Les Chrétiens d'Iran au XIXᵉ siècle (1800–1918): Une page se tourne', in R. Gyselen (ed.), *Chrétiens en Terre d'Iran: Implantation et Acculturation. Studia Iranica* 33. Louvain: Peeters, pp. 79–104.

—— 2007. *France-Iran: Quatre cents ans de dialogue. Studia Iranica* 34. Louvain: Peeters.

—— 2014. *Chroniques de massacres announces: Les Assyro-Chaldéens d'Iran et du Hakkari face aux ambitions des empires, 1896–1920*. Paris: Geuthner.

Joseph, J. 1961. *The Nestorians and their Muslim Neighbors: A Study of Western Influences on their Relations*. Princeton: Princeton University Press.

Kasravi, A. 1378h/1958. *Tarikh-e hedjdah saleh-ye Azerbaïdjan*. Tehran: Sepehr.

—— 1380h/1970. *Tarikh-e mašrouteh-ye Iran*. Tehran: Sepehr.

Lambeth Library Palace Archives, London (LLPA). Archbishop Mission to the Assyrian Christians.

LXIX, *Quarterly Papers*, Parry, O.H., October 1907.

XXV, *Quarterly papers*, October 1896.

Mauss, M. 1923–24. 'Essai sur le don: Formes et raisons de l'échange dans les sociétés archaïques', *L'Année Sociologique*: Seconde série, tome I, 30–186.

McDowall, D. 2004. *A Modern History of the Kurds*. London: I.B. Tauris.

Murre-van den Berg, H.L. 1999. *From a Spoken to a Written Language: The Introduction and Development of Literary Urmia Aramaic in the Nineteenth Century*. Leiden: Nederlands Instituut voor het Nabije Oosten.

Naby, E. 1977. 'The Assyrians of Iran: Reunification of a "Millat" 1906–1914', *International Journal of Middle East Studies* 8: 237–49.

'The Place of Islam in Persian Constitution'. 1911. *The Moslem World*, Part I, pp. 341–4.

Presbyterian Historical Society Archives, Philadelphia (PHSA)

—— CCVII, J.P. Cochran, *General Medical Report of Urmia Station*, 1 September 1903.

—— CCVII, Robert M. Labaree, Urmia, April 1906.

—— CCI, Shedd, Urmia, 23 November 1906.

—— CCII, Urmia, 27 August 1907.

—— CCVII, William A. Shedd, Urmia, 1 September 1907.

—— CCI, Urmia, 1 September 1907; 16 October 1907, *Report for the Year 1906–1907*.

—— CCIII, W. Shedd to W. Doty, Urmia, 25 April 1908.

—— 203, 19 May 1908.

—— W.A. Shedd, Urmia, 2 June 1908.

—— CCIII, W.A. Shedd, Urmia, 28 December 1908.

—— CCV, W.A. Shedd, *Report on Civil Affairs, 1910*, Urmia, 9 August 1910.

—— RG 91, W.A. Shedd, Urmia, 28 May 1913.

Reemtsma, J.P. 2008. *Vertrauen und Gewalt: Versuch über eine besondere Konstellation der Moderne*. Hamburg: HIS Verlag.

Semelin, J. 2005. *Purifier et Détruire, Usages politiques des massacres et génocides*. Paris: Seuil.

Teule, H. 2008. *Les Assyro-Chaldéens: Chrétiens d'Irak, d'Iran et de Turquie*. Brepols, Turnhout.

Vahakn, N.D. and T. Akçam. 2010. *Tehcir ve Taktil: Divan-i Harb-i Orfi Zabitlari-Ittihad ve Terakki'nin Yargilanmasi 1919–1922*. Istanbul: Bilgi Universitesi Yayinlari.

—— 2011. *Judgment at Istanbul: The Armenian Genocide Trials*. New York: Berghahn Books.

Vali, A. 2011. *Kurds and the State in Iran: The Making of Kurdish Identity*. London: I.B. Tauris.

Weibel, Y.C. 2007. *Surma l'Assyro-Chaldéenne (1883–1975), Dans la tourmente de Mésopotamie*. Paris: L'Harmattan.

Wigram, W.A. 1920. *Our Smallest Ally*. London: SPCK.

Wilson, S.G. 1913. 'The Russian Occupation of Northern Iran', *The Moslem World* III (July): 339–49.

Wratislaw, A.C. 1924. *A Consul in the East*. London: William Blackwood & Sons.

Yacoub, J. 1985. 'La Question Assyro-Chaldéenne, les Puissances Européennes et la Société des Nations, 1908–1938', PhD dissertation, Université Lyon II.

Yako, M. 1964. *Les Assyriens et les deux guerres mondiales*, trans. G. Bohas. Tehran (unpublished).

Yonan, G. 1989. *Ein vergessener Holocaust: Die Vernichtung der christlichen Assyrer der Türkei*. Göttingen: Gesellschaft für bedrohte Völker.

Zarzecki, S. 1914. 'La question kurdo-arménienne', *La Revue de Paris*: 873–94.

Chapter 4

Mor Dionysios 'Abd an-Nur Aslan
Church Leader during a Genocide

Jan J. van Ginkel

In academic research on the Sayfo, neither the position of the ecclesiastical hierarchy during the genocide nor the impact of the massacres on these church leaders and their policies after the event has been studied extensively.[1] Therefore, the time has come to pose the question: what was the response of the hierarchy during the massacres and in their aftermath? This leads on to the second question: to what extent did it influence their behaviour in organizing and administrating their church? How did the community respond to its leaders and their behaviour? In this chapter, I introduce a now more or less forgotten church leader of that time, Mor Dionysios 'Abd an-Nur Aslan, who at one time was Metropolitan of Harput, Homs and Diyarbakir respectively, in an attempt to illustrate some aspects of these questions. In his own time, Mor Dionysios was one of the highest-ranking officials in his community and church. His contacts within and outside his church make him a central figure in understanding the attitude and actions of the ecclesiastical elite during this crucial period. I will give a brief sketch of his career and position within the community before and after the Sayfo in order to highlight the challenges of these times and the way in which the hierarchy responded to these challenges.

Early Life

'Abd an-Nur Aslan was born in Urfa (Edessa) on 31 July 1851, the son of Ibrahim, son of Aslan, and of Rihan, a relative of Chorepiskos Paul.[2] After being trained in Syriac and Turkish by Deacons Elias and 'Abdallah, he joined the household of Patriarch Ignatius Jacob II (1847–71) who was then resident in Diyarbakir (Amid) in 1869. After the death of the patriarch, in 1871 he entered the Zafaran Monastery[3] and was ordained as a deacon by Julius 'Abdul Masih of Mardin. He was ordained as a priest by Cyril Giwargis, Bishop of Diyarbakir. There is some doubt about the date; G. Rabo states that this ordination occurred in 1875 (Rabo 2002, 2004: 250), but it seems that Cyril was only consecrated as Bishop of Diyarbakir in 1876 (Fiey 1993: 163). After being ordained as a priest, 'Abd an-Nur taught in Midyat for a year and half and later also had the opportunity to visit Jerusalem in 1879. In 1880 he was sent to Istanbul by Patriarch Ignatius Peter IV[4] (1872–94) to represent the Syriac Orthodox Church at the court of the sultan. This is the time in which the Syriac Orthodox were recognized and established as an independent *millet* (1882) (Atto 2001: 86),[5] distinct from the Armenian *millet*, of which they had been a part for centuries. 'Abd an-Nur became the first official *patrik vekili* (representative of the patriarch) of the Syriac Orthodox. As the official spokesman of his church at the palace, his duties went beyond maintaining contacts between the church and the Ottoman government. He also had opportunities to speak to the ambassadors of the Western countries.[6] During this period he spent in Istanbul, he was also in charge of the local Syriac Orthodox community. In that capacity he helped in the restoration of the Church of the Mother of God in Beyoglu, which had been burned down in the great fire of 1870.[7] He also tried to use the newly established contacts with the Anglican Church to acquire funding for a Syrian school in the capital (Taylor 2005: 55 [and n 15], 58–9 [and n 21]). After spending nearly eight years in Istanbul, 'Abd an-Nur was transferred to Hah in Tur Abdin in 1887 and little is known about his activities for the next ten years.

Harput

In 1896, the newly appointed Patriarch Ignatius 'Abdul Masih II (1895–1905) consecrated 'Abd an-Nur as Metropolitan of Harput (Elazig), whereupon he took the name Dionysios.[8] His consecration took place just a few months after the massacres of 1895/96 in that region.[9] Although there are only limited sources about his tenure as Metropolitan of Harput, there are at least various reports in the newly founded contemporary Syriac newspapers.[10] These reports leave little doubt that Dionysios 'Abd an-Nur was pastorally active and that he tried to help members of his community to withstand the pressures from outside. For example, he intervened in clashes about the remarriage of a Syriac Orthodox woman to a Kurd after her first (Armenian) husband had left to go to the US. The religious and social implications of this love triangle made it potentially very dangerous for all communities. The metropolitan was able to convince the government to annul the second marriage (Trigona-Harany 2009a: 159–60).

The fact that he was able to convince the government to annul the marriage may have had to do with other reports about his contacts with the Turkish state. In various instances, he was not remiss in showing his positive attitude towards that state. In 1910 he praised the new constitution as 'heroic' and, in his own diocese in 1912, he was actively involved in collecting money for the war effort (Trigona-Harany 2009a: 136, 138). Although this attitude reflects the 'normal' tendency of a minority to rely on the central state for protection against any potential upheaval within society (Atto 2011: 83–142), Dionysios 'Abd an-Nur seems to have taken this one step further.

To all intents and purposes, the metropolitan appeared to be anxious to distance himself, and his community, from the Armenians. As early as his time in Istanbul, he was already actively involved in seeking to achieve independence for the Syriac Orthodox from the Armenian *millet*. Although there were unquestionably theological and other grounds for the establishment of a separate *millet* for the Syriac Orthodox, the fact that the Armenians had already begun to acquire 'a bad name' in certain circles in Ottoman society could well have intensified that desire. This drive to be seen as different from the Armenians remained an important element in Syriac Orthodox ecclesiastical policy,[11] and among its champions Dionysios 'Abd an-Nur was one of the most prominent. The clearest expression of this desire for separation can be seen in his founding of the journal *Kekvo d-Suryoye* (*The Star of the Suryoye*), in Harput.[12] Undoubtedly, his decision to set up this journal was a response to other publications and concrete acts by his own parishioners, who mingled freely with the Armenians – intermarrying, using the language and espousing the culture. This interaction could even go as far as the 'conversion' of whole communities. For instance, when a particular village priest crossed swords with Dionysios 'Abd an-Nur, he and his parish 'changed churches' and became Armenians in the blink of an eye (Trigona-Harany 2009a: 201–2).[13]

The metropolitan also clashed with the modern and secular elite of the Syriac-speaking community. Best documented in various contemporary journals and essays are his conflicts with Aşur Yusuf.[14] A. Yusuf was a journalist and professor at the Euphrates College, an American mission school in Harput and a leading representative of this more secular cultural elite. He, for example, criticized Dionysios for the misappropriation of funding earmarked for educational purposes. Caution is advised here, as this accusation might simply be a reflection of an ideological conflict about whether education should be available to all young people, or should be reserved for a certain elite. Lurking behind this ideological conflict lies the clash between the elitist ecclesiastical hierarchy and the modernists, who took a more 'democratic' view.[15] In a report by Ernst Lohmann on a meeting with Dionysios, he states that the bishop had asked for assistance in establishing a seminary in Harput 'for suitable young men'. A German theologian would be in charge of the staff and its curriculum, but the bishop would teach the Syriac language and church history. It seems that Dionysios was making a determined effort to strengthen the clergy intellectually (Lohmann 1904).

Although Aşur and Dionysios clashed repeatedly, they both displayed a similar 'Ottomanist' attitude. Aşur was also assiduous in stressing the need to protect and develop the Syriac culture of his own community. There was a difference between the two men: unlike the metropolitan, Aşur seems to have focused on the inner strength of his community and less on the pressures from outside that threatened to assimilate the Syriac Orthodox culturally. Like Dionysios 'Abd an-Nur, Aşur Yusuf also displayed his loyalty to the state by participating in the war effort during the Balkan Wars (1912) and supporting the new constitution of 1908 (Trigona-Harany 2009a: 131–9). He even praised the metropolitan for his handling of the Syriac Orthodox woman and her two marriages (Trigona-Harany 2009a: 160; 'Abdünnûr has performed his duty rather well'). Nevertheless, his 1913 comment about the precarious position of Dionysios 'Abd an-Nur in Harput highlights both their mutual antagonism and the difficult character of the metropolitan:

> The conflict between the Italian and Balkan governments and the Ottomans have [sic] come to an end. But the years-long conflict happening between the Harput congregation and metropolitans has not. (Cited in Trigona-Harany 2009a: 160)

In fact, Dionysios 'Abd an-Nur seems to have antagonized so many members of his community that by 1913 he had to leave Harput. Whether or not he was officially deposed can no longer be ascertained.

Homs

After leaving Harput, Dionysios 'Abd an-Nur received orders from Patriarch Ignatius 'Abd ed-Aloho II (1906–15) to take care of the diocese of Syria and Homs in 1914.[16] Although little is known of his activities in this period, it was the seminal period in the history of the Syriac Orthodox community. Although many members of his previous diocese in Harput were killed or had disappeared (Naayem 1920: 146–8), Dionysios 'Abd an-Nur survived unscathed in Homs,[17] where he did leave a legacy. While in Harput, and possibly even earlier, Dionysios 'Abd an-Nur had been actively collecting manuscripts and copying them. His collection must have been impressive, as it contained several unique manuscripts.[18] He was in contact with various Western scholars and was acutely aware of their interest in the Syriac heritage. At least one manuscript was copied under his direct personal supervision for J. Rendel Harris. Several other manuscripts in Harris's library also originate from Harput. He also mentioned Syriac manuscripts in Western libraries and makes explicit reference to Western scholars in his own works. Several examples occur in his 1903 poem written in praise of the Indian Syriac Orthodox Metropolitan, Geevargese Mar Gregorios Parumala (1848–1902).[19] These works show his international connections, but his writing activities were also directed towards his own community. The poem about Mar Gregorios was used in a memorial service. He also composed a lengthy Lament on the Destruction of the Monastery of Mar Barsauma near Malatya.[20] When he was transferred from Homs to Diyarbakir in 1917, he left behind part of his collection, which is now part of the Homs Collection in the Patriarchal Library in Saydnaya.[21]

Diyarbakir

In 1917 Dionysios 'Abd an-Nur was consecrated as the new Metropolitan of Diyarbakir (Amid) by the new patriarch, Ignatius Elias III Shaker (1917–32).[22] As in 1896, he was transferred to a diocese that had suffered overwhelming losses in the preceding years. Again his mission was to rebuild a shattered community. The impact of the genocide was even worse than the trauma of the events of 1895/96, as a once flourishing community had now been reduced to a small remnant, which was subjected to constant pressure. Moreover, because of the devastating impact of the genocide in the region of Harput, this diocese had to be merged with the diocese of Diyarbakir as neither diocese had sufficient numbers left to function on its own.[23]

By now in his late sixties, it is known that Dionysios 'Abd an-Nur tried to provide pastoral care for his new community, but it seems he faded from history. He no longer seems to have been involved in church politics. There are also no traces to suggest that he was still using his international contacts. However, he did retain his old attitude towards the state. In a report on the situation in Eastern Anatolia by an English officer, Dionysios is said to have opted for the continuance of Ottoman rule and 'had prayers offered in the church for the sultan and his government, that their benign rule might continue' (Noel 1920: 'Note on Position of Syrian Jacobites').[24] This steadfastness is also reflected in the various honours awarded to him for his loyalty by officials of the Turkish Republic.[25] During the Sheikh Said rebellion (1925), his 'support' of the government was repaid by the award of the honorary title, 'Friend of the Turks'. This seems to reflect a continuation of attitudes from Ottoman times by both the metropolitan and the new state officials. The overriding idea seems to have been that the state was the best source of protection for a weak minority. The metropolitan certainly seems to have coveted its patronage by showing his unconditional loyalty.[26] It is unclear whether this was because of his closeness to the government or because of the small size of the community, which was not perceived as dangerous. There are certainly no references to the Diyarbakir community being threatened with expulsion, which was the eventual fate of the much larger community of Urfa (Edessa) and Azakh.[27]

Although the state seems to have honoured him, even though it is not possible to be precise about how exceptional these honours were, the metropolitan appears to have spent his last years in relative isolation, with only a limited number of believers. According to Günel (1970), there were stories about Dionysios 'Abd an-Nur riding through the city on a donkey and being pestered by youths. He was reduced to the condition of being an old man who waved his stick at them; there was not much else he could do (Günel 1970: 195).

Dionysios 'Abd an Nur died in 1933 and was buried in the Zafaran Monastery (Mardin), the last Syriac Orthodox Bishop of Diyarbakir. He seems to have left a substantial sum of money, some real estate and many books, manuscripts and religious silverware. His religious legacy, however, was limited as both within the community and within the church hierarchy few remember him.

Epilogue

The second half of the nineteenth century and the first decades of the twentieth century saw the imperial state of the Ottoman Empire alter into a patchwork of national countries in the Middle East and the Balkans. This process was both very painful and highly dramatic, and it changed the demographic and cultural setting of this region forever.[28] This demographic, cultural and ideological upheaval within the Ottoman Empire culminated in the events of 1915–16 (Gaunt 2006; Üngör 2009),[29] which are now referred to as the Armenian Genocide[30] and Assyrian Genocide or Sayfo.[31]

In this very challenging environment, under the leadership of its ecclesiastical leaders the Syriac Orthodox Church had to find a way to survive. For a while, Mor Dionysios 'Abd an-Nur, who represents this old ecclesiastical hierarchy, was an important player in the Ottoman and Turkish world. The course of his career can be used to highlight the problems and challenges the patriarchs and bishops faced and the various strategies and actions they adopted to guide their community. Dionysios 'Abd an-Nur was a prelate who was active in social affairs, and even established a journal. He had good connections with Western scholars and politicians, but within his community he clashed with the new, more secular elite, such as Aşur Yusuf, who had a more modern approach to communal identity. Whereas Dionysios seems to have been focused on the traditional social division within the community, which also relied on internal patronage, the new elites tried to further the cause of the community by educating anybody who was willing and capable. Nevertheless, despite his educational conservatism, he did try to activate his international contacts to improve the schools in Istanbul and Harput, to the extent that he was even willing to accept foreign teachers.

Twice Dionysios was consecrated a bishop in places where history had recently shown its most ugly and bloody face. Twice his mission was to help the shattered community to move on. In Harput his answer was to stress loyalty to the government, but simultaneously to emphasize the unique and distinct identity of the Syriac Orthodox. He seems to have actively tried to counter the assimilation process between his parishioners and the Armenians. His principal aim was to protect the identity of his community, but he might also have been inspired by an element of fear of the anti-Armenian attitude of large parts of Ottoman government and society.[32] Despite the exhortations to the Syriacs to show their loyalty, in the end both Armenians and Syriacs suffered the same fate during the First World War.

In his response to the massacres in 1916, Dionysios seems once again to have resorted to his previous model. He sought refuge for his community by remaining loyal to the government, which he felt was the only power that could protect them, even after the genocide.[33] Although in hindsight his attitude might be called into question, it should be noted that the majority of the leaders chose to follow the same path, most notably Patriarch Ignatius Elias III (Atto 2011: 83–100). Immediately after the First World War, at the peace conference in Paris (1919), the hierarchy had, through its delegate Metropolitan Ephrem Barsaum, tried to establish an autonomous area for the Christians, but it soon became clear that the other victorious countries were not interested in the concerns of this small community.[34] As a result, Ephrem Barsaum and the rest of the hierarchy turned back to focus even more on the local or regional governments, rather than on the West and global networks. The fact that the community of Diyarbakir was allowed to remain could even have been felt to be a vindication of that policy. The impact of the Sayfo – no matter how terrible it had been – did little to change the policies of the hierarchy; it might even have intensified them.

One reason for the attitude of these bishops was that they seemed to have run out of options. Although there were mass migrations in this period,[35] the vast majority of the survivors were unable to leave their newfound homes. They were as vulnerable as ever. The violence continued for several years,[36] for example in the expulsion of the Edessene Christian community or of the Syriac Orthodox patriarchate from the Turkish Republic.[37] However, other non-Turkish communities were forced to bear the brunt in these later decades, namely the Greeks and the Kurds. Just as after previous massacres, the community had to 'live on' as it had done for centuries. Dionysios was part of a tradition in more ways than he might have bargained for.[38]

Jan J. van Ginkel is Research Fellow at the Vrije Universiteit (VU University) in Amsterdam. He has worked – both as a researcher and as a lecturer – in the field of Syriac Studies and the History of Middle Eastern Christianity at various universities. His publications include *John of Ephesus. A Monophysite Historian in Sixth-Century Byzantium* (Groningen, 1995) and, as co-editor, *Redefining Christian Identity. Christian Cultural Strategies since the Rise of Islam* (Peeters Pubs. 2005) and *Syriac Renaissance* (Peeters Pubs 2010).

Notes

1. Note the relative lack of references to the higher ecclesiastical order in Gaunt (2006). Although members of the hierarchy were also massacred, the direct victims were predominantly ordinary community members and their local priests.
2. This part of the chapter is mainly based on Gabriel Rabo's articles (2002, 2004). For further information, see also 'Al-Sayid Dionosios 'Abd al-Nur Matran Diyarbakir' (1933) in *Al-majallah al-Batriyarkiyyah al-Suryaniyyah* (The Syriac Patriarchal Magazine), 1, pp. 168–9; (1982), no. 13, pp. 16–17.
3. Probably with the name Butrus (Peter); see Taylor (2005: 55, n 15, 58–9, and n 21).
4. In contemporary documents he is referred to as Peter III. For the change in his designation, see Taylor (2005: 15, n 1). The change of designation might well have occurred under the influence of Western scholarship.
5. Note that the community had gained more autonomy within the Armenian *millet* since at least the 1830s. In the *firman* confirming his appointment (1873), Patriarch Ignatius Peter IV was already treated as being *de facto* independent of the Armenian *millet*.
6. For some examples of his attempts to lobby with the British Foreign Office, see Destani (2007a and b); on a conflict over church ownership in Mosul, see Destani (2007a: 394–6); on Kurdish attacks on Syriac Orthodox near Siirt, see Destani (2007b: 290); and on requesting funding for a school, see (ibid.: 291).
7. One reason for the long delay in rebuilding the church seems to have been a property dispute with the Armenian Church. See Taylor (2005: 40 and n 58).
8. In manuscript CFMM 280 (Manuscript in Church of the Forty Martyrs, Mardin, http://www.hmml.org/) (retrieved 31 October 2016), he calls himself Metropolitan of the Diocese Melitene and Hisn Ziyad, which is "Khartbert" (Harput). I wish to thank Adam McCollum (Hill Museum & Manuscript Library) for providing me with this information. According to the colophon in Mingana (1933: Manuscript 535), it was written by Metropolitan Dionysios 'Abd an-Nur on 29 August 1895. However, his inauguration in Harput took place in 1896. In the colophon he refers to himself as 'nominally Metropolitan' ܚܣܝܐ ܒܫܡܐ, without mentioning his diocese. This phrase is usually an expression of humility. However, Dionysios never resorts to this phrase in other manuscripts and invariably mentions his diocese. Could it be an indication that he had already been consecrated in 1895, but not yet inaugurated in Harput (which took place in 1896)?
9. For a contemporary account of the impact of these massacres, see Harris and Harris (1897).
10. This part of the chapter is mainly based on B. Trigona-Harany's book, *The Ottoman Süryânî from 1908 to 1914* (2009a).
11. For some remarks, see Trigona-Harany (2009a), and see also Özcoşar (2006: ch. 2.2.3.3., pp. 171–8).
12. See also Trigona-Harany (2009b: 294–5).
13. Note that Aşur Yusuf also berated the priest, calling him 'ignorant, empty-headed and disobedient' (Trigona-Harany 2009a: 144–5).
14. See, for example, Trigona-Harany (2009a: 144 and n 406) on two lawsuits that Dionysios 'Abd an-Nur brought against Aşur Yusuf and his paper.
15. It should be noted that Aşur Yusuf was not anti-ecclesiastical hierarchy (Trigona-Harany 2009a: e.g. 160–61 and *passim*). Nevertheless, the hierarchy was traditional and elitist. For example, Serepiskopos Pavlos (*patrik vekili* in Istanbul at that time) only selected children from wealthy families for educational opportunities, as did

'Abd an-Nur (Trigona-Harany 2009a: 158). Note that Pavlos had a very good reputation among the 'secular' modernizers (ibid.: 154).

16. This part of the chapter is mainly based on Gabriel Rabo's (2002) article.

17. Research into the history of the indigenous Syriac Christians south of Aleppo is still a desideratum.

18. Johannes Gerber (1911: 1) refers to a collection of 'wertvolle' manuscripts in the hands of the 'syrisch-jakobitischer Erzbischof Abdun-Nur von Sis'. Ernst Lohmann bought two manuscripts from him, 'die der schlaue und kundige Orientale aber nur zu sehr hohen Preise feilbot' [a nice example of German Orientalism]. Hubert Kaufhold (1990: 115–17, 151) establishes that the bishop mentioned in Gerber's introduction is Dionysios of Harput. Ernst Lohmann (1933: 145–6) describes the contacts between the two men and the manuscript collection. Lohmann asserted that the collection, consisting of 'viel wertvollere' manuscripts than the one (or two, according to Gerber!) he had bought, had been destroyed in the 'Christenverfolgungen durch die Turken', i.e. the Sayfo. Also see *Auf der Warte* (Lohmann 1904), where Lohmann describes his meeting with Mor Dionysios and finding the Bar Wahbun manuscript.

19. According to J.F. Coakley (1993: 155–6), the text (JR Syr. 33 = *olim* Harris 142) is 'supplemented by lengthy notes in smaller writing. These notes also contain a good deal of miscellaneous information about the history and glories of the Syrian Orthodox church in India and elsewhere'. He also copied a polemical tract by Saliba, better known as Sleebo Mor Osthatheos, Metropolitan in India, denouncing a Syrian Catholic work (JR Syr. 30 = *olim* Harris 147). Dionysios's link with India also needs further research. There are other indications in this collection that manuscripts had reached Rendel Harris through the hands of Dionysios 'Abd an-Nur and are now in Manchester or Harvard.

20. I wish to thank Adam McCollum for providing me with this information.

21. Some examples of manuscripts that were part of his collection at some time: Garshuni version of the Chronography of Mor Michael Rabo (Chabot 1899–1924 : xlvii); various manuscripts of scientific and historical works of Bar `Ebroyo (see the index provided in Takahashi [2005]); Gospel of Hah (1227 AD); Bar Salibi's Commentary on the Letters of Paul (see Rabo 2002; Coakley 1993: 156–7); *Job of Edessa, Book of Treasures* (1221 AD; copies made for Rendel Harris and A. Mingana; the original [or an unknown copy] was copied again in 1964 in Elazig/Harput; I wish to thank Adam McCollum again for this information). This implies that at least some of his manuscripts remained in Harput and survived the turmoil of the twentieth century.

22. This part of the chapter is mainly based on Aziz Günel's book, *Türk Süryaniler Tarihi* (1970: 192–5). Note that this work was written in a highly nationalistic context in Turkey, which has probably influenced the presentation of some of the material.

23. Both dioceses had been linked before; see Fiey (1993: 163, 216). For the impact of the massacres, see Üngör (2009, 2011: 85).

24. This note might originally derive from Noel's (1919) *Note on the Kurdish Situation*, which was then integrated into Noel (1920). Dionysios is referred to as Mitran Abdul Nus [*sic*!].

25. Rabo (2002) states that he became a 'Provinzratsmitglied' (member of the provincial council).

26. As already mentioned our source for these events was written in Turkey in the early 1970s, a very Turkish nationalistic environment, which might well have influenced the author in his presentation and selection of anecdotes.

27. During the Kurdish rebellion, Azakh was located within the region held by the troops of Sheikh Said.

28. It was not only non-Turks who fell victim to these events. The expulsion of Turks and Muslims from the various newly created or expanded Balkan states has had an irreversible impact on the Turkish psyche and identity as well. For a study on the expulsion of Turks and Muslims from the Balkans, see McCarthy (1995). Note that his approach to the massacres of non-Turks, including the genocides of 1915–16, can and has been challenged. See also Pekesen (2012).
29. For a case study, see Üngör (2009). Many events in later years can and should be seen as part of this effort to homogenize 'Turkish territory', e.g. the removal of the Syriac Orthodox patriarchate from within the boundaries of Turkey, but also the ethnic cleansing of Kurds from parts of eastern Turkey.
30. For a chronology and literature, see Kevorkian (2008).
31. For a legal discussion of the use of the term 'genocide' for these events, see the 2002 memorandum, 'The Applicability of the United Nations Convention on the Prevention and Punishment of the Crime of Genocide to Events which Occurred during the Early Twentieth Century: Legal Analysis Prepared for the International Centre for Transitional Justice', retrieved 31 October 2016 from http://ictj.org/sites/default/files/ICTJ-Turkey-Armenian-Reconciliation-2002-English.pdf.
32. Although not explicit in the sources, it was this rejection of the Armenian cultural influence on his parishioners that seems to have caused most of the conflicts in Harput and eventually led to his removal from this See, not the clash with the modernists (who also opposed the cultural closeness).
33. For the survival of many who had been involved in the genocide in the Turkish Republic, see Üngör (2009) and his chapter in this volume.
34. This also seems to have led Ephrem Barsaum, when he had become patriarch in 1933, to commit fully to the cause of pan-Arabism rather than expect protection from the West.
35. Migration within the Middle East meant that the group was still living as a minority among – dominant – others. Migration outside the Middle East meant that these isolated communities usually assimilated to the surroundings and, for the most part, were swallowed up into the larger society.
36. For a very general overview, see Tachjian (2009).
37. See Atto and Barthoma's chapter in this volume for the expulsion of the Syriac Orthodox patriarchate.
38. This chapter is only a preliminary presentation on Mor Dionysios 'Abd an-Nur Aslan. The author would like to hear from anyone who has more information about this man and his career.

Bibliography

Anonymous 1933. 'Al-Sayid Dionosios 'Abd al-Nur Matran Diyarbakir'. *Al-majallah al-Batriyarkiyyah al-Suryaniyyah* (The Syriac Patriarchal Magazine), 1, pp. 168–9. Reprinted in 1982, no. 13, pp. 16–17.
Atto, N. 2011. *Hostages in the Homeland, Orphans in the Diaspora: Identity Discourses among the Assyrian/Syriac Elites in the European Diaspora*. Leiden: Leiden University Press.
Chabot, J.B. 1899–1924. *Chronique de Michel le Syrien, Patriarche jacobite d'Antioche 1166–1199*, 4 vols. Paris: Ernest Leroux.
Coakley, J.F. 1993. 'A Catalogue of the Syriac Manuscripts in the John Rylands Library', *Bulletin of the John Rylands University Library of Manchester* 75(2): 105–207.

Destani, B.D. 2007a. *Minorities in the Middle East: Christian Minorities, 1838–1967. Greek Orthodox Communities, Roman Catholic, Jacobite, Chaldean and Syrian Catholic Communities in the Levant and Iraq, 1844–1955*. Slough: Archive Editions, Ltd..

—— 2007b. *Minorities in the Middle East: Christian Minorities, 1838–1967. Protestant Communities in the Levant, 1841–1913*. Slough: Archive Editions, Ltd..

Fiey, J.M. 1993. *Pour un Oriens Christianus Novus: Répertoire des diocèses syriaques orientaux et occidentaux*. (Beiruter Texte und Studien 49). Stuttgart: Steiner

Gaunt, D. 2006. *Massacres, Resistance, Protectors: Muslim–Christian Relations in Eastern Anatolia during World War I*. Piscataway NJ: Gorgias Press.

Gerber, J. 1911. *Zwei Briefe Barwahbuns: nebst einer Beilage: das Schisma des Paulus von Beth-Ukkame [nach Joh. v. Ephesus, III. Teil]*. Halle a.S.: Friedrichs-Universität Halle-Wittenberg, Diss.

Günel, A. 1970. *Türk Süryaniler Tarihi*. Diyarbakir: n.p.

Harris, J.R., and H.B. Harris. 1897. *Letters from the Scenes of the Recent Massacres in Armenia*. London: James Nisbet & CO., Ltd.

Kaufhold, H. 1990. 'Zur syrischen Kirchengeschichte des 12. Jahrhunderts: Neue Quellen über Theodoros bar Wahbûn', *Oriens Christianus* 74: 115–51.

Kevorkian, R. 2008. 'The Extermination of Ottoman Armenians by the Young Turk Regime (1915–1916)', *Online Encyclopedia of Mass Violence*, retrieved 31 October 2016 from
http://www.sciencespo.fr/mass-violence-war-massacre-resistance/en/document/extermination-ottoman-armenians-young-turk-regime-1915-1916

Lohmann, E. 1904. 'Ein Besuch bei einem syrischen Erzbischof', in *Auf der Warte* (Separat Abdruck, with additional remark by the author) Freienwalde a. O.: n.p.

—— 1933. *Nur ein Leben: Lebenserinnerungen* (3. Aufl.). Schwerin: Verlag Friedrich Hahn.

McCarthy, J. 1995. *Death and Exile: The Ethnic Cleansing of Ottoman Muslims, 1821–1922*. Princeton: The Darwin Press.

Mingana, A. 1933. *Catalogue of the Mingana Collection of Manuscripts*, 3 vols. Cambridge: Heffer.

Naayem, J. 1920. *Les Assyro-Chaldéens et les Arméniens massacrés par les Turcs*. Paris: Bloud & Gay Editeurs.

Noel, E.W.C. 1919. *Note on the Kurdish Situation*. Baghdad: Government publication.

Noel, E.W.C. 1920. *Diary of Major Noel on Special Duty in Kurdistan*. Baghdad: Government publication .

Özcoşar, İ. 2006. '19. Yüzyilda Mardin Süryanileri', PhD thesis, Kayseri, retrieved 31 October 2016 from http://www.suryaniler.com/makalehavuzu/19_yuzyil_Mardin_Suryanileri.pdf

Pekesen, B. 2012. 'Expulsion and Emigration of the Muslims from the Balkans', *Europäische Geschichte Online*, retrieved 31 October 2016 from http://www.ieg-ego. eu/en/threads/europe-on-the-road/forced-ethnic-migration/berna-pekesen-expulsion-and-emigration-of-the-muslims-from-the-balkans.

Rabo, G. 2002. 'Aslan, Dionysius 'Ebednuhro ('Abdennur)', *Biographisch-Bibliographisches Kirchenlexikon*, retrieved 31 October 2016 from http://www.Bautz. de (registration needed).

—— 2004. 'Mor Dionysius ‚Ebednuhro Aslan (1851–1933)', in *Kolo Suryoyo, Zeitschrift der syrisch-orthodoxen Diözese von Mitteleuropa*, No. 144. Losser.

Tachjian, V. 2009. 'The Expulsion of Non-Turkish Ethnic and Religious Groups from Turkey to Syria during the 1920s and early 1930s', *Online Encyclopedia of Mass Violence*, retrieved 31 October 2016 from http://www.sciencespo.fr/

mass-violence-war-massacre-resistance/en/document/expulsion-non-turkish-ethnic-and-religious-groups-turkey-syria-during-1920s-and-early-1930s.

Takahashi, H. 2005. *Barhebraeus: A Bio-bibliography*. Piscataway, NJ: Gorgias Press.

Taylor, W.H. 2005. *Antioch and Canterbury: The Syrian Orthodox Church and the Church of England 1874–1928*. Piscataway, NJ: Gorgias Press.

Trigona-Harany, B. 2009a. *The Ottoman Süryânî from 1908 to 1914*. Piscataway, NJ: Gorgias Press.

———— 2009b. 'A Bibliography of Süryânî Periodicals in Ottoman Turkish', *Hugoye* 12(2): 287–300.

Üngör, U.Ü. 2009. 'Diyarbekir (1915–1916): Young Turk Mass Killings at the Provincial Level', *Online Encyclopedia of Mass Violence*, retrieved 31 October 2016 from http://www.sciencespo.fr/mass-violence-war-massacre-resistance/en/document/diyarbekir-1915-1916-young-turk-mass-killings-provincial-level.

———— 2011. *The Making of Modern Turkey: Nation and State in Eastern Anatolia, 1913–1950*. Oxford: Oxford University Press.

CHAPTER 5

SYRIAC ORTHODOX LEADERSHIP IN THE POST-GENOCIDE PERIOD (1918–26) AND THE REMOVAL OF THE PATRIARCHATE FROM TURKEY

Naures Atto and Soner O. Barthoma

Between 1918 (the end of the First World War) and 1926 (the resolution of the Mosul Question), the Entente, Turkey and the minority groups living there became enmeshed in a complex series of negotiations. Struggling to obtain a political foothold for their people in the aftermath of the First World War, Syriac Orthodox Church leaders – their effective civil leadership – were forced to negotiate their civil position and rights. Although the Syriac Orthodox Patriarch Ignatius Elias III Shakir (1867–1932) had deputized a delegation led by Archbishop Aphrem Barsoum to attend the Paris Peace Conference in 1919 to present a list of requests, Patriarch Elias had changed his standpoint and declared his loyalty to the Turkish Republic a few years later. Although Turkish elites looked on this gesture with favour, the patriarch was exiled at the end of 1924 and the official Patriarchal See of the Syriac Orthodox Church in Mardin was later officially moved and re-established in Homs by Aphrem Barsoum in 1932.

This brief storyline sets the scene for this chapter, which poses three questions: (1) How can the change in the political standpoint expressed by Patriarch Elias III in this period be contextualized and explained? (2)

What impact did his ambivalence have on the outcome of the Treaty of Lausanne for Assyrians?[1] (3) What were the principal reasons for the removal of the Syriac Orthodox patriarchate from Turkey?

A limitation in writing this chapter has been the availability of the few sources about this topic. In part, the explanation for this situation lies with the removal of the Patriarchal See which, it can be assumed, would have certainly been in possession of some strategic documents relating to the period concerned.

The Paris Peace Conference (1919) gave representatives of different groups affected by the world war the opportunity to submit their requests for the improvement of their situation to representatives of the Great Powers, and among them were Assyrian representatives who attached various petitions to their submissions.[2] The Syriac Orthodox patriarch deputized a delegation led by Archbishop Aphrem Barsoum (the successor to Patriarch Elias III) to attend the conference. In his petition, the archbishop presented six requests on behalf of his people. Among them were a case for granting them autonomy in Turkey, a plea for the recognition of the losses in the broadest sense suffered by Assyrians and a claim for compensation. The requested autonomous area is shown on the map 'Carte Ethnographique et Politique de la Nation Assyro-Chadéenne' (Atto 2011: Appendix 5). Its area stretched from Urmia (in the east) to Tikrit (in the south), Bitlis (in the north) and Adıyaman (in the west). Further attempts to negotiate the rights of Assyrians with Western countries are revealed in a letter (16 February 1921) from the Syriac Orthodox patriarch to the British Foreign Minister, George, Marquess Curzon of Kedleston.

Given the prevailing circumstances, it is feasible to link the request for autonomy to a feeling of insecurity under Muslim rule.[3] The dislocation that occurred during the war, more specifically in the appalling aftermath of the genocide, naturally inflicted a severe trauma on and caused an enormous crisis among the Assyrians. Their demand for autonomy can be interpreted as their perception of a glimmer of hope that might allow them to pick up the thread of their lives.

Although these proposals by the Syriac Orthodox Church leadership were made only a few years after more than half of their population in the Ottoman Empire had been massacred, none was accepted. Reflecting on the process of the negotiations years later, Archbishop Aphrem Barsoum (Bet-Barsawmo 1996) expressed his disappointment in the way Western powers dealt with the Assyrian proposals:

> There [at the Paris Peace Conference], I laid bare all the catastrophes which had befallen my people. I spared no detail in describing the oppression and

the horror. Even though I particularly emphasized how our casualties had been both massacred in cold blood and had perished from hunger and cold during the war, when I saw that not one of the Conference participants shed a tear or felt any compassion for us, I felt as if I had delivered my speech to statues carved from stone.[4]

This example illustrates how communal leadership could exert little influence on the macro-politics in which their geopolitical position had been formed. In the case of the Syriac Orthodox Church leadership, and also that of the Church of the East, their representatives realized at an early stage that Western countries would not be prepared to keep their word and meet their demands. Realizing the constraints within which they had to operate, they found themselves forced to find other allies to secure the position of their people.

As noted, at the Paris Peace Conference Archbishop Aphrem Barsoum presented a list of requests on behalf of Patriarch Elias III, among which autonomy for his people was of paramount importance. Three years later, during the Lausanne Peace Conference (1922–23) when the conditions for Turkish minority policy were being shaped, the patriarch remained silent about these earlier requests and adopted a more explicitly pro-Turkish stance. To put the change in the patriarch's political standpoint into context and explain the reasons behind it, it is enlightening to take a look at his biography.

Patriarch Ignatius Elias III (1867–1932)

Patriarch Elias III was born in Mardin in 1867. In 1908,[5] he had been consecrated Archbishop of Diyarbakır, where he continued to serve until his appointment as Archbishop of Mosul in 1912, a position he occupied until 1917 (Nuro 1972). After Patriarch 'Abded Aloho died (26 November 1915), Archbishop Elias was elected patriarch and assumed his throne in 1917. It is remarkable that for more than a year – a relatively long period during the Sayfo – the Syriac Orthodox community was without a leader. At the moment, no sources that might explain this hiatus are known, but in that period of severe crisis it would have been more difficult to organize matters. Patriarch Elias III was an important witness of the Sayfo and its aftermath because of his position as a bishop, first in Diyarbakır and later in Mosul, and thereafter as the patriarch of the Syriac Orthodox Church between 1917 and 1932. Nevertheless, so far, no specific writings about the Sayfo by him are known.

As the patriarch responsible for his community, he found himself in a difficult political situation, in which a whole series of negotiations about the future of Turkey, its geographical borders and the status of minorities were taking place between different powers. Although the Patriarchal See was officially in the Zafaran[6] Monastery in Mardin, the patriarch had chosen to live in Istanbul for more than three years,[7] presumably assuming he could use his influence in the political arena more effectively there. He was in contact with both Western diplomats, especially the British and French, and Turkish political elites (Nuro 1972). Among the very few writings by Patriarch Elias III that have survived is a letter he wrote to his church community in Malabar (India) during the time he spent in Istanbul (1920); Elias III 2011). He mentions the killing of his people, the destruction of villages and the people who had been forced to take refuge elsewhere. The patriarch also states that he had received some financial help from the Christians in Egypt and was also seeking financial help from his church community in India. This letter shows that he had been trying to find resources to help his community members who survived the genocide.

Another important piece of evidence that shows Patriarch Elias III was very much aware of the massacres and was trying to help the victims of the genocide is the list of requests he submitted to the sultan. On 26 September 1919, Patriarch Elias had an audience in Istanbul with the Ottoman sultan, Muhammad Rashid, at which he was presented with an official *firman* (decree) confirming his appointment as patriarch.[8] During this audience, the patriarch took the opportunity to submit a long list of requests to the sultan and these were discussed by his cabinet (*Meclis-i Vükelâ*) on 22 November 1919 (Oral 2007; Hür 2007).[9] One important request was that those people who had been deported during the Sayfo should be allowed to return to their homes with the restitution of their property. Furthermore, he asked that abducted women and children and all others who had been forcibly converted to Islam should be allowed to return to their own religion.

Although the patriarch also made these and other requests through his representatives at the Paris Peace Conference, throughout his career he never failed to demonstrate his loyalty to the Ottoman and later to the Turkish Republican authorities, which is aptly illustrated by the following anecdote. Even during the dreadful year (1915) of the genocide, Elias, then still archbishop, had been contacted by the Ottoman authorities who had demanded he use his influence to stop the 'revolts' by his community members in Midyad, Cizre and Diyarbakır (Kurtcephe 1993). Archbishop Elias's response to this demand is unknown. Cogently the official Turkish discourse made use of the term 'revolt', instead of defence, to legitimize the massacres.[10]

Outsiders have criticized the patriarch for his unswerving loyalty to the Turkish state. For example, Israel Audo (2004), Chaldean Bishop of Mardin, refers to his attitude in terms of 'voluntary slavery'. This sort of criticism is also found in the book by M.C. Holmes (1923), the principal of the American orphanage for Armenian children in Urfa at the time of the patriarch's visit to that city in 1919.

Several sources[11] indicate that after the war the patriarch told his community members to submit to Turkish policy and rule, and to refrain from any cooperation with the Armenians. During his visit to Urfa in 1919, he was criticized by some community members for his plan to visit the Turkish governor before he had paid his respects to the British governor. The patriarch reacted to this criticism with the comment: 'My Son, let me do my job. I know what I am doing. The English are guests, whereas the Turks are here to stay' (Nuro 1972).[12] Especially after the realization had dawned that the Western countries were indifferent to the plight of the Assyrians, the patriarch inclined even more towards the Turkish side and subsequently expressed his loyalty more explicitly to the members of the Turkish elite whom he met, among them Rauf Bey, İsmet İnönü and Fevzi Çakmak. The patriarch's secretary Zakaria Shakir confirms this (Nuro 1972):

> So when the Patriarch visits Turkish statesmen for the first time ... he speaks about and explicates his Turkish policy, '... We of the Syriac [Orthodox] denomination are loyal to the administration to which we are subject' ... 'We don't have any links with Western nations.' ... He [the patriarch] repeats this formula [to everyone he visits]. Rauf Bey [Prime Minister] thought it an overstatement.

The patriarch's cautious political approach was firmly rooted in a survival strategy and should be understood in the context of his own time. An excerpt from Abrohom Nuro's interview with Zakaria Shakir (Nuro 1972) leaves no doubt that the patriarch's intention was to deal with issues within the accepted political boundaries set by the Ottoman and Turkish rulers. Simultaneously, as the supreme leader responsible for his people, he negotiated political matters with Assyrian lay elites:

Nuro: At the time, Naum Faik[13] expressed his preparedness to serve the cause of the Assyrian Movement, did not Patriarch Elias implicitly object to the idea? What is your honest opinion about this?

Shakir: During his time in Diyarbakır, Naum Faik performed a national service by forming a nationalist association.

Nuro: The 'Irutho [Renaissance] Association, perhaps! ...
Shakir: Patriarch Elias did not oppose them [Naum Faik and his friends].
          Indeed, he supported them. But he warned them: '... Be careful of
          movements which impinge on the sensitivities of the Turkish State
          [CUP].' ... I see the Turkish State through the officials with whom
          I am in contact. They regard the Armenians with extreme caution,
          through a finely focused microscope. ... 'So, do not bring this rigid
          scrutiny to bear on us, ...'.
Nuro: Yet he used to give them fatherly advice. Yes, as a father; that is, a
          father who knows his duties and commitments.
Shakir: ... Yes! There was both friction and a dialogue between him and
          Naum Faik.

As a young monk, Patriarch Elias had already witnessed the massacres of Christians in 1894–96 during the reign of Sultan Abdul Hamid II. He had personally experienced the terrors a ruler could unleash on his subjects. Against this background, the patriarch's attempts to negotiate between the different powers and to meet the most urgent needs of his community, namely to save their lives, become more comprehensible. In his interview with Abrohom Nuro (1972), Zakaria Shakir mentions that the patriarch used to say:

> We have to safeguard [the lives of] the living because the dead are not going to come back. ... We want to ensure that the swords are at rest. This was the term [swords] he used.

In line with his cautious, obedient attitude, Patriarch Elias III maintained good relations with the new Turkish political elites. His secretary, Zakaria Shakir (Nuro 1972), says that he had three meetings[14] with Mustafa Kemal in Ankara. On 9 February 1923 – prior to his meeting with Mustafa Kemal – Patriarch Elias III was interviewed by Celal Nuri, the owner of the newspaper *İleri* and an MP who was very close to Mustafa Kemal. In an interview, the patriarch made a statement setting out his stance on the future position of Assyrians in the Turkish Republic:[15]

> So far the issue of minority rights has entered neither the minds nor the dreams of the community I represent. We shall defend this very vigorously. I, on behalf of my community, did not make any such demand, nor do I make it now, nor shall I in the future. *Süryaniler* [Assyrians] are the minority of the people living under the purview of the *Misak-i Milli* [National Oath]. They merely wish to live together with the majority [Turks] in good times and bad and to enjoy the benefits of this ...

It is remarkable that the patriarch had already disclosed so much in the interview before he actually met Mustafa Kemal. His expression of loyalty says something about the insecurity and fear besetting him; he had left himself no room for negotiations about the future of his people with the head of the Turkish state. During the second meeting, which took place on 3 March 1923 (Oral 2007: 288; Nuro 1972), Mustafa Kemal said to Patriarch Elias: 'I congratulate you on this policy of yours. ... I put ... excellent means of transportation to Beirut at your disposal ... from here to Beirut and from Beirut to Aleppo'. Zakaria Shakir says that a final meeting between the patriarch (whom he had accompanied) and Mustafa Kemal was held to take his leave and 'to be punctiliously and painstakingly provided with appropriate orders to take to Mardin, ... as the professional, respected leader of a *millet* in Turkey'.[16] Zakaria Shakir also mentions that in the same meeting the patriarch was told by a representative from Mardin, '... you have gained the trust of young and old in Ankara'. Moreover, the yearbook of Mardin (*Mardin İl Yıllığı* 1967: 87, in Dolapönü [Dolabani] 1972: 102) mentions the approving words spoken by Mustafa Kemal about Patriarch Elias:

> During the War of Independence, as a true son of this country, the *Süryani* Patriarch Elias III has shown himself to be one of its heroes by having taken a strong stand against the aggressors.

What the patriarch did or why the Turkish political elites in Ankara rewarded him with so much trust, and the reason he is referred to as one of the heroes of the War of Independence, are no longer known. Nevertheless, the idea that the attitude and subsequent policy of the Syriac Orthodox Church leadership affected the non-recognition of Assyrians in the Treaty of Lausanne does raise some questions. Even before the patriarch was interviewed by *İleri* and had met Mustafa Kemal, the Western powers had washed their hands of the minority question.

An analysis of the Lausanne Conference documents leaves no doubt that the Western powers never expended much time and effort on the 'Assyro-Chaldean Question' and certainly did not prioritize it.[17] Before the conference, the British Foreign Office prepared a list of British requirements, which were divided into two categories, '(A) Essential' and '(B) Most Desirable'. The protection of minorities, including their demands for a 'home', was categorized as 'most desirable' (Dockrill 1993: 4), which could be translated as meaning they could easily use the questions in this category to appease Turkish demands.

The Assyro-Chaldean question was tabled a few times during the conference in the context of 'protection of minorities' (in the 13th and 14th meetings, 13/14 December 1922), in the Report of the Sub-Commission

(19th meeting, 9 January 1923)[18] and during the discussions about the
'Mosul Question' (21st meeting, 23 January 1923).[19] The discussions
between Lord Curzon and Ismet Pasha reveal that from the outset the
Turkish delegation had adopted a very rigid standpoint on the 'Assyro-
Chaldean' question. Lord Curzon mentioned the Assyrians for the first
time in the 13th meeting:[20]

> There is also the important group of Nestorian or Assyrian Christians in dif-
> ferent parts of the Kurdish mountains and on the Turco-Persian border. A
> deep interest is taken in the fortunes of these people, particularly in Great
> Britain, France and America, and they suffered terribly in the havoc and ruin
> of the recent war. In so far as they are now settled within the borders of British
> influence they are assured of our friendly interest and protection. Wherever
> they may be found in Turkish territory, we must insist upon adequate mea-
> sures being taken to safeguard their religion, their industry and their life.

The Turkish delegation refused to discuss this question. Ismet Pasha
argued that the 'Nestorians and Assyrians on the eastern frontier of
Turkey had never made any complaint until the great war, and even
during the latter they had not had to endure any suffering peculiar to
themselves ...'.[21] In the first meetings, the Allied powers, especially
Lord Curzon on behalf of the British Empire, were insistent on the
demands of the minority groups. However, this standpoint changed in
later meetings. Michael Dockrill (1993: 7) says that the British government was committed to peace and retrenchment, and did not want any
complications outside Europe while it had to deal with a serious rift
with the French over Germany. Therefore, the British Prime Minister
urged Curzon to terminate the Lausanne Conference quickly on the
best terms he could get. The Turkish delegation was aware that the
breach in the Allied front would strengthen its hand at the conference.
Directly after this, prior to the Minorities Sub-Commission meeting on
9 January 1923, the Western delegates reached an agreement with the
Turkish delegation led by İsmet İnönü. Later, Curzon admitted that 'the
minority clauses were less than satisfactory and that the Armenians
[and with them the Assyrians] had been abandoned to their fate'.[22]

In his book *The Great Betrayal* (1924), Edward Hale Bierstadt
(Executive Secretary of the Emergency Committee for Near East
Refugees in 1923) also unequivocally indicates that the Allies were more
absorbed with economic and political imperialist interests rather than
protecting the rights of minorities. The fact that they had to compete
with each other for resources paved the way for Turkey to take a leading
role in the negotiations at the Lausanne Conference. Bierstadt (1924:
170) writes:

Two factions were conspicuous at Lausanne; one representing the oil interests, the other appearing in the interests of the Christian Minorities and America's philanthropic investment in Asia Minor. Oil won the day. Turkey refused to discuss concessions unless the minorities were excluded from the conversation, and not one of the Powers was willing to forego a possible economic advantage to see justice done. Knowing that the Allies were divided among themselves Turkey pitted the one against another.

Consequently, it would be wrong to take Patriarch Elias's loyalty as an explanation for the outcome of the Treaty of Lausanne in terms of how this affected Assyrians. The two most compelling factors in this decision were the fawning attitude adopted by the Western powers in their dealings with Turkey and the rigid policy imposed by the fledgling Turkish Republic in the wake of its military success. On account of its strong position, the Turkish state was able to presume to take the upper hand at the Lausanne Peace Conference. It requires no great stretch of the imagination to see how the Turkish delegation managed to thwart the participation of the delegations from minority groups.[23] The Turkish delegation did not attend the meetings at which the representatives of the Armenians and the Assyro-Chaldeans were heard.[24] Furthermore, during the meeting of the Minorities Sub-Commission on 6 January 1923, in a vehement reaction to the submissions[25] made by Western diplomats on behalf of 'Assyro-Chaldeans', Rıza Nur Bey, member of the Turkish delegation, walked out of the meeting (James 1923). In the discussion of its position on the 'Assyro-Chaldean Question', the Turkish delegation refused to budge an inch. The minutes and documents of the Lausanne Conference unequivocally reveal that when this matter was tabled by Western diplomats in the 21st meeting on 21 January 1923, the head of the Turkish delegation, İsmet İnönü, stated:

The Chaldeans,[26] and more especially the Assyrians of the Vilayet of Diarbekir, never let themselves be influenced by foreign agitation and they are still living on terms of perfect understanding with their Turkish compatriots.[27]

The Turkish delegation refused all the demands touching upon the Assyro-Chaldeans.[28] Consequently, the eventual upshot of the post-First World War negotiations was that, as a group of people, the Assyrians were no longer protected by any treaty. In contrast to the position they had enjoyed in the preceding era before the foundation of the Turkish Republic, the Assyrians had now lost their formal status as a self-contained community (*millet*). In the 'official' Turkish minority policy that was outlined in the Lausanne Treaty (24 July 1923), it was agreed that non-Muslims would be allowed to enjoy certain rights. Later, in

1932, Turkey inserted a clause that narrowed the definition of non-Muslim minorities to the Armenians, Greeks and Jews only.[29] The new clause made it officially possible for only the recognized non-Muslim minorities to establish their own schools, social organizations and magazines, which meant that the Assyrians were denied any access to these rights (Oran 2007: 38–9).[30]

The Removal of the Patriarchal See from Turkey

How was it that such a loyal leader who had won the praises of the Kemalist regime could be sent into exile? Oral and written sources infer that the patriarch's flight was the outcome of state policy. In 1924, an official decree issued by the authorities deprived Patriarch Elias III of his right to use his official title in his communications with them (Srayel [Israel Audo] 2004, in Bet Sawoce and BarAbraham 2009). Sources mention two different years for the order to move the Syriac Orthodox patriarchate from Turkey. Harry Charles Luke, once Assistant-Governor of Jerusalem for the British Mandated Government, wrote that the patriarch had already been expelled from his monastery in the spring of 1924 (Luke 1925: 28, 113). He also observes that, since February 1924, Assyrians in this region had been subjected to a renewal of the persecution they had suffered during the war. Abrohom Sowmy, an orphan in the Assyrian orphanage in Adana who joined Yuhanon Dolabani in Jerusalem and served the community there, told his son Peter Sowmy that the patriarch did not go back to Mardin after 1924.[31] Peter Sowmy says that in 1923–24 Patriarch Elias travelled between Jerusalem and Mardin on several occasions and, by the end of 1924, the patriarchate had been temporarily moved to Jerusalem. In contrast to these two sources, a letter in the Secret Archive of the Vatican mentions that the patriarch fled Turkey in late 1925.[32] Moreover, an oral account given by Archpriest Gabriel Aydin (Bar Yawno), who was a pupil at the Zafaran Monastery (Mardin) in the 1920s, says:[33]

> ... one day the governor[34] of Mardin came to the Monastery to deliver a telegram from Atatürk [Mustafa Kemal] which had been sent to him [the governor]. The telegram read: 'The clerical leader in the black cassock [the patriarch] should leave Turkey immediately and should never ever return!'

So far, no explanations have been found for the discrepancies about the year in which the patriarch permanently left Turkey. Archbishop Dolabani ([Dolapönü] 1972: 165) mentions the necessity for Patriarch

Elias III to leave the country in more general terms: '... that, after the death of Patriarch Elias III in India, it was absolutely necessary that the Patriarchate be moved to Homs in Syria in 1933 during the Patriarchate of Aphrem Barsoum'. It is generally known that Archbishop Dolabani had been subjected to crushing pressure by the Turkish authorities to do with what he could and could not publish. This reference to the removal of the patriarchate might provide an explanation for the censorship imposed on him.

After the patriarch left his residence in Mardin, he busied himself seeking a new home for the patriarchate of the Syriac Orthodox Church abroad. Initially Patriarch Elias attempted to settle the patriarchate in Jerusalem (Kiraz 2005),[35] where he lived for three years (Nuro 1972), but the patriarchs of the other denominations (the Latins, Greeks and Armenians) were unhappy about this plan. An oral source hints that King Faisal had forbidden any attempt by Patriarch Elias to establish the patriarchate in Mosul.[36] However, Archbishop Athanasius Yeshue Samuel (1968: 117), one of the monks who had accompanied the patriarch to Iraq and India, mentions that Patriarch Elias III had a meeting with King Faisal in 1931, but he does not mention what had been discussed. Kiraz (2005) writes that suggestions about settling the patriarchate in Mosul had to be abandoned because the patriarch died. An official decree[37] signed by the Turkish cabinet on 7 July 1931 deprived Patriarch Elias III of his Turkish citizenship on the grounds that he had acquired Iraqi citizenship without having first sought permission from the Turkish authorities – despite the fact that he had already been exiled – and as a consequence of this action his relations with Turkey were null and void.

On 16 February 1931,[38] Patriarch Elias journeyed on to his church community in India, where he was hoping to solve problems within the community, and where he died in 1932. A year later, in 1933, the official Patriarchal See of the Syriac Orthodox Church was established in Homs and since 1959 it has been based in Damascus. Homs was chosen because Elias's successor, Patriarch Aphrem Barsoum, was based there as Archbishop of Syria and Lebanon (Kiraz 2005). After Patriarch Elias left Turkey, the Turkish authorities forbade Patriarch Aphrem Barsoum from entering Turkey because he had argued the case for the rights of Assyrians in Turkey when, as an archbishop, he had been the church's representative in the postwar negotiations. A government decree of 7 June 1937, which was signed by Mustafa Kemal, Ismet Inönü and other cabinet members, banned the import into Turkey of any publication by Patriarch Aphrem Barsoum 'because of their dangerous content'.[39]

The contextualization of this period does offer some explanations for the expulsion of the patriarch. As Oral (2007: 294–5) writes, the removal of the Syriac Orthodox patriarchate from Turkey can be explained in the context of the Kemalist secularization policy that was adopted in 1923. In his speech in May 1924, Mustafa Kemal said that religious institutions constituted a discrepancy within a state that worked on the basis of a single jurisprudence (*Atatürk'ün Söylev ve Demeçleri* 1997: 102–3). He declared in no uncertain terms that '[t]he Orthodox and Armenian churches and Jewish synagogues which are based in Turkey should have been abolished together with the Caliphate'. The political arena in the mid-1920s also shows that relations between the community and the Turkish state worsened after what was known as the 'Nestorian Revolt' in the Hakkari mountains in 1924, and were exacerbated even further in 1925, after it emerged that some members of the Assyrian community had supported the Sheikh Said Revolt.[40] The Kemalist regime seized upon these revolts as a pretext to eliminate any potential opposition forces and, by doing so, weed out potential threats to the regime. Independence Tribunals (*İstiklal Mahkemeleri*) were used to facilitate the effectuation of this policy.[41] After the failure of the Sheikh Said Revolt, in 1926 the state launched a comprehensive elimination and disarmament programme,[42] whose purpose was to achieve stability within the borders of the *Misak-i Milli*. After they had been established, many people were arrested and brought to trial before these Independence Tribunals. A letter in the Secret Archive of the Vatican (*Archivio della Nunziatura Apostolica in Parigi*: Busta 392)[43] supplies the information that 150 Assyrians, both Syriac Orthodox and Syriac Catholics, were deported from Midyad, 'Iwardo, Anhel, Mzizah and Midin. Another hundred persons were deported from Hazakh. The lawyer Malak Barsaumo (a member of the Hanne Safar family in Midyad) was hanged in Elazığ in 1926 (Bet Sawoce 2009: 259-270).[44]

Conclusion

The political discourse of the Syriac Orthodox Church leadership in the nascent Turkish Republic has to be understood in the context of the early post-Sayfo period (1918–26), in which the Sayfo had obviously weakened their position drastically.

In the post-Sayfo period, having lost hope of being able to effectuate any real change in their status, Assyrians feared stigmatization. Given their precarious status, the representatives of the Assyrians never lodged any appeal against their status in the decades that followed the Sayfo, and hence they were left with little hope of being granted any formal status at a later date.[45] Their strategy, born of necessity, has been to develop tactics to accommodate to their new position in Turkish society;

consequently, it has been characterized by obedience to a succession of Turkish governments.

Patriarch Elias III certainly championed the demand for 'Assyro-Chaldean autonomy' at the Paris Peace Conference, lobbied with Western powers and presented a whole list of demands to the ruling sultan. Later, however, especially towards 1923, the patriarch spoke of his loyalty to the Turkish authorities in no uncertain terms. In seeking an explanation for this ambivalent attitude, the relational and contextual aspects in the process of decision making cannot be overlooked. The conclusion reached in this chapter is that the stance taken and decisions made by the Syriac Orthodox leadership during this transitional period can be explained in terms of the adoption of a 'survival strategy', although the term 'strategy' should not be taken literally. A 'survival strategy' should not be understood as a political approach developed in a context in which different choices can be made to maximize subsequent benefits. The 'survival strategy' discussed here was the product of a crisis situation in which individuals or groups encountered insurmountable obligations that necessarily limited their (political) choices and set the boundaries to their means of influence. Our contention is that the Syriac Orthodox Church leadership adopted this survival strategy in order to safeguard the future of its remaining community members. Hence, the discourses of loyalty professed by the church leadership should be seen in the context of their weak position and desperate straits, particularly in the post-Sayfo period. By and large, discourses of loyalty of clergymen with the governments under which they live have been characterized by the de-politicization of their community. A typical example of such a discourse of obedience can be seen in the speech of the former patriarch of the Syriac Orthodox Church, Zakka I Iwas, when he spoke to his community members in the Zafaran Monastery (Mardin) in 2004:[46] 'In order to be a true believer in God, above all a believer should be a good citizen. If a believer is not loyal to his country then it is not possible to be a true believer in God' (quoted from Akyüz 2005: 457). The patriarch's correlation between a 'believer' and a 'loyal citizen' provides a cogent illustration of how the clergy in particular have made use of loyalty discourses based on religious arguments to encourage the members of their community to become loyal and obedient citizens, a role they hope will ensure that they will be tolerated in the countries in the Middle East in which they live. This religious discourse of loyalty shows no deviation from the traditional line taken by Syriac clergymen, namely to convince the faithful to accept any hardship and persecution. This strong discourse of 'loyalty' betrays the fear they have experienced and should be seen in the light of a survival strategy.[47]

Another question raised in this study was whether the pro-Turkish stance of Patriarch Elias III affected the outcome of the Lausanne Treaty. It would be at worst wrong, at best an oversimplification, to assert a direct relationship between the pro-Turkish stance of the patriarch and the drawing up of the Lausanne Treaty in which the minority policy of Turkey was shaped. Even prior to the conference, theirs was a lost cause: Assyrians and their rights had already been abandoned. At the Lausanne Conference, the Western powers, Great Britain in particular, were not disposed to support the rights of minorities within the *Misak-i Milli* boundaries with any vigour. Angling to strengthen its own position in the negotiations on the Mosul Question, Great Britain accepted the Turkish stance on minority questions.

Considering the decision to move the Syriac Orthodox patriarchate from Turkey, the conclusion has to be that, although Patriarch Elias III repeatedly expressed his loyalty during the time in which the Turkish Republic was being established, his leadership was still perceived to be a 'potential threat' by the nascent Turkish regime. It was therefore inevitable that he was among the leaders who were expelled from Turkey in the mid-1920s.

Naures Atto is Senior Research Associate at the Faculty of Asian and Middle Eastern Studies and former Mellon Postdoctoral Fellow in World Christianities and their Diaspora in the European Context at the University of Cambridge. She is the author of *Hostages in the Homeland, Orphans in the Diaspora: Identity Discourses among the Assyrian/Syriac elites in the European Diaspora* (2011).

Soner O. Barthoma is Research Fellow at Freie Universität Berlin, and coordinator of the EC Horizon 2020 'Respond' project at Uppsala University. He is the author of several articles about the modern history of Assyrians in Turkey.

Notes

1. In this publication, although we use the name 'Assyrians' cross-denominationally, we focus on the case of the members of the Syriac Orthodox Church only. For further discussions about the use of different names for the same group of people, see Atto (2011).
2. See the introduction in this volume for more about the requests of different delegations. See further de Courtois (2004: 201–23) for a specific discussion of the Syriac Catholic and Syriac Orthodox delegations and their demands. See Yacoub ([1986]

1993) specifically for the Assyro-Chaldean delegations. See Aprim (2006) for a discussion of the above-mentioned delegations.

3. For instance, after the frightening expansion of the Islamic State in Iraq and Syria in 2014, Assyrians worldwide have launched a demand to the international community for a 'safe zone/heaven'.

4. The original of this citation was published in Arabic in Ignatius Zakka Iwas (1983), *The Syrian Orthodox Church at a Glance* (translated into English by E.H. Bismarji, Aleppo), and translated into Turkish by Jan Bet Sawoce in A. Bet-Barşawmo (1996). This is our translation of the Turkish translation.

5. Syriac Orthodox Resources, *Patriarch Ignatius Elias III*, retrieved 22 July 2011 from http://sor.cua.edu/Personage/PElias3/.

6. Earlier Syriac names for this monastery were Dayro d-Kurkmo and Dayro d-Mor Hananyo.

7. Zakaria Shakir (Nuro 1972) mentions that he remained in Istanbul for three and a half years. The patriarch mentioned three years in the interview 'Süryani Kadim Patrikíne göre Anadolu', *Ikdam* 9076, 23 June 1922, p. 1.

8. During this audience, Sultan Muhammad Rashid conferred the Ismania Medal on Patriarch Elias III. See further McCallum (2010) for a study on the Christian leadership in the Middle East.

9. For the official response to the patriarch's requests, see *Başbakanlik Osmanlı Arşivi Meclis-i Vükelâ Mazbataları* (217), No. 553, 22 November 1919.

10. See also Talay (2010: 242–4), who uses some examples to illustrate how the authorities misrepresented the situation.

11. For the patriarch's directive to the Adana congregation, see 'Süryani Kadim Patriğinin Bir Tebliği', *Ikdam*, 8921, 15 January 1922, p. 3. For the patriarch's decree to the Urhoy congregation, see Akyüz (2005: 445) and Nuro (1972).

12. Even today, all Christian minorities in the Middle East are caught in the same dilemma: they have to choose between cooperation with Western foreign powers or cooperation with local power groups. In both cases, the relations are problematic because they are either forced to show their 'loyalty' by the majority groups with whom they live or approached very pragmatically by Western powers.

13. Naum Faik (1868–1930) was a prominent Assyrian intellectual known for his patriotism (*umthonoyutho*).

14. An article detailing the patriarch's gratitude for the reception he had received appeared in the newspaper: 'Süryani Patriki'nin Şükranı', *Ikdam*, 9332, 9 March 1923, p. 1.

15. *İleri*, 9 February 1923. In some sources, the name of the newspaper is said to be *Yenigün*. This interview was republished in a press release sent by the president of the Syriac Orthodox Church Board in Istanbul, Ferit Özcan, to the Turkish daily newspaper *Milliyet* (19 November 1977) in reaction to a previously published secret US document about Turkey during the time of the War of Independence. For similar statements by Patriarch Elias III in Turkish newspapers, see 'Süryani Kadim ve Türkiye Patriki Ilyas Efendi Ankara'da', *Ikdam*, 9299, 4 February 1923, p. 2; 'Süryani Patriki'nin Beyanatı', *Akşam*, 1572, 6 February 1923, p. 1. See also 'Süryani Kadim Patriki tarafından Süryani cemaatinin sadakatini teýiden arz ve iblağ ediliyor', *Ikdam*, 9422, 10 June 1923, p. 2.

16. There is no record of the orders Mustafa Kemal gave to the patriarch.

17. See also Joseph (2000: 167–8) showing how Great Britain and other powers yielded to the Turkish claims in their desire to secure an agreement.

18. See the Annex (pp. 303–13) for the 'Report of the Sub-commission on Minorities', particularly pp. 307–8 about 'Assyro-Chaldeans' in *Lausanne Conference on Near Eastern Affairs 1922–1923* (1923).

19. See 'Mosul: Statements of Turkish and British Cases', in *Lausanne Conference on Near Eastern Affairs 1922–1923* (1923). Proposal made by Lord Curzon for reference to League of Nations (pp. 337–63), and in the Appendix, 'Correspondence between Lord Curzon and Ismet Pasha Regarding Mosul' (pp. 363–93).
20. See *Lausanne Conference on Near Eastern Affairs 1922–1923* (1923: 178).
21. See *Lausanne Conference on Near Eastern Affairs 1922–1923* (1923: 208).
22. Documents on British Foreign Policy (DBFP), Curzon to Lindsay, unnumbered tel., 5 February 1923, no. 370 in W. N. Medlicott et al. (eds), *Documents on British Foreign Policy 1919–1939 (DBFP)*, 1972, p. 505.
23. Agha Petros (as representative of the Assyrian delegation) participated in the opening ceremony of the Lausanne Peace Conference in November 1922 (Nirari 1989: 191).
24. See *Lausanne Conference on Near Eastern Affairs 1922–1923* (1923: 299).
25. These requests were discussed in conjunction with the quest for an 'Armenian homeland' undertaken by the same Western delegations.
26. Members of the Church of the East who have converted to Roman Catholicism are referred to as Chaldeans.
27. *Lausanne Conference on Near Eastern Affairs 1922-1923* (1923: 343). See also a similar statement in the 'Reply to the British Memorandum Regarding the Mosul Question' (p. 376), and in Turkish sources about the Lausanne Conference in Meray (1993: 347).
28. *Lausanne Conference on Near Eastern Affairs 1922–1923* (1923: 308).
29. For further reading about this limitation, see also Cengiz (2003).
30. For example, Archbishop Dolabani applied to the Turkish authorities on 19 October 1949 to obtain permission to commence a Bible study course in the Zafaran Monastery. The correspondence between the archbishop and the Turkish authorities illustrates the almost insurmountable difficulties the archbishop encountered when he made this application and how he eventually had to give up because he failed to make any progress. For more on this correspondence, see Akyüz (2005: 450–53).
31. Email communication with Peter Sowmy, February 2013. Peter Sowmy had been informed about this while growing up.
32. 'Letter from Hazakh, 4 January 1926', in *Archivio della Nunziatura Apostolica in Parigi* (Busta 392).
33. All translations are ours if not mentioned otherwise (Bet Sawoce and BarAbraham 2009). Since, as far as we know, Archpriest Gabriel was born in 1926, he probably heard this quotation from others after he had commenced his studies in the monastery. Otherwise his year of birth would have to be at least five or six years earlier. At the time of writing, Archpriest Gabriel's frail health prevented him from talking about this matter, so it was impossible to discuss it with him personally.
34. Other oral information commonly heard among Assyrians says that the governor of Mardin (1923–25), Abdülfattah Baykurt Bey, had a very good relationship with the patriarch and therefore informed the patriarch that it would be better for him to leave the country if he were not to forfeit his life. If he did not take this advice and leave, when the governor received the telegram from Ankara it would be too late to save his life. It is said that when he heard this news, the patriarch decided to flee the country.
35. Dolabani (1972) mentions that he travelled (first) to Aleppo to consecrate a church.
36. We have not been able to find a written confirmation for this source.
37. This document (7 July 1931, Başbakanlık Cumhuriyet Arşivi [BCA], Başvekalet, 036/16/01/02, 17-1-18) was signed by the president of Turkey (Mustafa Kemal), Prime Minister Ismet Inönü and other cabinet members.
38. Zakaria Shakir (Nuro 1972) mentions that they went to India at the end of 1930.

39. BCA, Başvekalet, 030/18/01/02, 75-50-1.
40. For an early source, see Sykes (1924: 473–4). See also Gaunt (2006, Appendix I, p. 341) and Bet Sawoce (2009: 259–70).
41. See more about the Independence Tribunals in Zürcher (2003: 179–80).
42. On 15 June 1926, there was a suicide assassination attempt against Mustafa Kemal in Izmir.
43. See also Luke (1925: 113), who mentions that the patriarch was expelled (spring 1924) from the Zafaran Monastery.
44. See also Joseph (1983: 102–3) about how the Syriac Orthodox became victims during the suppression of the Kurdish revolt.
45. On 30 March 1995, representatives of the Mor Gabriel Monastery in Tur Abdin and the Syriac Orthodox Bishopric in Istanbul requested the then incumbent Turkish president, S. Demirel, and Prime Minister T. Ciller to recognize Assyrians as a non-Muslim minority and to grant them the rights inherent in this status. A respondent who was involved in writing this application informed me that they never received an answer to this request. Assyrian activists in the diaspora have also run up against this wall of silence from Turkey in response to their requests, an indication that their requests have not been taken seriously.
46. Patriarch Zakka I Iwas was officially invited by the governor of Mardin to attend the meeting 'Kültürler Arası Diyalog Platformu', which was held in Mardin on 13 May 2004.
47. To give an example, many books written by Syriac Orthodox clergymen in Turkey have a frontispiece showing a picture of Mustafa Kemal.

Bibliography

Akyüz, G. 2005. *Tüm Yönleriyle Süryaniler.* Mardin: Mardin Anadolu Ofset.

Aprim, F. 2006. *Assyrians in the World War I Treaties: Paris, Sevres, and Lausanne.* Retrieved 29 June 2011 from http://www.christiansofiraq.com/TreatiesfredJune166.html.

Archivio della Nunziatura Apostolica in Parigi (Busta 392). 'Letter from Hazakh', 4 January 1926.

Atatürk'ün Söylev ve Demeçleri. Vol. III. 1997. Ankara: Atatürk Araştırma Merkezi.

Atto, N. 2011. *Hostages in the Homeland, Orphans in the Diaspora: Identity Discourses among the Assyrian/Syriac Elites in the European Diaspora.* Leiden: Leiden University Press.

Audo, I. 2004. *Maktbonutho cal Rdufye da Kristiyone d Marde, w d Amid, w d Sacërd, w da Gziro w da Nsibin d bi sato 1915.* Jönköping: Ashurbanipal bokförlaget.

Bet-Barşawmo, A. [Barsoum, A.]. 1996. *Tur-Abdin Tarihi.* Södertälje: Nsibin.

Bet Sawoce, J. 2009. 'Beth-Zabday Azech', *Vad hände i 1915?* –I. Norrköping: Azret Azech.

Bet Sawoce, J., and A. BarAbraham. 2009. 'Cumhuriyet Tarihi Boyunca Doğu ve Batı Asurlara Karşı – Baskı, Zulüm, Asimile, Kovulma', in F. Başkaya and S. Çetinoğlu (eds), *Türkiye'de Azınlıklar: Resmi Tarih Araştırmaları 8.* Istanbul: Maki Basın Yayın, pp. 152–251.

Bierstadt, E.H. 1924. *The Great Betrayal: A Survey of the Near East Problem.* London: Hutchinson & Co.

Cengiz, O.K. 2003. *Minority Foundations in Turkey: An Evaluation of Their Legal Problems.* Presentation for the working-level meeting of foreign embassies, organized by the Dutch Embassy in Ankara, 4 April.

de Courtois, S. 2004. *The Forgotten Genocide: Eastern Christians, the Last Arameans.* Piscataway, NJ: Gorgias Press.

Dockrill, M. 1993. 'Britain and the Lausanne Conference 1922–1923', in *The Turkish Yearbook of International Relations Vol. XXIII.* Ankara: Ankara Üniversitesi Basımevi, pp. 1–17.

Dolapönü, H. [Dolabani, Y.]. 1972. *Tarihte Mardin. Itr el-nardin fi tarih Merdin.* Istanbul: Hilâl Matbaacılık.

Elias III, I. 2011. 'Letter to the Church Community in Malabar', *The Patriarchal Journal of the Syrian Orthodox Patriarchate of Antioch and All the East* (Damascus, Syria) 49(309–10), 584–586.

Gaunt, D. 2006. *Massacres, Resistance, Protectors: Muslim–Christian Relations in Eastern Anatolia during World War I.* Piscataway, NJ: Gorgias Press.

Holmes, M.C. 1923. *Between the Lines in Asia Minor.* New York and Edinburgh: Fleming H. Revell Company.

Hür, A. 2007. 'Hoşgörü (!) Tarihimizden Bir Yaprak: Süryaniler', *Agos Newspaper*, 20 July.

James, Edwin L. 1923. 'Allies Consider Turks Insulting; Demand Apology', *The New York Times*, 7 January. Retrieved from http://umdearborn.edu/dept/armenian/bts/Oct_Jan_7_1923_NYT_AlliesConsiderTurksInsultingDemandAnApology.pdf.

Joseph, J. 1983. *Muslim–Christian Relations and Inter-Christian Rivalries in the Middle East: The Case of the Jacobites in an Age of Transition.* Albany: State University of New York Press.

—— 2000. *The Modern Assyrians of the Middle East: Encounters with Western Christian Missions, Archeologists & Colonial Powers.* Leiden: Brill.

Kiraz, G.A. 2005. 'Suryoye and Suryoyutho: Syrian Orthodox Identity in the Late Nineteenth Century and Early Twentieth Century'. Paper presented at the *PIONIER Project Seminar*, Leiden University.

Kurt, A. 2010. *The Secret Payment of Patriarch Elias Shaker for Denying the Assyrian Genocide Seyfo.* Retrieved 20 June 2011 from http://www.atour.com/forums/religion/48.html.

Kurtcephe, I. 1993. 'Birinci Dünya Savaşı'nda Bir Süryani Ayaklanması', *OTAM* 4 (January): 291–6.

Lausanne Conference on Near Eastern Affairs 1922–1923. Records of Proceedings and Draft Terms of Peace. 1923. London: HMSO.

Luke, H.C. 1925. *Mosul and Its Minorities.* London: Martin Hopkinson & Company Ltd.

McCallum, F. 2010. *Christian Religious Leadership in the Middle East: The Role of the Patriarch.* Lewistone: Edwin Mellen Press.

Medlicott, W. N., D. Dakin and M.E. Lambert (eds). 1972. *Documents on British Foreign Policy 1919–1939 (DBFP) First Series, Vol. XVIII, Greece and Turkey September 3, 1922–July 24 1923.* London: HMSO.

Meray, S.L. (trans.). 1993. *Lozan Barış Konferansı: Tutanaklar-Belgeler I.* Istanbul: Yapı Kredi Yayınları.

Nirari, N. 1989. *Agha Petros.* Chicago: Alpha Graphic.

Nuro, A. 1972. *Interview with Zakaria Shakir in Lebanon in 1972* (translated from Arabic into English for us by Salim Abraham). Unpublished.

Oral, M. 2007. 'Mardin'in Son Süryani Kadim Patriği Mar İgnatios III. İlyas Şakir Efendi', in I. Özcoşar (ed.), *Makalelerle Mardin IV.* Istanbul: Mardin Tarihi Ihtisas Kütüphanesi Yayınları, pp. 269–97.

Oran, B. 2007. 'The Minority Concept and Rights in Turkey', in Z.F. Kabasakal Arat (ed.), *Human Rights in Turkey.* Philadelphia: University of Pennsylvania Press, 35–56.

Samuel, A.Y. 1968. *Treasure of Qumran: My Story of the Dead Sea Scrolls.* London: Hodder and Stoughton Ltd.

Sykes, M. 1924. *Dar ul-Islam: Record of a Journey through the Asiatic Provinces of Turkey*. London: Bickers and Son.

Talay, S. 2010. 'Sayfo, Firman, Qafla: Der Erste Weltkrieg aus der Sicht der syrischen Christen', in R.M. Voigt (ed.): Akten des 5. Symposiums zur Sprache, Geschichte, Theologie und Gegenwartslage der syrischen Kirchen (V. Deutsche Syrologentagung), Berlin, 14–15 Juli 2006, pp. 235–250. *Semitica et Semitohamitica Berolinensia, 9*. Aachen: Shaker.

Yacoub, J. [1986] 1993. *The Assyrian Question*, 2nd ed. Chicago: Alpha Graphic.

Zürcher, E.J. 2003. *Turkey: A Modern History*. London: I.B. Tauris & Co Ltd Publishers.

——— 2010. 'Renewal and Silence. Postwar Unionist and Kemalist Rhetoric on the Armenian Genocide', in R.G. Suny, F.M. Göçek and N.M. Naimark (eds), *A Question of Genocide: Armenians and Turks at the End of the Ottoman Empire*. New York: Oxford University Press, 306–316.

Chapter 6

Sayfo, Firman, Qafle

The First World War from the Perspective of Syriac Christians

Shabo Talay

⌒⁓

For the massacres against the Christian population in the eastern provinces of the Ottoman Empire during the First World War, the *Suryoye*[1] – the Syriac Christians in Tur Abdin and in the surrounding regions[2] – most often use the terms *Sayfo, Firman* and *Qafle*. For this reason, the perspective of the victims and their descendants concerning the fate they suffered is presented in the following discussion with reference to these three terms.

Reassessing the Experience of Suffering

While the persecution and extermination of the Christians of the Ottoman Empire during the First World War is referred to in Western historiography as the 'Armenian Genocide', and has been and is still extensively treated as such in scientific, literary and artistic expression by both Armenian as well as other non-Armenian Western scholars, the extermination of the Syriac nation[3] awaits scientific and literary appraisal.

For instance, from among the Western Syriacs there have been until recently but a few extensive monographs concerning what they endured in this period. One among these is the work entitled *Spilled Blood: The Atrocities and Painful Events of the Christians within the Borders of Mesopotamia*,[4] by Abdulmasih Naaman Qarabashi (1999) who between 1915 and 1918, as a novice at the Syriac Orthodox Patriarchal See in the Zafaran Monastery (Syriac: *Dayro d-Kurkmo* and *dayro d-Mor ḥananyo*) near Mardin, recorded in Syriac the experiences of the refugees who arrived there, especially those from the regions around the cities of Diyarbakir[5] and Mardin. The second work is that of archpriest Sulayman Henno (Aramaic: Khori Slēmān Ḥənno) with the title *The Atrocities Committed against the Suryoye in Tur Abdin*.[6] His handwritten copy was made available in print in the Netherlands by the former Syriac Orthodox Archbishop Julius Yeshu Çiçek in 1987. Henno presents a collection of the terrifying events in particular Syriac Orthodox locations, most of which are in Tur Abdin.[7] In addition, one needs to mention the somewhat more comprehensive treatment of the topic by the Syriac Catholic priest Ishaq Armale (Aramaic: Isḥāq bar Amalto) from the year 1919. Armale published his account in Arabic under the pseudonym *Šāhid ʿIyān*, meaning 'eyewitness', in Lebanon using the title *The Ultimate in the Catastrophes of the Christians*.[8] Armale provides a comprehensive presentation of the persecution, which is ordered chronologically and supplemented by individual observations and accounts of events, at which he himself had been present. A further work, which has not yet been edited for publication, is the Eastern Syriac manuscript by Israel Audo, the last Chaldean bishop of Mardin, which is entitled *An Account Concerning the Horrors Committed against the Christians of Mardin, Diyarbakir, Siirt, Cizre, and Nusaybin in the Year 1915*.[9] Audo, who was born and grew up in Alqosh in northern Iraq, was consecrated in 1906 to become the Chaldean Catholic archbishop of Mardin, where he lived until his death in 1948. Just like Armale, Audo sees himself as an eyewitness. In the preface to his work, Audo makes his role explicit:

> I have not written this book hastily. Indeed, I have limited myself to what I have seen personally or what I have heard many times from others and what I have recorded is far removed from exaggeration. I have incorporated into this account nothing from what I have heard without accurate verification. (Audo 2004: 5)[10]

The events and the experience of suffering have been and are still expressed for the most part through the millennia-old literary tradition which began with St. Ephraem the Syrian. This tradition takes the form of the *memra* (pl.: *memre*), rhythmic poems of instruction.

Often, these *memre* concerning the atrocities of the Suryoye are sung
with a weeping voice. Julius Çiçek edited two volumes of such Syriac
poems, the volume *Saypē* in 1981, and *Tenḥoṭo d-ṭūrᶜabdīn* in 1987. The
fate of the Christians of Cizre (Aramaic: Gziro/Gzira) is immortalized
by Isho Sulayman Gharib (Aramaic: Išo Šlemon Ġarīb) in his lengthy
poem, *The Extermination of the Syriac Christians of Cizre in Turkey in
the Year 1915*.[11] Composed in modern, literary Eastern Syriac, Gharib's
poem describes in sixty-five four-line strophes the suffering that the
Christians of Cizre had to endure in 1915 while the First World War
raged on. Another *memra*, composed in the Modern Aramaic language
of Tur Abdin, is preserved as a recording by İsa İşler (Aramaic: ᶜIsa
Saqaṭ) on an audio cassette and released in Germany.[12] Similar record-
ings are available in Kurdish and Arabic.

Only in the past few years have Suryoye in the diaspora engaged with
their history during the First World War in a concerted way, which has
resulted in scores of projects.[13] For several reasons, including its many
eyewitness accounts composed in the language of Tur Abdin, the monograph *Sayfo b-Ṭurcabdin* (*Sayfo*[14] in Tur Abdin) by Jan Beth-Ṣawoce
from Sweden (2006) is a high point in coming to terms with this past.
Beth-Ṣawoce collected from across the whole of Europe the personal
histories of Suryoye survivors of the First World War. This publication is
largely composed in Turoyo, the Aramaic vernacular of Tur Abdin, and
is written in the Latin alphabet.[15]

Religious Dimensions of the Persecution

In their assessment of the massacres that took place during the First
World War, all of these works speak of a general extermination extending to all Christians by both Turkish and Kurdish Muslims. Although
the nuances distinguish each of these accounts one from the other, they
share this common assumption: that what was taking place was a general persecution of Christians. For this reason, Qarabashi, in his aforementioned book, places these massacres of Suryoye in a line of Christian
persecutions beginning with the massacres of Christians by the Roman
Emperors in the first four centuries, those conducted by the Sassanian
King Shapur (Shāhpur II, 309–379) and those of the Arab-Islamic armies
of the seventh century (Qarabashi 1999: 25–38). In the same way, the victims of the Sayfo are presented as witnesses for their faith, or, according
to Audo, as Christian martyrs.[16] The premise is that these Christians died
because they were Christians, not because they were not Turks or Kurds.
Many were offered to accept Islam instead of death. Each person who

accepted this offer and converted to Islam would be spared.[17] Audo (2004: 37) also stresses the religious motivation of the perpetrators of the persecution of Christians, who were 'invited before the slaughter to renounce their faith, but they did not renounce it'.[18] For this reason, Audo considers the murdered Christians martyrs (Syriac: *sāhḏē*). In contrast to this perspective, Archbishop Çiçek considers the political motivation of the war as primary. Nevertheless, he emphasizes immediately the religious motivations of the Muslim persecutors. He writes:

> It is known that the First World War in 1915 had political motives and in no way religious ones, but the Muslims and especially the Kurds were thirsty for the blood of Christians. They used this golden opportunity to relieve themselves of the Christians within the boundaries of the Ottoman Empire, and to appropriate for themselves the possessions and property of Christians for free. Thus there were more than 100,000 Syriac Christians and 1.5 million Armenians, who were killed and eliminated, in a terrible manner, without any justifiable cause, for no reason.[19]

Most Suryoye were of the firm conviction that, in the perspective of the immediate agents of these operations, who were mostly Kurds, all these actions that took place against Christians in the eastern provinces of the Ottoman Empire were without a doubt an instance of Islamic holy war (jihad) by which the adherents of Islam spread their religion among non-Muslims by the sword. It has been reported that the attackers fell upon Christian villages with calls of '*Allāhu akbar*'. Each survivor and contemporary witness who has been able to share his or her voice has spoken of a general extermination of all Christians by Muslims. For Audo (2004: 5), who describes the situation in Mardin and its surrounding areas, primarily 'two nations, the Arameans [that is, the Suryoye, Syriacs] and the Armenians' were affected by the extermination.[20]

This religious aspect of the extermination and deportation of Christians is concealed or completely rejected by many, especially Turkish historians, although the Turkish military used religious expressions in their telegrams.[21] Thus, according to one telegram dated 15 November 1915, the Syriac Christians (Turkish: *Süryani hiristiyanlar*) between the cities of Cizre and Midyat attacked Islam (Ottoman: *islam-a hücüm*) and massacred Muslims (Ottoman: *ahali islamiye-ye qatil*).[22] The national troops, who had the responsibility to put down this alleged uprising of Christians against Muslims, are referred to not with the Turkish word *asker*, 'soldier', but with the word *mücahit*, *mujāhid*, a fighter for Islam.[23]

In highlighting the religious dimension as an explanation for the events during the First World War in eastern Turkey, it also is in no way my intention to minimize the importance of nationalistic, political and strategic motives. It always seems to be a question of power.

Sayfo, Firman, Qafle

From the perspective of Syriac Christians, the fate they had to suffer during the First World War is unequivocally genocide. This is clear from the three most important expressions used by Syriac Christians in connection with the First World War, and which this chapter will now discuss in detail.

Sayfo: 'Sword, Extermination, Extinction'

The first word from the title of this chapter, *sayfo* is the Aramaic cognate of the Arabic *as-sayf*. The basic meaning of this word is 'the sword', but in this context the Syriac word is to be understood as the pendant for the fuller expression 'sword of Islam'. Since at least the tenth century, *sayfo* has had the secondary meanings 'extermination' and 'extinction'. The Syriac lexicographer Hassan Bar Bahlul from the tenth century glosses the lemma *sayfo* with the Arabic words *'ifnā'*, 'extermination, annihilation, destruction', *fanā'*, which has the same range of meanings, and *'ibāda*, 'extermination, elimination, extinction' (Bar Bahlul [1901] 2010: 1345). From this one can draw the conclusion that according to the viewpoint of the Suryoye, the massacres of the First World War were a religiously motivated war of extermination against Christians. Most of the perpetrators knew practically nothing of the regional or even international political strategies and interests of the Great Powers and the lesser participants, about which a great deal has been and continues to be written and discussed. For the Suryoye the persecution came, if not without some forewarning, by surprise. From official sources it was always claimed that Suryoye had done nothing wrong against the Ottoman authorities and for this reason would be spared.[24] Rather, according to these official Turkish sources, what took place was a war against the Allied Powers and their allies, the Armenians. Thus, one could witness the burning of the village of Isfis from the neighbouring village of Midən without fear of being attacked. One felt secure in Midən because one presumed that the residents of Isfis had committed some criminal act for which they were now being punished. A short time thereafter, Midən had its turn, with its three to five thousand inhabitants. When the situation had calmed down, of the more than five hundred large families in Midən, only around seventy remained; of the seven priests who were active in the village, there was only one left.[25]

Firman: 'Decree of the Sultan, Punishment, Extermination'

In the spring of 1915 my grandmother, Nise be Qasho Mirza, then fifteen years old, found herself together with her parents on the homeward journey from a pilgrimage to Jerusalem. Three years earlier, her father, Gawriye be Qasho Mirza, together with his wife and his daughter, had set out on foot for Jerusalem from Midən, the previously mentioned village in Tur Abdin, by way of Antioch, in order to visit the grave of the Lord, but also with the objective of settling in Palestine. After some time, at the request of his brother *Qasho* Yuḥanən be Qasho Mirza, who was one of the seven priests of the village at the time, he and his family packed up and intended to return to his village. Just as the caravan to which he had joined his small family reached Nusaybin (this is the famous Syriac city of Nisibis, in Aramaic *Nṣībīn*), the mullah, i.e., the Muslim muezzin (Arabic: *muʾaḏḏin*) who announces the call to prayer, called out from the roof of the mosque[26] not the call to prayer chanted in classical Arabic but rather in Kurdish, *geli muşilmano, firmana filliha-ya*, 'O Muslims, the *firman* of the Christians is at hand', inciting them to the extermination of the Christians.[27]

It is not my intent to burden the reader with an account of how my grandmother endured the war and survived. Rather, I would like to examine more closely the term the muezzin called out, namely *firman*. This important term is used by both Syriac Christians in Aramaic as well as Kurds in the Kurdish language to designate what was taking place at that time.

The Modern Aramaic term *firman* corresponds to the Turkish *ferman*, a borrowing from the Persian word *farmān* which has the basic meaning 'command, order, decree'. In Ottoman Turkish, *ferman* came to be a technical term for the decree of the sultan or of the government. During the Ottoman Empire and in the period of the Young Turk movement, an official *ferman* could only mean a command from the highest level of the state. That is to say, if the Kurds as 'co-perpetrators' and the Suryoye as 'victims' use the same term for what took place, then this means indeed that the whole set of operations was planned, ordered and organized from the highest levels of the Turkish state. Thus, when the Kurdish muezzin called out *firmana filliha-ya* (the *firman* of the Christians is at hand), it must be understood that he was announcing an official command to exterminate the Christians.

According to the Turkish dictionary published by the Association for the Turkish Language (Türk Dil Kurumu), a *ferman* was pronounced in order to punish anyone who had revolted against the state. Thus, it is also possible that the *ferman* was decreed against the Syriac Christians because they had rebelled against the state. In fact, there can be found in Ottoman archives pieces of evidence that speak of a revolt of Syriac Christians living in the villages between Cizre and Midyat, specifically in Midyat and in the villages of 'Iwardo (Syriac: ᶜAynwardo; Turkish: Gülgöze), Bsorino (Turkish: Haberli) and Azǝx (also spelled Azakh; Turkish: Idil).[28] However, survivors' accounts show that this is a misrepresentation of the facts.[29] There is no credible evidence for any such operations against the Ottoman Turkish state on the part of the Suryoye before the beginning of the genocide. On the contrary, telegrams sent from the Imperial German Embassy in Constantinople in July 1915 lead to the opposite conclusion:

> Since the beginning of the month [July 1915], Rashid Bey, the vali of Diyarbakir, has initiated the systematic extermination of the Christian population of the district under his authority, without distinction of race or confession, ... as a consequence of which ... the Christian population between Mardin and Midiat has risen up against the government and destroyed the telegraph circuit. (Yonan 1989: 277)

A telegram from Mosul dated 28 July reads, 'This uprising has been incited as a direct result of the extreme procedure of the vali of Diyarbakir against Christians in general. They are defending their own skin...'.[30] At approximately the same time on the eastern side of the Tigris River, the Eastern Syriac Tkhuma Tribe were also defending themselves from the raids of Turkish-Kurdish troops. Shlemon d-Tiyare, the *malik*, or leader, of the Tkhuma Tribe, is reported to have answered the demand to surrender with, '... we have no animosity towards the Turkish government, but we are forced to defend ... ourselves'.[31]

These three examples indicate that the three or four instances of the so-called 'revolt of Syriac Christians' – *Süryani ayaklanması* as the Turks present it – while the Christians were barricaded in their villages had nothing to do with an uprising against the Turkish state. On the contrary, this was an attempt to defend themselves against the ruthless and cruel murder of Christians by the military and paramilitary units of the Turkish-Kurdish alliance. This is indicated, moreover, by the fact that Christians survived only in those villages where they had barricaded themselves and defended themselves. This was not an act of rebellion against the forces of the state. I know of no operation on the part of Syriac Christians west of the Tigris River against the Turkish authority.

Qafle: 'Deportation Marches, Extermination through Deportation'

The last term, *qafle*, is a widely used term in the Christian Arabic dialects spoken around Diyarbakir and Mardin for the events that took place during the First World War. *Qafle* corresponds to the Arabic *qāfila*,[32] meaning 'caravan' or 'convoy'. *Qafle* designates first and foremost the deportation of Christians from their residences.[33] These deportation marches were not only towards the south, such as those suffered by the Armenians and the Pontus Greeks. *Qafle* also includes the situation in which all able-bodied men of the villages were assembled and transported to perform forced labour on the construction of roads,[34] at which time these Christian villages were raided by Kurds from the neighbouring villages, plundered, and burned down. This can be deduced from the description provided by a woman from the village of Mlaḥso in the district of Lice, a locality some 100 km north-east of Diyarbakir:

> Our Muslims, the Muslims from the neighbouring villages, were very good, but all at once they became like fire which consumed us. In fact it was not they, but the government, which became like fire. It was the government that carried the men away. (Jastrow 1994: 117f)

How were the men treated? They had to perform forced labour in stone quarries or on road construction for three or four months at a time, without provisions. The weakened and emaciated men were for the most part killed; at any rate, only a few individuals were able to survive these torments.

Syriac Christians understand the concept of *Qafle* as the extermination of Christians, on the one hand through the transport of the men, who were taken away in groups for forced labour and then killed, on the other hand through the subsequent laying waste of the villages in which there were no longer any men capable of mounting a defence, at the hands of the Kurdish units, the so-called *Hamidiye Alayları*, and of the Kurdish inhabitants of the neighbouring villages. According to the accounts collected by Audo, women, the elderly and children were not spared from the deportation marches.[35]

After the End of the First World War

According to the statistics provided by Gaunt (2006: 405–32), more than seventy per cent of Syriac Christians did not survive the First World War. In regions outside the core area of Tur Abdin, with the exception of the large cities, no single Syriac Christian community remained intact. All which they had left behind went to the Kurds. It was primarily they who had grabbed for themselves the cities and villages, property and possessions of the Christians and who to this day still hold on to them.[36] It was the same people who exterminated their Christian neighbours 'like fire', as has been portrayed above. The Suryoye have not yet recovered from this senseless murder and probably never will. The survivors have been silent for over eighty years. They have wanted to live in Turkey in peace. The unjust politics of the later, officially secular Turkish Republic against the Christian minority drove the survivors of the First World War out of Turkey between 1925 and 1995, and for this reason barely two thousand persons live in their homeland on Turkish territory.

Among Syriac Christians, there is still no public commemoration of the genocide of the First World War in the homeland, such as exists among the Armenians. Out of fear of reprisal, the tragedy and the suffering is spoken of only privately. Only in 2000–2001 with the case of the Syriac Orthodox priest of Diyarbakir Yusuf Akbulut, has this matter been revived among Syriac Christians in the West. Akbulut had told Turkish journalists that during the First World War not only were Armenians massacred, but also Syriac Christians. Until then, the discussion in the Western media was solely about the genocide committed against the Armenians, which in Turkey had been vehemently denied on the grounds that the Turks could not have committed genocide against the Armenians because, according to Turkey, the Armenians together with the Russians had first massacred the Turks. The Suryoye had no role in this discussion whatsoever, and it was to this fact that Akbulut wanted to draw attention. For this reason, he was charged with treason and brought before the notorious State Security Court in Diyarbakir. Due to the great interest in Europe concerning this case, the priest was released, not because he was found innocent, but because of a lack of evidence.

Since then, the Suryoye have become aware that they have to deal with their past and make known their painful fate to the wider public in both the West and in Turkey. They have emphasized that they do not wish to bring legal proceedings against Turks and Kurds of the third and fourth generation who bear no guilt for the crimes the Suryoye suffered. They only bear the great responsibility that such a crime never happens again in Turkey, and that the survivors may work through their mourning and their memory. Enough time has passed, and on the cusp of the accession of Turkey to the European Union it would be a good occasion for Turkey to free itself of this old burden. However, the discussion in Turkey concerning the fate of Syriac Christians during the First World War has only just begun. Neither the officials in Turkey nor the majority of the Kurds have officially apologized for their actions. Nevertheless, the Kurds no longer deny them and some of their organizations have even officially recognized the genocide.[37]

More than thirty per cent of the population of eastern Turkey was Christian before the First World War. Today, at most two thousand Christian individuals live there. When will anyone in Turkey be able to deal earnestly and without prejudice with the question of how this situation came to be? When once after a lecture in Nuremberg, Germany I asked the Turkish historian Kemal Çiçek, from the research group on Armenia in Ankara, about the whereabouts of Syriac Christians, he replied, 'They all went to Mosul' (Turkish: *Hepsi Musula gittiler*).

The First World War is a decisive point in the history of Syriac Christians. The Syriac nation lost the overwhelming part of its people and homes in the eastern provinces of the Ottoman Empire. According to the estimates of Afram Barsoum, the patriarch of the Syriac Orthodox Church, as published by Sleman Henno in 2005, over ninety thousand died during the First World War, and this number counts only those who were members of the Syriac Orthodox Church in Tur Abdin and its surrounding areas. It is against this background that the three concepts of *Sayfo*, *Firman*, and *Qafle* are to be understood. They express the perspective of the Syriac Christians with regard to what happened. Despite the clear relationships between 'perpetrator' and 'victim', the Suryoye attempted to bear the entire suffering as Christians and to understand it, to an extent, as the punishment of God. Thus, according to one song,

> Like wolves they howl and fall upon the Suryoye;
> They drive them from one place to another, like foreigners,
> On account of the sins of the children of the Church and of the monks
> Because they have not kept the divine commandments. (Ritter 1969: 692)

Those who have been affected by this catastrophe searched among and within themselves for the guilt for what had happened, in order to understand why they had to endure so much suffering. The discussion in this chapter does not attempt to indict anyone, but rather, as Amill Gorgis (2002: 12) writes in the conclusion to his preface to Qarabashi's *Spilled Blood*, it attempts to 'illuminate the dark areas in order to remember those who were the victims of religious and nationalistic fanaticism'.

Shabo Talay is Professor in Semitic Studies at the Freie Universität Berlin. Besides the linguistic research activities in neo-Aramaic

languages and Arabic dialectology, he has published on the history
and current situation of minority communities in the Middle East.
His publications include *Die neuaramäischen Dialekte der Khabur-
Assyrer* (Harrassowitz, 2008), *Texte in den neuaramäischen Dialekte
der Khabur-Assyrer* (Harrassowitz, 2009), 'Neben-, mit- und gegen-
einander: Zum Zusammenleben von Muslimen und Christen in
Ostanatolien', (*Der Islam* 2011), and 'Politische und gesellschaft-
liche Entwicklungen im Turabdin des 19. Jahrhunderts: Rolle und
Bedeutung der syrischen Christen' in M. Tamcke and S. Grebenstein
(eds.), *Geschichte, Theologie und Kultur des syrischen Christentums*
(Harrassowitz 2014).

Notes

1. I employ this term here where necessary as a synonym for 'Syriac Christians' solely
    in an attempt to avoid the politically charged words 'Aramean' and 'Assyrian'.
    Even if most activists still belong to the Assyrian camp, the vast majority of Syriac
    Christians living in Germany refer to themselves as Arameans. In choosing the
    expressions 'Syriac Christians' or 'Suryoye', I as a scholar would like to avoid being
    labelled as favouring one side or the other.
2. This chapter considers only the Syriac Christians of Tur Abdin and neighbouring
    regions. Thus, the situation of the Assyrians, that is, the Syriac Christians east of the
    Tigris River, is omitted here.
3. Afram Barsoum, patriarch of the Syriac Orthodox Church (1933–57), dedicated to
    this topic only some two pages in his book, ܡܟܬܒܢܘܬܐ ܕܥܠ ܐܬܪܐ ܕܛܘܪܥܒܕܝܢ (*Maktbōnūtọ
    ʿal aṭrō d-ṭūrʿabdīn*) [Account concerning Tur Abdin] (Barsoum 1964: 182–4).
4. The original title in Syriac is: ܕܡܐ ܙܠܝܚܐ ܓܘܢܚܐ ܘܫܪܒܐ ܡܚܫܫܘܢܐ ܕܡܫܝܚܝܐ ܕܒܐܬܗܘܡܐ ܕܒܝܬܢܗܪܝܢ
    (*Dmō zlīḥō: gunḥē w-šarbē mḥaššōnē ḍa-mšīḥōyē ḍ-ba-thūmē ḍ-bēṭnahrīn*). And the
    Syriac name of the author is ʿBedmšīḥō d-Qarabāš.
5. As one can also tell from his name, Qarabashi came from the Syriac village of
    Qarabash near Diyarbakir. Possibly for this reason, the events that occurred in and
    around Diyarbakir make up a significant part of his book.
6. Original title in Syriac: ܓܘܢܚܐ ܕܣܘܪܝܝܐ ܕܛܘܪܥܒܕܝܢ (*Gunḥē ḍ-suryōyē ḍ-ṭūrʿabdīn*).
    The author's handwritten copy was edited by Julius Yeshu Çiçek (1987), reprint:
    Sulayman Henno and Julius Yeshu Çiçek, *The Massacre of Syriac Christians at Tur
    Abdin*, Bar Ebroyo Kloster Publications 19 (Piscataway, NJ: Gorgias Press, forth-
    coming). Çiçek was the Metropolitan Archbishop of the Syriac Orthodox Church
    for Central Europe, resident in Glane/Losser, the Netherlands. He passed away in
    Düsseldorf in 2005.
7. This work has since been translated into Turkish (by Hanna Basut, 1993), German
    (by Amill Gorgis and George Toro, 2005) and Dutch (by Jan Jonk, 2005); full publi-
    cation details of these works are given in the bibliography.
8. The Arabic title is القصارى في نكبات النصارى (*Al-quṣārā fī nakabāt an-naṣārā*). On the
    back cover of the book, following the English title, the author, who calls himself
    'Eyewitness', writes, 'An authentic rare document which describes in affective,
    comprehensive details what was committed against Christians in Turkey and
    Mesopotamia, and particularly in Mardin; of oppressions, aggressions, kidnappings,

captivities, massacres and other sort[s] of scandalous crimes in the year 1895 and during the period extending from 1914 to 1919'.

9. ܡܟܬܒܢܘܬܐ ܥܠ ܪܕܘܦܝܐ ܕܟܪ̈ܣܛܝܢܐ ܕܡܪܕܐ ܘܕܐܡܝܕ ܘܕܣܥܪܬ ܘܕܓܙܪܬܐ ܘܕܢܨܝܒܝܢ ܕܗܘܐ ܫܢܬ ܐܛܝܗ (*Maktḇānūṯā ʿal rḏup̄yā ḏa-ḵristyānē ḏ-merdā wa-ḏ-ʾāmīd wa-ḏ-siʿird wa-ḏ-gāzartā w ḏa-nṣīḇīn da-hwā šnaṯ 1915*). All references in the present chapter are to the copy of this work in West Syriac script and published by Iliyo Dere (2004).
10. Unless otherwise indicated, all translations from foreign languages are my own.
11. Original title: ܩܨܬܐ ܕܩܛܠܐ ܕܣܘܪ̈ܝܐ ܕܐܬܪܐ ܕܓܙܝܪܐ (ܛܘܪܩܝܐ) ܫܢܬܐ ܕܐܛܝܗ (*Qəṣṣatta d-qəṭla d-sūrāye d-ʾatrā də-gzīrā (turkiya), šatta d-1915*).
12. Jan Beth-ṣawoce (2006: 284–8) published a transcription of the contents of this audio cassette recording. Meanwhile, hundreds of new songs and poems have been composed that address the subject of the First World War and which have awoken an interest in the topic even among Suryoye youth living in the West.
13. A further activity to be mentioned is the founding of the 'Seyfo-Centre' in Sweden, whose director and co-founder, Sabri Atman, has already dedicated many years of his life to the pursuit of this cause. He seeks to gain participants in the struggle through organizing talks and demonstrations both in nearly every capital in the West and in cities inhabited by many who have been affected by the genocide. His goal is to pressure Turkey to formally recognize as genocide the massacres against the Syriac Christian population in the Ottoman Empire. The same goal is pursued by the politico-cultural institutions of the Suryoye, among them the World Council of Arameans (WCA), the Assyrian Democratic Organization (ADO) and the European Syriac Union (ESU). These and other groups conduct events and political lobbying activities which are in general independent of one another.
14. Sayfo is here used with the meaning of 'extermination'.
15. Beth-Ṣawoce published several works in this Latin writing system for speakers of Turoyo (Surayt) Aramaic. Some of these texts can serve as important sources for research on Tur Abdin during and after the First World War. It should be noted here that Beth-Ṣawoce worked with David Gaunt as research assistant and provided him with empirical material for his book, *Massacres, Resistance, Protectors* (2006).
16. Syriac: ܣܗ̈ܕܐ ܕܟܪܣܛܝܢܘܬܐ (*sāhḏē ḏa-ḵristyānūṯā*).
17. Armale (1919: 355f) offers an example of Armenian Catholics from Mardin, who باعوا دينهم بدنياهم (*bāʿū dīnahum bi-dunyāhum*), 'sold their religion for their earthly lives'.
18. Audo (2004: 37): ܡܙܕܡܢܝܢ ܗܘܘ ܩܕܡ ܕܒܘܚܝܐ ܠܡܟܦܪ ܘܠܐ ܟܦܪܘ (*mezdammnīn (h)waw qḏām dḇuḥyā l-meḵpar w-lā ḵp̄ar(w)*).
19. In Qarabashi (2002: 16).
20. Audo (2004: 5): ܬܪܝܗܘܢ ܐܡ̈ܘܢ ܕܐܪ̈ܡܝܐ ܘ[ܕ]ܐܪ̈ܡܢܝܐ (*trayhōn emwān d-ārāmāyē w[ad]-ʾarmenāyē*).
21. Some of these telegrams, which come from Turkish archives and mention Syriac Christians, have been published by Dr Racho Donef, each accompanied by a photograph, with the original text in Romanized Turkish transcription and an English translation, in Gaunt (2006: Appendix 4, 445–94).
22. According to Donef, in Gaunt (2006: 472–3).
23. E.g. Donef, in Gaunt (2006: 457, 461).
24. Still in 1960 this was stated by the Turkish president of the time, Cemal Gürsel, in a conversation with Aziz Günel (Khori ʿAzīz), the priest of the Syriac Orthodox Church in Diyarbakir (in Ritter 1969 (= *Ṭūrōyo*, Teil A, Band 2), 334–43). According to Günel, Gürsel said, 'We love the Syriac Christians in particular because they have a clean record with us, and the Syriac Christians always behave in a manner that is genuine and loyal to us' (Ritter 1969: 337, sentence 24).

25. Slēman Ḥanna Maskōbi describes the events that took place in and about Midən and Bsorino, in which the people of Midən, after a siege of the village by soldiers and armed Kurdish paramilitaries from neighbouring villages, which lasted for many days, fled by night. According to him, most of the people of Midən had to give up their lives there. See Ritter 1971 (= *Ṭŭrōyō*, Teil A, Band 3), 446–55.

26. At that time, the mosque in Nusaybin, as typical elsewhere in Tur Abdin, probably did not have a minaret.

27. In Kurdish, the Christians are generally referred to as *fillah*, 'peasant, farmer', from the Arabic *fallāḥ* or the Aramaic *fallāḥā* with the same meanings.

28. Israfil Kurtcephe speaks in detail about this in his article, 'Biririnci dünya savaşında bir Süryani ayaklanması' [An Uprising of the Syriac Christians during the First World War] (1993). Kurtcephe took as a main source for this article material from the *Askeri Tarih ve Stratejik Etut Başkanlığı (ATASE) Arşivi* [The Archive of the Directorate for Studies on Military and Strategic History]. In his book *Savur* (1944), which is polemical with regard to Syriac Christians, Zeki Teoman describes how the Christians of Midyat rose up against the government and how four hundred armed men from Savur, a small regional capital city in the province of Mardin, 40 km north-west of Midyat, went out to put down the uprising. It is alleged that along the way to Midyat, from many Muslim localities which are listed by name, as well as from Mardin, 'everyone who could carry a weapon' (Turkish: 'eli silah tutan') joined them. Gallo Shabo also mentions the band of fighters, as published in Beth-Ṣawoce (2006: 115). Shabo was one of the leaders of the defence of ᶜIwardo (ᶜAynwardo) and according to him more than twelve thousand Muslim fighters of diverse origins surrounded his village and attacked it.

29. According to Slēman Ḥanna Maskōbi (in Ritter 1971: 446–55), the inhabitants of the village of Midən are said to have disarmed any soldiers who were present in the village at the start of the war and expelled them. They had earlier learned of the massacre committed by soldiers against the Protestant Christian family Hirmiz in Midyat. In this massacre, the soldiers stationed in Midyat had arrested all of the male members of this respected family on the charge of collaboration with the European powers and then murdered them between Estel and Midyat. The fear that the same fate would befall them led the inhabitants of Midən to this act of despair. The inhabitants of the village soon considered their act a mistake, returned their weapons to the soldiers, and permitted them to return to the village. With those same weapons, the soldiers took part in the subsequent attack on this village, which the villagers allegedly instigated.

30. The telegram was dated 28 July 1915; see Yonan (1989: 277).

31. Following Rudolph Macuch (1976: 238), a report from Malik Shlemon d-Tiyare.

32. Cognate to Syriac ܩܦܠܐ (*qāplā*) and Turoyo *qaflo*, pl. *qafle*.

33. Armale (1919: 184ff) describes one instance of deportation of the Christian notables in the city of Mardin; all Christian denominations represented in the city were affected.

34. Prior to this, the young men were drafted for war service in the context of the general mobilization. Of these young men, few returned to their families. See the reports from Midyat in Gaunt (2006: 331) and from Midən by Slēman Ḥanna Maskōbi in Ritter (1971: 446ff).

35. Fēṣal Mḥammad ᶜAbdirrahmān, a member of the ruling family of the Arabian Ṭayy Tribe, has recounted to me the tragic end of one of these deportation marches. According to his claims, a deportation march, consisting of approximately three hundred men, women and children, was driven into a cave in Margada, which lies in north-eastern Syria between Dēr iz-Zōr and Ḥasaka. The soldiers who accompanied the march, all of whom were Cherkessians, blocked the entrance to the cave with

wood, which they set alight. Only four people survived this act of martyrdom. See Talay (2007: 11f).

36. One exception is a Kurd with the pseudonym Berzan Boti from the vicinity of Siirt, who on 13 May 2009, in the context of an official press conference in the Swedish Parliament in Stockholm, bequeathed to the Seyfo-Centre everything his family had acquired from Christian owners. He apologized for the suffering his family had brought upon the Christians. He wanted no part in the crime, and for this reason he returned the wrongfully acquired property. Retrieved 11 August 2013 from http://www.seyfocentre.com/index.php?sid=2&aID=71.

37. According to Sarian (2011), some Kurdish organizations (these are the PKK, Kurdish Parliament in Exile, PRK/Rizgari) and several intellectuals officially recognized the genocide. In addition, more recently, at an election campaign event organized by his party in Midyat, the chairman of the pro-Kurdish Party for Democratic Society (Demokratik Toplum Partisi, DTP), Ahmet Türk, apologized to Syriac Christians for the crimes committed against them during the First World War. He emphasized that the Kurdish people too took part in these crimes. Retrieved 11 August 2013 from http://www.seyfocentre.com/index.php?sid=2&aID=500 and http://www.hurriyet.com.tr/english/ domestic/ 10672641.asp.

Bibliography

Anschütz, H. 1985. *Die syrischen Christen vom Tur 'Abdin: Eine altchristliche Bevölkerungsgruppe zwischen Beharrung, Stagnation und Auflösung*. Würzburg: Augustinus-Verlag.

Armale, I. 1919. *Al-quṣārā fī nakabāt an-naṣārā* [The Ultimate in the Catastrophes of the Christians]. Beirut: Al-Sharfe Monastery. Swedish translation in 2005 by Ingvar Rydberg, *De kristnas hemska katastrofer: Osmanernas och ung-turkarnas folkmor i norra Mesopotamien 1895/1914–1918*. Södertälje: Nsibin.

Atiya, A.S. 1968. *A History of Eastern Christianity*. London: n.p.

Audo, I. 2004. *Maktbānūṭā ᶜal rḏupyā ḏa-kristyānē ḏ-merdā wa-ḏ-ᵓāmīd wa-ḏ-siᶜird wa-ḏ-gāzartā w ḏa-nṣībīn da-hwā šnaṭ 1915)* [An Account Concerning the Horrors (Committed) against the Christians of Mardin, Diyarbakir, Siirt, Cizre, and Nusaybin in the Year 1915], ed. Iliyo Dere. Jönköping: Assyriska Riksförbundet i Sverige.

Aydin, K.N. 1997. *Geḏšē w šabṭē ḏ-ṭūrᶜabdīn: ḥuroḇo d-dayrōṭo w qeṭlo d-dayrē* [The Misfortunes and Scourges of Tur Abdin: The Destruction of Monasteries and the Murder of Monastics], 1st ed. Glane: Mor Ephrem Kloster.

Bar Bahlul, H. [1901] 2010. *Lexicon*, ed. Rubens Duval. Lexicon Syriacum Auctore Hassano Bar Bahlule, 2 vols. Paris: E Republicæ Typographeo, prostat Ernestum Leroux, 1901. Reprint: Rubens Duval, *The Syriac Lexicon Hasan Bar Bahlul [sic]*, 2 vols. Piscataway, NJ: Gorgias Press.

Barsoum, Afram. 1964. *Maktbōnūṭo ᶜal atro d-ṭūrᶜabdīn* [Account Concerning Tur Abdin], ed. (with Arabic translation: *Tārīḫ ṭūr ᶜabdīn* [History of Tur Abdin]) Bulus Bahnām. Jounie: Bībān.

Beth-Ṣawoce, J. 2006. *Sayfo b-Ṭurcabdin 1914–1915 (I)*. Södertälje: Nsibin, 2006.

Çiçek, Julius Yeshu (ed.). 1981. *Saypē. Mēmrē ḏ-ᶜal saypē ḏa-skal(w) mšīḥōyē ḇ-turkiyā men šnaṭ 1714–1914* [Poems about the Sayfo: On the Transgressions against Christians in Turkey in the Years 1714–1914]. Glane/Losser: Bar Hebraeus Verlag. Reprint: *Poems about Sayfo. What Happened to Christians in Turkey from 1714–1918*. Bar Ebroyo Kloster Publications 25. Piscataway, NJ: Gorgias Press, April 2005.

────── 1987. *Tenḥōṭō ḏ-ṭūrᶜaḇdīn* [Laments for Tur Abdin]. Glane/Losser: Bar Hebraeus Verlag. Reprint: *Voices of Tur Abdin*. Bar Ebroyo Kloster Publications 11. Piscataway, NJ: Gorgias Press, forthcoming.

Gaunt, D. 2006. *Massacres, Resistance, Protectors: Muslim–Christian Relations in Eastern Anatolia during World War I*. Piscataway, NJ: Gorgias Press.

Gharib, I. S. (Aramaic: Išo Šlemon Ġarīb), Original title: ܟܬܒܐ ܕܫܒܬܐ ܕܓܙܝܪܐ ܕܐܬܪܐ ܕܣܘܪܝܐ ܕܩܛܠܐ ܕܩܨܬܐ *(Qəṣṣatta d-qəṭla d-sūrāye d-ʾatrā də-gzīrā (turkiya), šatta d-1915).* [The Story of Extermination of the Syriac Christians of Cizre in Turkey in the Year 1915]. Unpublished manuscript.

Hage, W. 2007. *Das orientalische Christentum*. Stuttgart: Kohlhammer.

Henno, K.S. 1987. *Gunḥe ḏ-suryōyē ḏ-ṭūrᶜaḇdīn* [The Atrocities (Committed against) the Suryoye in Tur Abdin]. Abschrift des Mor Julius Yeshu Çiçek. Mor Ephrem Kloster/Glane: Bar Hebraeus Verlag. Turkish translation: Hanna Basut, *Farman, Tur Abdinli Süryanilerin 1914–1915 Katliamı*. Athens: n.p., 1993. German translation: Amill Gorgis and George Toro, *Die Verfolgung und Vernichtung der Syro-Aramäer im Tur Abdin in 1915*. Mor Ephrem Kloster/Glane: Bar Hebraeus Verlag, 2005. Dutch translation: Jan Jonk, *De vervolging en de uitroeiing van de Syro-Arameërs in Tur Abdin 1915*. Mor Ephrem Kloster/Glane: Bar Hebraeus Verlag, 2005.

Hoffmann, T. (ed.). 2004. *Vefolgung, Vertreibung und Vernichtung der Christen im Osmanischen Reich 1912–1922*. Münster: LIT-Verlag.

Jastrow, O. 1994. *Der neuaramäische Dialekt von Mlaḥsō*. Wiesbaden: Harrassowitz.

Kurtcephe, I. 1993. 'Birinci dünya savaşında bir Süryani ayaklanması' [An Uprising of the Syriac Christians during the First World War], *Ankara Üniversitesi Osmanlı Tarihi Araştırma ve Uygulama Merkezi (OTAM) Dergisi* 4: 291–6.

Macuch, R. 1976. *Geschichte der spät- und neusyrischen Literatur*. Berlin and New York: de Gruyter.

Merten, K. 1997. *Die syrisch-orthodoxen Christen in der Türkei und in Deutschland. Untersuchung zu einer Wanderungsbewegung*. Münster LIT-Verlag.

Qarabashi, A.N. 1999. *Dmō zlīḥō: gunḥe w-šarbe mḥaššōne ḏa-mšīḥōye ḏ-ḇa-ṯḥūme ḏ-ḇēṯnahrīn* [Spilled Blood: The Atrocities and Painful Events of the Christians within the Borders of Mesopotamia]. Mor Ephrem Kloster/Glane: Bar Hebraeus Verlag. German translation: George Toro and Amill Gorgis, *Vergossenes Blut: Geschichten der Greuel, die an den Christen in der Türkei verübt, und der Leiden, die ihnen 1895 und 1914–1918 zugefügt wurden*. Mor Ephrem Kloster/Glane: Bar Hebraeus Verlag, 2002. Dutch translation: Jan Jonk, *Vergoten Bloed. Verhalen over de gruweldaden jegens Christenen in Turkijke, en over het leed dat hun in 1895 en in 1914–1918 is aangedaan*. Mor Ephrem Kloster/Glane: Bar Hebraeus Verlag, 2002.

Ritter, H. Ṭūrōyo. 1990. *Die Volkssprache der syrischen Christen des Ṭūr ᶜAbdīn*. Teil A: Band 1, Beirut, 1967; Band 2, Beirut, 1969; Band 3, Beirut, 1971. Teil B: Wörterbuch, Beirut, 1979. Teil C: Grammatik. Stuttgart: Franz Steiner Verlag.

Sarian, Toros. 2011. *Kürt Aydınları ve Ermeni Soykırımı*. Retrieved 13 October 2014 from http://www.hayastaninfo.net/soykirim/1986-kuert-aydinlari-ve-ermeni-soykirimi.html#_ednd2.

Talay, S. 2001. 'Die Christen in der syrischen Ġazire (Nordostsyrien)', in M. Tamcke (ed.), *Orientalische Christen zwischen Repression und Migration: Beiträge zur jüngeren Geschichte und Gegenwartslage*. Hamburg: LIT-Verlag, 17–30.

────── 2007. 'Das Ṭayy-Arabische – Charakteristika eines Beduinendialekts', in R. Brunner, J.P. Laut und M. Reinkowski (eds), *XXX. Deutscher Orientalistentag, Freiburg 24-28. September 2007*. Online publication: http://orient. ruf.uni-freiburg. de/dotpub/talay.pdf. ISSN 1866-2943.

Tamcke, M. 2008. *Christen in der islamischen Welt: Von Mohammed bis zur Gegenwart*. Munich: C. H. Beck.

Teoman, Z. 1944. *Savur*. C.H.P. Savur Halkevi Yayını 2. Savur: n.p.

Yonan, G. 1989. *Ein vergessener Holocaust: Die Vernichtung der christlichen Assyrer in der Türkei*. Göttingen: Gesellschaft für bedrohte Völker.

CHAPTER 7

A HISTORICAL NOTE OF OCTOBER 1915 WRITTEN IN DAYRO D-ZAFARAN (DEYRULZAFARAN)

Sebastian Brock

Almost all accounts of the events of the Sayfo were written several years after the events. This gives an added interest to contemporary ones, such as the one translated below, taken from a liturgical manuscript written in October 1915, only four months after the commencement of the massacres on a large and organized scale. Copyists of manuscripts, at the conclusion of their task, have often added a colophon, giving details about their identity and the place and circumstances of their writing; in quite a few cases they have also provided important information about contemporary events, and this is the case with the colophon translated here. It is unlikely to be the only colophon of relevance for the Sayfo.[1]

Most accounts of events in Mardin come from Catholic sources,[2] and hitherto the only Syrian Orthodox one from Dayro d-Zafaran has been that by 'Abedmshiho Na'man Qarabashi, in his *Dmo zliho*. 'Abedmshiho Qarabashi (1903–83) was a student at the monastery at the time of the Sayfo, and kept a diary of events, which was written up and published many years later, in 1997, and then again in 1999, under the title *Dmo zliho* (German translation by G. Toro and A. Gorgis, *Vergossenes Blut*, 2002); included in this account is a short section concerning the attack on Dayro

d-Zafaran in the summer of 1915.[3] It is this event that is also the subject of
a historical note, translated below, to be found in a manuscript written in
the monastery just a few months later and dated 15 October 1915.

The Manuscript

Mor Philoksinos Yuhanon Dolabani (1885–1969; metropolitan of
Mardin from 1947), who had become a monk at Dayro d-Zafaran in 1908
(Dolabani 2007: 32), compiled a series of catalogues of Syriac manuscripts in different locations, which remained unpublished until 1994
when Mor Gregorios Yuhanon Ibrahim reproduced them photographi-
cally in three volumes (8–10) of his series Syriac Patrimony; the third
volume is devoted to small collections in different churches and monasteries, and among the manuscripts belonging to the churches of Mor
Hnanyo and of the Yoldat Aloho of Netpo, number 6 is a Fanqitho for
the Great Fast (Lent) (Dolabani 1994: 125–9). This was copied out in
the Monastery of Mor Hananyo (Dayro d-Zafaran) by the Monk Murad
(Awgen), 'son of Shmu'il, from the village of Hashas in the region of
Gurzan',[4] and it was completed in October 1915, on the Feast of Mor
Osyo and Mor Esha'yo (on the 15th). At the end of the manuscript, the
scribe has added a historical note, and fortunately Dolabani has copied
out the text in full;[5] it is this text, together with Dolabani's added note
about the scribe, that is translated below.

Translation of the October 1915 Note

Translator's note: words in round brackets are provided for the sake of
sense.

1. With grief and unspeakable suffering I am going to record the last
    Fathers who have survived, and the Fathers who have been martyred
    (lit. testified) in the persecution that the Kurdish Muslims (*Tayoye*)
    have started up [+ following the indication they had received][6]
    against our wretched people (*umtan*), not distinguishing between
    us and the children of Togarma [i.e. Armenians]. Those who have
    been held in the hope of some sort of life, that is the Fathers [+ in
    these regions of ours][7] (are):
2. Mor Qurillos Gurgis, epitropos of the Patriarchate in Mardin,
    Mor Qurillos Elias, abbot of Mor Mattai (Monastery) on the moun-
    tain of Alfaf,

Mor Iwannis Elias Halluli, universal metropolitan,
Mor Julius Behnam, of Gozarto d-Qardu,
Mor Dionysios 'Abednuhro, of Syria,[8]
Mor Iwannis Elias Shakr, of Mosul,
Mor Athanasios T'umo, of Amid,
Mor Qurillos Mansur of Kartbert (Kharput),
Mor Grigorios Afrem, of Jerusalem.

3. Those who have been martyred are:
Mor Athanasios Denho, metropolitan of Siverek,
Mor Anthimos Ya'qub, of Kerburan;
Mor Philoksinos 'A(bd)lahad of Tur 'Abdin, has fallen asleep in the Lord.

4. As for the monks and priests, I am unable to indicate the names of them all precisely, for this persecution was not raised up in a few villages, but in the entire region of Armenia, and people of our Church were put to the sword, from Bitlis as far as Gozarto d-Qardu; [p. 127] and along with them, the flock of our monastery, that is, the people of the villages of Qellet, Bafawah, Ma'sarteh, Qasro, Ibrahimiyeh and the rest of the villages: there only survive from them a remnant not worth counting.

5. O the suffering, bereft of any consolation! Whom should I counsel? Whom should I weep for? Whom should I pass over of those who were slain by the sword? Or of those who went off as prisoners and were slaughtered? Or those who ended their lives in different kinds of deaths? The time of the chastisement of wrath was stirred up alike against the guilty and the innocent.

6. But God's care preserved us when, on the seventeenth of June massed hordes of Kurds came against us from 'Ain Gurne to the mountain of Mor Ya'qub and Qurqus of the God-Bearer [sc. Mary]. God acted in (his) grace towards us when, on the day we were in straits, the governor of the town of Mardin heard (about it) and sent us some 90 valiant armed soldiers who drove (the Kurds) away from us. They remained with us for two days, after which they went away, leaving some ten soldiers for guarding the monastery; four of them are with us right up to the present. May the Lord deliver us from these chastisements and bring peace back to the land in his mercy, allowing everyone to live in quiet; and may he cause those driven out (lit. strangers) to return to their homes in peace and health, amen.

7. [p. 128] There are now residing in our monastery people from Hesno d-Anttho and Banabil, impoverished victims of plunder. (This has occurred) in the days of our Abbot, Abba T'umo, from Arzioglu,

and the inhabitants of our monastery (are): Abun Mor Quryaqos Shmu'il of Tur 'Abdin, Abba Sa'id of Mardin who was Abbot of (the Monastery of) Netpo, Abba 'Abedmshiho of 'Urdnus, Abba Elias Quri of Mardin, who was mentioned above, in charge of the (printing) Press; Abba Petros of Banabil, Abba Yuhanon of Mansuriyeh, Abba Shem'un Nasheph of Mardin who was Abbot of (the Monastery of) Mor Ya'qub, Abba Ya'qub of Mosul, Abba Mika'il son of Yeshu', Rabban Anton of Mosul; the novice brothers, Monk Shem'un So'uro of the church of Mor Hnanyo who is from Arzioglu, Monk Yawseph of Bartelli, Monk Yawsep of Ka'biyeh, Monk Yuhanon of Qarahbash, Monk Ya'qub Tanurgi of Mardin, Monk Saliba of Ka'biyeh, Monk Yuhanon Dawlabani of Mardin, Monk Melke of Mardin, the gate-keeper of the Monastery; together with the students, for whose individual names we have not got enough space for them to be mentioned.

8. [Note, evidently by Dawlabani] This writer was ordained priest by Mor Ignatius Elia, the Patriarch, who set him to be abbot of the Monastery of Mor Quryaqos. While he was still in charge, he was killed by the oppressors when he was standing up on behalf of some destitute people and was being questioned about them. This was at the time of the rebellion of Sheikh Sa'id in the year ... [left blank; in fact 1925]. [p. 129] And from among those people mentioned by him in the historical notice, indicated in 'gold water': on the day that the Monastery fell into dire straits, that is, 17th June, when the Kurds surrounded it with their firearms and were attacking it, when some-one was needed to be sent to the town to give news (of what was happening) to Mor Qurillos Gurgis, and to learn what was happening in the town, he [i.e. the scribe, Murad Awgen] volunteered gladly and courageously, while everyone else shrank from going. While the gate was locked, they lowered him from a window on the north side and he made the journey alone. God protected him so that he reached the town and informed Mor Qurillos; Mor Qurillos then went to the governor, who ordered troops to be sent as a guard. The governor then was Shafiq Bey.

Annotation

(Numbers refer to sections in the translation above)
The following annotation is very basic in character, and it is to be hoped that scholars more familiar with the sources for this period will one day be able to provide a much fuller prosopographical commentary.

1. 'children of Togarma': this designation for Armenians is based on the genealogy in Genesis 10:3, Togarma (Armenian T'orgom) being held to be the father of Hayk, the ancestor of the Armenians.
2. Mor Qurillos Gurgis: he features already in a colophon of 1895 with a list of bishops (Dolabani 1994: 182; see also 1990: 277).
   Mor Qurillos Elias: he too features in the colophon of 1895 (Dolabani 1994: 183; see also 1990: 277).
   Mor Iwannis Elias Halluli: he too features in the colophon of 1895 (Dolabani 1994: 183; see also 1990: 277); his title is given literally as 'metropolitan of the universe', presumably in the sense that he was not appointed to a specific see.
3. Mor Athanasios Denho: he is recorded in a manuscript of 1895 as already being metropolitan of Siverek (Dolabani 1994: 183; see also 1990: 277). For his fate, see Gaunt (2006: 261) and Henno (1987: 14–15).[9]
   Mor Anthimos Ya'qub: for his fate, see Gaunt (2006: 366) and Henno (1987: 147–8).
6. 'seventeenth of June': the number, which is written out, conflicts with that given by Qarabashi (1999: 103), namely 'Monday, 4th July'; Dolabani (2007: 37) gives '15th June'. The differences between these dates cannot simply be due to that between the Julian and Gregorian calendars.
   'Ain Gurne ... Qurqus of the God-Bearer: Qarabashi (1999: 103), has 'from 'Ain Gurne in the south-east as far as Qurqus of the God-Bearer in the north'. The area is also given in Dolabani (2007: 37), whose account shows a number of verbal similarities with the wording of the colophon, which he must evidently have had in mind.
   'some 90 soldiers': Qarabashi (1999: 104) gives 'about 100', providing several further details (see translation below). Dolabani (2007: 37) also gives '90' and adds that the commander was Nuri Effendi.
   'ten soldiers ... four': the same figures are given in Dolabani (2007: 37–8).
7. 'inhabitants of our monastery': the figures given by Qarabashi (1999: 105) only partially fit with the number of names given in the ensuing list.
   monks: several of the names are mentioned in Dolabani (2007: 36).
   Yuhanon Dawlabani: the future Metropolitan of Mardin and author of the Catalogue.
8. Mor Ignatius Elia: Patriarch Elia III (1917-1932).
   Monastery of Mor Quryaqos: in Beshiriyeh, north of the Tigris.
   'north side': the episode is also recorded by Dolabani (2007: 37).

'gold water': evidently 'tears' are meant.

'Shafiq Bey': for him, see Gaunt (2006: 171, 178).

Translation of the Account in Qarabashi's *Dmo Zliho*

Finally, for convenience of comparing the two accounts, I append a translation of the corresponding passage in Qarabashi's *Dmo zliho* (1999: 103–6):

> The Monastery was filled with thousands of men, women and children, refugees who had taken refuge, having fled from the Christian villages in the vicinity of the Monastery, such as Hesno d-Anttho, Banabil, Bkhereh etc., along with [refugees from] the nearby monasteries of the God-Bearer, of Netpo, and Mor Ya'qub. They were weeping and wailing for the men and the youths who had been killed, and those who had been scattered [in various places] for labour, and had perished.
>
> From one moment to another those living in the monastery were expecting attacks from the Kurds. Then, on the fourth of July, in the morning of Monday, the wild Muslims came against the Monastery, surrounding it from 'Ain Gurne in the south-east to Qurqus of the God-Bearer in the north. Some of them reached within a stone's throw of the Monastery's garden.
>
> [p. 104] Some of those living in the Monastery, who were from the villages and monasteries, fired shots at the Muslims from the rooftops, while others earnestly urged the soldiers [guarding the Monastery] to chase them away; others, again, were continually praying: how grievous and pitiful was the supplication, with the young boys standing lined up in front [sc. in the church] and making prostrations, crying out 'Lord, have pity, have mercy on us'.
>
> The guards from Hesno d-Anttho, on hearing the shots, signalled by horn to the town, that they should send a force, and at midday fifty soldiers from the Fiftieth Corps arrived. The faces of everyone were set for slaughter and destruction, but God in his grace preserved us. Because the Kurds who had come against the Monastery had previously made an agreement with the commander of the 50 soldiers, whose name was Farhan, that they would give him 200 gold dinars, so that he would hand over the Monastery to them for killing and plunder. When these soldiers wanted to enter the Monastery, some people did not want to open the gate, being afraid lest there happen what had happened in the village of Qasro; but bishop Elias Halluli and others allowed them to enter inside; however, before any bad trouble occurred from them, there turned up other soldiers from the fighting forces, sent by the governor of Mardin in response to a request from Mor Qurillos Gurgis. As soon as these other soldiers arrived, they turned out the treacherous ones from the 50th Corps. Thus those in the Monastery found peace in their hearts. In number there were about 100 soldiers. When they went up onto the roofs of the monastery buildings they saw the wild [Kurds] all around the Monastery.

Their commander was enraged and cast bitter insults at the contingent of the 50th Corps, and gave orders to drive the Kurds away and disperse them.

When the Kurds saw this, they retreated in defeat. The Abbot gave instructions to the attendants to slaughter some ten sheep and prepare a meal for the [soldiers from Mardin]; these remained in the Monastery for two days. As the general fighting was still going on and the soldiers' clothes became dirty, care was taken to have these washed, and to some of them new clothes were provided when it was seen that they were lacking some. Twenty dinars of gold were presented to their commander who distributed them among his troops. When they were released, the commander left ten of them to guard the Monastery of Mor Hananyo; these stayed there for twenty days, held in great respect by those living in the Monastery.

Even though the Christians who had taken refuge in the Monastery escaped [being killed], when it came to the onslaughts of famine and disease, because the provisions they had brought with them when they fled their homes ran out, and because they were unable to go outside the Monastery – since anyone who did so would immediately be killed by all the Kurds along the road – once all the provisions in the Monastery had been used up, it was a case of famine. Furthermore, as the facilities for washing were scarce, filth gave rise to sickness and disease. Accordingly, little by little they would escape to Mardin, under protection from the guard of soldiers in the Monastery; there they would manage to live either by working or by begging for alms. Then they got scattered in the desert regions around Mardin, in Beth 'Araboye, and kept alive (avoiding) famine and death.

To be found in the monastery then, at the time of affliction, was Patriarch 'Abedmshiho, who, after he had been wrongfully deposed and had joined the Catholics, had returned to the holy fold and motherly bosom [of the Syrian Orthodox Church]; also [present there were] Mor Iwannis Elias Halluli, Mor Sewerios Samu'il of Mor Melke [Monastery], eight priest monks and twelve novice monks; there were also something like forty students, quite apart from the villagers of Hesno d-Anttho, Banabil and Bekhereh, and some individual refugees from among the Christians of surrounding villages, such as Dara, Firan, Bafawah, Ma'sarteh etc. However, the brave men with weapons who guarded the monastery from the attacks of tyrannical [Kurds] were in particular young men of the village of Banabil who were renowned for their agility and valour; these men stood on guard night and day, holding their arms ready – but when troops turned up, they hid themselves, afraid lest they be arrested and sent off for forced labour – in fact, to be killed. This was especially the case if the troops should have found any weapon in the hands of these young men, seeing that this was not permitted, and any Christian found with a weapon on him was subject to sentence of death.

Sebastian Brock is Emeritus Reader in Syriac Studies at Oxford University and Emeritus Fellow of Wolfson College, Oxford. He has published widely in the field of Syriac Studies and has four volumes of articles reproduced in the Ashgate series of Variorum Reprints. He was one of the four editors of the *Gorgias Encyclopedic Dictionary of the Syriac Heritage* (2011), and his translation of Zacharias's Life of Patriarch Severos has been published in the Liverpool University Press series *Translated Texts for Historians*.

Notes

1. Two others are known to me; one is to be found in Dolabani's catalogue (see notes 5 and 6), the other is an East Syriac manuscript of 1919 in Baghdad, whose text is reproduced in Saliba (2003: 3–10, of Syriac pagination). An extended colophon concerning the massacres of 1895, in Mingana Syriac manuscript 95, is translated in Brock (2008: 36–8); there is also a German translation in Kaufhold (2007).
2. Notably Armalet (1919), Simon (1991) [the text dates from 1916], de Courtois (2004: 66–73, 160–70, 182–4, 246–8), and Rhetoré and Alichoran (2005) (P.V.M. 1996/7 and 2002/3 only concern the Armenians). According to a German source quoted in Naayem (1920: 4–5), the Syrian Orthodox in Mardin itself were much less affected, thanks to the payment of 'une somme énorme' as protection money.
3. Published in 1997 by the Assyrische Demokratische Organization (Augsburg) and in 1999 by the Monastery of Mor Ephrem, Holland; in the 1997 edition there is no chapter numbering, and the passage on Dayro d-Zafaran is on pp. 140–44, while in the 1999 edition it features as Chapter 4, section 18 (pp. 103–6); the German translation has a different numbering, and there it is section 31, on pp. 94–7.
4. Murad also wrote no. 10 in the same collection (Dolabani 1994: 132–3) where he is said to be from Arzon, rather than Gurzan. The manuscript was written in the monastery in 1916, and gives a partially overlapping list of names.
5. In view of Dolabani's mention of the revolt of Sheikh Sa'id in his note about the fate of the scribe, this particular entry must have been compiled by him between 1925 and 1928, the date when his catalogue was evidently completed.
6. This important information is given in brackets, which may imply it was added by Dolabani.
7. This is evidently added by Dolabani (and is given in brackets) to indicate that this is not a full list of bishops in 1915.
8. See Jan van Ginkel's chapter about Mor Dionysius 'Abednuhro/'Abd an-Nur in this volume.
9. Henno records that he was seventy-nine years old, and had been metropolitan for thirty-three years; Henno continues, 'He was arrested in the night and imprisoned; the next morning, after tortures that he endured with a true witness, his head was crushed by a stone; his two priests were killed along with him'.

Bibliography

Armalet, I. 1919. *Al-qusara fi naqabat al-Nasara*. Beirut: Al-Sharfe.
Brock, S.P. 2008. 'The Syrian Orthodox Church in Modern History', in A. O'Mahony (ed.), *Christianity in the Middle East: Studies in Modern History, Theology and Politics*. London: Melisende: 17–38.

Courtois, S. de. 2004. *The Forgotten Genocide: Eastern Christians, the Last Aramaeans.* Piscataway, NJ: Gorgias Press.

Dolabani, P.Y. 1990. *Patryarke d-Antyukya.* Glane/Losser: Monastery of St Ephrem.

Dolabani (Dolabany), Y. 1994. *Mhawyono da-ktobe srite d-botay arke d-dayroto wad-'idoto suryoyoto dab-madenho* (Yortuto Suryoyto 10), ed. G. Ibrahim. Damascus: Mardin Publishing House.

Dolabani, P.Y. 2007. *Tash'itho d-hayye d-Yuhanon Dolabani,* ed. E. Dere and T. Isik. Södertälje: Assyrian Federation in Sweden Press.

Gaunt, D. 2006. *Massacres, Resistance, Protectors: Muslim–Christian Relations in Eastern Anatolia during World War I.* Piscataway, NJ: Gorgias Press.

Henno, S. 1987. *Gunhe d-Suryoye d-Tur 'Abdin,* ed. Y. Çiçek. Glane/Losser: Bar Hebraeus Verlag.

Kaufhold, H. 2007. 'Zeitgenössische syrische Berichte über die Christenverfolgungen der Jahre 1895/6 im Osmanischen Reich'. *Oriens Christianus* 91: 25–43.

Naayem, J. 1920. *Les Assyro-Chaldéens et les Arméniens massacrés par les Turcs: Documents inédits recueillis par un témoin oculaire.* Paris: Bloud et Gay.

P.V.M. 1996/7. 'Documents sur les événements de Mardine 1915–1920', *Studia Orientalia Christiana, Collectanea 29/30*: 5–220.

P.V.M. 2002/3. 'Autres documents sur les événements de Mardine', *Studia Orientalia Christiana, Collectanea 35/36*: 33–88.

Qarabashi, A.N. 1997. *Dmo zliho.* Augsburg: Assyrische Demokratische Organization.

—— 1999. *Dmo zliho.* Glane/Losser: Bar Hebraeus Verlag.

—— 2002. *Vergossenes Blut,* trans. G. Toro and A. Gorgis. Glane/Losser: Bar-Hebraeus Verlag.

Rhétoré, J., and J. Alichoran. 2005. *Les chrétiens aux bêtes: souvenirs de la guerre sainte proclamée par les Turcs contre les chrétiens en 1915.* Paris: Le Cerf.

Saliba, G. 2003. *Makhtutat maktaba mutraniyah kanisat al-sharq fi Baghdad.* Baghdad: Church of the East Press.

Simon, H. 1991. *Mardine, la ville héroïque: autel et tombeau de l'Arménie (Asie Mineure) durant les massacres de 1915.* Jounieh: Maison Naaman pour la Culture.

CHAPTER 8

INTERPRETATION OF THE 'SAYFO' IN GALLO SHABO'S POEM

Simon Birol

⟢§§—⟢

For the explanation and interpretation of persecutions and defeats, all the great religions have their own scriptural sources to which they can refer. The different Christian confessions especially tend to have used varying degrees of moral theological thinking to seek an explanation for those events. Well grounded in both biblical and even more ancient motifs, Syriacs have endured experiences of encroachments and other catastrophes[1] that have led to the evolution of common patterns of interpreting and justifying such events as the inevitable outcome of their sins, a chastisement sent by God Himself (Harrak 2005: 60).

Not surprisingly, a significant number of the Syriac survivors of the 'horrific massacre'[2] (stanza 2) in 1915 used this paradigm to imbue their shattering experiences with a religious meaning (Beṯ-Ṣawoce 2006a: 9). Among the few eyewitnesses to write an interpretation of these events, Gallo Shabo stands out as the most significant. As one of its secular leaders, Gallo Shabo Beth Murad, from the village of 'Iwardo (Turkish: Gülgöze) in Tur Abdin, played an important role in the defence of his village.[3] He is one of the rare eyewitnesses to the events of 1915 in Tur Abdin to have captured his memories and experiences in a poem. In his

lament, he describes the Sayfo as Divine Judgement. Although, as Atto
(2008: 126) and Talay (2010: 237) point out, much of the Syriac literature about the events of 1915 is poetic and mournful, redolent with
prayers and supplications,[4] Gallo Shabo's approach to this event goes
further than those of other contemporary Syriacs from Tur Abdin.

Whereas authors such as 'Abdulmasih Ne'man Qarabashi (1999)
and Archpriest Sleman Henno (2005) have used religious language to
place their experiences in the context of persecutions of Christians in
the past, Shabo goes a step further and describes the visitation poeti-
cally as God's will. In his interpretation of the Sayfo of 1915, he identifies the Syriacs in this period as the 'eighth generation' (stanza 6), who
were doomed to be punished for their own sins and those of their ancestors. As well as its theological interpretation, this work also stands out
because 'one of the major figures of the events in Midyat and the defence
of 'Ayn-Wardo ['Iwardo]' (Gaunt 2006: 397) probably wrote this detailed
depiction of what had happened shortly after the Sayfo.[5] This presump-
tion emphasizes its significance as a source for a possible reconstruction
of the events. I will commence with a brief sketch of Shabo's personality
and what was probable in his mind when he was interpreting the events
of 1915 in the way he did.

The Author Gallo Shabo Beth Murad

The original version of Shabo's untitled[6] poem recounting the Sayfo in
1915 was written in Classical Syriac. It was collected and edited with
other poems as one of the first anthologies to be published by the newly
established Syriac Orthodox Diocese in Europe in 1981 by the late
Archbishop Julius Yeshu' Çiçek.[7] The book is entitled *Poems about the
Swords that Christians Had to Suffer in Turkey 1714–1914*. The date
of the poem cannot be determined with any certainty, but there can be
little doubt that Shabo composed his poem shortly after the Sayfo, probably in 'Iwardo. Gallo Shabo was born in 1875 in the village of 'Iwardo,
where he was educated in ecclesiastical doctrines and was imbued with
a fine command of Classical Syriac.[8] His education eventually led to
his appointment as Deacon of the Syriac Orthodox Church in 'Iwardo.
Here he pursued his studies in Syriac, Arabic, Persian and the Ottoman-
Turkish language. Even before the Sayfo,[9] as one of the secular leaders
of 'Iwardo, Shabo had been imprisoned twice in Midyat (stanzas 74–5)
and Mardin. According to Çiçek, Shabo copied many religious works,
especially the works of Bar Hebraeus, including parts of the latter's
Compendium Grammar and his *Treasury of Mysteries (Awsar Roze)*

during his incarceration.[10] Soon after the Sayfo, in 1920, Shabo had to flee from 'Iwardo to Mosul with his uncles. In 1923, he left Iraq for Qamishli in Syria, which was under French mandate. He died there in 1966.

The Poem and Its Interpretation

Although Shabo had the ability to speak and write different languages, because he chose to write his poem in Classical Syriac his immediate audience was limited to Syriacs and those few others who were able to read and understand the Syriac language. In short, Shabo saw his mission to be to write and share his memories and interpretation of the Sayfo in his poem from the perspective of his oppressed community. This poem consists of 207[11] stanzas, each of four lines and written in the twelve-syllabic meter of Jacob of Sarug. Despite its standard meter, readers may have failed to recognize Shabo's text as poetry. In fact, it seems to have been intended to be sung as a traditional dirge, in the manner of other poems about massacres and persecutions.[12]

The poem can be divided into six parts. Shabo begins his poem (stanzas 1 to 5) with a prayer, in which he beseeches God to grant him the power to be able to tell 'something about what happened at this time' (stanza 2). In this he complies with earlier Syriac writers such as Patriarch Behnam Hadloyo (d. 1454) in his poem about repentance (1987), Yuhanon Sbirinoyo (d. 1729) in his poem about the capture of Tur Abdin by Mir Shemdin (1981), Father Mirza of Midun (fol. 52) and Father Aphrem Safar of Midyat (1987) in the proem to his first poem about the massacres of 1895, who have all used the first stanzas of their poems to accentuate the mightiness of God and to depict God as the Creator (stanzas 1–2).[13] In his second step, Shabo prays, as did Giwargis Azkhoyo (1981) and Isa Işler (2006) in their poems, for 'the wisdom and knowledge' (stanza 2) to be able to report about the Sayfo. In his poem about his experiences in the newly established Turkish Republic, the late Bishop Mor Iwannis Aphrem Bilgiç (1981) used the same sort of introduction, whereas Monk Yuhanon Kafroyo (1981) dispensed with such a beginning and commenced his work with a description of his personal experiences at the time of the Sayfo. Taking a completely different tack to either of these poems, Shabo emphasizes 'What I saw and heard with my own deaf ears' (stanza 3), to underline both the authenticity of his depiction and the singularity of his poem 'about what happened at this time' (stanza 2). In the tradition of former Syriac writers and contemporary Syriac poets writing about the Sayfo, Shabo harks back to the

Seleucid Era,[14] hence forming a starting point for his remark that the mass murder of Christians results from a decree[15] issued by the Ottoman leader Muhammad Rashad[16] in the year 2226 after the Seleucid Era (1914/15 AD). In the poems in Çiçek's collection and Qarabashi's book, the Sayfo is consistently described as a regional event, whereas, right from the beginning of his poem, Shabo avers its initiation by 'command of that Muslim king', underscoring that it was a part of the imperial policy adopted against the Christians (see stanzas 4, 15, 16, 22, 23).[17]

Shabo claims that this decree, which was sent to 'all the Muslim heads' (stanza 6), described Christians as traitors, who 'had usurped uncounted pieces of land' (Gaunt 2006: 398), whose ultimate goal was to seize power from the Muslims throughout the length and breadth of the country. Consequently, the decree stipulated what should be done to restrain the power of the Christians: the mass killing. Rashad's hatred of the Armenians had been so fierce and deep-seated that, Shabo claims, the Chaldean, Syriac Orthodox and Syriac Catholic Christians were also doomed to be massacred (see stanza 5).[18] This was the spur that encouraged Shabo to compose the following stanzas in the form of a prayer that can also be interpreted as a cry for help and understanding:

> Behold Divine Revelation writes of it,
> How greatly the people called Christian shall be oppressed.
> Woe to us for everything is turned against us,
> This arrow has struck us and it is no more than we deserve. (Stanza 7)

In contrast to the other poems in Çiçek's collection, Shabo has linked these biblical prophecies to the experiences of the Sayfo. For the interpretation of this genocide he has depended highly on the prophets of both the Old and the New Testament, and his knowledge of various Syriac theological writings, including those of the *Lawij*. Although this statement is true, Shabo never quotes directly from his scriptural resources. For instance, in the 7th and 8th stanzas, it appears Shabo is referring to Luke's prophecy of persecution of Christians (cf. Luke 11:49 and 21:12), Isaiah's description of God's judgement and the destruction of the Earth (cf. Chapter 24). Perhaps this was also borrowed from the conclusion of the 11th stanza of the poem *Lawij*, in which the poet uses the words 'Would that I had never existed and had not seen that hour' and that when God 'does not deliver us, We shall find no other refuge' (stanza 15). This comes very close to Shabo's expressions (see stanzas 8, 17, 169, 197–8). The description of the wailing (see stanzas 9, 13, 19), sobbing (see stanzas 4, 6, 20) and the endless, hard-fought battles (see stanzas 29–30, 36) in Bishop Mor Qurillos Ya'qub 'Urdnusoyo's poem also seems to be influenced by Shabo's way of reporting and interpreting his experiences.

According to Gallo Shabo, this generation, who had been punished by the 'horrific massacre', had reached the eighth and last age of time, therefore they would suffer extreme torments until the advent of Divine Judgement.[19] These events occurred at the beginning of this age, but other Syriac writers, working from the eighteenth to the twentieth century, have also attempted to interpret the persecution and catastrophes that befell them as retribution for their sins, by making this connection between sinful deeds and having to bear the horrific consequences an unalterable concept.[20] For instance, this aspect is expressed in Bishop Ya'qub 'Urdnusoyo's words, which were still remembered by Syriacs decades after the Sayfo (Talay 2010: 247):

> And they will open their mouths such as beasts and rear up at the Syriacs. They persecute them from town to town as if they were strangers; weighed down by the sins of the church's people and the solitary monks, because they have not obeyed the Lord's Commandments. (Stanza 22)

Yuhanon Sbirinoyo interprets the massacres in his time in the same sort of words: 'The cause is because of our sins that afflict us, You, Lord, have mercy on us; and annihilate and forgive our frailties' (stanza 10). Giwargis Azkhoyo (see stanzas 42–4), Monk Yuhanon Kafroyo (see stanza 24) and Ne'man Aydin (see stanzas 23, 41) begin by describing their situation and concluding that this event was a punishment for their sins. They do this without making any reference to other writings, but adduce it as an irrevocable concept. Only Bishop Aphrem Bilgiç enumerated a few of the Syriac misdeeds in his poem (see stanzas 48–9).

Shabo underlines the singular experience of the Sayfo by saying: 'For this anguish is very cruel and there is none like it' (stanza 11) and 'This battle was like no other' (stanza 167), therefore only a learned prophet, of the likes of Jeremiah (see stanza 10), has the talent to 'compose piteous dirges for us' (stanza 10), because 'Neither hearing nor speech can comprehend it, Nor is the tongue able to tell of this massacre' (stanza 11; see also stanzas 38, 198). As well as Shabo, Isa Işler has also pointed out the uniqueness of the events (see stanzas 58, 84, 95), for instance when he describes the Sayfo as a greater act of cruelty than that which befell the Jews at the hands of the ancient Assyrians and Babylonians (see stanza 58). In spite of his loss for words, Shabo is able to speak about the Sayfo, because 'He [i.e. the Lord] gave me a full heart, a spring of water, And my eyes shall also be as sources which do not fail' (stanza 12). A similar statement can be discovered in the books of the prophets Isaiah (cf. 58:11) and Ezekiel (cf. 3:10). Shabo's statement serves to underline the authenticity of his report and of his interpretation.

The idea that the Syriacs sinned and consequently God punished them with the Sayfo runs through the poem like a thread. By and large, Shabo describes the Sayfo in general terms, but he does give more detailed information about Omid (Turkish: Diyarbakır), Midyat and 'Iwardo.[21] In the case of Midyat and 'Iwardo, he illustrates his interpretation by accepting God's chastisement without any critical challenge (Atto 2008: 130). When he focuses on God's chastisement, he uses the Syriac term for 'sin' ('Htitho') only three times.[22]

The Structure of the Poem

According to Judeo-Christian tradition, the author of the biblical Book of Lamentations, the prophet Jeremiah, mourned the destruction of Jerusalem and its temple by Nebuchadnezzar II (king of the Neo-Babylonian Empire) in 586 BC. It seems that by using the name Jeremiah, Shabo wants to express that the Sayfo was of the same proportions and had the same terrible effect on the Syriacs as did the destruction of Jerusalem and its First Temple on the Jews. The structure of the Book is close to the structure of Shabo's poem, although direct references to biblical texts are few and far between.

As Atto (2008: 129) has stated, in the first part Shabo describes the contemporary situation of Armenians, Chaldeans and Syriacs (*Suryoye*), who were being exterminated by the Muslims in the lands in which they had been living for so long; hence these lands had become bereft of Christian groups (see stanza 4). Significantly, Shabo ends his poem with a description of the actual situation of the Syriacs (see stanzas 203–6). At the beginning of his book, the author of the biblical Book of Lamentations also gives an overview of the actual situation in Jerusalem (cf. Lam. 1:1-11.15–17.22).

The second part, stanzas 6 to 42, deals with the causes Christians were killed and what plans the 'Muslim king' (stanza 4) and the 'Sultan of Islam' (stanza 22) had for the Christians. As his source, he mentions the Syriac refugees who had arrived in Tur Abdin from 'faraway lands' (stanza 41; see also stanza 96). God's judgement can be seen in both this part of Shabo's poem and in the Book of Lamentations (cf. Lam. 1:13-17.20–22; 2:2-8.17.20–22). Afterwards, he repeats what he has heard about the killings in Omid from eyewitnesses. Shabo expresses his astonishment when he hears of the defeat of Omid (Atto 2008: 128).

In stanzas 65 to 137, Shabo recounts the Sayfo in Tur Abdin in detail. He describes how he was imprisoned in Midyat and what he discussed with and asked the other imprisoned Christians. Afterwards, when

Shabo reports about Midyat, he begins by recording his talks with other Christians in jail. There, he expresses his first impressions of the sufferings of the Syriacs in Tur Abdin, because one of the persons being held in custody told him that there were no Syriacs left alive there and he should feel as if he too were dead (see stanzas 78–9).

Shabo propagates his idea that the events were the consequence of their sins in his description of the Sayfo in Midyat. It is noticeable that, especially in this description, he uses biblical references (cf., e.g., Luke 11:4 and Matthew 6:13) to help him set down detailed accounts of what happened there (see stanza 66). Furthermore, he makes various allusions to God (see stanzas 70, 71, 76, 93, 105, 108, 127, 133–7), and, as Atto (2008: 126) has also mentioned, he inserts a prayer in every fourth line between stanzas 114–24.

Initially, Shabo records that the people of Midyat were disturbed by the sound of shooting in the nearby village of Habsus (Turkish: Mercimekli), and that by order of the political leader of Midyat, three of the Muslim agitators were executed.[23] In his reaction to this, Shabo reveals that the 'heathens' (stanzas 2, 18, 25, 54, 63, 82, 84–5, 100, 109, 111, 113, 116, 121, 123, 135, 137, 139, 141, 154, 182, 195, 203; see also stanzas 44–5, 47, 55, 112, 159, 189, 200) were now enraged and the Syriacs were frightened by the response of the Muslims. Henno (2005: 76–7) says that the houses of Christians in Midyat were searched for weapons, and Christians of different denominations were imprisoned.

Both acts swelled the fear of the Christians, although the secular and religious leaders of the Syriacs in Midyat, Hanne Safar and Father Aphrem Safar, had assured them that there was no cause to be frightened. Henno and Shabo both report that after this incident, seven Syriac Orthodox Christians and Gallo Shabo himself were imprisoned but released sometime later. Apart from Shabo (stanza 82), both Armalto (Gaunt 2006: 177) and Henno (2005: 77–8) interpreted this as an act of bad faith in governmental policy, and Henno goes so far as to claim that the other imprisoned Christians were killed (2005: 77–8). Afterwards, Henno chose to describe the Sayfo in Midyat by quoting (stanzas 101–31) from Gallo Shabo's poem (2005: 79–81), because Henno considered him a reliable eyewitness (2005: 79), who with other armed men from 'Iwardo had participated in the defence of the city (see stanzas 100–30).[24]

Therefore, when Shabo heard the appeals for help from Midyat, twenty-five armed men, among them Shabo, left 'Iwardo on 6 July 1915 to go to the assistance of the people in Midyat (see stanzas 101–2). Over the next days, Shabo and dozens of strong men were witnesses to the very violent murders of Christians in Midyat (see stanzas 104, 107, 109–10). Although Shabo and the rest of the men from 'Iwardo were experienced fighters (Gaunt 2006: 196), they witnessed scenes of great brutality, that were later described by Shabo less emotionally, because he wanted to keep to what he had seen and did not want to embroider it. At this point, he evokes his sadness and horror elicited by the events in Midyat (see stanzas 115, 120, 122–4, 132–6). He goes as far as to compare the situation of the Syriacs (see stanzas 110–12) with God's wrath unleashed against Sodom and Gomorrah (cf. Genesis 19:24–28) and with the *Lawij*'s imagery of the trembling of the Earth (see stanzas 3–5, 8, 14–15, 18, 20–21, 27), inspired by 'the cries for help by the souls' (stanza 124).

As said earlier, in the whole poem he only uses the word 'sin' three times, but all three times consecutively in this part of the poem (see stanzas 134–6) to underline unequivocally that what happened was 'because we have sinned' (stanza 135).[25]

It is striking that he personalized the city of Midyat, because the Book of Lamentations also personalizes the city of Jerusalem as a broken widow (cf. Lam. 1:1; 2:12). Midyat is further characterized as a broken widow, but in Shabo's description Midyat is not to be outdone in cruelty by the personalized widow Jerusalem, as Midyat is not only a widow, her children have also been slain and all her friends have deserted her and 'they assault her' (stanzas 131–2). In his description Shabo tries to indicate that the Sayfo was more brutal and bitter than the ravage that Jeremiah describes. The outrages, especially in Midyat, were in his view so unique that the world had never before seen such inhuman slaughter and only a person of the stature of the Prophet Jeremiah (see stanzas 10–11) would be able to tell of the catastrophe he witnessed in such a way that he could convey his feelings to his readers.

In stanzas 137 to 203, Shabo reports on the battle in 'Iwardo. As a leader of this village, he gives an account of the defence strategy taken up by the Syriacs to counter the Muslim attacks. Shabo mentions twelve thousand[26] armed fighters, who were encamped on the high hill opposite the village (see stanzas 140–41), pitched against the Syriacs of 'Iwardo. Setting the context for his story of the assault, he depicts the social situation of the Syriac population in this village that was, like so many other villages, ravaged by famine and its aftermath. In this part he describes the Bishop of Qartmin, Mor Philoxenos Abdlahad Beth Mase from the village of Upper Kafro (Turkish: Arıca), as a highly significant figure during the Sayfo in 'Iwardo. He obviously played an important role at that time (Henno 2005: 89) and Shabo mentions him in several passages, adding more interesting details about the Sayfo.

Shabo describes the awkward and desperate situation one evening of the inhabitants of 'Iwardo, who were very afraid and low-spirited, bereft of any hope: 'All the people were immediately defeated, they gave up in despair and their knees trembled unceasingly' (stanza 152).

However, the next moment the Lord imbued the fighters with a new will to resist the Muslim attackers and they were able to defeat them (see stanzas 152–4). Bishop Abdlahad, who was given a sign[27] of victory by the fighters, used religious language to interpret this incredible victory: God has brought this victory, because it is easy for God to do so (see stanza 156). He also prays to God for a complete victory over the enemy (see stanza 152), in a passage that comes very close to Isaiah 4:4-6.

The next few days were incredibly difficult for the inhabitants of 'Iwardo; they had lost several places outside the village (see. stanzas 159–63, 175–8) but, after a time, they were able to retake them and explained their victory as a sign of God's mercy (see stanzas 179–82; see also Aydin 1990: 114–15 and Henno 2005: 89). Shabo keeps to his own interpretation and when describing the famine in 'Iwardo he writes:

> At the Lord's will, they strike us down with every chastisement.
> No blame is attached to the heathen peoples who now inflict
> punishment on us.
> Because of our iniquity and transgressions, they now scatter us,
> And hunger and death surround us on all sides. (Stanza 200)

The Syriacs had forfeited the 'Lord's mercy' (stanza 199), which had protected them: because of their 'wrongdoing' (stanzas 199, 201), God is incandescent with 'rage ... like an oven' (stanza 105). Shabo also borrowed this image from various biblical quotations (cf. Gen 19:28; Ez 22:22; Dan 3:6.11.17, Mal 3:19). Hence, the Muslims, often called the 'Heathens' (stanzas 2, 18, 25, 44, 54, 63, 82, 84–5, 100, 109, 111, 113, 116, 121, 123, 135, 137, 139, 141, 154, 182, 195, 203), were able to scourge and chastise them, because of the sins earlier committed by Syriacs before God.[28]

The Description of Muslims in the Poem

Shabo asserts that God would chastise the Muslims when their 'wrongdoing is greater than that of' (stanza 199) the Syriacs. Therefore, Shabo cried to God: 'Look down, O Lord, and see how much they [i.e. the Muslims] blaspheme against Thy Good Name', adding the request to 'help Your servants [i.e. the Syriacs] and suppress the fighting!' (both in stanza 160).[29]

Ever since the advent of Islam, some Syriac writers had interpreted the new Islamic rule as the fulfilment of a number of biblical prophecies

(Harrak 2005: 47). Nevertheless, they noted the different consequences for the people of both religions. For instance, Dionysios of Tell-mahre had done this, saying 'God, Whose purpose is to chastise us for our sins, nodded in assent while this [Arab] empire waxed in power' (Chabot 1916–37: 228, translated in Palmer 1993: 130–31).

Even Bar Hebraeus, who also used this idea in his writings, states critically: 'That someone, who has sinned seven times, will be punished, this is an old lesson; but when we sinned, we suffered, chastisement a thousand-fold. There is no end to our punishment and no respite, its character never changes' (my translation based upon Scebabi 1877: 114–16).

Shabo prays only once that God should gaze on the blaspheming and sins of the Muslims, and cries: 'O Lord, cause their swords to rebound wondrously onto themselves' (stanza 146). In accordance with these passages, he states that 'no blame can be attached to the heathen people, who chastise us' (stanza 200), because they are being used as temporary instruments by God (Harrak 2005: 47; see also stanzas 199–200). Shabo's message was that the dimension of the sins was so extreme, 'we are now at "ninth hour"' (stanzas 101, 113, 144), at which time 'as it is said, an unbelievably terrible event shall occur in the world' (stanza 144; cf. Mark 15:25). Right at the beginning of his poem, Shabo addresses the Muslims, especially the Muslim ruler, whom he calls 'a pig rolled in filth' (stanza 15), in an admonitory manner, telling them not to think they hold power over the Christians in the Ottoman Empire, because only God has the power to make decisions about the Syriacs:

> Woe to you [Muslim king!] oh mindless wretch and drunkard!
> How dare you try to emulate the sufferings of the End of the Time ...
> (Stanza 6)

It is obvious that the Muslims, respectively the Muslim king, should not have the power to defeat and kill the Christians; God chose the Muslims as the instrument of His chastisement, as He used different nations (e.g. Is. 10:5-34) as an instrument to chastise the Jews of Jerusalem. But why does he draw this parallel with what he believed had happened to the Jews of Jerusalem?

As said earlier, Shabo was not able to participate as a fighter in 'Iwardo, but he played an important role as a strategist. In this position, he was probably able to hear the slogans of the Muslims, uttered as a kind of psychological warfare, proclaiming that within a short time the inhabitants of 'Iwardo would be killed horrendously and that the lives of the Syriacs were in the hands of the Muslims (see stanza 168). Although slogans would have been yelled on both sides, the last call that remained unanswered was, according to Shabo, from the Muslim side (see stanza 169). Therefore, it is possible to understand this poem as the final and definitive answer to this exclamation: No, the life of the Syriacs is in the hands of God and the Syriacs accept God's punishment. Muslims were used by God to chastise the Syriacs just as the ancient Assyrians and Babylonians were interpreted to be God's tool in the biblical books. İşler interprets the Muslims' role in the same way: Muslims were directed by God (see stanzas 32, 62, 94). Therefore, he requests Him to stop the Sayfo and halt the troubles that He visited upon them (see stanzas 108, 124) and 'to break down the Muslims' power with the magnitude of the cross' (stanza 121).

Using a similar sort of language to that chosen by Shabo, the so-called 'Nestorian Lutheran' priest Luther Pera wrote about the situation of Syriacs in Urmia, underlining that both Shabo and Pera (Tamcke 2008: 206) interpreted the events in 1915 and in 1918 as God's wrath and the Muslims as God's instruments, without marginalizing or covering up the brutality of what happened.

This could explain why Shabo did not use many derogatory expressions about Muslims. Certainly he does not shun epithets such as 'evil and drunken fools' (stanza 4; see also stanzas 154, 178) and 'the cursed people' (stanzas 140, 155; see also stanzas 165, 169, 187–8) to describe the Muslims, but in comparison with other Syriac authors he is very restrained.[30]

Shabo's leniency when he describes Muslims arises from the fact that he regards their role to be only negligible figures, moved and used by God Himself. God was the principal factor in the realization of the Sayfo, according to Shabo. Another point for ignoring the significance of the Muslims in the events is that Shabo stated and justified that not Muslims, but only God Himself was able to change the situation of the Syriacs. Shabo observes that the thread of the way of life before the Sayfo cannot be picked up again, so the only salvation is the end of the world and salvation by God Himself. In reverse, the generation who had to face these events had been penalized for their sins by God Himself, who visited the Sayfo on them. Therefore, it should be the hope of Christians to be members of the eighth generation as they would be the recipients of God's salvation. Any return to a former life or a prolongation of the actual situation was beyond Shabo's comprehension.[31]

It is striking that Shabo emphasizes that the Sayfo was a unique,[32] unparalleled event (see stanzas 11, 38, 198). He achieves this by revealing the countless and previously unheard acts of ruthlessness and brutality, never before encountered in any former experiences of persecutions and catastrophes. Therefore, he concludes his poem with a description of the actual situation that contrasts starkly with the former flourishing situation in Tur Abdin. In the last four stanzas he points out that, as a whole, the mountains and the region of Tur Abdin have been engulfed in grief, caused by the destruction of churches, monasteries and the murder of the people, priests and monks.

> The scourge of famine has completely consumed the people,
> And a second scourge follows hard on its heels.
> Various illnesses have struck people down like the plague,
> And the third [has been] barbaric murder and Sayfo. (Stanza 202)
>
> Who shall not weep for the churches that the heathens demolished, ...
> They are reduced to ruins, the dwelling places of owls and conies.
> (Stanza 203)
>
> Woe to you, oh mountains, the home of hermitages!
> Now all that can be done is to mourn the monks. (Stanza 205)
>
> Where is the delightful, embellished beauty of Mor Gabriel,[33]
> Today nothing more than a den of all sorts of thieves? (Stanza 206)

Nevertheless, Shabo admonishes trust in God and His judgement, echoing the last part of the Book of Lamentations, especially its final words (cf. Lam. 5:19-22). It is striking that Shabo does not develop any idea of repentance; in contrast to the ancient Syriac tradition (Harrak 2005: 47) and also the *Lawij*, he does not even mention repentance as way to gain release from the chains of the sins that brought the Sayfo down upon the people.[34] It seems that he consciously ignored this concept, because what happened was so unique that any 'ordinary' return to a former life and rites would be unimaginable. The uniqueness of the Sayfo will only be comprehensible when the Syriacs, who faced this ruthlessness, have reached the eighth generation and will find salvation only by God Himself.

In his dolorous last lines, Shabo points out that the surviving Syriacs have had to bear the consequences of the Sayfo: disease, poverty, hunger, the breaking up of families and many who were forced to become servants to Muslims.[35] They had been ridiculed, victimized and degraded by the Muslims, and it was a terrible truth that some Christians had to live 'like animals' (stanzas 191, 195; see also stanzas 189, 190–91, 195, 197; see also Gaunt 2006: 337).

The end of the poem reveals the reason he interprets the Sayfo as 'Divine Judgement sent by God Himself'. As the events fit the biblical sources so well, he is hoping that God had chosen that actual generation to be the eighth generation, so that He will redeem the Syriacs and free them from their anguish. Indubitably, Shabo considers God to be the only path for such a miracle to be achieved, because Syriacs have 'No friends or relatives' (stanza 132), except God:

... They left not a single place where they did not massacre and deport them ... (Stanza 138)

Because of our iniquity the wall that surrounded us was breached. Our Lord's mercy that protects us, he distanced from us ... (Stanza 199)

Referring back to Jeremiah 30:11–16, he concurs with the *Lawij* (stanzas 15, 46) that God is the only hope of His people in this situation (see stanzas 66, 76, 121, 150, 160, 169, 198).[36] On account of their sins, Shabo's and all other poems in Çiçek's anthology, with the exception of those of Yuhanon Sbirinoyo (see stanza 19) and Bishop Ya'qub 'Urdnusoyo (see stanzas 39–40), exclude the idea of justice in paradise after their deaths. Nevertheless, Shabo does mention once that 'our death is fairer than life at this time' (stanza 153).

Though Shabo is able to reimagine the sufferings they had to bear, it seems clear for him that the gravity of the Sayfo cannot be rehabilitated by any human or governmental power. Effectively, the Sayfo can be described as a decisive break for the Syriacs in the Ottoman Empire (Talay 2010: 245), so it is coherent to see the salvation of those sufferings solely in the biblical prophecies.

Epilogue

A common theme in Syriac literature has been the interpreting of a catastrophe like the Sayfo in an eschatological way (Harrak 2005: 60). It was not unusual to expose an answer to persecution by referring to the scriptural sources of the community (van Ginkel 2007: 216). Obviously, Shabo had been extraordinarily distressed by the events of 1915 and their aftermath, and he was also continually being asked by other people why this calamity had befallen them (see stanzas 35–42). Drawing on his education in and inspiration from religious texts, he thought that such an event was so unique it could only be the beginning of the End of Time, described in several books of the Bible and by the Church Fathers.

His intention was not only to cast light on the sufferings of 1915; he was also eager to interpret what had happened for his people in their language as a sign of hope. In a situation characterized by the degradation

of Christians into near slavery and abject poverty, obviously the only
hope could come from some power more powerful than the enemy: God.
Therefore, it was God and God alone who brought the battle in 'Iwardo
to an end:[37]

> After 60[38] days had passed, as said,
> The Lord sent a command to the shameful people. (Stanza 187)

In his explanation of the events in 'Iwardo, Shabo continues his argument by saying that God had allowed the Syriacs to become the servants
of the Muslims. Therefore, in comparison with the works of other Syriac
authors, Shabo's poem is very specific as he is the only Syriac writer who
describes the Sayfo of 1915, and explains and interprets this genocide in
a way that is therapeutic.

The only way to interpret any change in this situation is to believe
that the events were God's chastisement, that after the anguish, judgement would lead to salvation. Especially in stanzas 157–61, he tries
to prove how suddenly God's salvation can come: just as Good Friday
meant a decisive break for the Lord's followers, loyalty to Jesus led to
their salvation on Easter Sunday (see stanza 157). Despite this message of hope, Shabo concludes his poem with a description of the actual
situation, providing an unvarnished, authentic picture of what it was
like. All knowledge, prayers and belief indicated that the situation
of the Christians of Tur Abdin seemed to mark the End of Time (see
stanza 202).

All in all, Gallo Shabo presents his audience with an image of a calam-
itous, almost inconceivable Sayfo, one that far exceeded all former persecutions and massacres, leaving just one interpretation, that the events
of 1915 were a visitation of God's wrath. All that was left was to utter a
helpless cry and plead that they might be the eighth generation, as this
event would signify the end of their atrocious situation.

Simon Birol is a PhD candidate at the Ruhr-University Bochum. He
is the author of several articles about Syriac Church history, Christian-
Islamic coexistence and migration/diaspora: 'Die Ambivalenz des 21.
Jahrhunderts: Syrische Christen in der Türkei zwischen bekannten
Repressionen und neuen Hoffnungen?' in M. Tamcke, S. Grebenstein
(eds), *Geschichte, Theologie und Kultur des syrischen Christentums*,
(Harrasowitz 2015), 'Einige Bemerkungen zu der Schrift "Lawij" des
Basilius Šemʿūn II.' (*Parole de l'Orient* 2015) and 'Syrisch-orthodoxe
Christen in Deutschland' in T. Bremer, A. E. Kattan, R. Thöle (eds),
Orthodoxie in Deutschland (Aschendorff 2016).

Notes

1. For example, famine and drought have also been interpreted as the retribution for the sins of the people by Syriac Church fathers (Tamcke 2009: 267).

2. Gallo Shabo generally refers to the 1915 events in terms of 'Massacre' (see stanzas 2, 9–11, 41, 54, 56, 105–6, 111, 137, 163, 202) and does not refer to it as 'Sayfo' (see note 9). I am indebted to Naures Atto for the whole English translation of Gallo Shabo's poem, translated for her by Nicolas Al-Jeloo. If not otherwise marked, all texts have not been previously translated and all translations are my own. The transcription is based on the traditional pronunciation of the Surayt Aramaic language of Tur Abdin (also called Turoyo). Diacritical signs have been reduced to a minimum.

3. Because of three wounds received during the fights in Midyat (stanza 126; see also Gaunt 2006: 334), Gallo Shabo was not able to participate as a defender, but he was one of the main strategists of the resistance (Gaunt 2006: 348, 397) and of domestic matters (Aydin 1990: 115) in 'Iwardo.

4. The cassette by Isa Işler (1992) from Belgium is full of prayers dedicated to the Christians killed and those who survived and of execrations heaped on their Muslim killers. In his recording, Isa Işler narrates his own experiences and also recalls the eyewitness accounts that he heard from the different villages in the melancholy dirge with which Syriacs mourn the death of relatives. His poem has been published in J. Beṯ-Ṣawoce (2006a: 291–319).

5. Gallo Shabo's leadership role in 'Iwardo has also been recorded by Archbishop Çiçek (1981: 69) in the last stanza of Shabo's poem (see note 11). Additionally, Gallo Shabo's father Shabo Murad is listed at the top of the Syriac Orthodox Patriarchal Register of Dues of 1870 for 'Iwardo (Bcheiry 2009: 52), which underlines the leading role of Gallo Shabo's family in the village of 'Iwardo at least since 1870.

6. The late Archbishop Çiçek added the title, 'This Poem Describing the Slaying of Syriacs' (W-honaw mimro d-som 'al-qatlo d-Suryoye). I thank Naures Atto for this information. Jan Beṯ-Ṣawoce has given me a manuscript that was in the possession of Archpriest Gabro Beth Yawno. This manuscript contains a number of poems narrating horrific events written by eyewitnesses, among them an unedited poem ascribed to Gallo Shabo (fol. 1–19), poems by Priest Hanno Qufar (fol. 20–44; publ. in Çiçek 1981: 141–63), Monk Yuhanon Kafroyo's poem (fol. 46–50; publ. in Çiçek 1981: 17–21), Priest Mirza of Midun (fol. 52–61; unedited) and also the here discussed poem by Gallo Shabo (fol. 62–100), although this poem has been transmitted without mentioning its author. According to this manuscript, the title of this poem is 'About the Destruction and the Sword that the Sons of Hagar Stroke against the Syriacs and Armenians' ('al-harbo w-sayfo da-mhaw bnay Hogar b-Suroye w-Armenoye). The unedited poem has been ascribed to the late Gallo Shabo (fol. 1) and has a similar title. The name of Gallo Shabo was added later with a different colour to the manuscript, ascribing the poem to him. According to the manuscript, this poem was written in 1916 (fol. 1). Because of the uncertainty about the authorship, I refer to this poem as the poem written by Pseudo-Gallo Shabo. The aforementioned poem by Father Mirza of Midun recorded 'the manslaughter and devastation inflicted by the sons of Mir Sevdin by Izzadin Sher and Massur Beg' (fol. 52) in 1855 (cf. Barsoum 2008: 131).

7. Jan Beṯ-Ṣawoce recorded Father Yuhanon Shamcunki's translation of this poem (from the first stanza up to stanza 191) into Surayt Aramaic on tape in Hannover (Germany, 1981). It has been published in Beṯ-Ṣawoce (2006a). Father Yuhanon's recording has been transcribed and also translated into English and published in

Gaunt (2006: 398–404). In her article 'Remembering the Seyfo; Re-reading the Poem by Gallo Shabo', Naures Atto (2008) presents several stanzas of this poem in English.

8. The main information in his biography has been taken from Çiçek's introduction to Shabo's poem. According to Atto (2008: 125) and Çiçek (1981: 32), a longer, unpublished biography is preserved by Shabo's grandson, His Eminence Mor Julius Abdlahad Shabo, Archbishop of Sweden and Scandinavia.

9. Contrary to Atto's perception (2008: 124), Gallo Shabo twice used the term 'Sayfo', in stanzas 146 and 202. This can be taken as evidence of an earlier rather than later composition of the poem, because in the years after the mass murder, the term 'Sayfo' was not immediately taken to refer to this event (Beṯ-Ṣawoce 2006a: 9–11). In contrast, in two (see stanzas 3, 20) of the sixty-nine stanzas in the unedited poem about the Sayfo in 'Iwardo which was ascribed to Gallo Shabo and probably written later (see note 14), Shabo uses the term 'Sayfo' explicitly referring to the events in 1915.

10. Bar Hebraeus's writings especially, such as the above-mentioned *Awsar Roze*, can be considered to be a collection of short notes on all the books of the Syriac Bible giving a complete text, other historiographical and liturgical texts as well as orally trans-mitted hymns and poems, such as the famous poem *Lawij* in Kurdish by Catholicos Basilios Shem'un (transcription and translation into English in Kreyenbroek 1995: 29–53), have indubitably left their mark on Shabo's poem and his way of interpret-ing the Sayfo as a punishment for the sins of the Syriacs. In the tradition of the Syriacs, the Catholicos of the Syriac Orthodox Church, Basilios Shem'un (1710–40), was forced by a Kurdish clan chief to chant a song. The Catholicos began to compose the poem *Lawij*, in which he laments the transgressions of mankind and speaks of the End of Time. This poem was written in both Arabic and Syriac script and was one of the most popular sung lamentations among the Syriacs until very recently (Çiçek 1987: 99; see also Birol 2015: 65–100).

11. Atto (2008: 128) states that the last stanza of Shabo's poem seems to have been added by Çiçek. In the manuscript of Archpriest Gabro Beth Yawno (see note 6), Gallo Shabo's poem ends abruptly in the middle of stanza 190.

12. Father Yuhanon Shamcunki did not recognize the melodic traits of this poem, there-fore Beṯ-Ṣawoce did not identify Shabo's work as a poem and identified it as prose (see note 7). In contrast to Çiçek's uncritical edition, the manuscript of Archpriest Gabro Beth Yawno records that the present poem was written in the twelve-syllabic meter of Jacob of Sarug (fol. 62). Isa Işler's poem and the poem *Lawij* have also been sung in different variations. Syriacs generally performed their poems as a sort of recitative. Hence, Shabo's poem was probably also intended to be delivered in this fashion. Interestingly, Çiçek makes mention of Shabo's sweet and mournful voice (Çiçek 1981: 32).

13. Archbishop Çiçek collected and edited the poems of Father Aphrem Safar of Midyat, Patriarch Behnam Hadloyo and Bishop Ya'qub 'Urdnusoyo (d. 1804) and put them into an anthology with other poems under the title *Tenhotho d'Tur'Abdin* (English: The Groans of Tur Abdin).

14. In Pseudo-Gallo Shabo's unedited poem, he uses the Gregorian calendar, and this supports the statement that Shabo's edited poem was written earlier than his unedited work (see note 9).

15. It is possible that Shabo seized upon the widespread assumption (Talay 2010: 241–4) of a command (stanza 4) resp. decree (stanza 15) issued by the sultan and other Ottoman authorities (see stanza 173) as a connecting point to his theological inter-pretation that the Lord's command to the 'shameful people' (stanza 187) stopped the Sayfo in 'Iwardo after sixty days (see stanza 6, 187; see note 38). Furthermore,

it should be mentioned that a belief in the existence of a decree from the sultan that heralded the event in 1915 was widespread among Christians (Gaunt 2006: 328, 364, 368–9) and also among Muslims (Gaunt 2006: 305).

16. Muhammad Rashad, whose regal name was Mehmet V, was 35th Sultan of the Ottoman Empire from 1909 to 1918.

17. At the beginning of the second chapter of Sleman Henno's *Gunhe d-Suryoye d-Tur 'Abdin* (translated into German in 2005), he refers to Shabo by quoting this stanza of Shabo's poem verbatim. This is an indication of the widespread popularity of this poem. In the poem 'Aqafto' by Ne'man Aydin (1981: 70–90), he refers to 'the foolish people of Hagar, who were incited by a command issued by the Byzantine [i.e. Ottoman] king' (stanza 24). In Yusuf Bilan's poem (1981: 97–107) about the Sayfo in Azakh (Turkish: Idil), he writes that 'King Enver Rashad' (stanza 4), probably a mixture of Ottoman Sultan Rashad and War Minister Enver Pasha, issued this anti-Christian command. Father Aphrem Safar interpreted the command of the 'pagan Byzantine [i.e. Ottoman] king' as being prompted by the spread of the apostasy of the rulers of Constantinople (stanzas 5–6; in the second poem stanza 10).

18. He distinguishes the different known Christian communities in his immediate environment as ethno-Christian groups. In comparison to Yusuf Bilan's poem, Shabo also mentions 'Franks' (he most probably means the Chaldean Catholics and Syriac Catholics) in later stanzas (see stanzas 27, 89), who also fell victim to the Sayfo.

19. In his *Church History*, Pseudo-Zacharias Rhetor also interprets his own generation as 'the last generation' and reports on what had befallen them and what they will experience in accordance with strong eschatological expectations based on biblical revelations: 'And it showered itself upon stones and fell upon walls; and discerning men were in fear and trepidation and anxiety, and instead of the joy of the Passover they were in sorrow, because all the things that are written had been fulfilled against us on account of our sins' (my translation based on Brooks 1919: 135–6, 199–200).

20. In Syriac literature this concept is also strongly represented, e.g. Dionysios of Tellmahre was quoted in the Syriac Chronicle of Michael the Great: 'God turned His face away. And when we cry, He does not listen, because we have angered Him with our deeds' (my translation based on Chabot 1899–1924: 108).

21. In Pseudo-Gallo Shabo's other poem, he focuses more on the village of 'Iwardo, but also gives information about other villages in Tur Abdin, such as Bote (Turkish: Bardakçı) (see stanzas 30–33) and Kfarze (Turkish: Altıntaş) (see stanzas 51–8).

22. In these stanzas he is talking in terms of sin: 135 ('Because we have sinned'), 136 ('We shall leave these for Io, ... For all who sin have to deserve the wine of this') and 147 ('... they requested God's mercy upon the sinners'). The basic meaning of sin in the Syriac language is to miss the mark (Sokoloff 2009: 442–3), so it was irrevocable that in retribution for their sinful way of life, the people were not able to reach God, and they were punished with God's chastisement.

23. Henno (2005: 76) also reported on this event, but he says that only two men were killed.

24. Aydin (1990: 113–14) also reports about Syriac warriors from 'Iwardo, who participated in the defence of Midyat (Gaunt 2006: 195 and 203).

25. In 1914, the deposed Syriac Orthodox Patriarch 'Abdulmasih II angrily left the city after a quarrel with the Syriac community of Midyat, with the words: 'I hope and pray that Midyat will be turned upside down' (Bet-Şawoce 2006b: 272). It should be mentioned that the following generation of Syriacs had also made a connection between the brutality of the Sayfo in Midyat in 1915 and the curse of the deposed patriarch. Hence, it is possible that Shabo believed that the extreme brutality used

against the Christians in Midyat compared to other locations was the result of this curse.

26. Yawsef Babo-Rhawi also mentioned around twelve thousand Muslim fighters (Gaunt 2006: 349), whereas Resqo Gawwo-Afrem counted ten thousand government soldiers aided by twelve thousand Kurds (Gaunt 2006: 353).

27. According to Henno (2005: 90), Resqo Gawwo-Afrem (Gaunt 2006: 353) and Aydin (1990: 115), the sign was a flag. Resqo Gawwo-Afrem described it as 'the green Muslim flag' (Gaunt 2006: 353).

28. In his unedited poem, Pseudo-Gallo Shabo indicates that 'our sin was in front of the cloud' (stanza 59), also in front of God (cf., e.g., Ex 20:21, 24:16, 34:5; Num 9:17).

29. In Pseudo-Gallo Shabo's poem, he cites more accusations of transgressions against the Muslims and says in no uncertain terms that the Muslim fighters had also sinned (see stanza 13).

30. In contrast to the poems by Mirza of Midun (fol. 61) and Monk Yuhanon Kafroyo (see stanza 24), Bishop Ya'qub 'Urdnusoyo's poem (see stanzas 21–3, 30–32), Father Aphrem Safar's poem (in the first poem see stanzas 2, 8, 22; in the second poem see stanzas 21, 23, 26, 44), Ne'man Aydin's poem (see, e.g., stanzas 24, 26, 32, 37, 38, 39, 90, 97) and Işler's poem (see stanzas 3, 14, 16, 30, 53, 56, 69, 80, 87, 94, 101–2, 104, 109, 111, 116, 120), Shabo uses only the fairly mildly denigrating expressions 'fool(s)' (stanzas 22, 23, 24) and 'shameful people' (stanzas 169, 188). However, it is striking that Shabo does call Muhammad Rashad 'a pig rolled in filth' (stanza 15) and also 'evil' (stanza 4), as is the railroad (stanza 193), betraying his knowledge of imperial policy. Moreover, he calls the fate of the Syriacs (stanzas 51, 108), the judge in Midyat (stanza 82) and also his opponents in 'Iwardo 'evil' (stanzas 137, 181–2). Closer to home, Shabo calls the Muslim clan chief 'Abdal'aziz from Midyat 'the Antichrist' (stanza 87). Resqo Gawwo-Afrem also refers to him as 'a sworn enemy of the Christians' (Gaunt 2006: 354). In contrast, in his unedited poem Pseudo-Gallo Shabo is not loath to use more denigrating epithets such as 'evil' (stanzas 4, 11, 28–9, 60), 'drunkard' (stanza 5), 'tyrannical people' (stanza 7), 'Mohammed … Satan's friend' (stanza 18) and 'Forgetters' (stanzas 42–4, 51).

31. In a note at the end of the earlier mentioned apocalyptic poem by Bishop Ya'qub 'Urdnusoyo about the end of the world, included in manuscript 144 of the Church of the Forty Martyrs in Mardin (fol. 47v; copied 1915), the copyist Monk Yuhanon [the later Bishop Mor Philoxenus Yuhanon Dolabani (d. 1969)] advances a similar view, cf. Birol (forthcoming).

32. It is obvious that the blowing of the horns (stanza 175) and trumpets (stanzas 173–5), the sound of the people (stanzas 175–6, 178) and the gunfire (stanza 175), the battle call 'Muhammat salawat' (stanza 173), the trembling of the Earth (stanza 173) and the countless bodies of the dead recall apocalyptical topics, underlining the singularity of these events.

33. Henno (2005: 103) as well as Qarabashi (1999: 132) has underscored Shabo's statement that Mor Gabriel had become a 'den of all sorts of thieves' (stanza 206). It had been occupied by the Kurdish family 'Azzam between 1917 and 1919 (Henno 2005: 100–103; Aydin 1988: 78–9; Gaunt 2006: 231, 247). Henno (2005: 103) says that the first priest to return to Mor Gabriel in 1919 was Father Yuhanon of 'Iwardo. Therefore, Shabo must have written his poem before 1919 (see note 9).

34. Although he did not explicitly mention repentance, the poem does refer to people beseeching God to forgive them (see stanzas 123, 147, 150), a theme repeated in Pseudo-Gallo Shabo's unedited poem (see stanza 22).

35. Resqo Gawwo-Afrem (Gaunt 2006: 354), Gawriye Beth Mas'ud (Gaunt 2006: 386), Henno (2005: 92–3) and Aydin (1990: 116) have also presented an authentic depiction of condi-

tions in 'Iwardo after the battle, all fitting in well with Shabo's description. Moreover, Aydin (1990: 116) and Resqo Gawwo-Afrem (Gaunt 2006: 354) have confirmed Shabo's statement that, after the battle in 'Iwardo, families left 'Iwardo for Anhel (Turkish: Yemişli) and the village of Kafro in Mount Izlo (Turkish: Elbeğendi) (see stanza 188).

36. On further examination the German Protestant missionary journal *Hermannsburger Missionsblatt* of 1916 reveals that Syriacs from Urmia (Iran), namely the Lutheran minister Luther Pera, interpreted their own situation in a similar way: 'We were taught the important lesson not to trust in human power and help, but only in the Almighty and Living God. In His Hands lies the fate of the people. He has used the imperial powers, for either to punish or to rescue Oriental Christians' (my translation, based on Tamcke 2008: 205).

37. In his poem, Pseudo-Gallo Shabo gives more details about the end of the battle in 'Iwardo. It is striking that in his edited poem Shabo ignores the significant role of Sheikh Fathallah, but Pseudo-Gallo Shabo emphasizes it in four out of sixty-nine stanzas (see stanzas 63–7).

38. Apart from Shabo (stanzas 183 and 187) and Aydin (1990: 114), Henno (2005: 93) says that the siege of 'Iwardo went on for sixty days, but Ishaq Armalto mentions fifty-two days (Gaunt 2006: 205) and Resqo Gawwo-Afrem said sixty-two days (Gaunt 2006: 352).

Bibliography

Atto, N. 2008. 'Remembering the Seyfo: Re-Reading the Poem by Gallo Shabo', in *The Harp* 23: 123–136.

Aydin, H. 1988. *Das Mönchtum im Tur-Abdin: Das Leben der Mönche im Tur-Abdin in der Gegenwart*. PK Glane: Bar Hebraeus Verlag.

Aydin, H. 1990. *Die Syrisch-Orthodoxe Kirche von Antiochien: Ein geschichtlicher Überblick von Diakon Hanna Aydin*. PK Glane: Bar Hebraeus Verlag.

Aydin, N. 1981. 'Aqafto', in J.Y. Çiçek (ed.), *Memre d-'al Sayfe da-sbal Mshihoye b-Turkiya men shnath 1714–1914*. Holland: Diocese of the Syriac Orthodox Church in Middle Europe, pp. 70–90.

Azkhoyo, G. 1981. 'Al-Ruwandez maroho shnath 2146 d-yawnoye', in J.Y. Çiçek (ed.), *Memre d-'al Sayfe da-sbal Mshihoye b-Turkiya men shnath 1714–1914*. Holland: Diocese of the Syriac Orthodox Church in Middle Europe, pp. 8–15.

Barsoum, A. 2008. *The History of Turabdin*, trans. Matti Moosa. Piscataway, NJ: Gorgias Press.

Bcheiry, I. 2009. *The Syriac Orthodox Patriarchal Register of Dues of 1870: An Unpublished Historical Document from the Late Ottoman Period*. Gorgias Eastern Christian Studies 17. Piscataway, NJ: Gorgias Press.

Beṯ-Ṣawoce, J. 2006a. *Seyfo b Tur Abdin 1914–1915*, Vol. 1, 2nd ed. Södertälje: Nsibin Förlag.

—— 2006b. 'The Fall of Medyad. Midyat in the Time of Sayfo 1914–15', *Parole de l'Orient* 31: 269–77.

Bilan, Y. 1981. 'Memro d-'al shgushye gawonoye da-shnath 1914', in J.Y. Çiçek (ed.), *Memre d-'al Sayfe da-sbal Mshihoye b-Turkiya men shnath 1714–1914*. Holland: Diocese of the Syriac Orthodox Church in Middle Europe, pp. 97–107.

Bilgiç, I.A. 1981. 'Al ksef-risho u-ihtiyat d-folhutho turkoyto', in J.Y. Çiçek (ed.), *Memre d-'al Sayfe da-sbal Mshihoye b-Turkiya men shnath 1714–1914*. Holland: Diocese of the Syriac Orthodox Church in Middle Europe, pp. 22–31.

Birol, S. 2015. 'Einige Bemerkungen zu der Schrift "Lawij" des Basilius Šem'ūn II.', *Parole de l'Orient* 40: 65–100.

—— (forthcoming). 'Forgotten Witnesses: Remembering and Interpreting the 'Sayfo' in the Manuscripts of Tur 'abdin' (working title) in S. Talay (ed.), *Sayfo 1915 – The Assyrian/Aramean Genocide*. Piscataway/NJ: Gorgias Press.

Brooks, E.W. (ed.). 1919. *Historia Ecclesiastica Zachariae*. Louvain: Peeters.

Chabot, J. -B. (ed.). 1899–1924. *Chronique de Michel le Syrien, Patriarche Jacobite d'Antioche (1166–1199)*. 4 vols. Paris: Ernest Leroux.

—— (ed.). 1916–37. *Anonymi auctoris: Chronicum ad annum Christi 1234 pertinens I*. Corpus Scriptorum Christianorum Orientalium 81, 109 and 56. Leuven: Peeters.

Çiçek, J.Y. (ed.). 1981. *Memre d-'al Sayfe da-sbal Mshihoye b-Turkiya men shnath 1714–1914*. Holland: Diocese of the Syriac Orthodox Church in Middle Europe.

—— (ed.). 1987. *Tenhotho d-Tur'Abdin*. PK Glane: Bar Hebraeus Verlag.

Gaunt, D. 2006. *Massacres, Resistance, Protectors: Muslim–Christian Relations in Eastern Anatolia during World War I*. Piscataway, NJ: Gorgias Press.

Hadloyo, B. 1987. 'Al-tyobutho', in J.Y. Çiçek (ed.), *Tenhotho d'Tur'Abdin*. PK Glane: Bar Hebraeus Verlag, pp. 1-14.

Harrak, A. 2005. 'Ah! The Assyrian is the Rod of My Hand! Syriac Views of History after the Advent of Islam', in J.J. van Ginkel, H.L. Murre-van den Berg and T.M. van Lint (eds), *Redefining Christian Identity: Cultural Interaction in the Middle East since the Rise of Islam*. Leuven: Peeters, pp. 45–65.

Henno, S. 2005. *Die Verfolgung und Vernichtung der Syro-Aramäer im Tur Abdin 1915*, transl. G. Toro and A. Gorgis. PK Glane: Bar Hebraeus Verlag.

Işler, I. 2006. [Untitled], in J. Beṯ-Ṣawoce (ed.), *Seyfo b Tur Abdin 1914–1915*, Vol. 1, 2nd ed. Södertälje: Nsibin Förlag, pp. 291–319.

Kafroyo, Y. 1981. 'Al qatle da-Mshihoye 1914', in J.Y. Çiçek (ed.), *Memre d-'al Sayfe da-sbal Mshihoye b-Turkiya men shnath 1714–1914*. Holland: Diocese of the Syriac Orthodox Church in Middle Europe, pp. 16–21.

Kreyenbroek, P.G. 1995. 'The Lawîj of Môr Basîliôs Shim'ûn: A Kurdish Christian Text in Syriac Script', *Journal of Kurdish Studies* 1: 29–53.

Palmer, A. 1993. *The Seventh Century in the West-Syrian Chronicles*. Translated Texts for Historians 15. Liverpool: Liverpool University Press.

Qarabashi, 'A.N. 1999. *Dmo zliho: Gunhe w-sharbe mhashone da-Mshihoye d-bethnahrin*. PK Glane: Bar Hebraeus Verlag.

Safar, A. 1987. 'Al qatle da-Mshihoye shnath 1895', in J.Y. Çiçek (ed.), *Tenhotho d'Tur'Abdin*. PK Glane: Bar Hebraeus Verlag, pp. 129–142.

Safar, A. 1987. 'Al qatle da-Mshihoye shnath 1895', in J.Y. Çiçek (ed.), *Tenhotho d'Tur'Abdin*. PK Glane: Bar Hebraeus Verlag, pp. 143–148.

Sbirinoyo, Y. 1981. 'D-'al shbitho d- Tur abdin da-hwoth b-yadh Mir Shemdin', in J.Y. Çiçek (ed.), *Memre d-'al Sayfe da-sbal Mshihoye b-Turkiya men shnath 1714–1914*. Holland: Diocese of the Syriac Orthodox Church in Middle Europe, pp. 1–7.

Scebabi, A. (ed.). 1877. *Gregorii Bar Hebraei Carmina*. Rome: Typographia Polyglotta.

Shabo, G. n.d. Tub 'al-sayfo u-harbo da-mnoh bnay Hogar ba-qritho d-'Aynwardo d-Tur abdin. Unpublished.

—— 1981. 'W-honaw memro d-som 'al-qatlo d-Suryoye', in J.Y. Çiçek (ed.), *Memre d-'al Sayfe da-sbal Mshihoye b-Turkiya men shnath 1714–1914*. Holland: Diocese of the Syriac Orthodox Church in Middle Europe, pp. 31–70.

Sokoloff, M. 2009. *A Syriac Lexicon. A Translation from the Latin, Correction, Expansion, and Update of C. Brockelmann's Lexicon Syriacum*. Winona Lake, IN: Eisenbrauns; Piscataway, NJ: Gorgias Press.

Talay, S. 2010. 'Sayfo, Firman, Qafle – Der Erste Weltkrieg aus der Sicht der syrischen Christen', in R. Voigt (ed.), *Akten des 5. Symposiums zur Sprache, Geschichte, Theologie und Gegenwartslage der syrischen Kirchen*. V. Deutsche Syrologentagung, Semitica et Semitohamitica 9. Aachen: Shaker Verlag, pp. 235–250.

Tamcke, M. 2008. 'Diesem furchtbaren Gottesgerichte gegenüber, das wir gesehen und erlebt haben: Theologische Deutungen der Verfolgungen der ostsyrischen Christen aus ostsyrisch-lutherischen Berichten während des Ersten Weltkrieges', in M. Tamcke (ed.), *Christliche Gotteslehre im Orient seit dem Aufkommen des Islams bis zur Gegenwart*. Beiruter Texte und Studien 126. Würzburg: Ergon-Verlag, pp. 203–212.

———— 2009. 'Was die Dürre lehren kann', in L. Greisiger, C. Rammelt and J. Tubach (eds), *Edessa in hellenistisch-römischer Zeit. Religion, Kultur und Politik zwischen Ost und West*. Beiruter Texte und Studien 116. Würzburg: Ergon-Verlag, pp. 267–78.

'Urdnusoyo, Q.Y. 1987. 'Al-qrobe d-zabne hroye', in J.Y. Çiçek (ed.), *Tenhotho d'Tur'Abdin*. PK Glane: Bar Hebraeus Verlag, pp. 115–23.

van Ginkel, J.J. 2007. 'The End is Near! Some Remarks on the Relationship between Historiography, Eschatology, and Apocalyptic Literature in the West-Syrian Tradition', in W.C. van Bekkum, J.W. Drijvers and A.C. Klugkist (eds), *Syriac Polemics. Studies in Honour of Gerrit Jan Reinink*. Leuven: Peeters, pp. 205–17.

CHAPTER 9

THE PSYCHOLOGICAL LEGACY OF THE SAYFO

AN INTER-GENERATIONAL TRANSMISSION OF FEAR AND DISTRUST

Önver A. Cetrez

⸻⸸⸺

Background

My personal link to the Sayfo (meaning 'sword' in Assyrian; other terms used are *Fërman*, meaning 'order' and *Qafle*, meaning 'deportation') is related to a childhood memory of my grandfather Seǧo. I was around seven years old and would accompany my grandfather as he did his regular agricultural work. On the road, he would tell stories that provided the most inspiring material for my childhood fantasies. One of these stories was about the spirits of people from the past, hidden in the caves in the mountains we used to pass by. The stories were not told to scare me, but to tell me something about the past, about people's experiences, and their suffering.

Why is the psychological dimension of a trauma such as genocide important? Is it not better to try to forget, instead of dealing with issues that are past? Duran, Firehammer and Gonzalez (2008: 288) point out the importance of understanding how history affects our present mental well-being when they write: 'If the historical soul wounding is not effectively dealt with, each person, as well as her or his descendants, is doomed to experience and perpetuate various forms of psychic and spiritual suffering in the future'. After all, as Duran et al. remind us, the term *psychology* itself literally means the study of *the soul*.

To acquire a thorough background to the historical and political dimensions of the Sayfo, I refer to the other chapters in this book as well as to previous research (Travis 2010; Gaunt 2006). It is important to note that the Sayfo in the Ottoman Empire in 1915 was not the last, but was followed by other massacres, among them the massacre at Simele (Iraq), including the Dohuk and Mosul districts, in 1933, the homogenization campaigns of the Ba'th era in Iraq and Syria after the 1940s (Donabed and Makko 2012), the civil war in south-east Turkey after the 1980s, and the trauma of migration *en masse* to Western countries after the 1970s (Cetrez 2011a; Deniz 1999). All these events in the recent past have contributed to an accumulation of trauma among Assyrians. But now, today, various parliaments have recognized the Sayfo and memorials are being erected in Australia, the United States, Armenia, Wales, France and Belgium, among others. The inscription on the monument in Belgium expresses the inter-generational suffering well: 'Virgin of the Poor, pray for Assyrian (Syriac) Martyrs of the Seyfo genocide perpetrated by the Ottoman Empire in 1915 and relieve the suffering of their children'. In a study conducted among Assyrians (n = 241) in Sweden in 2010, ninety-one per cent responded that they had a relative who had been killed during the Sayfo, seven per cent said they had no relatives who had been killed, and two per cent who did not know (Cetrez 2011b).[1] The memory of the Sayfo is commemorated in different ceremonies on 24 April each year, and a number of painters and writers have expressed their personal interpretation of the Sayfo in creative ways. A large project of interviews was also conducted by Jan Bet-Şawoce in Sweden during 1990–2000, for the purpose of gathering material about the Sayfo. The Assyrian Federation of Sweden produced a documentary about the Sayfo, called *Exodus*, at the end of the 1980s, and the Seyfo Center (http://www.seyfocenter.com) collects information and works on the political level for the recognition of the Sayfo.

Previous Research

A research review using scientific electronic databases limited to the English and Swedish languages was conducted in 2013. A broad search, using the keywords 'trauma' and 'genocide,' revealed a total of 221 hits. On the basis of the abstracts, forty-six sources were chosen for further reading. Previous studies have focused mainly on survivors of the Holocaust, the Armenian genocide and the more recent genocides in Bosnia and Rwanda. Their results relate to first-generation survivors and such health issues as well-being (Nadler and Ben-Shushan 1989) and psychopathology, revealed in such symptoms as social withdrawal and suspicion, which lead to difficulties in forming close emotional attachments (ibid.). Research has also been carried out into inter-generational trauma and health, examining emotional difficulties in dealing with the Holocaust (Chaitin 2002), obsessive storytelling or deep emotional silence (Jacobs 2011), secondary traumatization (Van IJzendoorn, Bakermans-Kranenburg and Sagi-Schwartz 2003), personal, social and family impacts of the Holocaust (Lazar, Litvak-Hirsch and Chaitin 2008), transmission of distrust and fear (Teshuva 2010; Chaitin 2002) and the psychological impact on Armenian survivors (Karenian et al. 2010). Research has also focused on the inter-generational transmission of narratives and their contribution to identity construction (Azarian-Ceccato 2010). Other studies have looked at how child survivors have dealt with extreme trauma (Sternberg and Rosenbloom 2000) and at how children absorb their parents' psychic conflicts (Urlic 2004). Other research has been interested in person-object relations and the transmission of the genocidal past (Kidron 2012) and the role of ritual in the cross-generational transmission of trauma (Jacobs 2011). Another perspective has concentrated on post-conflict reconciliation, trust and constructive attitudes (Geneviéve 2010), revenge and forgiveness (Van Noort 2003) and aesthetic ways of dealing with trauma (Connolly 2011).

Research on trauma and its consequences reveals that the *trauma* of 'extreme experiences throughout the lifecycle can have profound effects on memory, affect regulation, biological stress modulation and interpersonal relatedness' (Connolly 2011: 608), and also giving way to feelings of depression and guilt (ibid.). Connolly goes on to write that, following the Holocaust survivors, trauma has an impact on future generations, notably with a long period of *silence*, characterized by denial and repression. Hence, the children of survivors have had a greater tendency than their parents to display emotional problems. They have also shown 'characteristic deficits such as a failure of metaphorization with subsequent difficulties in distinguishing between reality and fantasy, and a disturbance of temporality, all of which lead to the typical disturbances of memory and of identity' (Connolly 2011: 610). Furthermore, research has also revealed among survivors the incapability to remember, to mourn and to symbolize the trauma. This inability to symbolize mental structures is also transmitted to future generations. Findings in neuroscience have also confirmed the inter-generational transmission of trauma, with lasting hormonal changes among Holocaust survivors as their Post-Traumatic Stress Disorder (PTSD) is replicated among their adult children (Connolly 2011). According to DSM-IV (American Psychiatric Association 1994), PTSD is defined as the persistent re-experiencing of a traumatic event, the persistent avoidance of stimuli associated with the trauma or numbing of general responsiveness and persistent symptoms of increased arousal, including hyper-vigilance and irritability. The symptoms are chronic, and the disturbance causes impairment in social, occupational and other important functioning (Connolly 2011). If PTSD is left untreated, the long-term psycho-social effects can be transmitted from generation to generation (Kidron 2012). Trauma survivors and their descendants are widely encouraged to express their repressed and silenced past both verbally and non-verbally (ibid.).

Psychological research on the Sayfo has yet to be undertaken. Nevertheless, a historical approach by Gaunt (2006) included interviews with survivors of the Sayfo and their children, conducted in the decade 1990–2000. One category in this study was lessons learned from the Sayfo, expressed through stories and proverbs retold by survivors, which served as lessons for own conduct. Cetrez (2011b) analysed material from an Assyrian electronic newspaper in Sweden, *Hujådå* (www.hujada.com). A search for the keyword 'Sayfo' from 2001 to 2011 resulted in forty-seven articles, in which two relevant themes occur, one of *self-image*, including *victimization* and *vulnerability*, and the other of *remembrance* of the Sayfo.

Aims and Questions

My aim in this chapter is to demonstrate how a trauma such as the Sayfo has ongoing effects on Assyrian individuals who have had to face the new traumas of the Iraq and Syria War. The Iraqi individuals had settled in Sweden during 2012–13, while the Syrian individuals were refugees in Istanbul, Turkey, during 2013–14. Two general research questions run through this chapter as a scarlet thread: (1) What stories have Assyrians heard about the Sayfo and how has this information affected their experiences both in Iraq, Syria and in Sweden today? (2) On the basis of the stories the participants tell about the Sayfo, what can a psychological analysis, primarily from an object-relation perspective, tell us about the cultural construction, including in- and out-group perceptions, of Assyrian-Iraqis and Assyrian-Syrians in particular and Assyrians in general?

Theoretical Framework

Object-Relation Theory

My theoretical starting point will be the object-relation theory, more specifically the concepts of image and imagination described in the approach of the Dutch-born clinical psychologist Paul W. Pruyser (1916–87) to human development. The discussion of *images* and *imagination* has, Pruyser (1983) says, a number of reference points, one being the external reality and its impact on the human mind, a second being the mind itself generating mental images and a third reference point being cultural work, for example religion, art, literature, music and science. This cultural work comprises a wealth of systems of symbols transmitted inter-generationally. They also constitute a world of their own, transcending both the external and the internal worlds. The verb 'to imagine' denotes a mental process that produces a variety of images. Viewing intentionality as a characteristic of the human mind in search of meaning, the imagination produces images. In other words, a human being actively forms images in an attempt to create reality through culture. Pruyser's most important contribution is his theoretical concept of what he calls the *illusionistic world*, a liminal space between subjectivity and objectivity, or an intermediate area of experience.

Pruyser's approach provides a good basis for an understanding of the role of image and imagination in early human development. Other concepts in object-relation theory add to this approach by indicating that the child learns early to differentiate itself from other people and from the outer world, by forming an image of itself in relation to others (Psychologists for Social Responsibility 1989). Volkan (1985, referred to in Psychologists for Social Responsibility 1989) points out that very early in its life the child characterizes experiences into distinct *good* and *bad* categories. From the child's point of view, an object, such as the self, cannot be both good and bad at the same time. Therefore, the mind finds ways around this dichotomy, including outlets for externalizing bad aspects of the self-image. By the time the child learns to integrate the opposite images of others and of itself, and as its cognitive ability develops, it finds ways to deal with these binary categories, for example by understanding that people can be both good and bad (Jones 2008). Nevertheless, certain images remain divided in a dualistic relationship, as all-good or all-bad, and are then projected onto other people or objects, for example through the externalization of negative parts of the self onto specific objects in the surrounding area (ibid.). By doing this, the child manages to build up an inner sanctum of safety and strength for itself, in which are included those who are close to it and its own group. Although this process distorts our ability to make more nuanced judgements and contributes to the formation of stereotypes of other people (Psychologists for Social Responsibility 1989), as human interaction is its focus, object-relation theory can be advanced through a concept from practice theory, *misrecognition*. The ritualization theorist Bell (1992: 87) writes that '[p]ractice sees what it intends to accomplish, but it doesn't see the strategies it uses to produce what it does actually accomplish, a new situation'.

Inter-generational Transmission of Trauma

In inter-generational trauma two fields are of relevance to the survivors: *the death of time* and *the death of language* (Connolly 2011). The *death of time* refers to the discontinuity between past, present and future among survivors, and this is transmitted to their children. Connolly (2011) also refers to research by Kijak and Funtowicz (1982) showing that this dissociation in temporality leads to the simultaneous coexistence of two aspects of the ego, one part continuing 'to live' in the death camp, stripped of all its defences, and the other part 'adapted' to the new reality, and behaving as if it can love, hate and work. Connolly refers to other research in which parents and children identify with each other in what has been called a 'vampiric identification'. The children become imprisoned in the parents' trauma, in an imageless, timeless condition, condemned to repeat what they themselves have not experienced. This death of time creates dissociation between history and memory, which is purely subjective, mythical and ineffective for the creation of meaningful narratives (Connolly 2011). The children of survivors have memories which are transmitted to them, but of which they have no personal experience. Consequently, they acquire a repetitive, static and coercive character. Instead, these non-experienced memories accumulate an amalgam of images from personal experience and stereotyped images of the history of the family or the social group (ibid.).

The *death of language* refers to an extreme physical deprivation, in which the threat of extinction and the process of dehumanization lead to a 'world without metaphors', Connolly (2011) postulates. Metaphor itself lies at the heart of our capacity to think imaginatively and to perform dream work; this has profound effects on symbolization, which also lies at the core of Pruyser's (1983) approach to human development and creativity through the illusionistic world. Dreaming is important to the consolidation of memory as well as to the metabolization of emotions and sensations, as shown by neuro-physiological research. Without the ability to ritualize and symbolize, the cultural content is being distorted into an unhealthy condition, or what Pruyser calls the inner autistic or the outer realistic worlds. Both survivors of intense trauma and their children, Connolly writes, report disturbances in dreaming, sometimes an inability to dream, or when dreaming having hallucinations in sleep as well as nightmares, which are sometimes repetitive. Connolly also postulates that the less the parents remember, the more these experiences are transmitted to the children in less representable and elaborative forms. *Narrative* is a central aspect of inter-generational trauma and it requires the capacity to use metaphor in order to fashion the experiences into a comprehensible and meaningful whole for oneself and for others.

To elaborate further on the death-of-language concept, we need to look at theories of inter-generational narratives and trauma that focus on the relationship between storytelling, personal or others', and perceptions of worldview, self and identity formation in a cultural context. Azarian-Ceccato (2010: 107) points out that narrative scholars look at the protection of self and the conception of identity relating to the stories told. He also examines the role of culturally specific narratives in the making and the articulation of collective identities. In their work, narrative scholars have also looked at the recounting of historically laden traumatic narratives about the Holocaust. These studies have shown how the appropriation of others' stories helps individuals to comprehend their own world, and their place in it. However, narrative scholars, Azarian-Ceccato argues, have not focused so much on the inter-generational transmission of narratives as it relates to the maintenance of ethnic identity. Narrative theory can help to explain how we bridge the past and the present linguistically and how certain events remain seminal to a group's idea of existence (2010: 107). This is connected to the idea of *collected stories*, indicating an individualized articulation of stories, which are not discovered through direct experience, but vicariously encountered (2010: 112). In collected stories, the lines of authorship and storyline lineages and origins are blurred, giving the impression that the person telling the story has actually lived through the experience recounted (ibid.).

Remembering and Trauma

Traumatic events can lead to the failure of memory, leaving the traumatic experience in an indescribable and unknowable condition (Kidron 2012). It is a human characteristic to remember and, as relational beings, we then want to share those memories with others. *Collective memory* refers to the sharing of memories within a community, creating a sense of identity among its members (Bourguignon 2005). A definition of collective memory, by Schiff, Noy and Cohler (2001) referred to in Azarian-Ceccato (2010: 112), is 'the property of social groups who talk about, and reconfigure, defining moments of a group's history through the frame of present day concerns', being the cultural fabric of a society and its stock of significant stories and events. Another definition is 'shared representations of the past, involving the meanings and forms ... through which the past is remembered and influences action in the present' (Foner and Alba 2010: 800). Remembering can be in many forms – oral, written, images and ritualistic. Stein (2009) relates remembering to *memory work*, which assumes that remembering is an active process mediated by culture. Memory work can be travelling to one's parents' place of origin, collecting oral histories from survivors or producing films and memoirs narrating the biographies of the survivors. As feelings of loss are transmitted inter-generationally, Stein writes, individuals undertake memory work in an act of solidarity with the trauma of their parents. By engaging with their parents' traumatic past through memory work, the children are addressing the loss of both memory and continuity caused by genocide. Stein points out that any act of remembrance takes place from a specific point of time and place. The parents' traumatic experiences also leave the children with a loss of history, growing up knowing little about their roots.

Lazar, Litvak-Hirsch and Chaitin (2008, referring to research by Alexander 2004) present an important concept, cultural *trauma*, defined as those phenomena occurring 'when members of a collective feel they have been subjected to a horrendous event that leaves an indelible mark upon their group consciousness, marking their memory for ever and changing their future identity in fundamental and irrevocable ways' (Lazar, Litvak-Hirsch and Chaitin 2008: 98). Referring to Smelser (2004), another perspective is added to the concept of cultural trauma, as follows: '... for an event to be considered a cultural trauma, the memory of the event is culturally and publicly represented as obliterating, damaging, and as a threat, both to the existence of the culture the individual identifies with, and to one's own identity and self' (Lazar, Litvak-Hirsch and Chaitin 2008: 98).

Method

The empirical material for this study is drawn from two separate studies. The first one is a larger study conducted in 2012–13 among

Assyrian-Iraqis residing in Södertälje, Sweden, among which five interviews (three females and two males, the youngest twenty-seven and the oldest sixty, who arrived in Sweden between 2005 and 2008) included material related to the Sayfo, collected from the interviewees who all had ancestors who had survived the Sayfo and had emigrated from Turkey to Iraq soon after 1915. The second study was conducted among Assyrian-Syrians, still refugees in Istanbul or South East Turkey, and included 25 individuals (equally divided by gender, age ranging from 18 to 70 years) and five focus group semi-structured interviews. The interviews in both studies followed a semi-structured pattern, inspired by a life-story method, focusing on whether the interviewees had heard stories about the Sayfo from their parents or grandparents and whether this has had any relevance to how they have interpreted their situation either today or in earlier periods of their lives. The interviews were carried out face to face, either in Assyrian, Arabic, English or Swedish, and were tape-recorded and then transcribed verbatim. As the research team included well-trained Assyrian and Arabic speaking colleagues the use of translators was not needed (also recommended by Hassan, et al., 2015). Ethical approval was granted by the Uppsala regional board, in Sweden, for both studies. As in other studies with refugees, we created a written information letter, both in Arabic and English that we shared with each participant before an interview was conducted. This was also read aloud for them before the interview. They were informed about the purpose of the study, how the interview was being structured, the benefits and possible risks of the study, and that the participants could at any moment withdraw from the study, without any questioning or hindrance. The participants were also informed about the level of confidentiality of the study and how the data material was kept, who had access to the material, and how it would be analysed and presented. The possible risks identified in both studies were the fact that the interview questions may awaken difficult memories among the participants. It could be memories of the war or memories of fleeing Iraq or Syria. With questions of trauma experiences in the past and challenges during their present vulnerable conditions, the participants could be exposed to short term risks. Though questions about previous difficulties were limited, questions regarding experience of trauma, physical and psychological conditions of themselves and of their children were needed. In order to meet the need of the participants a psychiatrist was on hand, whom the participants could consult after the interview. An interpreter was available for them if needed. Though none of the participants consulted the psychiatrist, it was a service provided without any cost.

In coding the interview material, the principal method used was an inductive approach. The Assyrian-Iraqi material will be presented first in overall coding and then through two distinct cases, one female and one male. The Assyrian-Syrian material will only be used to clarify or confirm some of the conclusions. A deductive approach is used in the theoretical analysis.

Empirical Findings

First, the overall empirical result related to the Sayfo will be presented, giving the density and the co-occurrence of the codes. Following this, two cases from the interviews with Iraqi-Assyrians are presented. One is by a female, reflecting the theme of *dlo awla* (distrust), and the other by a male, reflecting the theme of *zëcto* (fear).

Presentation of the Overall Material

An analysis of the distribution of codes reveals that the code *the Sayfo and its consequences* is the most common one (with its sub-codes, n = 44), among which religious differentiation is the most frequent (n = 14). This is followed by the code *fear* (with its sub-codes, n = 35), among which social consequences is the strongest (n = 8). Furthermore, the code *inter-generational relations* occurs frequently (n = 15), as well as *stories* (with its sub-codes, n = 12), *distrust* (n = 10), *meaning* (with its sub-codes, n = 10) and *self-image* (with its sub-codes, n = 8).

One of the sub-codes of *the Sayfo and its consequences* is *qaṭlo d marduto* (cultural genocide). Cultural genocide is concerned with political, religious and ecological dimensions referring to the situation in Iraq and Syria. This is exemplified by a female Assyrian-Syrian woman, who reflects on this as a collective experience:

> I don't feel safe because of the situation in my country, and because I belong to an Assyrian minority. We are under the threat of being murdered by IS. I can't talk anymore. I had enough of the miserable situation we live in. (Woman, born 1965)

One informant from Iraq describes it in terms of systematic killing, discrimination and deportation, as well as destruction of infrastructure and archaeological sites and the use of radioactive material for the purpose of ridding Iraq of Christian people. The arrival of the Americans in Iraq in 2003 is also referred to as the beginning of genocide and extermination, opening the way for gangsters, extremists and sectarians who wanted revenge to kill people indiscriminately. There is also a fear of the increased awareness of ethnic and national differentiation. The rising use of national labels and separatist movements increases the risks of genocide, or as one informant puts it (text excerpt, Simon 12: 152–6):[2]

> Politics, [that's] what's happening now, this very minute – there is a genocide coming; it began two–three years ago. Kurds want to take the Christian area. I have told you, separatists surrounded Mosul.

This prediction is more or less what took place just one year after the interviews were conducted, perpetuated by religiously motivated terrorism. Cultural genocide also includes the exodus of the intellectuals, who are subsequently scattered throughout different countries. The informant refers to this as *genocide of a demographic character*. There is also frustration that the world community takes note of some wrongdoings against other groups, but does not pay attention to the genocide now being perpetrated against the Assyrians in Iraq and Syria.

A code co-occurrence analysis provides information about how each code is used across all project excerpts and whether it has been coded together with other codes. The results present the frequencies with which all code pairings were applied to the same excerpt. Such a display can expose patterns in which two codes were (or were not) used together.

Stories and distrust: seven overlapping excerpts from the interviews were coded with both 'feeling of distrust' and 'stories as *madǧo rwiho*' (lessons to be learned). The relatively high frequency of this pairing indicates that, as participants are thinking and reporting on distrust, they often discuss thoughts about lessons to be learned. These codes also co-occur with such codes as inter-generational relations, religious connotation, social consequences of the Sayfo and gender.

Inter-generational relations and religious differentiation: another seven overlapping excerpts were coded with both 'inter-generational relations about stories of Sayfo' and 'impact on life attributable to *far-qiye d dino*' (religious differentiation).

Stories and inter-generational relations: another group included six overlapping excerpts, coded with both '*hkeyat*' (stories) and '*i calaqa d bayn daj jilat*' (inter-generational relations), indicating that the relations between the generations frequently take place through stories.

Stories as lessons to be learned and inter-generational relations: five overlapping excerpts were coded with both 'stories as lessons to be learned' and 'inter-generational relations'. The case of Sitto, to be presented below, is one example of how inter-generational relations and lessons to be learned, and distrust and religious differentiation, are intertwined. Inter-generational relations and stories as lessons to be learned are also linked to the feeling of distrust and feeling unsafe, as well as the impact on life as the consequence of religious differentiation, again as in the case of Sitto (10: 687–8). An Assyrian-Syrian female who had escaped to Turkey after her husband had been decapitated in Syria, tells in the interview of her grandmother, who grew up as an orphan and who would tell stories about her memories from the Sayfo: 'When I was out in the field my uncle shouted loud from a distance that I should hurry.' The whole village had been killed. She would be told by older people, '*Aloho lo mahwalkhuyo*' ('May God not let you experience this'). But, the mass killings, the burning of churches and driving out people is a new genocide, just like Sayfo, taking place, she says repeatedly.

Inter-generational relations and distrust: five overlapping excerpts were coded with both 'inter-generational relations' and 'distrust'.

Feeling unsafe and religious differentiation: five overlapping excerpts were coded with both '*šcoro lo m'amno*' (feeling unsafe) and 'impact on life attributable to religious differentiation'. Sitto's case (10: 30–39) is one of these examples, which also highlights the gender dimension. The same person also tells of how she felt unsafe, together with religious differentiation and the social impact of what has happened in Iraq (10: 716–21).

Inherited fear from the Sayfo: five overlapping excerpts were coded with both 'fear related to the Sayfo' and '*wëroto d zëcto*' (fear inherited from the elderly).

Fear of history being repeated: five overlapping excerpts were coded with both 'fear based on past conditions' and 'fear being repeated'.

Internal fear: four overlapping excerpts were coded with different sub-codes for fear, namely '*zëcto d lawğël*' (internal fear), 'past conditions' and 'societal consequences', plus effects on relationships today in Sweden.

Existential questions: four overlapping excerpts were coded with meaning on a cognitive level and as a religious dimension, as well as religious differentiation and the feeling of being vulnerable.

The Case of Sitto: The Feeling of Distrust

Sitto is female, fifty years old and a third-generation Sayfo survivor. She speaks about the lack of safety being suffered by her family in Iraq, specifically highlighting the gender dimension and the religious differentiation from other groups, and the fact that the lack of safety was the main reason for her emigration to Sweden. She says:

I cannot feel it's safe for my daughter. I cannot feel it's safe for my children. So, this is what makes us always want to get out of Iraq ... And there is something very important to us as a Christian people. We never feel safe in Arab countries. Because we are always the target, because of the idea that it's *halal*[3] ... to kill us, because we are not Muslims. And this is the thing which really, really makes us constantly worried about our families, our children, our daughters. (Sitto 10: 30–39)

Sitto also gives this as a reason for her depression, which began twenty years ago and have still not been alleviated in Sweden. Speaking about her relatives, she remembers her grandmother, who was very close to her. This grandmother was born in Turkey and experienced the genocide in 1915. As a result, she had her own nose cut off. Sitto's grandfather was killed in the same period. Sitto would hear from both her grandmother and her father about the many relatives they had lost during the Sayfo. The grandmother was proud of being a Christian, even though that was the reason for the atrocities. Sitto says that her grandmother did not feel safe either, and, as a lesson for life, she would tell Sitto not to trust Muslims, no matter how good they were to her. Instead, Sitto was told to put her trust in God, to be strong and not be afraid or do anything that deviated from the norms in the Bible.

During the latest American invasion (2003), Sitto could sense how people around her had changed and had begun to see her not primarily as Iraqi, but as Christian. This reminded her of the stories told by her grandmother and her father, with the moral not to trust Muslims.

Sitto links her experiences in life with what is happening to her group, affecting her socially and making her feel unsafe:

I always helped them [neighbours], stayed beside them in good times and in bad times. We never did anything bad to them. ... When the Americans came to Iraq, they [neighbours] began to blame us. It's not our fault. 'No, it's your fault, because you are Christian like them.' They began to avoid us. They began to see us as an enemy. One day my neighbour told me 'You are rubbish, because you are Christian'. This is what really hurt and I did not feel safe. (Sitto, 10: 716–21)

Sitto continues on the *dlo awla* (distrust) theme, making it clear that although they have relations with Muslims, there are social and gender-specific limitations:

We did not let them into our houses. For example, my sons, in Iraq they had Muslim friends, but they never let them inside the house. They tried to keep their sisters away from them. (Sitto, 10: 691–3)

Sitto is aware that she is passing on to her children the same lessons in life she learned from her grandmother and father:

> I tried, but my children did not believe it. They thought that the times are changing and everything is changing. But [after] what happened in Iraq, they began to think that I might have got something right. I tried to tell them, be friends with them but do not trust them, do not give them everything, do not involve them in your life, your personal life. When you want to involve someone in your personal life, they must be trusted, and I do not trust them. (Sitto, 10: 696–700)

Sitto's distrust of Muslims is not only attributable to stories about the Sayfo, but also to conditions in contemporary society in general. Furthermore, the distrust did not end with the situation in Iraq, but continues in the post-migration situation in Sweden and towards Muslims globally. Sitto connects what happened during the Sayfo with what is happening to her people today in a very clear way, through the existential question she is formulating, linking it to a religious dimension and to her vulnerable social position and that of her people:

> They will be satisfied to kill us for no reason. ... I read from time to time [about the Sayfo], but why, why did they kill them? It's the same now. We're always the target and the object with which they make a sacrifice. ... They will kill us. Why? Because we are Christians. Are they bad people, the Christians? Yes, because they are not Muslim. They do not judge us because we are doing good things, doing bad things, are good people, are evil people. No. (Sitto, 10: 707–14)

The Case of Simon: Feeling of Fear

Simon is a forty-eight-year-old male and belongs to the fourth generation of Sayfo survivors. As he reached adulthood, Simon could sense an ethnic differentiation in Iraq, where his group was seen as inferior. This sparked his interest in the history of his people, and through the internet he learned about the persecutions of his group and of other minorities. This self-study led him to establish an image of his in-group as a weak one.

When talking about his situation in Sweden and establishing friendships, Simon, as do many other Assyrian-Iraqis, mentions that he does not have any ethnic Swedish friends. However, he is definite that this is not because of any difficulty in establishing friendships with Swedes; instead, it is related to his own *zëcto* (fear), which is internal and has social consequences, creating a feeling of exclusion from society. He says:

There is something inside us. This element is called fear. This fear pushes us away from society and from Swedes. This fear is not limited to the way we are treated; it includes everything and it makes us draw back. We always feel that Swedes hate us or do not want us here because we are migrants, whereas in reality Swedes are not like this. This fear is planted inside us, but it is only illusion and not reality. (Simon, 16: 119–23)

The fear he feels is attributable to past conditions, which have consequences for all aspects of life today, according to Simon:

We have been taught about this fear from the beginning. I have reached a level of fear which makes me feel scared whenever there is a knock at the door, whenever the post is delivered. I get scared. Fear is inside us because our past is built on fear. Our [education] is built on fear; our life is built on fear because we have spent a long period [caught up] in wars. I took part in a war and I was wounded. So fear is inside us and it is very difficult to get rid of. (Simon, 16: 127–32)

This fear, Simon says, is not only related to the war in Iraq or to being a minority; it is deeper, embedded in the culture and society. First and foremost, it is built on the primary socialization at home:

This fear begins at home ... Our families taught us about fear even before [we began] school. 'Do not do this or he will do this to you. Do not go there otherwise the car will run over you. Do not be late otherwise you get killed.' Fear is implanted inside us in this way. (Simon, 16: 140–43)

The internalization of fear continues in the secondary socialization, for instance at school. Simon elaborates on this aspect in more detail, stressing that this fear was also present in his parents, who in turn had inherited it from their families, the legacy of past experiences. When asked what past he is referring to, he says it is related to the Sayfo, and what happened then forced them to migrate to different countries:

It is related, since the survivors of such massacres as the Sayfo and the Armenian massacre fled to Syria, Lebanon and Iraq. They even went as far as the south of Iraq. It is something they inherited. I have not met any of the old people who witnessed those events, but I met their children. The same families were broken up and dispersed to different places, so half the family was in Syria and the other half went to Iraq. (Simon, 16: 156–60)

Simon tells of his own village and other villages as examples of this fear. Villagers have built their lives in the fear that atrocities against them will be repeated:

Because of the fear they built our village in a location [not benefiting most from] the surrounding area. This was so that the village could not to be seen from a distance, for example, if an army happened to pass by the village. ... Up to the present we have villages in the north of Iraq where people live in groups, as if the people wanted to hide themselves ... Old people still have the same fear. They are afraid of history repeating itself. They build a cellar in their houses in which they store a lot of food. They always think that a famine or some similar calamity might occur. (Simon, 16: 165–72)

Simon links the past with the present by indicating that the history of the Sayfo will be repeated and this makes him feel unsafe:

Nowadays we see that same situation has been re-awakened. The changes in our region are indicating that the old situation will return. Extremism has recently come to the fore again and if they do not get it under control, the same event can be repeated again. ... It could happen, this is not far-fetched. The West considers these events isolated actions and they are not bothered by it. (Simon, 16: 270–74)

As Simon's case shows, fear has been a dominating theme, both as an internal inherited phenomenon linked to the Sayfo, and as an external aspect influencing social life.

Theoretical Analysis

In the following analysis, specific concepts from object-relation theory will be used, more specifically imagination as a practice. This is followed by some additional concepts found in the research review.

Image and Imagination

In any consideration of the Sayfo, the mental process of imagining is linked to such healthy cultural work as annual commemorations, the symbolic monuments erected, the seminars and conferences held, the popular and scientific writings, the poetry, novels, paintings, music and documentaries. These practices can perform the function of healthy ritualizations of the Sayfo.

However, as Pruyser (1983) notes, imagination in the illusionary world runs the risk of intrusion from the autistic and realistic worlds, when imagination is connoted with either good or bad categories, rather than the complex relationship between these two dimensions. On the one hand, images and imagination are creating prototypes that are inflated and self-images characterized by being *victims* and *vulnerable* and, on the other hand, generalizing stereotypes of others. These images are formed through relationships and objects in the outer world, including *role models* and *social identities* to which the individual can relate, as they stand as models for *enmity* or *allies*. Therefore, the risk of a different kind of ritualization of the Sayfo is great. In the search for a meaningful interpretation of this historical trauma, a one-sided process of imagination, either internal or external, runs the risk of creating all-bad images of the *gërup baroyo* (out-group) or *hënne* (them) and all-good images of the *gërup gawoyo* (in-group) or *ahna* (us). This dichotomization of images creates a culture connoted with processes of projection, externalization, distortion and stereotyping. Furthermore, not only does this construct a wrong image of the other, as a consequence it also builds up a wrong image of the self, creating an inflated self- or group-image as not only all-good but also as 'vulnerable' and the 'victims' of history. Despite the strong stereotypes of Muslims as hostile, there are some exceptions, among them Shaykh Fathallah, who played an important role in saving Assyrians during the Sayfo (see Gaunt 2006). What object-relation theory teaches us is that any individual or group needs to learn to integrate opposite images of others and of the self by understanding that these images can be both good and bad. The hegemony today is still that of fear, victimization and vulnerability. This is why it is so crucial that the individual and the community liberate themselves from the strong dichotomization of 'us' and 'them'.

Without a balanced ability to imagine or an ability to use metaphors, it is impossible to shape personal experiences in a comprehensible and meaningful way. The material reveals that, when describing the experiences of the Sayfo, the interviewees' relatives used only fragments of narratives. It is impossible from this study to draw any conclusions on the presence of trauma among earlier generations. However, what we do know is that PTSD, which was very probably evident as a result of the Sayfo, was left untreated or, at best, the culture-specific treatment that was perhaps given did not include the need for a re-ritualizing or re-imagining of the consequences of the Sayfo, and this has resulted in long-term psycho-social effects for the self and for succeeding generations. Some of the psychological effects today are fear, distrust, victimization and feelings of vulnerability. Fear is accentuated by different conditions in the outer social world, among them primary processes of family stories and secondary processes of school and societal practices. There is also a sense of *worry* generated by the conditions in which relatives and a person might find themselves because of the current war. This is exacerbated by a feeling of *distrust*, formed by the stories told within the family and community. These inner feelings of worry and distrust, made worse by misgivings about victimization and vulnerability born of unhealthy imagining and brooding, are woven together and acquire meaning through the narratives available in the cultural surroundings. The context of narratives has already been influenced by certain hegemonic positions, in which certain narratives are dominant, dictating what is being transformed and what can and cannot be said: so-called lessons to be learned. One of these narratives is the understanding of contemporary living conditions as a cultural genocide taking place today, constructing a world of meaning and the elaboration of existential questions. During the previous Iraq War, the attitude towards the Christians deteriorated to the negative; informants were affected by the stories told by their elders, teaching them not to trust outsiders, specifically Muslims. From our perspective of image and imagining, the contemporary war, accentuated by the stories of the Sayfo, constitutes the images which trigger the imagination to conjure up social relations fraught with distrust and fear.

Fear is expressed in culture-specific ways. Historically, among Assyrians, external groups have played the role of inserting fear as part of the socialization of children. Examples used are *Rëmoye* (Romans),[4] the Muslims or the *Jandërma* (military police). Different periods and places have had their own specific object for the externalization of fear. Recently, in countries of immigration, the externalization of fear is exercised through warnings against *fšoro* (assimilation) and *ha dë mwayëc i marduto d këtle* (losing one's culture). Consequently, the Sayfo is not the sole narrative of cultural work; earlier narratives have preceded it and new ones are being formed in the diaspora. However, what makes the Sayfo unique is that the traumatic dimension has not been healed. Nor does the damage stop there. The binary oppositions used also reflect and are upheld by those in the surrounding societies, namely the distinctions between Christians and Muslims, Western and Eastern, liberal and traditional. Such practices as fear and distrust follow a dualistic construction of binary oppositions, strongly set in a religious discourse today. The content of these practices is externalized into an object to construct the Self in relation to the Other; constructing the good and the bad, the oppressed and the oppressor. Therefore, there is a need for the enemy to be bad in order to maintain the positive view of oneself as good. The upshot is that the more vulnerable the self is, the stronger the need for enmity. In cultural work, negative images of the enemy as well as positive images of the in-group are created and sustained. Around this cultural work of distrust and fear, narratives are woven and passed on inter-generationally. One of the functions of these narratives is to connect the past, the present and the future, as exemplified in the two cases in this study.

The Death of Time and Death of Language

The informants reveal a simultaneous coexistence in their countries of origin and in Sweden, in terms of worry about private property left in Iraq or Syria or anxiety about relatives scattered all over the world. Other Assyrians continue to hide in their villages (prior to the recent war), partly, but not solely, on the basis of a fear inherited from previous generations, thereby repeating a pattern based on a fear they have not experienced themselves. As the *death-of-time* concept indicates, they have memories of which they have had no personal experience. However, they are being reminded of the legacy of fear from the Sayfo by the new atrocities and traumas that were perpetrated during the last and recent wars. These non-experienced and transmitted memories, sensations and emotions, namely images formed only by external sources, create a coercive behaviour, including not letting outsiders get too close to their private spheres. In other words, the non-experienced happenings of the Sayfo become personal, through the new atrocities committed during the war and accentuated by the stories told, linking the past with the present.

More so than ever before, the conditions among the Assyrians, such as the *silence* surrounding the Sayfo, have resulted in a world without metaphors and the inability to achieve a balanced or healthy imagination, in other words, the *death of language*. In Connolly's words, on account of the radical break between trauma and language, or in Pruyser's words, because of the inability to ritualize and symbolize, neither the victims of the Sayfo nor the succeeding generations have been able to find categories of thoughts or words to describe their experiences.

In the results of this study, in which narratives of 'victimization' and 'vulnerability' in relation to the Sayfo are told and passed on to younger generations, we see a construction and maintenance of individual and collective identity in a larger societal context. However, the *collected stories* used in these narratives do not need to be experienced personally; lineages of authorship and origins are blurred. The upshot is that it is as if the person telling the story had actually lived through the experience recounted, a reaction also identified in previous research on the Sayfo (Cetrez 2011b). The inter-generational silence about the Sayfo, the limited recognition of the Sayfo, as well as the present misrecognition of the cultural genocide by the world community, limit the ability to express and articulate feelings of trauma in a constructive way linguistically.

Remembering and Trauma – Loss of History and Continuity

In the Assyrian case, we see a collective form of memory work in the sense of practices related to the Sayfo. Memory and remembrance, as inner-psychological practices, are dependent on *stories collected* in the outer world, as well as on the information available. However, a strong tendency towards *silence* in the outer social world means that the processes of remembrance are limited. The practice of remembering is taking place in a specific contemporary time and place, and in this study the context is that of exodus, in which Assyrian-Iraqis and Assyrian-Syrians in particular and Assyrians in general constitute a minority group. The Swedish context is also one of a politically open society, in which they can articulate their rights for recognition, a situation helpful to the healing process of remembrance. However, in the Turkish context, the discussion of the Sayfo is more limited and the genocide itself not recognized. As an example, early in the Syrian war a specific camp was built for Christians and Yazidis in Midyat, South East Turkey. However, during my own visit to the camp in 2013 only one family had taken refuge there. Others preferred to live in the surrounding villages, justifying this by saying they could not trust the Turkish government. At the same time as they felt gratitude towards the Turkish society, they also felt ambivalence and distance due to the historical experiences and stories told by their grandparents. Consequently, the remembering of the Sayfo becomes the cultural fabric of significant stories and events, to borrow terms used by other researchers (Azarian-Ceccato 2010). By remembering the Sayfo and through the different practices related to this, Assyrians as individuals and as a collective are simultaneously conducting cultural work, by producing documentaries, writing books, creating music and arts and so on. But, by engaging with their parents' traumatic past, the act of remembrance among Assyrians is also a sign of loss of history and continuity attributable to genocide, which, as described by some of the participants in this study, has left them with only a limited knowledge of their own collective roots. The interpretation among individuals in this study, of being subjected to a horrendous event and experiencing a threat to the existence of individual and cultural identity, points to what Lazar, Litvak-Hirsch and Chaitin (2008) call *cultural trauma*.

A Culture of Binary Oppositions

On the basis of this empirical analysis of the Sayfo and its consequences, is it possible to say something about Assyrian culture in general? For a

behavioural science approach to culture, I propose the following broad
definition:

> Cultures consist of how people from a specific frame of reference perceive,
> interpret and classify visible artefacts (e.g., food, clothes, architecture, envi-
> ronment), visible behaviour (rules, code systems for language, social roles,
> rituals), fundamental attitudes, values and beliefs (evolving around family
> relations, relations to friends, to society, to the transcendent), on different
> dimensions (psychological, physical/biological, social, ecological and existen-
> tial) and on a scale from joyful to painful, good–evil, desirable–undesirable,
> acceptable–unacceptable. The cultural content reflects generativity and con-
> tinuity, as this is passed on from one generation to another, and dynamism,
> as it changes, mixes with other cultures, and is adaptable to innovative
> solutions.[5]

From the empirical material on the Sayfo, we can discern a pattern
emerging, namely a culture positioned between the poles of binary
oppositions; strongly dualistic in interpreting reality and one's position within this reality. It is a dualism of *aḥna* (us) and *hënne* (them),
the former being *aḥna a mšiḥoye* (us Christians) and *u camaydan*
(our people), who are vulnerable, the victims of history who have been
unjustly treated. The latter are the Muslims, the Arabs, the Kurds or
the Turks, who are the oppressors. Whereas the former is connoted with
good and positive; the latter is connoted with bad and negative. Such a
culture draws strong boundaries in social relations, accepting certain
relations but not others; a strong boundary between intimacy within
the in-group and distance from the out-group, as well as trust shown
towards the in-group and distrust towards the out-group. Subsequently,
such other cultural work as images and imagining, as well as narratives, memory and remembrance, follows a similar dualistic pattern of
good and evil, desirable and undesirable, acceptable and unacceptable.
History has been harsh towards the Assyrians, and for survival purposes,
it is not difficult to understand the development of a culture with strong
stereotypes about the out-group and strong prototypes of the in-group,
at times exaggerating the differences from the out-group while mini-
mizing the differences within the in-group. All human practice can be
classified into binary oppositions of inner and outer processes, and they
are dynamic in nature. Although they might be static for a period, for
the purpose of survival, when a culture is too strongly based on similar
binary oppositions it loses its ability to change, to be creative, to adapt
and to be innovative.

Discussion

Just as revealed in the studies by Jacobs (2011) and Azarian-Ceccato (2010), the present study also shows that storytelling and inter-generational transmission of narratives have both played a role in causing the situation of Assyrian individuals today, especially in their relationships with other people. Furthermore, individuals recount the genocide narrative with little linguistic differentiation between the past and the present. As in the case of the study of the Armenians, the informants in our study rework, reshape and interpret narratives of the past from their own context at hand. Their interest in increased knowledge and teaching about the Sayfo is comparable to the findings of Chaitin (2002) about third-generation Holocaust survivors.

Cultural trauma, as described by Lazar, Litvak-Hirsch and Chaitin (2008), is also apparent among Assyrians in their attitude to the Sayfo, including such characteristic features as being subjected to a horrendous event and leaving an indelible mark upon group consciousness, but the memory of the Sayfo is most clearly represented culturally and publicly as obliterating, damaging and as a threat to the existence of individual and cultural identity. Silencing the Sayfo past has also been found in previous research, among third-generation Holocaust survivors (Lazar, Litvak-Hirsch and Chaitin 2008; Connolly 2011). Distrust of non-family members or others is another topic that crops up, which is also demonstrated among Holocaust survivors for three generations (Chaitin 2002).

Fear is a strong reaction found among the participants in this study, as is also seen among the fourth-generation Armenian survivors (Karenian et al. 2010) and third-generation Holocaust survivors (Lazar, Litvak-Hirsch and Chaitin 2008). The results of this study indicate that fear is one of the hindrances to attachment with people in the forming of social relations, which can be compared to Nadler and Ben-Shushan's results (1989). The fear of annihilation as a real threat found in this study is comparable with the results among third-generation Holocaust survivors (Lazar, Litvak-Hirsch and Chaitin 2008). The perception of some groups as a potential threat to their own survival is also comparable to the study by Lazar, Litvak-Hirsch and Chaitin (2008). Both fear and distrust are common consequences among genocide and mass trauma survivors, as shown in a study among Holocaust and Cambodian survivors in Australia (Teshuva 2010).

It is very important to highlight that the Sayfo and the generational reactions need to be understood in relation to the relevant political

and societal conditions and developments in those countries in which
Assyrians have been living, including Turkey, Iraq and Syria. These
conditions differ from those of the Israelis and Armenians, on which
much research has been conducted, not least because after the Sayfo
Assyrians have had to continue to live as a stateless minority.

Recommendations and Suggestions for Future Research

As this study has demonstrated, the Sayfo still affects the lives of many
Assyrians. But a general psychological approach is not enough. It is
also crucial to approach the issue from the perspective of *liberation psychology*, which is grounded in *liberation theology* influenced by Freire's
ideas of *conscientization*, that is, a change in consciousness (Duran,
Firehammer and Gonzalez 2008). The aim of this process is that the
entire community that is affected by systematic forms of oppression
and injustice can begin to liberate itself and, as a result, to liberate the
oppressor (ibid.). Consequently, instead of seeing itself as a victim of
trauma and genocide, the community needs to find a balance in its relationship with the trauma. As the individual and the community establish a relationship with the trauma, instead of remaining a trauma, a
new narrative emerges, which is liberating (ibid.). Although the empirical material in this study has not dealt with issues of reconciliation or
other ways of dealing with the trauma of the Sayfo, the research review
provides information that is useful to communities to which the Sayfo is
relevant. Reconciliation needs to be both inwards within the community
(see more in Cetrez 2012), between the different political organizations,
and outwards, towards the Turkish, Kurdish, Syrian and Iraqi societies.
The focus in reconciliation needs to be on individual, community and
national levels simultaneously (see more in Geneviéve 2010; Van Noort
2003). A critical cultural evaluation of images, enmity and stereotypes
needs to be conducted on both individual and community levels. Future
studies need to depict pathways towards liberation from the negative
psychological consequences of the Sayfo and to contribute to healing the
wounds passed on from one Assyrian generation to another.

The psychological approach to the Sayfo is very new and a great deal
of research remains to be done. One possible focus in such research is
to examine primary and secondary sources, including family processes
and structures over generations and time, for example through theories
of *life-course perspective*. Another approach can be through *partial relevance*, studying the stages that cover the elaboration among the younger
generations. *Socialization processes* are also useful to understand how

younger generations are influenced by family values linked to the Sayfo. Further research can focus on the inter-generational transmission of trauma and personality development among the grandchildren of survivors, either through a *psycho-analytical viewpoint, social learning and family system theories, object-relation theory, self-in-relation perspective* or *ritual theories*. Other research topics can focus on well-being and coping, behavioural health concerns and problems, reconciliation, trust and enmity, the contribution of literature, poetry, art and film to memory, and converts and religious identity.

In conclusion, those trips with my grandfather, to which I referred at the beginning of this chapter, were perhaps the happiest moments of my childhood. Today, having read books and accumulated additional information about the Sayfo, as well as having practised new ways to ritualize the past, I view my grandfather's stories in a new light and with a different effect. I understand now that they were not made up, nor were they innocent stories to tickle a child's fantasies, but were part of a collective remembrance of historical happenings during the Sayfo, with a concern on the part of my grandfather to guide, nurture and establish an act of care towards the next generation. Today, they have given me the inspiration to immerse myself in this difficult topic of genocide, trauma and psychological effects among Assyrians, a community with which I have a personal connection.

Önver A. Cetrez is a senior lecturer at Uppsala University and during 2014–16 was Deputy Director of the Swedish Research Institute Istanbul. He has led several research projects on Assyrian migration and refugee research projects in Sweden and Turkey. His published works include: 'The Next Generation Assyrians in Sweden: Religiosity as a Functioning System of Meaning within the Process of Acculturation', *Mental Health, Religion & Culture* (2011) and, as co-editor, *The Assyrian Heritage – Continuity in Rituals, Symbols, and Language* (Uppsala University Press, 2012).

Notes

I am grateful to all those interviewed for sharing their personal life stories. Also to Jan Bet-Şawoce for translating some of the keywords into Modern West Assyrian, and to the peer-reviewers for their valuable comments. The Assyrian-Iraqi study was part of the project 'Gilgamesh – Mental health, meaning-seeking, and integration processes among Iraqi immigrants in Sweden', financed by the Swedish Research Council and conducted during 2010–13. The Assyrian-Syrian study was part of the project 'Religion as support or burden – Syrian Christian refugees in Turkey, their overall health and resilience', financed by a national grant awarded to the multidisciplinary research programme, Impact of Religion: Challenges for Society, Law and Democracy, established as a Centre of Excellence at Uppsala University and funded by the Swedish Research Council 2008–2018. Önver Cetrez is a member of this Centre of Excellence, within the theme Well-Being and Health.

1. The study was conducted among Assyrians in several cities in Sweden, and the respondents were asked if the Sayfo should be recognized as genocide and if they had any relatives killed during the Sayfo.
2. The first number indicates the specific interview person, followed by the row in the transcribed document.
3. *Halal* in Arabic connotes a practice whose performance is ritually clean.
4. Romans in Assyrian cultural narratives refer to Byzantines; that is, Eastern Rome.
5. The definition has been developed with inspiration from Rudmin (2009), Marsella (2005), Erikson (1982) and Ruesch et al. (1948).

Bibliography

American Psychiatric Association. 1994. *Diagnostic and Statistical Manual of Mental Disorders*, 4th ed. Washington, DC: American Psychiatric Association.

Azarian-Ceccato, N. 2010. 'Reverberations of the Armenian Genocide Narrative's Intergenerational Transmission and the Task of not Forgetting', *Narrative Inquiry* 20(1): 106–23.

Bell, C. 1992. *Ritual Theory, Ritual Practice*. Oxford: Oxford University Press.

Bourguignon, E. 2005. 'Memory in an Amnesic World: Holocaust, Exile, and the Return of the Suppressed', *Anthropological Quarterly* 78 (1): 63–88.

Cetrez, Ö.A. 2011a. 'The Next Generation Assyrians in Sweden: Religiosity as a Functioning System of Meaning within the Process of Acculturation', *Mental Health, Religion & Culture* 14(5): 473–87.

——— 2011b. 'Assyrian View of Turkey from the Perspective of Immigration: The Construction of the Other', Keynote speech, *European Society for Intercultural Theology and Interreligious Studies Conference on the Study of Religions in a Changing Europe: Integrity. Translation and Transformation*. Istanbul, 26–29 April.

——— 2012. 'Assyrian Identification as a Body of Power Politics: A Practice-Oriented Analysis', in Ö.A. Cetrez, S.G. Donabed and A. Makko (eds), *The Assyrian Heritage: Threads of Continuity and Influence*. Uppsala: Uppsala University Library, pp. 221–42.

Chaitin, J. 2002. 'Issues and Interpersonal Values among Three Generations in Families of Holocaust Survivors', *Journal of Social and Personal Relationships* 19(3): 379–402.

Connolly, A. 2011. 'Healing the Wounds of Our Fathers: Intergenerational Trauma, Memory, Symbolization and Narrative', *Journal of Analytical Psychology* 56: 607–26.

Deniz, F. 1999. *En minoritets odyssé: upprätthållande och transformation av etnisk identitet i förhållande till moderniseringsprocesser: det assyriska exemplet*. Uppsala: Uppsala University.

Donabed, S.G., and S. Makko. 2012. 'Between Denial and Existence: Situating Assyrians within the Discourse on Cultural Genocide', in Ö.A. Cetrez, S.G. Donabed and A. Makko (eds), *The Assyrian Heritage: Threads of Continuity and Influence*. Uppsala: Uppsala University Library, pp. 281–95.

Duran, E., J. Firehammer and J. Gonzalez. 2008. 'Liberation Psychology as the Path Towards Healing Cultural Soul Wounds', *Journal of Counselling & Development* 86 (Summer): 288–96.

Erikson, E.H. 1982. *The Life Cycle Completed*. New York: W.W. Norton.

Foner, N., and R. Alba. 2010. 'Immigration and the Legacies of the Past: The Impact of Slavery and the Holocaust on Contemporary Immigrants in the United States and Western Europe', *Comparative Studies in Society and History* 52(4): 798–819.

Gaunt, D. 2006. *Massacres, Resistance, Protectors: Muslim–Christian Relations in Eastern Anatolia during World War I*. Piscataway, NJ: Gorgias.

Geneviéve, P. 2010. 'Reconciliation and Justice after Genocide: A Theoretical Exploration', *Genocide Studies and Prevention* 5(3) (December): 277–92.

Hassan, G., L.J. Kirmayer, A. Mekki-Berrada, C. Quosh, R. el Chammay, J.B. Deville-Stoetzel, A. Youssef, H. Jefee-Bahloul, A. Barkeel-Oteo, A. Coutts, S. Song, and P. Ventevogel. 2015. *Culture, Context and the Mental Health and Psychosocial Wellbeing of Syrians: A Review for Mental Health and Psychosocial Support Staff Working with Syrians Affected by Armed Conflict*. Geneva: UNHCR, 2015.

Jacobs, J. 2011. 'The Cross-Generational Transmission of Trauma: Ritual and Emotion among Survivors of the Holocaust', *Journal of Contemporary Ethnography* 40(3): 342–61.

Jones, J.W. 2008. *Blood that Cries out from the Earth: The Psychology of Religious Terrorism*. New York: Oxford University Press.

Karenian, H., M. Livaditis, S. Karenian, K. Zafiriadis, V. Bochtsou, and K. Xenitidis. 2010. 'Collective Trauma Transmission and Traumatic Reactions among Descendants of Armenian Refugees', *International Journal of Social Psychiatry* 57: 327–37.

Kidron, C.A. 2012. 'Breaching the Wall of Traumatic Silence: Holocaust Survivor and Descendant Person-Object Relations and the Material Transmission of the Genocidal Past', *Journal of Material Culture* 17: 3–21. Kijak, M. and S. Funtowicz. 1982. 'The syndrome of the survivor of extreme situations: definitions, difficulties, hypotheses', *International Review of Psychoanalysis*, 9: 25–33.

Lazar, A., T. Litvak-Hirsch and J. Chaitin. 2008. 'Between Culture and Family: Jewish-Israeli Young Adults' Relation to the Holocaust as a Cultural Trauma', *Traumatology* 14(4): 93–102.

Marsella, A.J. 2005. 'Culture and Conflict: Understanding, Negotiating and Reconciling, Conflicting Constructions of Reality', *International Journal of Intercultural Research* 29: 651–73.

Nadler, A., and D. Ben-Shushan. 1989. 'Forty Years Later: Long-Term Consequences of Massive Traumatisation as Manifested by Holocaust Survivors from the City and the Kibbutz', *Journal of Consulting and Clinical Psychology* 57(2): 287–93.

Pruyser, P.W. 1983. *The Play of the Imagination: Towards a Psychoanalysis of Culture*. New York: International Universities Press.

Psychologists for Social Responsibility. 1989. *Enemy Images: A Resource Manual on Reducing Enmity*. Retrieved 2 August 2010 from http://www.psysr.org/about/pubs_resources.

Rudmin, F. 2009. 'Constructs, Measurements and Models of Acculturation and Acculturative Stress', *International Journal of Intercultural Relations* 33 (2009): 106–23.

Ruesch, J., A. Jacobsen, and M. B. Loeb. 1948. 'Acculturation and Illness', *Psychological Monographs*, 62(5): 1–40.

Stein, A. 2009. 'Trauma and Origins: Post-Holocaust Genealogists and the Work of Memory', *Qualitative Sociology* 32(3): 293–309.

Sternberg, M., and M. Rosenbloom. 2000. '"Lost Childhood" – Lessons from the Holocaust: Implications for Adult Adjustment', *Child and Adolescent Social Work Journal* 17(1) (February): 5–17.

Teshuva, K. 2010. *Caring for Older Survivors of Genocide and Mass Trauma*. Melbourne: Australian Institute for Primary Care & Ageing, La Trobe University.

Travis, H. 2010. *Genocide in the Middle East: The Ottoman Empire, Iraq, and Sudan*. Durham, NC: Carolina Academic Press.

Urlic, I. 2004. 'Trauma and Reparation, Mourning and Forgiveness: The Healing Potential of the Group', *Group Analysis* 37(4): 453–71.

Van IJzendoorn, M.H., J.M. Bakermans-Kranenburg and A. Sagi-Schwartz. 2003. 'Are Children of Holocaust Survivors Less Well-Adapted? A Meta-Analytic Investigation of Secondary Traumatisation', *Journal of Traumatic Stress* 16(5): 459–69.

Van Noort, M. 2003. 'Revenge and Forgiveness in Group Psychotherapy', *Group Analysis* 36(4): 477–89.

CHAPTER 10

SAYFO AND DENIALISM

A NEW FIELD OF ACTIVITY FOR AGENTS OF THE TURKISH REPUBLIC

Racho Donef

In 2007 I was in London as a guest of the Assyrian Firodil Institute to launch Ahmet Refik's *Two Committees, Two Massacres (Iki Komite Iki Kitâl 1998)*, which I translated (originally published in 1919 in the Ottoman script). I was also to give a talk on the Assyrian and Armenian genocide. Turkish consulate officials and their associates also attended this seminar. Their aim was clear from the outset: they were there to make a show of strength and disrupt the lecture. While I was talking, a member of this group asked the following question: 'You allege that genocide was committed against the Armenians and Assyrians in the east. So, why did no such incidents take place in Western Turkey? How is this possible? Can you explain?'

I thought this to be a strange question. The person posing the question was basically saying there was a war going on in the east, which did not affect anyone in Western Anatolia. I said, 'What do you mean? In the Aegean region, the Special Organization (*Teşkilatı Mahsusa*) gangs attacked Greeks, massacred many people and forced others to emigrate'. 'Do you have sources for this information?' he asked. I said, 'There are plenty of sources' and continued:

There are reports of the Danish Consul in Turkey on this topic. I uploaded them to the Internet. These documents of the Danish Consulate are not the only ones; other reports from the Swedish consulate also depict the same picture. Those documents also show forced deportations of Greek citizens. One report by the Swedish Consulate, dated July 21, 1915 states that those subjected to persecution were not just the Armenians; Greeks of Turkish citizenship were subject to the same persecution. About 60,000 Greeks, mostly women, children and elderly men, were forced to leave their homes in the Marmara Sea coast villages. (Donef 2009: 253)

In reality, what I thought to be a strange question at the time, I should have regarded as a normal occurrence. Turkish citizens are deceived by the often repeated mantra of minorities living in 'comfort and security' and being told that anyone who says to the contrary is either a traitor, an agent of a foreign government, ignorant, unqualified, one-sided or ideologically or politically biased. Those who came to the seminar did not do so to listen to the speaker or engage in a dialogue. Their objective was to protest and ask prepared questions. The group sent the following information to a number of online forums and to the Islamist daily in Turkey, *Zaman*:

Donef, who in his speech talked about the collapse of the Ottoman Empire in the early 1900s, and the Union and Progress Society, described this society as responsible for massacres. Donef said that the Union and Progress Society membership consisted of Young Turks and alleged that it had the mentality of wanting to create a community consisting of Turks only, rather than an ethnically diverse society.

Donef alleged that Circassian Ahmet who lived in the Eastern Anatolia region of Turkey during the First World War, killed two Armenian deputies and many Armenians and read to the participants part of Refik's book describing the incident. After his talk, in the question and answer section, he was asked many questions by the Turkish scholars participating in the seminar, and Donef found himself in a difficult situation. When he was asked if he was a historian, Donef said that he had only completed a doctorate and that he had translated Ahmet Refik's book into English. He was also angry that a Turkish citizen took a picture of him. When a Turkish scholar asked him why Armenians were not massacred in the west and why it is alleged that Armenians were only massacred in the east, Donef alleged that Greeks were massacred in Western Turkey. When a Turkish citizen asked a question using the phrase 'the so-called Armenian genocide', the tension increased. In the meantime, it has been observed that Dr Donef did not know the issue very well. (*Zaman*, 15 January 2007)[1]

The obsession with the official history thesis (*Türk Tarih Tezi*) and the continuation of producing official history in Turkey goes hand in hand with denialism. Official history is not just the history produced through the efforts of the state. Its scope is not restricted to the publications supported, printed and distributed by the Ministry of Education, the Ministry of Culture, the Turkish Historical Society (*Türk Tarih Kurumu*) and so on. History manufactured by scholars, journalists, researchers and writers, designed within the framework of the official ideology, is also part and parcel of 'invented history' (Başkaya 2006: 8). In the example discussed above, a seminar was held that was contrary to the official views. Consequently, it needed to be undermined, and a group of people were sent to perform the task. This is because in those circles there is no tolerance of alternative opinions and thoughts. Rather than examine the evidence and dispute it scientifically, it is thought best to attack and vilify the person delivering the message. Unfortunately, this is the only path they are willing to take.

One of the foundation myths of the official thesis that the Assyrians, and other ethnic groups for that matter, were living in peace and harmony, is a myth created very early in the history of the Republic. At the Lausanne Conference, the head of the Turkish delegation and later Prime Minister and President of the Republic İsmet [İnönü] read the following statement in which the seeds of denialism were already sown:

> The Christians in the subject areas are mainly Nestorians, Assyrians and Chaldeans. The Nestorians, during the occupation of Van by the Tsarist Russian army, acted with such treachery and cruelty against their Muslim compatriots with whom they lived in peace, that during the Russian retreat they felt obligated to go with them. As to the Chaldeans and especially the Assyrians in the province of Diyarbakır, they were never influenced by external provocations, they lived in full harmony with their Turkish compatriots. (Kürt Halk Kültür Derneği 1981: 18–19)

In contrast to the current policy of denialism, before the Republic was formed there was some soul-searching about what had transpired during the preceding war. The aforementioned testimony by Ahmet Refik [Altınay], *Two Committees, Two Massacres*, is but an example. After the end of the war, the massacres perpetrated against Christians were not the taboo subject they were to become later. A government functionary such as Ahmet Refik published an account of what he witnessed, and expressed his disgust with the party of the Young Turks, Ittihat.[2] In the trials that were conducted in Istanbul for war crimes, the perpetrators were identified and found guilty, albeit in absentia (Kocahanoğlu 1998). An article that used disparaging expressions about Reşit Bey was published in the 7 November 1918 edition of the newspaper *Hadisat*. The *Vali* (governor) of Diyarbakır Reşit, who was

responsible for masterminding massacres against the Christian population in the province, was arrested for crimes committed during the war
and a *Hadisat* correspondent conducted an interview with him. The
correspondent did not make any effort to conceal his disgust with the
former *Vali* and his actions:

> ... we were in the presence of a degenerate, remains of Envers, who was once
> in authority in Diyarbekir, Mosul and Ankara, that is Reşit Bey. The afore-
> said responded begrudgingly to all of our questions, with a smile of contempt,
> as though his power and genius was not understood, held captive by his high
> seclusion of his soul, habitually indifferent to the miserable and ungrateful
> people and derision of the press, with a regal attitude of certainty about the
> just and categorical judgement of justice, civilization and history. At the same
> time he spoke with an expression peculiar to great people like Napoleon,
> ironic and swift, scattering ridicule and derision against newspapers. Only,
> from time to time, his glances to Tevfik Hâdi Bey, excitedly and secretly,
> asking for help made us doubt Reşit Bey's lofty infallibility. Whatever the
> consequences, we asked him:
> – It is said that you killed more than 50,000 men, women, children, inno-
> cent people and among them three *kaymakams* [governors of districts] and
> usurped from them 300 thousand lira of gold and jewellery of equal value.
> How much exaggeration is there in these [allegations]?
> – They are all lies, all lies ...
> – Apparently you retained a murderer, a major by the name of Rüştü
> Bey, in your retinue as gendarme commander and you employed about 30
> Circassians from Rüştü Bey's own tribe and killed these poor people.
> – I don't know.
> – It is said that you ordered to kill the *kaymakam* of Lice and a distin-
> guished writer known in literary and publishing circles, Giridî Ahmed Nesimi
> Bey and deputy *kaymakam* of Beşiri, a Baghdad notable and a graduate of the
> Civil Administration School, Suveydizâde Sabit Bey, for not following your
> orders for massacre. Your defence?
> – All wrong accusations. In any case, aren't newspapers a source of slander
> and anarchy?
> – They say that as soon your predecessor, the incumbent Department of
> Interior Undersecretary Hamid Bey, left because of your immorality when
> you were police chief in Diyarbekir, you were called up from Mersin and
> restored to the position of police chief and without any distinction of religion
> or sect you destroyed the poor people. Weren't these people who worked on
> these matters, your gendarmes?
> – I have no information about these things.
> ...

Because of the action of people such as the detestable Reşit Bey, whom
no religion, sect or profession will claim [as its own], the world civilization
sees us as 'the murderers of the oppressed' and this stain will be present
from our ancestors' grave to the cradle of our children. Our correspondent
thought that Reşit Bey should account for besmirching not only the name of

the public law officials but the whole nation and dared to continue to ask his questions. (Bilgi 1997: 80–81)

This critical attitude regarding the massacres perpetrated during the war, and even the acceptance of collective responsibility, can be contrasted with the attitude adopted after the formation of the Republic. The rewriting of Turkish history along the desired lines started in the early years of the Republic. In a book published in 1930, *Outline of Turkish History*, the anonymous author poses a rhetorical question, 'Why is this book written?', and offers the following response:

> Up to now, in most of the history books published in our country and in the French history books given as a source in those books, the role of the Turks in world history is understated, whether consciously or not. Such false information about the ancestors of the Turks has been harmful in the development of self-identity of the Turks. (Anon. 1930: 25)[3]

In short, effort was made to 'correct' what was regarded to be 'harmful'. The state, or rather the new regime, redesigned, spread and imposed a new version of any facts and historical events they did not agree with. According to Fikret Başkaya (2006: 7), 'official history is a made-to-order version of history founded on lying, tampering, denial ... censorship and self-censorship'.

Until the Armenian genocide emerged as a thorn for the Turkish Republic, the massacres of Christians were something to be proud of and boastful about. In a brochure published by the then governing Turkish Republican Party's Mardin People's House (CHP Mardin Halkevi), entitled *Mardin: Before and After the Republic*, the writer boasted:

> The greatest, the most happy and dignified joy the Turkish Mardin felt in her ancient history, going back for centuries and during her existence, happened in 1915. For the people of Mardin, this joy, which was more valuable, more precious than life itself, happened during the autumn months of that year.
> So, Mardin reached another joyful occasion in 1915, which our other cities and towns had not managed to, and its unkempt and devastated face was enlightened with the light it received from the Source of [Divine] Light and found itself progressing with great speed on the path of progress and development. (CHP Mardin Halkevi 1938: 24–5)

These thinly veiled references to massacres of Assyrians were promoted as a source of pride. Much like the attitude displayed by the Republican People's Party, Committee of Union and Progress, the party of the Young Turks, was very open about its plans to exterminate the Christian minorities. In 1912, in Giresun, the May issue of a local newspaper published by the Committee of Union and Progress heralded that '[n]ow it is not the time for politics, it is time for the *sword!*' (Fotiadis 1993: 201). The US ambassador in Constantinople between the years 1913 and 1916, Henry Morgenthau, in his *Secrets of the Bosphorus*, revealed that the Constantinople Police Director Bedri Bey said to one of Morgenthau's secretaries that 'the Turks exiled the Greeks with an outstanding success. The Empire needs to apply the same method' (Donef 2009: 258).

After the issue of the Armenian genocide came to the fore and could no longer be suppressed, the official policy of denialism was consti- tuted. Academics were trained to deny that such an event took place; the Turkish Historical Society focused on publishing books that pur- portedly showed that the Turks themselves were victims of aggression by the Armenians. To that an army of journalists could be added who, being uninformed about the events in question, repeated the official mantras. The journalists embraced this policy and promoted it, without any special knowledge of the events of the First World War. In the next decades, the state was prepared to refute Armenian accusations.

In short, the denial of the Armenian genocide was a well-established framework in Turkey, relying as it did on the Turkish Historical Society and academics producing material to counteract the Armenian claims. When the issue of the Assyrian genocide emerged, the establishment was caught unawares. Other than Salâhi Sonyel, there were few academics with sufficient knowledge of Assyrian history to refute the claims of genocide. Journalists from such nationalist and denialist newspapers as *Hürriyet* or *Türkiye* had no idea of the complexity of the issues involved, or even understood the history of the Assyrian communities during the war – although this did not stop them from writing about it.

The impetus for the Assyrian genocide claims came from abroad, from the diaspora and certain scholars, but the catalyst was Reverend Father Yusuf Akbulut's statements regarding the Sayfo in 2000. Yusuf Akbulut, a Syriac Orthodox priest serving in Diyarbakır, in Turkey's south-east, was charged with inciting hatred for his declaration that the Assyrians were also subjected to genocide in 1915: 'At that time it was not only the Armenians but also the Assyrians [*Süryani*] who were massacred on the grounds that they were Christians' (Yavuz, 4 October 2000). Already having to counteract Armenian and Hellenic genocide claims, the Turkish authorities now found themselves in a situation where they had to negate Assyrian genocide claims as well.

During September and October 2000, the United States Senate was also discussing a resolution on the genocide, which eventually did not pass. It was not clear at the time whether the resolution would be adopted. Nevertheless, Turkish newspapers felt obliged to print another volume of articles attacking Armenians and any other ethnic group or institution viewed as suspicious. One such paper, *Olay*, went to extract a statement from the Assyrian priest Yusuf Akbulut. It was suspicious that they chose to obtain a statement from a priest with a very small congregation in Diyarbakır, when they could have spoken to religious leaders in Tur Abdin or Istanbul. It is also likely that they went to extract the kind of statement the Armenian patriarchate issued from time to time, in order to appease Turkish authorities. For example, on the occasion of the resolution in the French Senate, the Armenian patriarch, who, it should be pointed out, had no choice in the matter, issued a statement to placate the authorities and avoided incurring the wrath of the press.

The priest in question, however, Reverend Father Akbulut, did not perform the assigned role and instead made a statement confirming that the genocide took place and that Assyrians were massacred, as well as Armenians. The following day, two journalists from the populist tabloid *Hürriyet*, from Istanbul, went to confirm Father Akbulut's statement. Akbulut was chatting (with journalists) off the record. Clearly, he did not think he was going to be reported. Nonetheless, he did not deny that he made the statement. Furthermore, the journalists had secretly recorded the interview on video.

The next day, the vilification campaign against the priest started in earnest. *Hürriyet* called him a 'traitor' (*hain*). This is a charge worth analysing. What is the act of treason that Akbulut had actually committed? Who did he betray by these statements? He simply stated what he believed to be the truth. It is certain that what *Hürriyet* means by 'traitor' is 'a traitor to the Turkish nation or state'. However, Father Akbulut is not a Turk, although a Turkish citizen. He is a Syriac Orthodox, an Assyrian; a member of a dwindling minority. One could argue that were he to deny that the genocide took place, he would have been a traitor to his own nation. Under the circumstances, nobody would have blamed him had he simply issued a denial of the genocide for fear of his own and his family's safety.

The indictment summarized Father Akbulut's statement:

> At that time it was not only the Armenians but also the Syrians who were massacred, on the grounds that they were Christians. Christians were massacred in groups, the Kurds were used in the massacres ... The homeland of the Süryani is Mesopotamia. Whereas the Armenians' is Muş, Erzurum, Van, Erzincan and Sıvas. Armenians lived in these lands. Why is it that there were so many Armenians then and now there are not any? In our area, it is called the 'kafle time'.[4] What does kafle mean? It means destruction *en masse*. All

people living in the region know the truth. ... I look at Diyarbakır, many people say my grandmother is Armenian or Süryani. From this we understand that at that period our men have been massacred but our young girls were not touched. (Donef 2001a)

The underlying message in the Turkish press is that everyone who lives in Turkey owes gratitude to the Turkish government, state and nation. If they do not show this gratitude in some way, they will be considered traitors. Three journalists showing a complete lack of consideration for any ethical standards secretly recorded Akbulut, furnished the tape as evidence to the court and appeared as witnesses for the prosecution. They acted as agents of the state rather than independent observers of events, facts or truths. In effect, they fabricated the event in order to report it.

While the case was in progress, a report on the Assyrians was presented to the National Security Council (Milli Güvenlik Kurulu, MGK). The compilation of 'the Assyrian report', a report on the activities of the Assyrian diaspora, was almost certainly precipitated by the publicity the Akbulut case attracted. It may have also partly accounted for the circular issued by the then Turkish Prime Minister Bülent Ecevit on Assyrians, to facilitate their return to Turkey from the diaspora (see Appendix A). The Turkish government must have realized that the traditional methods of denialism may no longer be sufficient to neutralize claims of Assyrian genocide.

Calls for recognition of the Sayfo have obviously raised alarm bells in the higher ranks of the Turkish political, academic and military establishment. The Assyrian genocide has emerged as yet another historical reality swept under the proverbial carpet. At the same time, the Assyrian diaspora has been able to organize, set up institutions, community organizations, political parties to lobby on their behalf and express their criticism of governments in the Middle East whose policies and practices coerced them into exile. As the diaspora is becoming more articulate, more efficient and more effective, it is able to pressure governments in the West to sensitize them to this historical reality; Turkey has found itself in yet another quandary.

The activities of the Assyrian diaspora worried the authorities to such an extent that, in 2001, Turkey's National Security Council commissioned the aforementioned report on the Assyrians. Visibly, the report was commissioned because Turkey felt under a metaphorical siege. The National Security Council ordered the report to get a clear picture of in which organizations (partly named), who (also partly named) and where the Assyrians were active. An article by journalist Sabahattin

Onkibar appeared on 6 March 2001 in the fundamentalist *Türkiye* newspaper under the title, 'MGK'ya Süryani Raporu' (Assyrian Report to the National State Security Council). The State Security Council was a mechanism through which the military used to keep an eye on politicians (it has since been reformed).

Reportedly, the report was fourteen pages long. Only a short section of it was published, however. A cursory glance at the report would suggest that the Turkish National Intelligence Organization (MİT) monitored Assyrian and other websites that publish information about Assyrians (Donef 2001b).

Another example of attacks on opinions contrary to the official thesis is exemplified by journalist Özdemir İnce, who in a series named 'Lies in Syriac' in 2003 named anyone not agreeing with the official thesis a 'mercenary', i.e., a paid soldier (İnce 2003). This series of articles was written for the purpose of attacking Assyrians who were seeking recognition of the Assyrian genocide.

In this extraordinary series of twenty articles, İnce accused perished Assyrians and Armenians of treason. According to this viewpoint, it is the murdered party that is at fault, not the murderers themselves. In this series of articles, the only party that is not at fault over the events that took place in 1915 is the Turkish nation and the *Ittihat ve Terakki* government. Everyone else is guilty of something or other – the missionaries, the Armenians, the Assyrians, the Greeks, the Protestant Church, the Hamidiye regiments (i.e. Kurds), the French, the English and the Russians (Donef 2003).

The methods of the practitioners of the official thesis are so flexible and adept that they can integrate any document or study into this system. For example, Osman Selim Kocahanoğlu, who transliterated Ahmed Refik's *Two Committees, Two Massacres* from the Ottoman Turkish version to the Latin script, claimed 'there were no Armenian massacres or Armenian genocide' (Kocahanoğlu 1998: 17). Yet the book is directly related to the Armenian deportation and massacres. The transliterator hopes that those who read his preface will not go beyond the preamble to read the actual text, and that what will remain in the reader's mind is that the book proves there was no genocide.

Currently, two academics who are employed in the service of Sayfo denialism are Mehmet Çelik and Bülent Özdemir. Mehmet Çelik wrote a book on early Syriac Orthodox history, which, it must be said, is well researched. Yet, Mehmet Çelik, who must have knowledge of what happened during the First World War, does not hesitate to mislead. In an interview he gave to the newspaper *Zaman* (Akman 2008), he stated that the Interior Minister Talât Pasha, the governor of the east and south-east during the *tehcir* [deportation] sent seven circulars to provincial and district governors [*valis* and *kaymakams*]. In these circulars, he said: 'Oh, be very careful, not to bleed the nose of a single *Süryani*'. Therefore, the *Süryanis* were not subjected to deportation. While the Armenians were fooled by the Western imperialists and preferred adventure to the peace and tranquillity of several centuries, the *Süryanis* who lived with the Armenians in the same regions did not betray the Turks, with whom they had lived together peacefully for centuries. They did not respond to the fanciful proposals of the Russians, the French or the British.

The assertion that the Assyrians were not subjected to deportation is not a serious proposition warranting comment. Studies have been published in Turkish and anyone who works in this field would be aware of them. At the very least, one can consult publications in the Ottoman Archives, which cannot conceal the upheaval of 1915:

> It is understood that communication with departments and institutions associated with the Ministry of Justice and Sects has been taken in order to address the actual requests of the return to their homes of those *Süryanis* deported and the return of their property to them, help from the government and the special appropriation of revenue from the education aid to *Süryani* schools, the acceptance for gratis of two *Süryani* children every year as boarders for the Galatasaray Imperial School and each state school and the closure of the brothels that opened up around Istanbul.
>
> It has been communicated by the Ministry of the Interior to the provinces that by way of legal allocation of allowances the condition of the *orphans* and *widows* of those congregation members who *died* in the war is being improved, of the orphans who did not take advantage of this to be paid 750 lira as one-off [payment] from the appropriation of unforeseen expenses and if there are orphans of those deported, to be handed over to the congregation of which they are members, not to prevent those who want to change their religion and that although no communiqué or complaint about any interference on this matter has been received, [it is necessary] again to give requisite advise to relevant officers about this appeal of the patriarchate and in order to provide special assistance by the government, the provision of five thousand qurush a month from an appropriate allocation from the Ministry of Interior budget to the patriarchate has been considered and approved. (Gökbilgin 1965: 206–8, emphases added)

The most bizarre proposition is that 'not even a single Assyrian's nose bled in 1915'. Employing Goebbels' propaganda method, a lie is perpetuated until it becomes the truth; a false truth only for domestic audiences, to be sure. Admittedly, it is the interviewer that comes up with the proposition; it is not stated clearly as such by Mehmet Çelik, but the tenor of the interview encourages the reader to believe nothing happened to the Assyrians.

This outlandish assertion is then used as a source for other denialists with minimal historical knowledge or research experience. For instance, Sadettin Abaylı (2011), another denialist, quotes Mehmet Çelik as though it is now proven that nothing happened to the Assyrians. This type of simplistic message plays to domestic audiences only; the more outlandish the statement, the better. For instance, Kâzım Karabekir's (Commander of the Eastern Army during the First World War) daughter used similarly crude statements asserting that orders were given to provide Armenian convoys with doctors and milk, and she then wonders 'how can you have genocide with doctors and milk?' (*Zaman*, 9 March 2009). This rather naive assertion is, in turn, used as a source to deny the event of genocide.

It is not surprising that these assertions have not been translated into English for Turkish diplomats or academics to use abroad when they refute allegations. The audience for this type of rather simplistic message is Turks only. As Halil Berktay argued, '[o]n this issue Turkey is living in total, almost hermetic isolation from the rest of the world. The endless repetition that no such incident occurred, that this is a matter of groundless "Armenian falsification", forms a type of sweet lullaby for our public opinion. This lullaby is not putting the rest of the world to sleep, but it is putting Turkey to sleep' (Alpay 2000).

The 9th of September is celebrated in Turkey as 'the reconquest of Izmir'. In the official narrative the enemy, the Greeks, are thrown into the sea. No one survives. On the one hand, Turkey denies that genocide took place; on the other hand, school textbooks speak proudly of killing Greeks.

Is it any wonder that the Turkish audience (both at home and abroad) who grew up and became familiar with manufactured and invented history then overreacts when facing an alternative viewpoint? A case in point is the Assyrian genocide monument erected in south-west Sydney, in the suburb of Fairfield, where there is a sizable Assyrian community. The monument was vandalized: a crescent and star sign was painted on the monument and derogatory comments, not worthy of reproduction here, were written on its base. People who wish to deny that their grandparents committed a violent crime do so through violent means. The paradox is lost on them; so is the irony that the vandalism brought about further publicity for the Sayfo.

The term *sözde soykırım* ('so-called genocide') in Turkish is invariably used when referring to the Armenian genocide, and now to the Sayfo, in the Turkish press and by politicians, academics and bureaucrats, as though using the term genocide without the addition of 'so-called' would amount to an admittance on their part. The Turkish state has convinced itself that, more or less, this policy of denial is the only path to follow. This is unfortunate. Prime Minister Erdoğan apologized for the Dersim genocide perpetrated in 1939 by the Republican government (*Zaman*, 10 August 2011). This was a genocide against the heterodox Alevi Kurds residing in the province of Dersim. Perhaps Erdoğan's move signals a leap in the state policy in relation to denialism. It is hoped that Erdoğan will take the next step and break from the established norms in relation to recognition of the Sayfo, *Aghet* and *Megali Katastrofi*, though in light of recent events this seems unlikely. [5]

Racho Donef is an independent researcher. He holds a doctorate in anthropology and various qualifications, *inter alia*, in social sciences, languages and ancient history. He delivers lectures and teaches a number of courses related to the Middle East in the Workers' Educational Association. He has published a number of articles in Greek, Turkish and English related to the Assyrian genocide and minorities in Turkey. He is the author of *Assyrians Post-Nineveh: Conflict, Identity, Fragmentation and Survival: A Study of Assyrogenous Communities* (Tatavla Publishing, 2012), and *The Hakkâri Massacres: Ethnic Cleansing by Turkey 1924–25* (Tatavla Publishing, 2014).

Notes

1. All translations from foreign languages in this article were done by the author.
2. Ittihat ve Terakki Cemiyeti [Committee of Union and Progress].
3. This pseudo-historical account of Turkish history was produced by members of the Turkish History Committee (*Türk Tarihi Heyeti*). The thesis reflected the Kemalist ideology of the period.
4. The term *Qafle* from the Arabic *qāfila* (*qāfla* in Syriac and *qaflo/qafle* in Turoyo) literally means convoy, but in the context of the Sayfo it refers to the destruction during the deportation of the Assyrians (see Shabo Talay's chapter in this volume).
5. *Aghet*, Genocide in Armenian; *Megali Katastrofi*, the Great Disaster, Greek term referring to 1922 massacres of Greeks in the Pontus region and elsewhere in the Ottoman Empire.

Bibliography

Abaylı, S. 2011. 'Büyüklere masallar 2'. *Gerçek Medya*, 19 March. Retrieved from http://gercekmedya.com/yazar/buyuklere-masallar---2-123.html

Akman, N. 2008. '1915'te bir tek Süryaninin burnu bile kanamadı'. *Zaman*, 27 April. Retrieved from http:/zaman.com.tr.

Alpay, Ş. 2000. 'Serinkanlı olalım'. *Milliyet*, 20 October. Retrieved from http://www.milliyet.com.tr/2000/10/20/entel/ent.html

Anon. 1930. *Türk Tarihinin Ana Hatları*. Istanbul: Kaynak Yayınları.

Başkaya, F. 2006. 'Neden Resmi Tarih?' in F. Başkaya and S. Çetinoğlu (eds), *Resmi Tarih Tartışmaları, Volume 2*. Ankara: Maki Basın Yayın.

Bilgi, N. 1997. *Dr Mehmed Reşid Şahingiray: Hayatı ve Hatıraları*. İzmir: Akademik Kitabevi.

CHP Mardin Halkevi. 1938. *Mardin: Cumhuriyetten Önce ve Sonra. Halkevi Broşürü*. Istanbul: Resimli Ay Matbaası.

Donef, R. September 26, 2001a. 'The Assyrian Genocide and Article 312 of the Turkish Penal Code: The Case of an Assyrian Priest in Turkey'. *Atour*. Retrieved from http://www.atour.com/government/docs/20010926a.html

——— March 21, 2001b. 'Turkish National Security Council's report on the Assyrians'. *Atour*. Retrieved from http://www.atour.com/government/docs/20010321b.html

——— 2003. 'Yalanın Türkçesi veya yalancının mumu yatsıya kadar yanar', in *Nsibin*, Stockholm.

——— 2009. 'Resmi Tarih ve Rumlar', in F. Başkaya and S. Çetinoğlu (eds), *Resmi Tarih tartışmaları*, Volume 8. İstanbul: Özgür Üniversite Yayınları, pp. 253–82.

Fotiadis, K. 1993. 'Oi Ellines tou Pontou os ti Sinthiki tis Lozannis', in Charalamidis, M. (ed.), *I Poliethniki Tourkia*. Athens: Gordios, pp. 237–58.

Gökbilgin, M.T. 1965. *Millî Mücadele Başlarken: Sivas Kongresinden Büyük Millet Meclisi'nin Açılmasına*. Ankara: T.İ.B. Kültür Yayınları.

İnce, Ö. 9 May 2003. 'Süryanicenin yalancası'. *Hürriyet*.

Kocahanoğlu, O.S. 1998. *İttihat Terakki'nin Sorgulanması ve Yargılanması*. Istanbul: Temel Yayınları.

Kürt Halk Kültür Derneği. 1981. *Lozan Konferansı´nda Kürdistan Sorunu*. Uppsala.

Morgenthau, H., 1918. *Secrets of Bosphorus*, London: Hutchinson & Co.

Refik, A. 1998. *Kafkas Yollarında İki Komite iki Kitâl*. Istanbul: Temel Yayınları.

Talay, S. 2006. 'Sayfo, Firman, Qafle: Der Erste Weltkrieg aus der Sicht der Syrischen Christen', in R. Voigt (ed.), *Akten des 5. Symposiums zur Sprache, Geschichte, Theologie und Gegenwartslage der syrischen Kirchen*. Aachen: Shaker Verlag, pp. 235–49.

Yavuz, R. 'The traitor among us', *Hürriyet*, 4 October 2000. Retrieved from http://www.atour.com/news/assyria/20001127a.html

Zaman. 15 January 2007. 'Sözde soykırım iddialarına ilişkin konferansta tartışma yasandı'. Retrieved from http://www.zaman.com.tr/.

——— 9 March 2009. 'Ermeniler mezalim yaptığı için "tehcir" kararı alındı'. Retrieved from http://www.zaman.com.tr/.

——— 10 August 2011. 'PM Erdoğan Apologizes over Dersim Massacre on Behalf of Turkish State'. Retrieved from http://www.todayszaman.com/news-263658-pm-erdogan-apologizes-over-dersim-massacre-on-behalf-of-turkish-state.html

Appendix A

Press Statement by Prime Minister H.E. Bülent Ecevit Concerning Turkish Citizens of Assyrian Origin

Turkish citizens of Assyrian origin who emigrated abroad on their own will as a consequence of intense terrorist activities in their region have reportedly been facing certain difficulties in returning to their homes in Turkey.

It has also been claimed that they encountered certain restrictions in their efforts to return to their villages in exercising their real property rights and in visiting their relatives. It was also reported that they were not allowed to receive religious education and that foreigners were prevented from visiting Assyrian villages.

Certain administrative errors may have been made due to misinterpretations at local level. However, instructions have been given to the local authorities to act within the law.

Constitutional, legal and democratic rights of all Turkish citizens of Assyrian origin are under the full guarantee of the State.

Our dear citizens who have settled in other countries for various reasons can return to our country and their villages without any difficulty or restrictions. (Donef 2001a)

CHAPTER 11

TURKEY'S KEY ARGUMENTS IN DENYING THE ASSYRIAN GENOCIDE

Abdulmesih BarAbraham

It is well documented that the genocide of 1915 was a state-organized and state-sponsored campaign of destruction, aimed at eliminating from the emerging Turkish Republic the native Christian populations and wiping out evidence of their culture, which dated back more than three thousand years. This genocide is viewed as the precursor to the Jewish Holocaust in the Second World War. Turkey, until today, vehemently denies having committed this genocide.

According to Richard G. Hovanissian (1998: 201), the denial strategy for the genocide of 1915 has changed 'from one of absolute negation of intentional mass killing to that of rationalization, relativization, and trivialization'. But, he continues, all of these approaches are intended 'to create doubts and cloak disinformation by appealing to a sense of fair play and of giving a hearing to the other side of a misunderstood and misinterpreted issue'.

Under the guise of historical debate, Turkey has institutionalized the genocide denial. Hovanissian (1998: 202) says that the 'rationalizers pretend to pose a plausible, scholarly viewpoint, and a reasonable proposal', though the ultimate objective remains 'historical deception' instead of 'absolute negation'. Books of the Turkish Historical Society dealing with genocide denial are often regarded as groundbreaking in Turkey because they try to dismiss the 'claims' of Armenians (Akcam 2005: 257) – and, in recent years, the 'claims' of Assyrians as well. Such publications supposedly apply a scholarly approach using archival sources to disprove genocidal intent or impact. The argumentation outlined in the publications is, to some extent, adopted by universities in Turkey focused on the historical issues raised; it is exploited for political purposes and propaganda abroad.

Before we review two of the publications of the Turkish Historical Society on Assyrians, it would be helpful to shed some light on the society's background. The Turkish Historical Society (Türk Tarih Kurumu, TTK) was established as Türk Tarihi Tetkik Cemiyeti (Society for the Research of History) by a directive of Mustafa Kemal, Turkey's first president, on 15 April 1931. Its aims are defined by the Turkish constitution, and it has carried its current name since 1935. The society's mission is 'to research Kemalist thinking, the principles and reforms of Atatürk, Turkish culture, the Turkish history and the Turkish language by scholarly means, to make known and disseminate it as well as to distribute publications on it' (Rumpf 2004, 2016). Furthermore, it deals with various topics of Turkish, Ottoman and pre-Ottoman history of the region. For various controversial topics (e.g. Turkish-Russian history), the society established what they call international commissions of historians. One of the most important research fields of the society is the 'genocide' of the Christian population of the Ottoman Empire at the beginning of the twentieth century.

Victims of Major Power Policy?

The first book to be discussed here is written in English by Dr Salahi Sönyel (2001) under the title *The Assyrians of Turkey – Victims of Major Power Policy*. In the preface to the book, the author, whose speciality is the Armenian case, reveals in harsh language the so-called scholarly stance of the Turkish Historical Society:

> A number of Assyrians, particularly a few extremists, who have emigrated to West Europe and North America from Turkey, mainly for economic reasons, have indulged in propaganda, spreading rumours intermittently that they were compelled to leave their homeland because they were oppressed by the Turkish authorities. They also draw parallels between themselves and the Armenians of Turkey, and claim that they have shared the same fate with them.

Apparently some of these extremists are cooperating with numerous secessionist and terrorist organizations whose aim is to destabilise and dismember Turkey. They are supported and aided in this venture by some Turcophobe organizations. (Sönyel 2001: xi)

It is evident, beginning with the preface to his book, that in his zeal to discredit Assyrian claims of Turkish culpability, Sönyel resorts freely to any and all means. This includes derogatory language for those who hold a different position, attribution of ulterior motives to Turkey's critics unsupported by evidence, and facile indulgence in reciting 'history' according to a version intended to coincide with Sönyel's exculpatory thesis. Sönyel's intemperate approach to the central issue falls short of what one expects in terms of scholarship. His self-serving remarks seek to change the subject rather than to meet the challenge honestly.

About one third of Sönyel's book tries to establish the notion that Assyrians prior to the First World War lived in security and peace within the borders of the Ottoman Empire, benefiting from Ottoman Muslim toleration. Through a sequence of selective citations, Sönyel attempts to establish the claim that 'the appearance of missionaries in the Ottoman Empire, despite some of their humanitarian and other welfare activities, brought a catastrophe to the Eastern Churches, including that of the Assyrians' (2001: 25). He goes on to blame the missionaries for having created a rift between the Christians and the Ottoman government, which was 'not pleased with the activities of the missionaries, and saw them as enemies of the regime', since the missionaries, he continues, 'gave rise to dissatisfaction that did not previously exist, and urged the Christians against Ottoman laws, which they claimed were repressive' (ibid.: 26) This seems to be an after-construction invented in Kemalist times, since all missionaries in the Ottoman Empire were working with the explicit and formal permission of the sultan and they were very closely watched. If there was any suspicion at the time that they were inciting trouble, there is little evidence of this.

Focusing entirely on the Eastern Assyrians,[1] Sönyel tries to portray them as pawns of Britain and France, while also involved in intrigue with Russia. In addition, he portrays the events of 1914–18 partially as civil war between Muslim and Christian populations, and elaborates concerning the Assyrians that they were misled by false promises of independence, first by Tsarist Russia and then by Britain, into joining the war against the Ottoman Empire, and were deceived by both allies.

Sönyel does not touch on the root cause of the problems of the non-Muslims and the question of why Assyrians, after centuries of loyalty to the government, were desperately seeking such protection from the Great Powers. In fact, he mentions that Mar Shimun earlier rejected requests from the Kurdish leader Uebeydullah asking for assistance to become an independent ruler. Mar Shimun replied that 'he would not join in a rising against the government, and that, if he were to consent to do so, his people would not obey him' (2011: 71). Sönyel even contradicts himself as he cites as the reason for the Assyrians' persistent effort to seek the protection of the powers, that 'Turkish authorities (mostly Kurdish aghas and beys) did not protect them, but they demanded from them military taxes, poll tax, and other moneys ... As the Turks did not protect their person, property, and honour, from the Kurds, it was difficult for the Nestorians to pay them taxes' (Sönyel 2001: 52).[2]

Sönyel's nationalistic filter prevents him from questioning any of the motives of the Ottoman government or the Young Turks. He does not mention any of the massacres of the late nineteenth century perpetrated by the Hamidiye irregular regiments, armed and paid by the sultan, even though he dedicates a section to the reign of Sultan Abdulhamit, nor does he touch on any systematic killing during the First World War with the support of the regular Ottoman army. Instead, he portrays the Assyrians as potentially dangerous insurgents and traitors, capable of threatening the existence of the empire. His distorted scholarly view goes so far as to depict the victims as perpetrators (Sönyel 2001: 90).

As David Gaunt (2007: 30) summarized, Sönyel's key denial thesis is that, 'since the Nestorians of the Hakkari mountains declared war on the Ottoman state in May 1915, the violent ethnic cleansing of the region was justified'. In fact, Sönyel fails to provide any formal documentary evidence of the so-called 'war declaration' and he does not mention that 'in October 1914, Talaat Pasha sent a decree to the Vali of Van ordering the deportation of the Assyrians on the border' to Iran (Gaunt 2006: 128).

Through his nationalistic stance, Sönyel not only excludes any statements in those archival documents he is citing, which certainly would give a different picture of the events, but he even ignores contemporary Turkish events regarding the matter. The case of the Syriac Orthodox priest Yusuf Akbulut from Diyarbakir in Turkey is worth highlighting in order to demonstrate how free speech, for instance, was respected in Turkey at the beginning of the twenty-first century, just as Sönyel was writing his denialist thesis. In October 2000, the priest Yusuf Akbulut was charged with inciting hatred for his privately made statement to a journalist of the nationalistic newspaper *Hürriyet* (2000), that 'not only Armenians, but Assyrians too' were subjected to genocide in 1915. The next day the newspaper published an article titled 'The Traitor Among Us'. The priest was arrested and after various trials (pursuant to the infamous Article 312 of the Turkish Penal Code), in which Akbulut never denied making that statement, and under increasing international pressure, he was finally cleared of the charges (Donef 2001).

Sayfo – Creation of a Myth?

The author of the second publication by the Turkish Historical Society that deals with the Assyrian genocide is Professor Bülent Özdemir (2009). He is head of the Assyrian section at the society, which was apparently established in 2007. The book is entitled *Süryanilerin Dünü Bugünü: I. Dünya Savaşı'nda Süryaniler* [The Assyrians Past and Present: The Assyrians during World War I]. It was published in 2008, and its second extended edition appeared in 2009. Both of these editions are published in Turkish. As of 2013, an English translation of the book has been published under the title *Assyrian Identity and the Great War. Nestorian, Chaldean and Syrian Christians in the 20th Century*.[3]

It is no surprise that this book also reiterates the core thesis of 'Assyrian treason' and makes reference to Sönyel's thesis. While playing down the negative effect of the events of the late Ottoman Empire on the Assyrians, it differs in style from Sönyel's publication and addresses broader issues. Obviously, the Turkish side's argumentation is evolving and worth reviewing in more detail.

The book consists of six main sections. The first two sections establish the historical context of the Assyrians in the Ottoman Empire prior to the First World War, and are much better researched than Sönyel's book. The second section elaborates on the Assyrian–Armenian and Assyrian–Russian relations (Özdemir 2009: 66–70) to argue for a continuous historical relationship. Section three deals with the role of the Assyrians on the side of the Allies in the First World War, while section four briefly deals with 'The World War and Claims of Genocide' (ibid.: 111–25). Two further sections deal with the situation of the Assyrians after the war and during the Turkish Republic. The book concludes with various attachments of copied documents (ibid.: 175–221) and a bibliography.

In his foreword, the author points to the standard Turkish thesis regarding the role of missionaries; similar to Sönyel, Özdemir reiterates that the 'activities of Western Christians, and especially those of the evangelical missionaries in the nineteenth century, alienated the Assyrians from the Ottoman administration; the relationship with the Kurds, with whom they lived for many centuries, was negatively influenced and the sense of "others" was nurtured' (2009: vii). Özdemir differentiates between the situation of East and West Assyrians, while stating that Nestorians, 'with the encouragement of the Russians, allegedly took sides and became a "small ally" of the Entente states' (2009: vii).

The book's approach to dealing with the Sayfo is outlined as follows: to refute the Assyrian claims regarding the 'events of 1915'. This is based on the study of various external archives while comparing Assyrian claims with documents in the Ottoman archives.

Initially, Özdemir's reasoning sounds rational; in the introduction he says, '... the Assyrians, despite the marginality of their case, took their place in history during the discussed period, though they left behind a "sad history". At last and with "claims of genocide" in 1915, the topic grew to a political issue between states' (2009: x). However, along with his denial arguments, Özdemir occasionally adopts a partisan tone, for example in describing the Assyrian approach to providing numbers of victims, which he regards as too high, as 'fascistic' (2009: 51). In another context, he states that today's claims that a genocide was perpetrated against the Assyrians are based on 'encouragement and collaboration' with the Armenian diaspora; '[the allegation,] however, cannot be proven by documents in archives' (ibid.: 170). This Turkish predication certainly bears no relation to any reality and overestimates the Armenian diaspora's impact on the Assyrians. The Sayfo and the Assyrian suffering during the massacres have been burned into the consciousness of Assyrians since childhood,[4] independently of what happened to the Armenians. After their emigration to Europe, Assyrians were without any repression able to talk more freely about their history, the Sayfo and human rights issues concerning their people in the Middle East. These topics are still difficult or impossible to address openly in Middle Eastern countries, including in today's Turkey.

Özdemir attempts to differentiate between the position of the Nestorians and Jacobite Assyrians during the war, saying that the latter 'stayed loyal to the Ottoman regime and generally maintained silence during the war' (2009: ix). Going further, he says that the Assyrians who lived in Mardin, Urfa, Diyarbakir and Mosul, 'with few exceptions, lived in peace during the Armenian deportations – before and even after the war' (ibid.: 169). However, the Assyrians who lived in Van, Hakkari and Urmia did 'join the Russians along with the Armenian bandits and fought against the Ottoman Empire in the frontline in Caucasus and made sacrifices', he continues. This is a simple logic based on the discretionary categorization by the perpetrators to justify the mass killing of people by referring to an alleged role of a group during the war: those who eventually defended themselves and resisted are labelled as rebels and punished by death, and those who remained peaceful died as victims of war, but were not killed.

Of course, the aim of the book remains to deny any wrongdoing by the Turks.[5] Özdemir places blame on external powers, missionaries and even the Assyrian victims for what happened. These arguments are repeated over and over again. He makes no mention of the Teşkilât-ı Mahsusa (Ottoman Turkish for Special Organization), which carried out killing in major cities in south-eastern Anatolia. Regarding the Jihad, Özdemir offers a naïve interpretation of this Ottoman holy war decree, which became the root cause of most of the annihilation of the Christian population at the local level in south-eastern Anatolia during the First World War. The book can be also regarded as a first reaction to recent Sayfo research (particularly to David Gaunt's book) and lobbying by the Assyrian diaspora for the recognition of the genocide.

In regards to the current Assyrian demands to recognize their genocide, Özdemir observes that in the context of emigration and their life in the Western diaspora, the Assyrians are confronted with social and societal problems, the most important of them being the identity problem, and makes the claim that in modern publications the events of the First World War are interweaved with myths while 'claims of a genocide are utilized as historical reality' in forming a collective identity (Özdemir 2009: 114). For the Assyrian diaspora, Özdemir's assessment is that, as they emphasize being an ethnic group, 'they attach the claim of a lived genocide' in order to build unity and identity around it (ibid.: 162). With that, he claims, the question is answered 'why they have been forced to live abroad'. Ultimately, he concludes that the events prior to and after the First World War form key experiences in the historical tradition of the Assyrians, while they 'believe they have not achieved what they deserved in the postwar Middle East state configuration', and hence face a frustration that they still cannot overcome.

Certainly, this is a new quality in Turkish argumentation. The Sayfo is undoubtedly key to Assyrian identity all over the world and across the denominational borders of the Syriac churches, just as the Armenian genocide or Aghet is for Armenian identity and the Holocaust or Shoah is for Jewish identity. But what Professor Özdemir obviously confuses is cause and effect. It is legitimate for people to have learned lessons from their past, even if the lessons are as disastrous as a genocide. Özdemir's claim that 'most of the narratives are based on "oral tradition" and "hearsay"' is, in addition, a distortion, and reflects ignorance of the fact that some of the initial books on Sayfo were written by eyewitnesses, not to mention the numerous neutral bystanders from outside the community (Armalto 1919; Bryce and Toynbee [1916] 2000; Lepsius 1919;

Naayem 1920; Gaunt 2007). Considering the fact that Turkey since the establishment of the Republic systematically prohibited any discourse on the events of the First World War from an Assyrian perspective, the oral sources shedding light on the events cannot be underestimated or undervalued. Özdemir might criticize the methodology – in case there is a methodological problem with the validation of such oral sources – but not the use of oral sources as evidence.

As evidence of a so-called war declaration against the Ottoman Empire, Özdemir refers to a statement in a petition to the Paris Peace Conference, while he fails to provide any Ottoman archival documents as proof or confirmation of such an important fact. He reiterates the thesis that the Assyrians at the start of the war fought against the Ottoman Empire jointly with Russia and later with Britain, and made sacrifices. As proof of this collaboration, the author concludes that Assyrians did not remain neutral during the First World War, which is, according to him, 'a fact' that is 'clearly expressed by the title of Wigram's book, *Our Smallest Ally – A Brief Account of the Assyrian Nation in the Great War*' (Özdemir 2009: 8). Here again, Özdemir applies the same logic of discretionary categorization to indirectly justify mass killings, by labelling part of the victim group as 'neutral' and others as 'non-neutral'. In fact, he seems to be unaware of contradicting himself, as he labels the West Assyrians 'neutral', while neglecting to explain why they too lost a large portion of their population in the Diyarbakir province (de Courtois 2004: 196) even though they lived in the cities and villages not directly at the front of the war.[6]

Özdemir confirms that the Assyrians sought help from the British consulates or missionary centres, for the purpose of representing their interests and taking note of their complaints. However, 'their collaboration with Russia prior to the First World War and during the war as well as Assyrian entry into Russian military service along with the Armenians made their position against the Ottoman Empire particularly clear', he continues (2009: 67). According to the author, the archival materials emphasize that the Assyrians stood 'in enmity with the Kurds, with whom they lived for centuries as neighbours', and that Assyrians were regarded as a 'Trojan Horse' by Russia, Britain and France and utilized as such during the First World War (ibid.: 170). He argues that the Armenian claims in the context of 1915 against Turkey are for the Assyrians 'an example and point of departure' to raise 'similar' demands (ibid.: 169). Needless to say, Özdemir and other genocide deniers in general have a problem studying the Armenian genocide in the same context, because they disavow the evidence that the genocide during the First World War was committed against all Christian populations in the Ottoman Empire.

In conclusion, Özdemir states that 'the claims and the accusations brought against Turkey, that in 1915 and similarly to the Armenians, Assyrians were also victims of a genocide, cannot be proven by historical facts' (2009: 170). In stark contrast to the Turkish trivialization of the events, on 16 December 2007 the International Association of Genocide Scholars (IAGS), an organization of the world's foremost experts on genocide, passed a resolution affirming that the massacres and death marches of the Armenian, Assyrian and Greek populations during the First World War were genocide.[7]

Özdemir does not neglect to discuss both prewar and postwar statistics (2009: 50–65). He compares and comments on the various statistics, including those from American, French and British archives, while confronting them with McCarthy's minimalistic approach based on the Ottoman census of 1914. The number of Assyrians the author comes up with prior to the First World War in the different provinces varies from 144,483 (according to McCarthy) up to 435,000 according to the population statistics prepared in 1918 by David Magie (Özdemir 2009: 57–8),[8] who was advisor to the American President Woodrow Wilson and participated as a member of the US delegation to the Paris Peace Conference in 1919. Özdemir does not attempt to resolve obvious contradictions in the numbers he provides, even though such a discussion is quite necessary. For instance, one statistic from the Syrian-Orthodox Church in the 1870s provides a list that claims there were 236,380 West Assyrians living in the various regions of the empire (ibid.: 59), whereas in other statistics this number has been claimed to be much lower. Özdemir appears to accept the fact that considering different sources, around 360,000 to 430,000 Assyrians lived within the borders of the Ottoman Empire prior to the First World War. However, he dismisses population statistics provided to the Paris Peace Conference on 26 July 1919 (ibid.: 64) and documented in British Foreign Office archives that indicate there were 811,000 Assyrians in Turkey alone.

Regarding the number of victims, Özdemir tries to compare different statistics, though cursorily. He remarks that 'according to claims, the Assyrian losses within the Ottoman borders amount to 200,000', while adding that it is impossible to verify those numbers (2009: 61–6). Based on that statistic, however, Özdemir asserts that the West Assyrians' 'claims about losses' during the First World War are not in line with their population numbers prior to the war – which should mean that the number of victims is higher than the Ottoman statistics for the population prior to the First World War.

On some other important events of the war, Özdemir (2009: 169) states that:

- the Nestorians 'decided to fight on the side of the Russians and later deliberately moved from Hakkari to Urmia';
- 'in Mardin-Midyat, the Assyrians did not participate in the war and they have not been deported by force';
- the Assyrians were 'victim of difficulties that accompanied the war, such as illness, armed robberies and other clashes';
- 'only during the Armenian resettlement did some local resistance occur, which caused losses';
- however, 'there was no planned or organized genocide at any time'.

In a short subsection, Özdemir elaborates on the relations between the Assyrians and the Armenians and Russia during the First World War, mentioning the former two fighting alongside the latter, which was the 'protection power' in the Caucasus region until the Russian revolution of 1917. He says that ultimately the withdrawal of Russia 'caused panic among the Assyrians' (2009: 70). With regards to Britain, he raises the question of whether there were any promises for independence after the war, without giving a conclusive answer (ibid.: 82).

One important subsection is about the Sayfo – as the 'effort to establish a myth' (Özdemir 2009: 112). Certainly this is a new dimension in Turkish genocide denial research, arguing that the Sayfo includes 'claims' of massacres during 1915 by the Ottoman military power and irregular Kurdish troops against the Christian population of Mardin-Midyat. However, according to Özdemir, there is no proof, either in the Ottoman archives or in the foreign archives, that would support such claims. He explains that oral traditions, 'telling from father to son within the family', have over time developed to an important level in the diaspora and helped to 'construct a myth'. According to him, the 'resistance in Hazakh[9] and Aynwardo[10] in particular is transmitted in an exaggerated way' (2009: 113). Here Özdemir, like other Turkish historians, denies Assyrians even the right of self-defence (partially successful, as we know) against a powerful alliance of armed irregulars, mostly Kurds, and Turkish army units intending to destroy them, instead he portrays those sieges and the resistance as uprisings against the government.

Özdemir (2009: 114) touches briefly on the call for Jihad in the context of the First World War and comes up with a very strange interpretation. According to him, the declaration of Jihad, which was announced along with mobilization, has been 'misinterpreted' due to a lack of context. And the author explains that context: the call for Jihad against Christians during the First World War was 'targeted to mobilize Muslims in other countries' and was 'a political manoeuvre', as 'Jihad cannot be declared against [one's] own population'. 'The researchers, 'who do not know the legal basis of the decree, interpreted this as war and a call for destruction of the Christian population', he concludes.

The Ottoman government declared Jihad – holy war against the 'infidels' – in November 1914 by the Sheikh-ul Islam, Hayri Effendi, in order to unify the non-Turkish non-Christian population and mobilize it against the Christians in Anatolia. In fact, non-Muslims have always been considered 'internal enemies', not dignified members of the Ottoman population. Özdemir chooses to ignore the fact that the Jihad declaration (Yonan 2000)[11] was trumpeted throughout the country and in the streets based on government orders, and he tries to detract from its implications. Is this simply a new Turkish historian's attempt to misinterpret Jihad? Today, Kurdish people in Turkey refer to the order as the *Firmane Fillah* (Christian's Decree), which was the call to kill the Christians. A *firman* or *ferman* was a royal decree issued by the Ottoman sultan.

Özdemir touches on a statement in a 1919 report by the British officer E. Noel, who was sent on a fact-finding mission to Northern Mesopotamia immediately after the war. Evidently, Noel visited Mardin on 20 April 1919 and had talks with local religious leaders of the city. Özdemir (2009: 113) cites from the report that the Assyrians in Mardin suffered the 'least impact from the events and counted the least victims to grieve about'. In addition, he states that the Assyrians reconfirmed their loyalty to the Ottoman regime, while neglecting to mention the losses they had endured (Gaunt 2006: 176, 441).

In a conclusion as to the presumed intent of the Assyrians after any Turkish apology, Özdemir hints that once Turkey, seen as the heir of the Ottoman Empire, 'stops denying the claims of the genocide and apologizes', high 'claims for reparations would follow' (2009: 116). In the context of Turkish–European negotiations for EU accession, he argues that Assyrians 'aim to receive the minority status' they failed to obtain with the Treaty of Lausanne. Ultimately, and 'without doubt', he asserts that the aim of the Assyrians is to 'establish a state of their own in Northern Mesopotamia as their ancestral homeland, which is partially Turkish territory'. Indeed, this is an unnecessarily extreme stretch of Assyrian demands seeking recognition and justice.

Conclusion

It is not surprising that both books of the Turkish Historical Society have the same message, although they differ in style, breadth of the issues covered, and the archive materials utilized. Both stress the claim that there was no systematic or organized killing of Assyrians by the Ottoman government during the First World War. Furthermore, both argue that Assyrians are to be blamed for their destiny during the war and for the resulting sacrifices, because 'they joined the war against Turkey'.

While Sönyel focuses on the Eastern Assyrians and selectively cites mainly British archives, Özdemir broadened the selective archive utilization to include French, Russian, US and Ottoman sources, and also widened the focus to cover the events in Upper Mesopotamia and Tur Abdin. Both books are cited today in studies of Turkish university students on the Assyrians, meaning that the denial arguments are being actively used as reference and guidance for future research. In addition, the claims of the authors, though disputed by independent scholars, extend into public discourse in Turkey and most recently even into high school textbooks.[12] This is exactly the purpose of both books discussed here. In its concerted efforts to deny the genocide orchestrated by the Ottoman government during the First World War against the Christian population – Assyrians, Armenians and Pontic Greeks – today's Turkish government is clearly not hesitant to distort historical events by inverting victim and perpetrator in order to create what in German is called a *Dolchstoßlegende* ('stab in the back' legend). More seriously, the government is not afraid to carry a historically disputed matter to the public and confront Assyrians with hatred and open attacks. Assyrian organizations in Turkey and from abroad have protested against this initiative.

Abdulmesih BarAbraham holds an MA degree from the University of Erlangen/Nürnberg. He is Chairman of the Trustee Boards of the Yoken-bar-Yoken Foundation and of Mor Afrem Foundation. He has published numerous articles on the situation of the Assyrians in the Middle East. His publications include *Cumhuriyet tarihi boyunca doğu ve batı Asurlara karşı- baskı zulüm assimile ve kovulma* (Özgür Üniversite Kitapliği, 2009) and *Verbreitung des Nationalgedankens unter den syrisch-aramäischsprachigen Christen* (LIT Verlag, 2004).

Notes

1. The author uses the denominational term 'Nestorians' throughout the book, meaning the Eastern Assyrians.
2. Sönyel cites from an unreferenced letter of Mar Shimun, Patriarch of the Church of the East, to Russian Grand Duke Michael. By 'difficult', it is obviously meant that the Nestorians had no reason or motivation to pay taxes.

3. As the English version of the book was not available when the initial paper was prepared and presented, all translations from Turkish into English are mine.
4. It is worth pointing out that my grandfather, a survivor of the Sayfo, lost his parents during the events.
5. With respect to Kurds, Özdemir (2009: 35–42) emphasizes the clan-based interrelations with Assyrians and depicts conflicts among the groups as being mainly of economical character rather than religiously motivated. However, and without becoming specific, he admits that the establishment of the Hamidiye regiments (formed from selected Kurdish tribes) 'impacted' the relations between Assyrians and Kurds and 'brought an imbalance to the relationship'.
6. Figures of victims presented by the Syriac Orthodox Patriarchate to the peace conference after the war state that 77,963 West Assyrians were killed in 278 villages of the Diyarbekir province alone.
7. The full text is available at http://www.genocidetext.net/iags_resolution_supporting_documen tation.htm.
8. Providing a table with statistics of different denominations of Assyrians (Nestorian, Jacobite, Chaldean, Catholic) with reference to David Magie, 'The Christian Sects of the Turkish Empire', undated, at NARA, Inquiry Documents, Roll 47, No. 1010. The Magie Source seems to be undated, but was presented to Paris peace conference (see: http://www.oac.cdlib.org/findaid/ ark:/13030/kt496nd9gt/entire_text/).
9. Hazakh (today's Turkish name for the city is Idil), a larger village with a mostly Syriac Catholic population near Midyat, was under siege by Kurdish irregulars with the support and partial involvement of the Ottoman army between July and November 1915. For a detailed account of the events, see Gaunt (2006: 273–90).
10. Ayn-Wardo (today's Turkish name for the village is Gülgöze), an Assyrian village near Midyat in Tur Abdin, was under siege by Kurdish tribes and irregulars between July and October 1915. For a brief account of the events, see Gaunt (2006: 200).
11. According to the German historian Gabriele Yonan, 'the genocide carried out by the Muslim forces against Assyrians and Armenians would never have been possible without the declaration of Holy War (Jihad), by which the Muslims sought to destroy all Christian peoples in the name of the prophet Mohammed'.
12. The Turkish National Education Ministry in Ankara has recently published the third edition of a history textbook (Cazgir 2011) used in tenth grade high school classes. The book presents distorted historical information about Assyrians and denounces them as traitors who rebelled against Turkey. The subsection which deals with Assyrians is titled 'The Assyrian minority's situation under the Ottoman Empire'. It states: 'During the First World War, the Assyrians rebelled [against the Ottoman Empire] at the encouragement of Russian and other European states. Since these rebellions did not succeed, most of the Assyrians traveled from areas governed by the Ottoman Empire' (Cazgi 2011: p. 65).

Bibliography

Akcam, T. 2005. 'Anatomy of a Crime: The Turkish Historical Society's Manipulation of Archival Documents', *Journal of Genocide Research* 7(2), 255–277.

Armalto, I. 1919. *Al-Qousara fi Nakabat Al-Nasara* [The Calamities of the Christians]. Lebanon: Al Sharfe; reprinted Beirut 1970.

BarAbraham, A. 2011. 'Turkish High School History Book Portrays Assyrians as Traitors'. *Assyrian International News Agency*. Retrieved 2 October 2011 from http://www. aina.org/releases/20111002110757.htm.

Bryce, J., and A. Toynbee. [1916] 2000. *The Treatment of Armenians in the Ottoman Empire, 1915–1916*, ed. A. Sarafian. Princeton, NJ: Gomidas Institute.

Cazgir, V., I. Genc, M. Celik, C. Genc, and S. Turedi, S. 2011. *Ortaöğretim, Tarih 10 Sınıf, 3. Baskı (Middle Grade Education, History, 10th Grade*, 3rd edition), Ankara: Devlet Kitapları Döner Sermaye Işletmesi Müdürlüğü.

de Courtois, S. 2004. *The Forgotten Genocide: Eastern Christians, the Last Arameans.* Piscataway, NJ: Gorgias Press.

Donef, R. 2001. *The Assyrian Genocide and Article 312 of the Turkish Penal Code: The Case of an Assyrian Priest in Turkey.* Retrieved 2 August 2011 from http://www. atour.com/government/docs/20010926a.html.

Gaunt, D. 2006. *Massacres, Resistance, Protectors. Muslim–Christian Relations in South-East Anatolia during World War I.* Piscataway, NJ: Gorgias Press.

—— 2007. '1915: Ottoman Bystanders', *Report for Forum för Levande Historia,* December. Retrieved 2 September 2011 from http://www.atour.com/~history/1900/ 20110208a.html.

Hovannisian, G.R. 1998. *Remembrance and Denial: The Case of the Armenian Genocide.* Detroit: Wayne State University Press.

Hürriyet. 2000. 'İçimizdeki hain' [The Traitor among Us], 4 October. Retrieved 18 October 2011 from http://arama.hurriyet.com.tr/arsivnews.aspx?id=-186566.

Lepsius, J. 1919. *Deutschland und Armenien. Sammlung diplomatischer Aktenstücke.* Potsdam: Tempelverlag.

Naayem, J. 1920. *Les Assyro-Chaldéens et les arméniens massacres par les Turcs. Documents inédits recueillis par un témoin oculaire.* Paris: Bloud et Gay.

Özdemir, B. 2009. *Süryanilerin Dünü Bugünü: I. Dünya Savaşı'nda Süryaniler.* Ankara: Türk Tarih Kurumu Yayınları.

Rumpf, C. 2004. *Einführung in das türkische Recht.* 1. Auflage. Munich: C.H. Beck.

—— 2016. *DieVerfassung der Republik Türkei, Stand 1.6.2016* [The Turkish Constitution of the Turkish Republik as of 2016]. Retrieved 20 October 2016 from http://www.verfassungen.eu/tr/tuerkei82.htm

Sönyel, S.R. 2001. *The Assyrians of Turkey – Victims of Major Power Policy.* Ankara: Turkish Historical Society Publications.

Yonan, G. 2000. *Holy War Made in Germany – New Light on the Holocaust Against the Christian Assyrians during World War I.* Retrieved 2 August 2011 from http://www. nineveh.com/Holy%20War%20Made%20in%20Germany.html.

CHAPTER 12

WHO KILLED WHOM?

A COMPARISON OF POLITICAL DISCUSSIONS IN FRANCE AND SWEDEN ABOUT THE GENOCIDE OF 1915

Christophe Premat

In France, since the beginning of the 1990s, there has been a wave of historical laws passed to help cast light on past crimes. The role of the French state during 1940–44 was the starting point for the political discussion about the responsibility of the French administration in the Holocaust (Andrieu 2000). The same mindset is also revealed in the instituting of a national day set aside to commemorate the victims of anti-Semitic and racist crimes (law of 10 July 2000) and the abolition of slavery (10 May 2001), both telling outcomes of the development of public memory policies (Michel 2010: 91). The Algerian War, the role of *harkis*[1] and other groups have also been dealt with in these discussions. The debate on the abrogation of Article 4 of the law of 23 February 2005 (debate on the effects of French colonization)[2] exposed a gap between those who want to construct a status for the victims and those who refuse the logic of repenting (Michel 2010: 153). During this same period, the symbolic commemoration of past events has become a ritual (Nora 1997). The Republic has to deepen its foundations and enhance its social links by instigating these different acts of commemoration (Ozouf 1976). Memory governance has grown up in this context.

Recognition of the Armenian genocide has taken place in France in the specific context of the politicization of memory. The Armenian community is well integrated into the country, a number of different artists and political leaders among them helping to reaffirm its identity and its roots.[3] It is no wonder that they are able to influence the parliamentary discussions about the recognition of the genocide of Armenians in 1915. Moving the field of play slightly, it is interesting to note that the debate about the events of 1915 has gained in importance in a country with a different perception of communities, to wit, Sweden. Sweden is often viewed as a tolerant and liberal country that has invariably welcomed many political refugees since the 1960s. Although the first Oriental Christians came to Sweden at the beginning of the 1960s, their issues only began to be debated at the end of the 1990s. One of these groups of Oriental Christians referred (and refers) to themselves in English as Assyrians, but at a later stage some of them began to call themselves Syriacs or Assyrians/Syriacs (Swedish *Assyrier/Syrianer*) (Atto 2011). In this chapter, I use the term Assyrian as a cross-denominational name, inclusive of all the different Syriac churches.[4] Assyrians is a name that covers different Christian denominations whose roots lie in the northern part of Mesopotamia (Lundgren and Barryakoub 2010: 13). The Assyrians have arrived in Sweden in different waves of migrations from the mid-1960s to the present day.

The principal goal of this chapter is to understand how the genocide issue has been dealt with in the political discussions held in two different national traditions: France and Sweden. The idea is to compare two national narratives on the genocide. I shall adopt a discursive methodology (Thornborrow and Coates 2005: 6), analysing how representatives in both countries put this issue on the political agenda. Who killed whom? Who is the aggressor and who the victim? What categories do these political debates produce in these historical events? What are the main terms used in both national political debates? The controversy gives an unparalleled opportunity to highlight a historical question. The material is composed of legislative texts that illustrate the state of the political debates on this question. Both countries experienced a wave of immigration due to the events of 1915. The analysis of parliamentary texts is all the more important as it reveals the construction of new categories to qualify what happened.

In France, the Armenian community is the main party concerned with this issue, and in Sweden the majority of the groups of victims are Assyrians but do include other Christian communities. There is a difference between Armenians, who are a community in France linked to a state (Armenia), and Assyrians, who are a stateless community.

In France, most Armenians arrived in the 1920s, still in flight from the massacres of 1915 (Björklund 2011), but the first Assyrians came to Sweden only in 1967, as invited stateless refugees from Lebanon. A second wave arrived later as they too attempted to flee the growing religious and political tensions that were affecting Assyrians living in Turkey.

I argue that controversies aroused by the genocides in general help to identify and recognize the wounded identity of some social and ethnic groups. Maurice Halbwachs (1925: 391) has drawn up a social framework of memories. Accordingly, social groups recollect parts of the past in their struggle to strengthen their identity.[5] The parliamentary discussions are of paramount importance as they reflect the way this battle for social recognition is tackled by the representatives of the people and inserted into two different national narratives. The first part of the chapter is a description of the international context of the recognition of the genocide. The discussion then continues with a description of the historical background to these debates in France and in Sweden. In the last part, the debates and the laws related to the genocide in both countries will be compared.

The International Context

The concept of genocide and mass crimes dates back to 1948 when Raphael Lemkin, one of the first historians of genocide, founded the Convention on the Punishment and Prevention of the Crime of Genocide, part of the United Nations Commission on Human Rights. Although he had written about the Armenian genocide in the 1930s, he was actually inspired to create this institution as an immediate consequence of the Holocaust (Schaller and Zimmerer 2005: 448). Nowadays, it is obvious that this convention must be taken as the starting point for the official history of genocides. Although overshadowed by the Holocaust, the controversial question of the recognition of the Armenian genocide is nothing new. Many countries and various non-governmental bodies have recognized the Armenian genocide, and the Armenian Genocide Resolution was passed unanimously by the Association of Genocide Scholars of North America in 1997. In some parliamentary texts (Sweden, Northern Ireland and Scotland), the naming of the victims is not restricted to Armenians, but also includes Assyrians. The European parliament recognized the genocide of Armenians on 18 June 1987. The accompanying text is all the more striking as it insists on the need to acknowledge the history of the Armenians and it also refers to the shadow side of the matter: the terrorist acts committed by radical groups of Armenians between 1973 and 1986. The text regrets the continued denial of this genocide that has been historically proven.[6]

France and Sweden have two big Christian communities and counted among them are 600,000 Armenians in France and more than 100,000 Assyrians in Sweden (Gaunt 2010: 4). The proportion of these two communities in their new homelands is quite similar and their not inconsiderable presence has unquestionably influenced the historical and political reflections on the events of 1915 in both countries. In France, the debates on the historical genocides have been enshrined in the statute books in a series of historical laws passed since the beginning of the 1990s. Naturally enough, in French thinking the question of the role of the Vichy regime in the Second World War and its collaboration with the Nazi regime, as well as the massacres in the Algerian War, has taken centre stage in these historical debates. The way parliament has treated these historical laws has not been without controversy; some historians, such as Jean-Pierre Azéma (2006), have criticized political interference in what is considered a historical matter. On occasion, the controversy has been so heated that on 18 November 2008 the French National Assembly published a report on the question of memory laws (Rebérioux, 2008). Dealing as it does with such a delicate subject, the expression 'memory laws', first used in 2005, is imbued with negative connotations and theoretically could impinge on all the laws that have been passed in France. Many historians fear that in the future it will be the political powers-that-be that will decide what is worth being commemorated.

Under the Fifth Republic, the French parliament had its power to honour important past figures abrogated. This power is now vested in the person of the president. The mainspring behind this ideology is that historical persons should be celebrated if they have performed actions that have a collective meaning.[7] Some events, such as the French Revolution, are regularly celebrated to enhance the image of the Republic. The idea was to solidify new links between French citizens in the post-revolutionary period. When the first memory laws of 13 July 1990 allowed those who denied the Holocaust to be punished, two important historians, Pierre Vidal-Naquet and Madeleine Rebérioux, reacted angrily and declared that, if certain crimes should be punished, parliament did not have the legitimacy to decide what was historically true. Madeleine Rebérioux (2008: 20) writes that this idea of historical truth would certainly be extended to other genocides. The debate was both juridical and historical and the law of 13 July 1990 was only the first step in this discussion.

The argument about the recognition of the Armenian genocide in this controversy is being waged between those who are determined not to allow the political sphere to interfere with historical laws and those who are fighting for symbolic recognition. Many thinkers and politicians fear that the image of the Republic will be fragmented into as many pieces as there are different interpretations of history. The first parliamentary reactions to the question of the Armenian genocide date back to the end of the 1990s. In Sweden, the first reactions to the genocide of Christian communities came at the end of the 1990s, although a general bill of 1964 punished those who denied such genocides as the Holocaust. In fact, this bill was a transcription of the international convention on genocides and it was passed before the establishment of the Assyrian community in the country. Generally speaking, its purpose was to punish every crime committed against any community in Sweden.[8] In both cases it is important to sift through the facts to analyse whether parliament was simply passing a bill or whether it was expressing symbolic recognition of the crime of genocide.

A Brief History of Armenians in France and Assyrians in Sweden

As an aid to better understanding the background to the political debates in France and Sweden, a summary of the history of the Armenian and the Assyrian communities in both countries will not be out of place at this point. In 1966, after a request by the United Nations High Commissioner for Refugees and the World Council of Churches, the Swedish government decided to welcome Christian refugees living in Lebanon. Most of these refugees in Lebanon were stateless, but had actually come from Turkey. Consequently, the first Assyrians came to Sweden in 1967. Between 1967 and 1976, there were several waves of Assyrian migrants, and the communities already established in Sweden were able to take care of the new migrants. At the time the first Assyrians arrived in Sweden, there was no adequate categorization of refugees. In 1982, there were around fifteen thousand Assyrians in Sweden, four thousand of them living in the city of Södertälje (Svanberg and Runblom 1988: 31). These Assyrians had been anxious to flee from religious tensions in south-eastern Turkey. Most of them came from this region, specifically from the cities of Mardin and Midyat and from the villages in Tur Abdin; Sweden was the first destination for this diaspora.

As said, after the 1960s Sweden received several waves of Assyrian and Oriental Christian migrants. The last arrival of Oriental Christians was the group who were forced to flee in response to the deteriorating situation in Iraq after the conflict of 2003. Under the dictatorship of Saddam Hussein, the Christian communities had been relatively well protected and the fall of the regime had destabilizing consequences for them. In 1981, the Iraqi government had officially recognized seventeen communities, including four non-Muslim communities (Christians, Jews, Sabeans and Yazidis) (Yacoub 2010: 146). After 2003, many Christian leaders in Iraq were murdered (among them the Chaldean archbishop Paul Faraj Rahho in February 2008), but considerable numbers of Christians had already left the country (Yacoub 2010: 141). The situation is now repeating itself in Syria, where the civil war has already had tragic consequences for the Christian communities that had been relatively protected by the Baath regime. The migration of Christian communities from the Middle East is a symptom of the political instability in the area.

After their arrival in Sweden, the integration of Assyrians progressed smoothly, even though their collective integration might be considered problematic (Gaunt 2010). Against the odds, they have managed to build a community with their own media (including Suroyo TV, Suryoyo SAT and Assyria TV). Within a relatively short period, they have produced some influential politicians such as Ibrahim Baylan, the former Minister of Education under the government of Göran Persson, the former General Secretary of the Social Democrats under the leadership of Mona Sahlin and the present Minister of Energy. Nevertheless, the identification of this Christian community remains a disputed theme. For instance, there is not even consensus among the group itself or among outsiders about what name should be used to refer to them. The two main protagonists, *Syrianer* and *Assyrier*, have built up competing churches, associations and football teams (respectively Syrianska and Assyriska). Hence, for now, there is still a need to recognize the genocide of 1915 and its consequences on the diaspora of Assyrians under a plurality of names.

The main difference between the Armenians and the Assyrians is that the Armenians came to Europe, to France in particular, in the immediate aftermath of the events of 1915. The Assyrians came to Europe and Sweden much later, after the 1960s, when they were feeling threatened by the growing political instability and threats in the Middle East. In their case, the trauma of 1915 was actually reawakened in the 1960s. Among the Assyrians, the word *Sayfo* (sword) is used when referring to the massacres of 1915, whereas in Armenian the term *Meds Yéghern* (the Great Crime) is used. To the Assyrian community that developed in Sweden in the 1970s and 1980s, the Sayfo is a constitutive fact (Weibel-Yacoub 2009: 61), a factor that has to be borne in mind continually when making any analysis of the parliamentary debates on this question. In France, the establishment of the Armenian community dates back to the end of the 1910s, when large numbers of Armenians fled the massacres that had occurred in the Ottoman Empire. They organized themselves and began to settle in France.

The Armenian issue was a hot topic throughout the 1920s. The Western Armenians present in Turkey (they were called this to distinguish them from the community in Russia, the Oriental Armenians) numbered around 2.1 million in 1912 according to the Armenian Patriarchate of Constantinople, and 1.3 million in 1914 according to the Turkish authorities (Ter Minassian 2000: 135). The number of victims is contested, as the Turkish authorities claim there were around 600,000 victims, whereas the Armenians assert there were 1.5 million victims (Kévorkian 1999). A great many books have been published on the question of the genocide. The more radical theories claim that Turkey only came into the First World War to get rid of this community, finishing off the work begun with the first massacres of Armenians at the end of the nineteenth century. Tchalkhouchian (1919: 7) states, 'Turkey tolerated Christian populations. It could not admit that the Christian element would grow up and be important. History shows ... that Turkish politicians governing the country decided on massacres in order to diminish the number of Christians'.[9] In other words, the decision to unleash the genocide was taken by Ottoman Turks in 1915 (Dadrian 1995). Some historians place more emphasis on the objectives of the Turkish government. On 5 November 1918, Woodrow Wilson declared that Turks were imitating the actions of the German Kaiser when they killed the Armenians (Tchalkhouchian 1919: 106). The responsibility for who killed whom is shared between Turks, Tartars and Kurds (Tchalkhouchian 1919: 78). Although the Kurds might also have been responsible for executing the decision to commit massacres, they themselves were not left unscathed by the decisions of the Young Turks. They were also victims and removed from some regions; although they did take part in the massacres, they cannot be systematically associated with the genocide (Schaller and Zimmerer 2008: 8; Levene 1998).

The parliamentary discussions in France and Sweden have focused on the massacres of Oriental Christians but have never resulted in a collective accusation. The MPs only go as far as insisting on the necessity for the Turkish authorities to acknowledge this genocide so that there can finally be some clarification on what really happened.

The Parliamentary Climates in France and Sweden

It is easy to work with the archives of parliamentary debates as they are open access. In France, the National Assembly has a *rédacteur des compte-rendus* whose duty is to transcribe all parliamentary debates.[10] The job of analyst of debates is a prestigious one. The persons selected are supposed to transcribe texts and note the varying reactions in parliament. The importance of having full transparency on the debates cannot be stressed highly enough (Coniez 2008). The Senate also employs people who are in charge of publishing the debates.[11] The French parliament is composed of two assemblies, the Assemblée Nationale and the Senate, whereas the Swedish parliament has only one chamber. This difference is important because in France a law can only be adopted if both chambers agree on it. The discussions in both chambers are therefore very important; the debate has time to evolve and some initial positions can be strengthened after the discussion in the Senate. In Sweden, the parliament has one chamber; there is also a policy of full transparency in the debates and in the administration of the archives.[12] It is possible to have full access to everything related to the work of parliamentarians (committees, motions and also the different budgetary pieces linked to the action of the parliamentarians). At this point, the digital archives in Sweden provide sufficient information to establish the comparison.

The massacres of the Armenians were already a topic for discussion in France at the end of the nineteenth century. In France, the first MP to denounce the massacres of Armenian populations was the socialist Jean Jaurès in his speech in the Chambre des Députés on 3 November 1896 (Ter Minassian 2000: 136). The first of what are now known as the Hamidian massacres occurred between 1894 and 1896, preceding the massacres in Cilicia that were unleashed in 1909. The word 'genocide' had not yet appeared in international law, and the lack of a specific term created difficulties for some parliamentarians in France who wanted to draw attention to the massacres of Armenian populations as a reprisal for their claims to more autonomy. As the growth of a historical process, and given enormous impetus by the Holocaust, by the end of the 1990s the issue of the genocide was being fiercely discussed simultaneously in France and in Sweden. The first memory laws in 1990 punishing denial of the genocide cast the first stone in a juridical process. Aware of the ethical issues at stake, some political leaders were keen to reinforce the juridical framework. The Republic has always been a majority regime whose duty is to protect wounded minority communities. Their goal was to build a secure status for the victims (Michel 2010). On 29

May 1998, the National Assembly unanimously adopted a principle acknowledging the reality of the Armenian genocide. In October 2000, some Conservative MPs proposed a bill that would pave the way for the French parliament to recognize the genocide of 1915 officially.[13] On 29 January 2001, a law for the public recognition of the Armenian genocide of 1915 was passed in parliament. There is a large consensus in parliament on the necessity of recognizing the existence of the genocide, and it was heavily supported by the lobby of the Armenian diaspora. The final report of the parliamentary committee refers to some specific events in 1914 and 1915: when the city of Van established an Armenian government on 7 April 1915, the Young Turks reacted mercilessly. The first acts in the genocide were perpetrated on 24 April, when the Young Turks arrested 650 Armenian leaders in Constantinople.[14] The discussions focus on historical facts and provide accurate details on the construction of the evidence of the genocide. At the end of the 1990s, the National Assembly in France had a left-wing majority but the Senate was Conservative (the senators are not directly elected). Although the bill was proposed by Conservative senators, it was also accepted without difficulty in the Assembly, showing just how deep the consensus on this issue was. Work in committees is the appropriate way to reach a sensible debate on this question and share a consensus.

In Sweden, the debates on the recognition of the genocide began at the end of the 1990s. Although there was already a law to punish people who denied genocides (law of 1964), the principal purport of this law was to punish denial of the Holocaust. In the debate on the genocide of the Oriental Christians, the idea of punishing those who denied the genocide of 1915 was not raised. The parliamentary debates were concentrated on acknowledgement of the genocide: in 1999, an MP from the leftist party, Murad Artin, submitted a written question to the former Minister of Foreign Affairs, Anna Lindh. He wanted the Social Democrat government to offer a perspective on the Armenian genocide in a forthcoming conference in Sweden about the Holocaust (24–28 January 2000).

> One of the aims of the conference is to increase awareness and knowledge of the Holocaust, its meaning and causes. Particularly important is how the recognition of the Holocaust was handled by different states when it happened. Turkey is invited to the conference although the question of the genocide is not recognized in this country. When the Turkish state was created, genocide of Armenians was committed. The number of persons killed was between 1 million and 1.5 million.[15]

The MP wanted questions about genocide to be expanded so that the concept would no longer be restricted to the Holocaust. Murad Artin, who was an MP of the leftist party (Vänsterpartiet) between 1998 and 2002, is an Armenian who was born in Iraq and was one of the first politicians to talk publicly in Sweden about the genocide of the Armenians and Assyrians. He was a member of the parliamentary Foreign Affairs Committee, which is why he addressed himself to Anna Lindh. She replied that the topic of the conference was not about genocides in general but specifically about the Holocaust. In a way she was reaffirming the historical position of Sweden on the Holocaust. Turkey was permitted to take part in the conference on account of its role during the Second World War when it welcomed many Jewish refugees.[16] In France, it was the left wing (socialists, communists and ecologists) who passed the first memory laws, but the Conservatives had no hesitation in joining them in calling for acknowledgement of the genocide of Armenian populations. At the moment, there is a relative consensus on the recognition of the genocide, but not on the punishment of those who deny it.

The presidents of the friendship groups (France-Armenia) in the parliament (Senate and National Assembly) are the most active in working for the recognition of the genocide. A proposal for a bill condemning people who deny the Armenian genocide was submitted to the National Assembly as early as 12 October 2006,[17] but the Senate never debated this text. In the French National Assembly session of 22 December 2011, the debate showed the sensitivity that still surrounds this question. Valérie Boyer, a French Conservative MP, was the author of the proposal. She was the president of the French-Armenian friendship group in the National Assembly. She cited the last presidential visit of Nicolas Sarkozy on 6 October 2011[18] as proof of the very close relationship between France and Armenia. According to Valérie Boyer:

> The democratically elected national representation does not act under the threat of a state, whatever it is, especially on topics related to the defence of human rights in our country. These archaic methods, which I call diplomacy of threat, do not honour this great country which is Turkey; it strengthens my desire to vote for it to protect people who have now the French nationality'.[19]

The French MP insisted on the idea of the defence of human rights. The recognition of the genocide and the fight against the denial of this fact should not be influenced by diplomatic relations with another country. Valérie Boyer regretted the pressure exerted by Turkey in these issues. After naming Turkey, she referred to the general fact that historical debates should never be influenced by diplomatic relations with another country.[20] Parliament adopted this law, but the Constitutional Council declared that it was not legal in February 2012. After the shift of power and the election of the socialist François Hollande in May 2012,

the new parliamentary majority skirted around the issue. The socialist Minister of Foreign Affairs, Laurent Fabius, answered the questions
of the Foreign Affairs Committee of the National Assembly on 17 July
2012 in these words:[21]

> Regarding the issue of Armenian genocide and Turkey, we have to be careful
> with our words. A law that several of you voted aimed at punishing those
> who denied the existence of the genocide. The Constitutional Council which
> evaluated the text declared that it was contrary to the spirit of the constitu-
> tion. During the campaign of presidential elections, the two main opponents
> accepted the idea of repressing the denial of the genocide, if I remember it cor-
> rectly. The government is working on it. The task is not that easy as we have
> to honour the engagement of the president and respect the constitutional
> and juridical framework.

Most politicians are in favour of this recognition but are afraid of a
repeat of what happened with the first laws of 1990.

In Sweden, the leftist parties are the most engaged in the recognition
of this issue. In 2000, Yilmaz Kerimo, a Social Democrat MP, asked a
question about the recognition of the genocide of the *Assyrier/Syrianer*
and *Kaldéer*: would the Swedish government consider the genocide a
historical fact?[22] In his question, Yilmaz Kerimo, who is also politically
engaged in the municipality of Södertälje, claimed that the government
should sustain research in this domain if it really wants to understand
the migration process of the Assyrian community. He also pointed out
the fact that the parliamentary Committee of Foreign Affairs had asked
Turkey to open its archives to researchers on this issue. Anna Lindh
answered this question with the announcement of the creation of an
institute whose task would be to study all forms of genocide.[23] In 2001,
the Living History Forum (Forum för levande historia) was established
by the government and was keen to reinforce democratic values by
studying all forms of genocide.[24] The lessons of history should be more
focused on all forms of racism and intolerance. In France, the private
actors, among them the association Le Mémorial de la Shoah, concen-
trate on a specific memory issue (how to teach young generations about
the Holocaust). Sweden is now one step ahead with its creation of an
institute dealing specifically with genocides.

The Living History Forum was created to combat all the racist prej-
udices that were to be found in different Swedish schools (Lange et al.
1997). The motion 2002/03:U213 was drafted by Yilmaz Kerimo and
Tommy Waidelich. The debate on the genocide of the Assyrians was
introduced by the leftist parties in parliament. The name *Svärdets år*
(the Year of the Sword in Swedish) is quoted several times and various

names crop up in the debate: *Assyrier, Syrianer, Kaldéer* and *Armenier*. The motion states that two million *Assyrier/Syrianer* were living in the south-eastern part of Turkey at the beginning of the twentieth century. Many of them were killed during disturbances surrounding the collapse of the Ottoman Empire.[25] Naturally, the post-genocide generations of Assyrians and Armenians have been affected by what happened and this argument is central to the motivation behind the proposal. The need to have proper research outcomes to help clarify this matter is fundamental to the future of this community. This is the first time we have been able to see the link between genocide, identity and generation among the Assyrians and Armenians. Yilmaz Kerimo was very active in raising the debate on the situation in Iraq in 2006; he addressed a question in writing to the Conservative government. In it he used the term 'genocide' to qualify the events engulfing Iraq in which Christian populations were being subjected to kidnapping and murder.[26] He declared that around 300,000 Christians had disappeared from Iraq since 2003, either because they had been killed or because they had fled the country.[27] He also refers to the murder of the Syriac Orthodox priest, Paulos Iskandar. The word 'genocide' is used several times and the victims are named as *Assyrier/Syrianer/Kaldéer*. Yilmaz Kerimo is heavily engaged in these issues. He is the MP who proposed most of the texts (questions, motions) to do with the question of the Christian genocide. In 2007/08, he signed a motion with two other Social Democrats (Tommy Waidelich and Christina Zedell) that was rejected by parliament.[28]

The recognition of the Armenian genocide is in fact a strong political issue that indubitably influences the relationship between Turkey and France. During a parliamentary debate on 4 May 2011, Serge Lagauche, a socialist MP who was in favour of the punishment of those who denied the Armenian genocide (Proposal no. 607, 2009–10), declared:

> Our colleague, René Rouquet, concluded in his report [which would lead to the recognition of the Armenian genocide in 2001], transmitted to the Foreign Commission of the parliament: 'France is not taking any action against Turkey with which it has a long tradition of friendship. Indeed, the contrary is the case, France would like to establish a sustainable peace between Turks and Armenians. The peace has to be built on solid foundations and not on the occultation of history that threatens every democracy'.[29]

The French MPs insisted on the fact that this call for recognition is not addressed to the present Turkish government, which is not responsible for what happened under the Ottoman Empire. Nevertheless, during this parliamentary discussion, the aggressor is clearly defined: anyone who supported the racist and nationalistic ideology of pan-Turkism was accountable for these massacres. Serge Lagauche accuses the Turkish authorities of supporting an approach based on denial and of refusing to recognize the reality of these massacres. He refers to the murder of Hrant Dink, a Turkish-Armenian journalist who was assassinated in 2007 because of his fight for recognition of the Armenian genocide. The proposal of 2011 was devised to raise the pressure on genocide deniers. The deniers of the Armenian genocide would be punished just as those who deny the Shoah are punished. The Deputy Prime Minister of Turkey, M. Bülent Arınç, declared that French–Turkish relations would improve if the French parliament and the government did not try to go any further than the decision of the Constitutional Council that rejected the draft proposal for the 2011 bill.[30] This is a fine example of how political relations interfere with the way parliamentarians see historical facts.

In 2007, the Green MP Mats Pertoft asked the Conservative Minister of Foreign Affairs (Carl Bildt) whether he was prepared to launch an initiative to obtain recognition of this genocide.[31] In his question, he referred to *Assyrier/Syrianer*, *Armenier* and *Kaldéer*. The genocide was perpetrated in Eastern Anatolia at the end of the collapse of the Ottoman Empire. In his question to the Swedish government, the MP touched upon the diaspora of *Assyrier/Syrianer* and *Armenier* throughout the world. France is cited as being the homeland of a strong Armenian community. Last but not least, he explicitly referred to the acknowledgement of the Armenian genocide by the French National Assembly (18 January 2001). Another 2009 motion also referred to the Pontic Greeks. In his motion, Nikos Papadopoulos, a Social Democrat MP, described all the massacres of Pontic Greeks (they once numbered 750,000, but 350,000 of them were killed between 1915 and 1920). Hence, Pontic Greeks were introduced into these parliamentary debates as additional victims. The motion was strongly motivated by an analysis of the historical facts. Papadopoulos quoted the French archives with reference to this question. They contain the accounts of some of the eyewitnesses: 'This was the culmination of a series of attacks against and massacres of Christian populations, they eradicated the Christian civilization in the area'.[32] The interest of some Christian Democrats and Liberals was also quickened by the question. Cecilia Wikström, a Liberal MP from Uppsala, asked a question about the genocide of 1915. She referred to some figures about the massacres: 1.5 million Armenians, between 250,000 and 500,000 *Assyrier/Syrianer* and 350,000 Pontic Greeks. It is interesting to note that all the victim groups of the genocide were named in the Swedish parliamentary debate. This is in contrast to the parliamentary debates in France, in which only Armenians are referred to. It also has to be said that the motions and texts proposed in Sweden in 2008 were more accurate in their qualification of the genocide. For instance, Wikström mentions that the genocide was carried out in April 1915. In her argumentation, she also draws attention to the recognition of the genocide by several countries since 1965. She firmly states that the recognition accorded by the European parliament on 18 June 1987 was a step forward that Sweden could follow. She adds that, after the Holocaust, the genocide of 1915 was one of the most studied genocides.

At the moment, there is irrefutable scientific evidence obtained by independent researchers that should be made known to a broader audience.[33] Interestingly, the parliamentary discussions in both countries are very well documented by citing historical facts (in France) about the Armenian genocide and (in Sweden) about the Assyrian, Syriac, Pontic, Armenian and Chaldean genocides. A variety of victims is dealt with in Sweden because of the presence there of a number of different Oriental Christian communities.

A consensus is shared among different political parties in Sweden, even though the Conservatives do tend to drag their heels when it comes to recognizing the genocide, as they are worried about the follow-through for Swedish–Turkish relations. Of all the evidence, motion 2008/09:U332 on the genocide of Armenians, Assyrians, Syriacs, Chaldeans and Pontic Greeks is certainly the most documented text on the nature of the genocide. The motion was signed by different left-wing parties (leftists, Social Democrats and Greens) as well as by MPs from the Christian Democrats and Liberals. The text insists on recognition of the international texts pertaining to the genocide and the research area, acknowledging the role of the Living History Forum. Certainly some arguments are accurate, for instance the one stating that the genocide was discussed from 1918 until the rise to power of the nationalistic movement of Mustafa Kemal. The idea of genocide is discussed in a historical perspective, with the founder being the man who put forward this idea, Raphael Lemkin. The convention of 1948 is adamant that the category of genocide does apply to the cases mentioned in the document. To the text of the motion are appended other documents, including the testimonies of the Swedish ambassador Per Gustaf August Cosswa Anckarsvärd and the defence attaché Einar af Wirsén, who were serving in Constantinople at the time. Wirsén (1942) devotes a chapter to the genocide in his memoirs, *Minnen från fred och krig*. He writes that the official purpose of the deportations was to remove the Armenian populations from Mesopotamia, but in fact he reveals that the deportations were a means to wreak widespread slaughter among the Christian communities.[34] The motion points out that the Turkish authorities had a political responsibility to recognize the genocide. The former Swedish Prime Minister denounced these massacres as early as 26 March 1917. Different witnesses are quoted, among them the missionaries Alma Johansson (Johansson 1930), Maria Anholm (Anholm 1906), Lars Erik Högberg, E. John Larsson (Larsson 1919), Olga Moberg[35] and Per Pehrsson (Pehrsson 1896). Per Pehrsson and Maria Anholm had both witnessed different massacres at the end of the nineteenth century.

The motion was accepted by the Swedish parliament, which had recognized the concept of genocide in March 2010, in opposition to the position of the government, which wanted nothing to do with memory laws.[36] The Conservatives (*Moderaterna*) constantly rejected this type of motion and from 2002 until 2010 people managed to get by with a political construction of the recognition of the genocide. Although left-wing parties were more outspoken on their position on this question, some other MPs did not hesitate to join them in supporting these motions asking for recognition. In France, the reverse was true as the Conservative parties were more engaged with the question than the socialists. Here it was not parliament that voted a law against the will of the government; the government, with the president taking the lead, was in favour of such a law.[37]

In France, the parliamentary discussion of 22 December 2011 favoured the same arguments put forward for the international recognition of the Armenian genocide; the other communities are not named in the text. 'The genocide of Armenians is recognized in Russia, Canada, Argentina, Italy, Sweden and Germany. Its denial is repressed in Switzerland, Slovakia and that will be the fact in other states.'[38] The question of genocide has been handled in the context of the deep friendship between Armenia and France. France has a long history of interaction with Armenian people. Nicolas Sarkozy recently declared: 'Armenia is a sister country to France. Our relationship is more than friendship. These very close links are reinforced by the presence of a large community of Franco-Armenian citizens. It explains why we are a driving force in these matters in Europe'.[39] This quotation is peppered with highly emotive words and phrases such as 'sister' and 'more than friendship'. The Armenians are not a community like any other, as they are the descendants of the many who came in the 1920s after the genocide. The relationship between the two countries is very close and explains why the recognition of the genocide is a strong political statement. The genocide of the Armenians had already been recognized in France, but the purpose of this new law proposal is to punish those who deny it (*New York Times*, 13 October 2006).

The open attitudes of denial, the destruction of remembrance monuments and the diffusion of revisionist opinions in the press and on the internet can develop in France without being punished. The question of the opportunity to pass memory laws is a real and large topic to which no MP, neither lawyer nor historian, has a definite answer. The government respects all opinions, whether they are for or against the passing of these laws. Nevertheless, in the present case, I repeat that the question is neither to recognize nor deny any genocide; instead it is whether or not to draw up a penalty for those who would contest a genocide that has already been recognized by the French law. The text does not target anybody; it completes our legal system.[40]

The choice of words is particularly striking in this instance. The MP who proposed it did not want to harp on who killed the Armenians; his aim is to bring the legal system full circle in order to punish those who deny the reality of the genocide.

Conclusion

In both countries, the parliaments have debated and discussed the concept of genocide over the last decade. There has been a special parliamentary appropriation of the question fired by the motions, the questions addressed to the government and the laws. In France, the debate revolves around the memory laws, as many historians do not want parliament to define what is or is not true. The mention of Turkey does not crop up very often; instead the MPs have focused on the recognition of a community that is well integrated in France. The left-wing parties initiated the memory laws at the beginning of the 1990s, stealing a march on the Conservatives, who had not yet got round to tackling the question of genocide. In Sweden, all groups of victims were mentioned progressively between 2002 and 2010; the MPs studied the details of the massacres, backed up by historical facts, reports and books. When a political party is in government, it tends to tread more cautiously (as is the case for Social Democrats and Conservatives in Sweden), as it is anxious to maintain closer links with Turkey. The evolution towards a more pragmatic attitude might explain why there is a deviation between the governmental attitude and the debates in parliament. In all these texts, the authors of the motions have clearly underlined the role of Turkey in this genocide. In France, even if a few isolated MPs have referred to the genocide of other Christian communities, the texts focus on the Armenian genocide. The geopolitical aspect (the relationship with Armenia and Turkey) is all the more important as the French presidents have always expressed a special friendship with Armenia. The institutional framework (half-presidential system with a strong parliament in France versus a parliamentary system in Sweden) has also influenced the way the debate is tackled in both countries. In France, the arrival of the Armenians dates back to just after the genocide, whereas the Oriental Christians in Sweden only arrived in the 1960s. The genocide was not a direct reason for the migration, although it did play a role. Christians lived with the fear that those massacres could happen again. In that sense, we can say that the genocide has played a major role in their collective identity. Assyrian Christians need to develop this if they are to educate the younger generations of Assyrians born in Europe, and this is why they need official recognition of what happened in 1915 so badly. In the 1960s, they also came because of religious conflicts: they were afraid of falling victim to new massacres. In this tangential way, their migration can also be traced to the events of 1915, hence why it is so important to them to be given official recognition of the genocide. The collective trauma is still present; it cannot be forgotten. Both Armenians and Assyrians are well integrated in France and Sweden, but even so, the discussion of the genocide of 1915 has been raised under the influence of the political leaders from these two diasporic communities. In fact, the discussion of the genocide is also part of European history, because these migrations have led to permanent settlements.

Christophe Premat is Lecturer in Cultural Studies in the Department of Romance Studies and Classics at Stockholm University, and Associate Researcher in Political Science at the Institute of Political Studies of Bordeaux (Centre Émile Durkheim). Since 2014, he has served as deputy for the Third constituency for French residents overseas in the Assemblée Nationale in Paris. He is a member of the editorial board of the review *Sens Public*, an international online journal of social sciences. In 2015, he co-edited a handbook on French–German relations, entitled *Handwörterbuch der deutsch-französischen Beziehungen* (Nomos) and in 2014 he published a book entitled *L'idée d'une nouvelle représentation politique* (Edilivre).

Notes

1. The name *harkis* refers to Muslim Algerians who served in the French Army during the Algerian war between 1954 and 1962.
2. http://www.ladocumentationfrancaise.fr/dossiers/loi-memoire/termes-debat.shtml (retrieved 28 November 2013).

3. Among them are various well-known artists such as the singer Charles Aznavour and the filmmaker Robert Guédiguian. Some other politicians, such as the Conservative Patrick Devedjian, are also very influential in France.
4. The Syriac Orthodox Church, the Church of the East, the Chaldean Church, the Syriac Catholic and the Syriac Protestant Churches.
5. The old French word 'remembrance' is close to the word 'remember'. To remember means to recollect pieces of the past. Both groups are trying to establish the historical truth about the events of 1915.
6. The exact quote is: 'Whereas the recognition of the Armenian genocide by Turkey must therefore be viewed as a profoundly humane act of moral rehabilitation towards the Armenians, which can only bring honour to the Turkish government'.
7. Examples of this republican tradition in France can be illustrated by some historical ceremonies. In 1964, André Malraux, the French writer and the former Minister of Culture under De Gaulle, delivered a speech on Jean Moulin, the famous resistance fighter who died after being tortured by the Gestapo. His ashes were transferred to the Pantheon, in which people who have accomplished extraordinary acts for the Republic are buried. In 1995, Jacques Chirac led the transfer of the ashes of André Malraux.
8. http://www.riksdagen.se/sv/Dokument-Lagar/Lagar/Svenskforfattningssamling/Lag-1964169-om-straff-for-f_sfs-1964-169/ (retrieved 25 November 2013).
9 Unless otherwise indicated, all translations into English were made by Christophe Premat.
10. http://www.assemblee-nationale.fr/concours/index.asp (retrieved 25 November 2013). Before that date, the *rédacteur des compte-rendus* was a secretary of debates.
11. http://www.senat.fr/adresse/annuaire-direction-des-comptes-rendus-analytiques.html (retrieved 28 November 2013).
12. http://www.riksdagen.se/sv/Sa-funkar-riksdagen/Forvaltningen/Allmanna-handling ar-och-arkiv/ (retrieved 15 August 2012).
13. http://www.senat.fr/leg/ppl00-060.html (retrieved 20 April 2013).
14. http://www.senat.fr/rap/r12-716/r12-7164.html (retrieved 23 July 2013).
15. http://www.riksdagen.se/sv/Dokument-Lagar/Fragor-och-anmalningar/Fragor-for-skriftliga-svar/Turkiet-och-folkmordet-pa-arme_GN11454/ (retrieved 25 November 2013).
16. http://www.riksdagen.se/sv/Dokument-Lagar/Fragor-och-anmalningar/Fragor-for-skriftliga-svar/Turkiet-och-folkmordet-pa-arme_GN11454/ (retrieved 25 November 2013).
17. http://www.assemblee-nationale.fr/12/ta/ta0610.asp (retrieved 11 August 2012).
18. http://www.lepoint.fr/politique/nicolas-sarkozy-en-armenie-06-10-2011-1381523_20.php (retrieved 24 November 2013).
19 http://www.assemblee-nationale.fr/13/cri/2011-2012/20120094.asp (retrieved 19 October 2016)
20. The proposal states that people who deny the genocide should pay a fine of up to 45,000 euros.
21. http://www.assemblee-nationale.fr/14/cr-cafe/11-12/c1112004.asp#P11_185 (retrieved 19 October 2016)
22. http://www.riksdagen.se/sv/Dokument-Lagar/Fragor-och-anmalningar/Fragor-for-sk riftliga-svar/historieforskning-om-folkmord-_GO111006/ (Question no. 2000/01: 1006) (retrieved 25 November 2013).
23. https://www.riksdagen.se/sv/dokument-lagar/dokument/svar-pa-skriftlig-fraga/historieforsk ning-om-folkmord-i-turkiet_GO121006(11 April 2001) (retrieved 19 October 2016)

24. http://www.sweden.gov.se/content/1/c4/14/28/b30bd3a9.pdf (retrieved 23 November 2013).
25. Motion 2002/03:U213, retrieved 12 May 2012 from http://www.riksdagen.se/sv/ Dokument-Lagar/Forslag/Motioner/Forskning-om-assyriersyrianer_GQ02U213/ ?text=true.
26. The word is not appropriate here as there was no systematic plan to get rid of the Christian communities in Iraq. This argument weakens the demonstration of Yilmaz Kerimo.
27. Skriftlig fråga 2006/07:44, 'Genocide in Iraq'. Retrieved 25 November 2013 from http://www.riksdagen.se/sv/Dokument-Lagar/Fragor-och-anmalningar/Fragor-for-skriftliga-svar/Folkmorden-i-Irak_GU1144/.
28. Motion 2007/08:U339. Retrieved 25 November 2013 from http://www.riksdagen.se/ sv/Dokument-Lagar/Forslag/Motioner/Forintelsekonferens-om-folkmor_GV02U339/.
29. Senate meeting of 4 May 2011 (compte-rendu intégral des débats).
30. http://www.senat.fr/rap/r12-716/r12-7164.html (retrieved 28 June 2013).
31. Interpellation 2007/08:41. Retrieved 25 November 2013 from http://www.riksdagen. se/sv/Debatter--beslut/Interpellationsdebatter1/Debatt/?did=GV1041&doctype=ip.
32. Interpellation 2009/10:105. Retrieved 13 August 2012 from http://www.riksda-gen.se/sv/Dokument-Lagar/Fragor-och-anmalningar/Interpellationer/Erkanna ndet-av-folkmordet-pa-p_GX10105/.
33. Anna Lindh's (Minister of Foreign Affairs) answer 1999/2000:454. Retrieved 15 August 2012 from http://www.riksdagen.se/sv/Dokument-Lagar/Fragor-och-anmalningar/ Svar-pa-skriftliga-fragor/Turkiet-och-folkmordet-pa-arme_GN12454/.
34. Motion 2008/09:U332. Retrieved 16 August 2012 from http://www.riksdagen. se/sv/Dokument-Lagar/Forslag/Motioner/Folkmordet-1915-pa-armenier-a_ GW02U332/?text=true.
35. http://www.armenian-genocide.org/Affirmation.414/current_category.7/affirmation_ detail.html (retrieved 18 August 2012).
36. Answer by Carl Bildt to the written question 2009/10:696. Retrieved 14 August 2012 from http://www.riksdagen.se/sv/Dokument-Lagar/Fragor-och-anmalningar/ Svar-pa-skriftliga-fragor/Utrikesministern-och-riksdagen_GX12696/.
37. In both countries, the schoolbooks clearly refer to the genocide of the Armenians (Larsson, Almgren and Almgren 2012: 128); see also the different official pro-grammes in France (Centre National de Documentation Pédagogique 2003, http:// ecehg.ens-lyon.fr/ECEHG/enjeux-de-memoire/le-genocide-des-armeniens/le_geno-cide_armenien_a_l-ecole.pdf). Retrieved 19 October 2016.
38. Meeting of Thursday 22 December 2011. Retrieved 25 November 2013 from http:// www.assemblee-nationale.fr/13/cri/2011-2012/20120094.asp#INTER_0.
39 Meeting of Thursday 22 December 2011. Retrieved 25 November 2013 from http:// www.assemblee-nationale.fr/13/cri/2011-2012/20120094.asp#INTER_0.
40. Meeting of Thursday 22 December 2011.

Bibliography

Andrieu, C. (ed.). 2000. *La persécution des Juifs de France 1940–1944 et le rétablissement de la légalité républicaine, Mission d'étude sur la spoliation des Juifs de France.* Paris: La Documentation française.
Anholm, M. 1906. *De dödsdömda folkens saga.* Stockholm: Godtköpsförlaget.

Armbruster, H. 2014. *Keeping the Faith: Syriac Christian Diasporas*. Canon Pyon: Sean Kingston Publishing.

Atto, N. 2011. *Hostages in the Homeland, Orphans in the Diaspora: Identity Discourses among the Assyrian/Syriac Elites in the European Diaspora*. Leiden: Leiden University Press.

Azéma, J.P. 2006. 'Faut-il abroger les lois mémorielles?', *L'Express*, 2 February. Retrieved 6 August 2012 from http://www.lexpress.fr/actualite/societe/histoire/faut-il-abroger-les-lois-memorielles_483148.html.

Björklund, U. 1981. *North to Another Country: The Formation of a Suryoyo Community in Sweden*. Stockholm: Stockholm University Press.

——— 2011. *Armenien, sex essäer om diaspora*. Stockholm: Carlsson.

Bjurling, C. 1982. 'Vallbys syrianer i Västerås: En kristen minoritets flykt till "himmelriket" Sverige', Ph.D. Dissertation. Uppsala: Sociologiska institutionen.

Caloz-Tschopp, M.C. 2003. 'Les sans-État "Ni minoritaires, ni prolétaires, en dehors de toutes les lois" (H. Arendt)', *Tumultes* 21–22: 215–42.

Coniez, H. 2008. *Écrire la démocratie, de la publicité des débats parlementaires*. Paris: L'Harmattan.

Dadrian, V. N. 1995. *Autopsie du génocide arménien*. Brussels: Editions Complexe.

Deniz, F. 2001. *En minoritets odyssé, det assyriska exemplet*. Uppsala: Sociologiska institutionen.

Fabius, L. 2012. 'Compte-rendu Commission des Affaires étrangères', *14th Legislative Period, Report no. 4* [French Parliament], 17 July.

Gaunt, D. 2010. 'Identity Conflicts among Oriental Christians in Sweden', *Sens Public*. Retrieved 4 October 2010 from http://www.sens-public.org/spip.php?article767.

Hajjar, J. 1962. *Les chrétiens uniates du Proche-Orient*. Paris: Editions du Seuil.

Halbwachs, M. 1925. *Les cadres sociaux de la mémoire*. Paris: Alcan.

Johansson, A. 1930. *Ett folk i landsflykt: Ett år ur armeniernas historia* (facsimile).

Kévorkian, R.H. 1999. *Parler les camps, Penser les génocides*. Paris: Albin Michel.

Knutsson, B. 1982. *Assur eller Aram: Språklig, religiös och nationell identifikation hos Sveriges assyrier och syrianer*. Norrköping, Stockholm: Statens invandrarverk (SIV), Statens kulturråd.

Lange, A., H. Lööw, S. Bruchfeld and E. Hedlund. 1997. *Utsatthet för etniskt och politiskt relaterat hot m.m., spridning av rasistisk och antirasistisk propaganda samt attityder till demokrati m.m. bland skolelever*. Stockholm: Centrum för invandringsforskning.

Larsson, E.J. 1919. *Vid Ararats fot*. Stockholm: Svenska Missionsförbundets förlag.

Larsson O., H. Almgren and B. Almgren. 2012. *Alla tiders historia 2–3*. Stockholm: Gleerups.

Levene, M. 1998. 'Creating a Modern "Zone of Genocide": The Impact of Nation- and State-Formation on Eastern Anatolia, 1878–1923', *Holocaust and Genocide Studies* 12(3): 393–433.

Lundgren, S., and A. Barryakoub. 2010. *Assyrierna, frågor och svar*. Sweden: selfpublished.

Madra, Ö. 1982. 'Were the Assyrians Really Persecuted? A Critical Appraisal of a Study on the Assyrian Migration from Turkey to Sweden', *Invandrare och Minoriteter, Scandinavian Migration and Ethnic Minority Review* (3), May: 165–73.

Michel, J. 2010. *Gouverner les mémoires. Les politiques mémorielles en France*. Paris: PUF.

Mouradian, C. 2000. *L'Arménie de Staline à Gorbatchev. Histoire d'une république soviétique*. Paris: Ramsay.

New York Times. 13 October 2006. 'French Pass Bill that Punishes Denial of Armenian Genocide'. Retrieved 25 November 2013 from http://www.nytimes.com/2006/10/13/world/europe/13turkey.html.

Nora, P. (ed.) 1997. *Les lieux de mémoire*. Paris: Gallimard.

Ozouf, M. 1976. *La fête révolutionnaire 1789–1799*. Paris: Gallimard.

Pehrsson, P. (1896). *Armenierna och deras nöd*. Uppsala University: Archives of the Student Association of Uppsala University.

Rebérioux, M. 2008. 'Rapport d'information au nom de la mission d'information sur les questions de lois mémorielles no. 1262'. Treizième législature, Assemblée Nationale, 18 November.

Ringren, H., and A.V. Ström. 1967. *Religions of Mankind, Yesterday and Today*. Edinburgh and London: Oliver & Boyd.

Schaller, D.J., and J. Zimmerer. 2005. 'Raphael Lemkin: The Founder of the United Nations Genocide Convention as a Historian of Mass Violence', *Journal of Genocide Research* 7(4): 447–52.

——— 2008. 'Late Ottoman Genocides: The Dissolution of the Ottoman Empire and Young Turkish Population and Extermination Policies – Introduction', *Journal of Genocide Research* 10(1): 7–14.

Svanberg, I., and H. Runblom (eds). 1988. *Det mångkulturella Sverige, en handbok om etniska grupper och minoriteter*. Stockholm: Gidlunds Bokförlag.

Tchalkhouchian, G. 1919. *Le livre rouge*. Paris: Veradzenount.

Ter Minassian, A. 2000. 'Les Arméniens au 20ᵉ siècle'. *Vingtième Siècle* 2000: 135–50.

Thornborrow, J., and J. Coates (eds). 2005. *The Sociolinguistics of Narrative*. Amsterdam: John Benjamins Publishing.

Weibel-Yacoub, C. 2009. *Surma l'Assyro-chaldéenne (1883–1975). Dans la tourmente de Mésopotamie*. Paris: L'Harmattan.

Wirsén, E. 1942. *Minnen från fred och krig*. Stockholm: Bonnier.

Yacoub, J. 2010. 'Du traitement des minorités en Irak: le statut des chrétiens'. *Études interculturelles* (3), April: 139–54.

INDEX

War and Genocide

General Editors: Omer Bartov, Brown University; A. Dirk Moses, University of Sydney

In recent years there has been a growing interest in the study of war and genocide, not from a traditional military history perspective, but within the framework of social and cultural history. This series offers a forum for scholarly works that reflect these new approaches.

"The Berghahn series Studies on War and Genocide has immeasurably enriched the English-language scholarship available to scholars and students of genocide and, in particular, the Holocaust." —**Totalitarian Movements and Political Religions**

CPSIA information can be obtained
at www.ICGtesting.com
Printed in the USA
LVHW030025080120
642879LV00015B/596/P

9 781789 200515